Researching the Recognition of Prior Learning: International Perspectives

Edited by Judy Harris, Mignonne Breier and Christine Wihak

promoting adult learning

Published by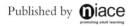

Copyright © 2011 National Institute of Adult Continuing Education
(England and Wales)

21 De Montfort Street
Leicester LE1 7GE

Company registration no. 2603322
Charity registration no. 1002775

NIACE has a broad remit to promote lifelong learning opportunities for
adults. NIACE works to develop increased participation in education and
training, particularly for those who do not have easy access because of class,
gender, age, race, language and culture, learning difficulties or disabilities, or
insufficient financial resources.

For a full catalogue of all NIACE's publications visit http://shop.niace.org.uk/

Cataloguing in Publications Data
A CIP record for this title is available from the British Library

Print ISBN 978 1 86201 460 2
ePub ISBN 978 1 86201 498 5
AER ISBN 978 1 86201 499 2
Online ISBN 978 1 86201 500 5

Edited, designed and typeset by 4word, Bristol

Contents

Foreword

JUDITH MURRAY, VICE PRESIDENT, OPEN LEARNING, THOMPSON RIVERS UNIVERSITY

It is my very great pleasure to contribute this brief Foreword to *Researching the Recognition of Prior Learning: International Perspectives*. Prior Learning Assessment and Recognition (PLAR) is an important component of Open Learning at Thompson Rivers University, British Columbia, Canada. In offering this service to students, we build on the outstanding legacy of one of our 'parent institutions', the British Columbia Open University and its more than 25-year history of innovation in this field. This intellectual heritage is now reflected in the Thompson Rivers University Act, the legislation which created our institution in 2005.

Thompson Rivers University – Open Learning is fully committed to collaborating with the global community to advance both the theory and application of PLAR, and to the development of best practices and international standards. In keeping with this commitment, Dr Christine Wihak, Director of PLAR, convened an invitational meeting of internationally known scholars to seek their participation in our Prior Learning International Research Centre (PLIRC) in July 2009. That inaugural meeting resulted in PLIRC's first significant accomplishment, the publication of this edited collection of the papers presented at the meeting.

I am deeply gratified to see our support for the PLIRC initiative bear fruit in this volume. My sincerest thanks go to all of the PLIRC-associated scholars who contributed, and especially to Dr Judy Harris and Dr Mignonne Breier for their excellent editorial efforts. I am hopeful that this significant contribution to the evolving field of PLAR will indeed stimulate innovative, provocative and rigorous research in the future.

Information about the authors

Judy Harris is Adjunct Professor at Thompson Rivers University (TRU), British Columbia, Canada, and was the first Visiting Scholar to be hosted by the Open Learning division of TRU in 2010. Her research interests include the curricular and pedagogic implications of the Recognition of Prior Learning (RPL), work-based learning and widening participation in higher education. She was Editor (with Per Andersson) of *Re-theorising the Recognition of Prior Learning* (Leicester: NIACE) (2006) and has many years of policy-related academic research in South Africa. As a freelance researcher, she has recently acted as a consultant to the Vice-chancellor of the University of Salford and is an Associate of the Centre for Higher Education Research and Information at the Open University, UK.

Mignonne Breier is in the Research Office at the University of Cape Town, South Africa, where she manages university-wide research development programmes. She was previously a Researcher at the Human Sciences Research Council and the Centre for the Study of Higher Education at the University of the Western Cape. Her research straddles informal learning, higher education, professional education (in teaching, nursing, medicine particularly) and student dropout, but Recognition of Prior Learning (RPL) has been a key theme. Her publications include the monograph *The RPL Conundrum: Recognition of Prior Learning in a Teacher Upgrading Programme* and journal articles that draw on her PhD research on the recognition of prior experience in the pedagogy of university courses in labour law.

Christine Wihak is the Director of Prior Learning Assessment and Recognition (PLAR) at Thompson Rivers University, British Columbia,

Canada. In that capacity she is responsible for a PLAR department that serves the university's on-campus and distance education students. She is founder and Director of the Prior Learning International Research Centre (PLIRC), and has taken a leadership role in developing Canadian and international communities of scholarship in PLAR. Her personal research interest is cross-cultural issues in PLAR in higher education. She has given invited workshops on this topic to open universities in Malaysia and China. Previously, she was Assistant Professor in Workplace and Adult Learning, Faculty of Education, University of Calgary, where she also taught graduate courses in qualitative and quantitative research methods. As a licensed psychologist, she has also specialised in psychological assessments for work-related issues.

Per Andersson is Associate Professor of Education in the Department of Behavioural Sciences and Learning, Linköping University, Sweden. His main research interests are educational assessment, particularly in relation to the Recognition of Prior Learning (RPL) and the professional development of adult educators. He was Editor (with Judy Harris) of *Re-theorising the Recognition of Prior Learning* (Leicester: NIACE, 2006) and has published recent work in *Adult Education Quarterly, Asia-Pacific Journal of Teacher Education, International Journal of Lifelong Education, Journal of Education Policy, Assessment and Evaluation in Higher Education,* and *Vocations and Learning: Studies in Vocational and Professional Education.*

Rachel Bélisle is Associate Professor in the Department of Vocational Guidance and a Researcher in the Équipe de recherche sur les transitions et l'apprentissage (ÉRTA) at Université de Sherbrooke, Québec, Canada. Her main research interests are the recognition and validation of out-of-school learning, the transitional learning of adults without a secondary diploma, the literacy practices of those adults and of the practitioners who work with them. She was Editor (with Jean-Pierre Boutinet) of *Demandes de reconnaissance et validation d'acquis de l'expérience. Pour qui? Pour quoi?* (2009, Presses de l'Université Laval) and (with Sylvain Bourdon) of *Pratiques et apprentissages de l'écrit dans les sociétés éducatives* (2006, Presses de l'Université Laval). She has published in French journals such as *Lien social et politiques, Ethnologies* and *Carriérologie.*

Roslyn Cameron is a Senior Lecturer in the School of Management and Marketing at Central Queensland University (CQU), Australia. She teaches Human Resource Management at CQU, elsewhere in Australia and in South-East Asia. Her research interests span recognition systems, e-portfolios, workforce planning and development, skilled migration, and mixed-methods research. She is Editor of the *International Journal of Mixed Methods in Applied Business and Policy Research,* a Standing Committee member of the *Society of Interdisciplinary Business Research* and President of the Asia Pacific Mixed Methods Network. She is also Project Leader on an Australian Cooperative Research Centre (CRC) for Rail Innovation research project, *Skilled Migration for the Rail Industry*, and a member of the research team of *A Skills Recognition Framework for Rail.*

Andreas Fejes is Associate Professor of Education in the Department of Behavioural Sciences and Learning, Linköping University, Sweden. Drawing mainly on poststructuralist theory, his research explores lifelong learning, workplace learning, Recognition of Prior Learning (RPL) and adult education. He was Editor (with Katherine Nicoll) of *Foucault and Lifelong Learning: Governing the Subject* (London: Routledge), and his articles have appeared in the *Journal of Education Policy*, *Educational Philosophy and Theory*, *Journal of Advanced Nursing, British Journal of Sociology of Education, Studies in the Education of Adults*, and *Teaching in Higher Education*. He edits the *European Journal for Research on the Education and Learning of Adults* (RELA) and is Secretary of the European Society for Research on the Education of Adults (ESREA).

Helen Pokorny is Principal Lecturer in Learning and Teaching at the University of Westminster, London, England, where she is the Course Leader of the MA in Higher Education. Her interests are in promoting inclusion particularly through assessment. She has written on feedback cues and relationships, group-work assessment, widening participation, raising the attainment level of Black and Minority Ethnic students through inclusive assessment practice, and the Assessment of Prior Experiential Learning (APEL). Her work on APEL derives from over a decade working with students and staff in higher education. She has presented conference papers, contributed to Andersson and Harris (2006) *Re-theorising the Recognition of Prior Learning* (Leicester: NIACE), and with colleagues has developed an APEL website – http://apel.londonmet.ac.uk/ – which records student and staff experiences of the process.

Nan Travers is the Director of the Office of Collegewide Academic Review at the State University of New York (SUNY) Empire State College, USA. In this role, she focuses on the policies and practices of self-designed student degree programmes, and on the assessment of prior college-level learning. Over the years, Dr Travers has been extensively involved in conducting research and presenting workshops in adult learning, including Prior Learning Assessment (PLA), college-level learning and ways in which students develop self-regulated learning. She is also the founding Co-editor of *PLA Inside Out: A Journal in Research, Theory and Practice of Prior Learning Assessment*, a premiere peer-reviewed journal showcasing scholarship in PLA to be released in spring 2011. She received her PhD in Adult Learning from the University of Connecticut.

Joy Van Kleef is a Researcher and Consultant with the Canadian Institute for Recognizing Learning (CIRL), and a Senior Associate of the Prior Learning Assessment (PLA) Centre in Halifax, Nova Scotia. She has specialised in PLAR consulting since 1989, and has completed over 80 research and implementation projects for local, regional, national and international organisations. Her main research interest is quality in Prior Learning Assessment and Recognition (PLAR), which is also the subject of her current doctoral studies at L'école des hautes études en sciences sociales in Paris, France. Joy was principal author of the cross-Canada research, *A Slice of the Iceberg* (1999) and *Feedback from Learners* (2003), two longitudinal studies of PLAR in Canadian colleges.

Patrick Werquin is an independent consultant based in Paris, France and Senior Lecturer at the University of Neuchâtel, Switzerland. He is a member of the Centre d'études sociologiques et politiques Raymon Aron (CESPRA, École des hautes études en sciences sociales [EHESS]). From 1999 to 2010, he was Senior Economist in the Directorate for Education at the Organisation for Economic Co-operation and Development (OECD), and in that capacity contributed to many publications on adult learning, adult literacy, qualifications systems and frameworks, and the Recognition of Non-Formal and Informal Learning. He is currently working for GHK Limited (for the European Commission) on lifelong learning policy, the Department of Education of Madeira, the University of Vilnius, the Moroccan Ministry of Education, and the Kyoto School for the Promotion of Non-formal and Informal Learning. He has a PhD in Economics.

Ruth Whittaker is Head of Widening Participation and College Liaison and Deputy Director of the Centre for Research in Lifelong Learning (CRLL), Glasgow Caledonian University, Scotland. She is also Chair of the Scottish Universities Recognition of Prior Learning (RPL) Network; Universities Scotland representative on the Scottish Credit and Qualifications Framework (SCQF) RPL Network, and a member of the recently launched European RPL Network. She undertakes research in recognising prior informal learning, credit transfer, transition and progression, and directs research and development projects at a national and European level at the policy/practice interface. Her RPL research interests are located within the context of widening participation, workforce development and national qualifications frameworks.

Angelina (Angie) Wong is Professor Emerita in Education at the University of Saskatchewan, Canada. As Director of the university's Centre for Distributed Learning and Instructional Design Group, she was involved in research and development projects with colleagues from Chile, China, Mozambique, Palestine and Thailand. She has published in the areas of blended learning and the assessment of experiential learning. She was Coordinator of an Online Master of Continuing Education programme and Instructor on the programme's Workplace Learning Internship. Since taking early retirement in 2008, she has continued to pursue a proactive interest in Prior Learning Assessment and Recognition (PLAR) and the application of its philosophy to curriculum and faculty renewal in higher education.

Glossary

ABET	Adult Basic Education and Training
ACDEAULF	Association canadienne d'éducation des adultes des universités de langue française
ACE	Adult and Community Education
ACE	American Council on Education
ADMEE	Association pour le développement des méthodologies d'évaluation en éducation
ANTA	Australian National Training Authority
APEL	Assessment of Prior Experiential Learning
AQF	Australian Qualifications Framework
AQFAB	AQF Advisory Board
AQFC	Australian Qualifications Framework Council
AUCC	Association of Universities and Colleges of Canada
BFUG	Bologna Follow-Up Group
CACE	Certificate in Adult and Continuing Education
CACSL	Canadian Alliance for Community Service-Learning
CAEL	Council for Adult and Experiential Learning
CAPLA	Canadian Association for Prior Learning Assessment
CATS	Credit Accumulation and Transfer Scheme
CAUBO	Canadian Association of University Business Officers
CCL	Canadian Council on Learning
CDEACF	Centre de documentation sur l'éducation des adultes et la condition féminine
CEDEFOP	European Centre for the Development of Vocational Training
CIQ	Conseil interprofessionnel du Québec

CIRL	Canadian Institute for Recognizing Learning
CIRRAC	Centre d'information et de recherche en reconnaissance des acquis
CLD	Community Learning and Development
CLEP	College Level Examinations Program
CLFDB	Canadian Labour Force Development Board
CNAA	Council for National Academic Awards
COCDMO	Coalition des organismes communautaires de développement de la main-d'œuvre
COSATU	Congress of South African Trade Unions
CRLL	Centre for Research in Lifelong Learning
CSL	Community Service Learning
CST	Conseil de la science et de la technologie
DACUM	Developing a Curriculum
DANTES	The Defense Activity for Non-Traditional Education Support
DBIS	Department for Business, Innovation and Skills
DEST	Department of Education, Science and Training
EC	European Commission
ECVET	European Credit System for Vocational Education and Training
EHEA	European Higher Education Area
EQF	European Qualifications Framework
ÉRTA	l'Équipe de recherche sur les transitions et l'apprentissage
ESC	Empire State College
ESRC	Economic and Social Research Council
ETDP	Education, Training and Development Practitices
ETS	Educational Testing Service
EU	European Union
EUCEN	European University Continuing Education Network
FD	Foundation Degree
FET	Further Education and Training
GCU	Glasgow Caledonian University
GED	General Education Development
HE	Higher Education
HEFCE	Higher Education Funding Council for England
HEI	Higher Education Institutions
HRD	Human Resource Development

HRDC	Human Resources Development Canada
HRSDC	Human Resources and Skills Development Canada
HSRC	Human Sciences Research Council
ICÉA	Institut canadien d'éducation des adultes
IEPDS	Integrated Post-secondary Education Data System
ILO	International Labour Office
INRS	National Institute of Scientific Research
IRAHE	Institute for Research and Assessment in Higher Education at the University of Maryland University College
JET	Joint Education Trust
LET	Learning from Experience Trust
LLP	Lifelong Learning Programme
NCVER	National Centre for Vocational Education Research
NESB	Non-English Speaking Background
NFROT	National Framework for the Recognition of Training
NPDE	National Professional Diploma in Education
NQC	Australian National Quality Council
NQF	National Qualifications Framework
NRF	National Research Foundation
NSF	National Science Foundation
NSSE	National Survey of Student Engagement
NUM	National Union of Mineworkers
NUMSA	National Union of Metalworkers of South Africa
NVQ	National Vocational Qualification
OECD	Organisation for Economic Co-operation and Development
PDP	Personal Development Planning
PLA	Prior Learning and Assessment
PLAR	Prior Learning Assessment and Recognition
PLIRC	Prior Learning International Research Centre
QAA	Quality Assurance Agency
RAC	Reconnaissance des acquis et des compétences
RNFIL	Recognition of Non-formal and Informal Learning
RPL	Recognition of Prior Learning
RPLC	Recognition of Prior Learning and Competencies
RPLO	Recognition of Prior Learning Outcomes
RSA	Republic of South Africa
RTO	Registered Training Organisation

RVCC	Portuguese National System for Recognising, Validating and Certifying Competencies
SAQA	South African Qualifications Authority
SCOTCATS	Scottish Credit Accumulation Transfer Scheme
SCQF	Scottish Credit and Qualifications Framework
SEEC	South East England Consortium
SETA	Sector Education Training Authority
SIG	Special Interest Groups
SME	Small and Medium-sized Enterprise
SQA	Scottish Qualifications Authority
SSHRC	Social Science and Humanities Research Council of Canada
SSSC	Scottish Social Services Council
SUNY	State University of New York
SVQ	Scottish Vocational Qualification
TAFE	Technical and Further Education
TECEP	Thomas Edison College Examination Program
TRU	Thompson Rivers University
TVET	Technical Vocational Education and Training
UCT	University of Cape Town
UMUC	University of Maryland University College
VAE	Validation des acquis de l'expérience
VET	Vocational Education and Training
VNFIL	Validation of Non-formal and Informal Learning
WBL	Work-based Learning

CHAPTER ONE

Introduction and overview of chapters

Judy Harris and Christine Wihak

There are two parts to this opening chapter. The first part gives readers the background to the collection and to the pivotal work of the Prior Learning International Research Centre (PLIRC). The second part is a synthesis and commentary of the main messages that emerge from the chapters in the volume.

Background to this collection

What is the Recognition of Prior Learning?

The Recognition of Prior Learning (RPL) is the practice of reviewing, evaluating and acknowledging the knowledge and skills that adults have gained through experiential, self-directed and/or informal learning as well as through formal education (Thomas, 2000). Typically, such learning involves achievement and performance in the workplace, community, artistic or other life activities, as well as learning through non-accredited workshops and training programmes.[1]

RPL offers significant benefits to individual adults: having workplace learning translated into an easily transferable format, enhancing reflective

---

[1] RPL is also known as the Prior Learning Assessment and Recognition (PLAR), Prior Learning Assessment (PLA), the Assessment of Prior Learning (APL), the Assessment of Prior Experiential Learning (APEL), the Validation of Non-formal and Informal Learning (VNFIL), and by many other acronyms in languages other than English. In this volume, the term RPL is used to refer to practices in a general way. Each chapter author uses the term with which s/he is most familiar and comfortable.

capacity and building confidence (Morrissey *et al.*, 2008). It is used in post-secondary contexts for admission and/or advanced standing, as well as for occupational and professional certification and in workforce development more generally. Since the mid-1990s, many governments around the world have closely linked RPL with national qualification frameworks and lifelong learning policies.

The Prior Learning International Research Centre

Although RPL is gaining momentum in policies and in terms of the range of practices, the research base lags behind. Research at the level of individual students, institutional policies and practices, and national initiatives, is critically needed to ensure RPL achieves its full potential in relation to lifelong learning. It is also the case that RPL raises complex issues around knowledge, learning, qualifications and power, which are all too often glossed over in the face of the exigencies of policy and practice.

Scholars, practitioners and managers at Thompson Rivers University (British Columbia, Canada) recognised this compelling need, and created an international research centre and an RPL network to facilitate, coordinate and disseminate scholarly research on theoretical foundations and practices in the field. The goal of the Prior Learning International Research Centre (PLIRC) is to stimulate innovative, provocative and rigorous research into the theory, policy and practice of RPL.[2]

The PLIRC inaugural meeting was held in July 2009, at Thompson Rivers University in Kamloops. Internationally recognised RPL scholars were invited to represent a range of academic disciplines (adult education, economics, educational psychology, educational policy, human resource development) and geographic locations and jurisdictions, including Australia, Canada, England, the European Union, the Organisation for Economic Co-operation and Development (OECD), Scotland, South Africa, Sweden and the United States. For pragmatic reasons, participation was limited to scholars publishing in English, although PLIRC recognises the meritorious research being conducted in other languages (see Bélisle's chapter in this volume). Each invitee was invited to present a paper summarising the state of RPL research in his or her geographic area. It is those papers that provided the basis for this book. Edited by Dr Judy Harris, with Dr Mignonne Breier and Dr Christine Wihak as co-editors,

---

[2] See the PLIRC website: http://www.tru.ca/distance/plirc.html.

Researching the Recognition of Prior Learning: International Perspectives is a companion volume to Dr Harris' previous book *Re-theorising the Recognition of Prior Learning*, Andersson and Harris, 2006.

Aims of this collection

In the 'Endword' to *Re-theorising the Recognition of Prior Learning*, Professor Michael Young, a well-known sociologist of education at the Institute of Education, University of London, offered the RPL research community a challenge. He wrote: 'RPL is not only a practice that needs *re-theorising* but one which offers the possibility of *new theorising*' (Young, 2006, p. 326). This book takes up that challenge. Because it is not advisable to begin new theorising without a clear sense of what has gone before, this collection is a stock-take of the current state of RPL research around the world.

Each author has surveyed considerable amounts of research, over a hundred items in some cases. On that basis, each chapter is a contextualisation and explanatory analysis of the state of the research field. To expand the scope of the book, chapters were invited from Rachel Bélisle, a Canadian Francophone scholar, and Per Andersson and Andreas Fejes, Swedish scholars. In addition, the final two chapters are issue-based papers from Canada, included as illustrations of the type of research being conducted in PLIRC's home country. So, although we cannot aim to be comprehensive in reviewing all of the RPL research, we have tried to be thorough. The collection therefore aims to encourage the development of RPL as a community of scholarship by laying the groundwork for 'new theorising'.

The brief for the authors

The brief given to the scholars in preparing their chapters was deliberately broad. We wanted to know: Who is doing research? What kinds of questions are they asking? How are they doing it? Why are they doing it? Where are the gaps? Each person approached the task in a slightly different way and this was fine, as we did not want to impose conformity. We made an editorial decision to retain complexity; for example, some of the authors delineated boundaries to inform what research to include/ exclude in their chapters, while others worked more organically with what was there in terms of research. The chapters are organised and structured

3

in different ways – historically and chronologically, thematically, and so on. Some authors 'typologise' the research, others do not. The result is a set of chapters that tell rich and complex stories about researching the Recognition of Prior Learning.

Synthesis and commentary

The authors found it difficult to write about research without discussing practice. As a result, themes pertaining to the state of RPL *practice* in the countries and regions surveyed are discussed first. Attention then turns to *research* and presents our sense of what we can say with confidence about the state of RPL research internationally. Thereafter, we focus on 'islands' of good research practice, followed by a consideration of research directions needed to advance the RPL field internationally. Finally, some further questions are raised in relation to issues not directly addressed in the chapters, but which are also worthy of research attention.

The state of RPL practice in the countries and regions studied

Werquin and Wihak's chapter notes the extensive efforts made to document practices in the OECD countries, while Harris' chapter contains similar information on work in the European Union. What we see in these chapters, and across all chapters, is evidence that governments are increasingly embracing RPL as part of public policy, particularly with respect to lifelong learning, qualification frameworks, credit systems and the development of learning outcomes. It is also the case that RPL is growing *without* such stimuli; for example, in the United States. There has, however, been a shift in RPL discourse and practice from a concern with the redress of socio-economic inequality to a more explicit economic focus on RPL in relation to efficiency, workforce development, labour mobility and the recognition of overseas qualifications. RPL linked to workforce development is particularly evident in Scotland and in Australia. Canada is a country that is explicit about the need to grow its labour force through immigration, and RPL is seen as a way of supporting the portability of skills and knowledge. Other countries are using RPL with refugee populations (particularly in Europe).

In general, though, practice lags behind policy. Most countries report disappointingly low take-up overall, despite policy commitments and funding, and in some cases compulsory requirements that RPL be offered;

for example, in relation to qualifications and programmes registered on the Australian Qualifications Framework. However, we do learn from the United States that uptake can increase over time.

It is also the case that implementation is uneven – uneven in terms of the extent of 'embeddedness' in government policy, uneven in terms of the extent of practice within and across educational sectors, and uneven regarding uptake in employment contexts. As discussed in Wong's chapter, the resistance of higher education to RPL is an issue that refuses to go away, except in newer institutions (in England and Scotland) or in institutions designed to be adult-friendly in the United States. The chapters also provide evidence of differing levels of responsiveness depending on discipline or area of study, with professional education in health, nursing and social services taking the lead in most contexts, usually led by professional body policy and, in the case of Canada, 'fairness legislation'. In Sweden, Canada and Australia, most RPL takes place in vocational education and training and/or community colleges. In some contexts practices are developing in relation to senior secondary school qualifications and careers guidance services.

There is increasing differentiation in types of RPL practice, most noticeably in Scotland and in European Commission policy and projects, where distinctions are made between formative and summative RPL. These are organised as separate practices, with the former used in relation to hard-to-reach candidates. Conversely, in Australia, RPL policy is moving practice towards summative, credit-focused processes and away from formative developmental provision.

Further differentiation is taking place in terms of course-based RPL and more generic approaches. The former tends to require matching of prior learning against the specified content of modules and learning outcomes; the latter adopts broader notions of 'equivalence' whereby prior learning and adults' intellectual capacities are assessed against generic competencies or level descriptors, leading to the award of 'general' rather than 'specific' credit. Assessing against generic competencies makes it possible to recognise valuable knowledge that is not taught in a formal way (cf. the Aristotelian notion of *phronesis* deployed in the South African research).

Work in the European Union is advocating two routes to all qualifications, with no distinction made between the RPL route and the 'taught' route. Scotland is seeking to develop opportunities for individuals to benchmark their prior learning against national standards, not necessarily for the purpose of gaining credit, but to aid formative RPL; for example. to give people an idea of their own level of competence in particular careers or occupations.

Chapters report growing interest in quality assurance and in the validity and reliability of RPL assessment. This cluster of concerns is felt as far apart as Sweden, South Africa and Canada. Some of the early, and very valuable, research into the validity and reliability of RPL was undertaken in the United States, enshrined as 'principles' and subsequently used as a basis for 'showcasing' best practices. This research is hard to locate 35 years later, pointing to a real danger of losing sight of our existing evidence bases.

Professional education and training programmes for RPL assessors and facilitators are being developed. These vary in size and scope. Some take an academic character; others orientate to occupational and national standards; some are one-off, in-house, skills-based programmes; and others aim to embed RPL modules into initial teacher training and continuing education for lifelong learning educators of various kinds.

Several chapters cite a shift away from 'front-end' pre-enrolment RPL to procedures that take place further into an educational programme, allowing learners and facilitators more time to gauge their prior learning in relation to formal content. The South Africa, Sweden and Australia chapters report such practices and suggest that they are potentially more successful and effective than 'traditional' RPL.

Finally, terminology and definitions are very unstable, both within and between contexts. Almost every chapter uses a different acronym and, even where the same term is used, the meanings attributed to it can differ.

What can we say with confidence about the state of RPL research *internationally*?

RPL researchers and scholars are few and far between. This was noted by all chapter authors. In Mignonne Breier's chapter on South Africa, the RPL community is referred to as 'introverted' and 'introspective' – often researching itself – a situation that is replicated in other countries. These small communities usually comprise key individuals who make important contributions. Research is frequently undertaken by academics in university departments of education, and there is sometimes a sense of people *doing* the research and people and practices *being* researched; for example, academics in higher education researching RPL in vocational education and training.

What counts as 'research' is a vital question identified in Van Kleef's chapter. Indeed, each author has a slightly different understanding of research and different perspectives on it, depending on their professional location, their particular relationship with RPL practice and their own prior experience of research; for example, as a university-based researcher, as a researcher in an international organisation such as the OECD, or as an RPL practitioner-researcher. Some authors exclude non-empirical theoretical work, others include it; some include important unpublished reports; others focus on research published in peer-reviewed journals. There are also different understandings of 'conceptual'. Although we deliberately kept the brief for writing the chapters open so that each author could include what s/he determined was relevant, a point for discussion is whether we want to develop a common language and, if we do, how this might be done.

Although there is a substantial amount of RPL research, the field remains fragmented. Researchers often do not know much about research beyond their own countries or context, and sometimes even within them. Importantly, research is not cumulative; it does not build on what has gone before.

Most recent research is policy-driven. Not surprisingly, it has followed the parameters and contours of available funding, and in most countries governments, government bodies and/or research councils have funded policy-related RPL research and development activities. This is particularly the case in Scotland, Australia, South Africa and the European Union. Federal monies were initially available in Canada, but funding now comes from a mix of public and private sources. In the United States, much of the RPL research is commissioned by the Council for Adult and Experiential Learning (CAEL) which receives its own funding from foundations (in the main). Government policy in the UK has diverted attention (and funding) from RPL to widening participation in higher education (for younger learners), and to work-based learning initiatives involving collaboration between employers and higher education institutions.

Much of the RPL research is a-theoretical and uncritical; there is either an absence of theory or an unproblematised acceptance of experiential learning or situated learning ideas (in the case of research conducted by educationists) and human capital theory (in the case of research undertaken by the OECD and the European Commission). South Africa is an exception to this (see below).

In terms of methodology and methods, the chapters in this volume make it abundantly clear that most of the RPL research is qualitative, small-scale and retrospective, consisting, for example, of action research, case studies and/or evaluations of pilot projects. Some larger-scale multi-institutional qualitative studies have been undertaken in the US. Australia, Canada, the US and South Africa have conducted large-scale quantitative studies, but most of them are descriptive rather than explanatory or pre-dictive. Pan-country research (e.g. the OECD and European Commission inventories) and comparative studies tend to deploy mixed methods, usu-ally surveys, progressively focusing to case studies.

'Islands' of good research practice

There are many of these. South Africa provides the international commu-nity with the most theoretical and critical research, undertaken alongside policy implementation. This is partly because imported models of RPL have not worked well there. Most of the South African research is pub-lished in peer-reviewed academic journals. England and Sweden also have a fair amount of research published in academic journals; the US, Canada and Australia less so. Somewhat paradoxically, the US has the most post-graduate study, with over 30 master and doctoral dissertations since 1974, but these have not in the main been published.

As discussed in Whittaker's chapter, Scotland is home to very gener-ative 'development-focused' research. This involves a dynamic and iterative dialogue between policy, implementation and research. A recent tradition has developed whereby an approach to RPL is developed and trialled, evaluated, refined, retried, and so on. It is this very thorough and pragmatic approach to the development of research- and theory-informed practice which is building confidence amongst diverse stakeholders and effectively rebranding RPL – forging a distinct break with the 'remembered pain' of cumbersome portfolio-based approaches in favour of more streamlined and flexible practices.

The United States has led the field in terms of going to scale with standardised and challenge testing, and is home to most of the impact studies assessing the actual benefits and outcomes of RPL for individuals, as discussed in Travers' chapter. There is hard evidence that RPL works in that context in terms of student persistence, success in study, increased self-concept and longer-term academic and career outcomes. Cameron's chapter notes that research in Australia makes use of statistical datasets capable of monitoring RPL activity nationally; for example, take-up by different social groups.

Wihak and Wong's chapter is a model of research that could easily be replicated in other contexts and in relation to other RPL topics. In undertaking and reporting on an empirical study into the conundrum of 'Why no PLAR in university adult education departments in Canada?', it represents a good example of small-scale, low-cost research that tells us something new.

As noted in Pokorny's chapter, specialist RPL research literatures are developing in England, most particularly in relation to nursing and other areas of health. A similar trend is seen in Canada and is developing around the world; indeed, all of the chapters make reference to articles in a range of professional journals.

Research directions to advance the RPL field internationally

This is very important if the field is to develop as an area of scholarly activity. It is vital to consolidate the fragmented nature of current research in favour of more cumulative effort. There is a real need for research that deepens our knowledge base by building on earlier research in a systematic way. One way to do this, for example, would be to undertake qualitative meta-analyses and syntheses of existing case studies.

As noted, most of the RPL research is qualitative and retrospective, and the methods used tend to be narrow. Alongside the ubiquitous case studies and evaluations of practice, there is real scope for the deployment of different methods; for example, more critical and historical inquiry, more discourse analysis (to complement general qualitative theme analysis), more ethnographies, and more phenomenological enquiries to capture data regarding the 'lived experience' of RPL for candidates, assessors and facilitators. As discussed, quantitative research is largely inventory-like, descriptive and concerned to answer 'extent to which' questions such as the extent of implementation, the extent of take-up, the extent of barriers and the extent of credit awarded. The quantitative research field, if developed, could move from descriptive research to drawing simple correlations, and from there to multivariate, explanatory studies capable of making evidence-based claims. Mixed methodologies and methods could also be used more creatively; for example, beginning with qualitative research and moving to surveys, rather than always the other way round. More methodological variety would make it possible to ask different types of questions and learn different things about our field.

RPL research would benefit from a broader range of theoretical perspectives being brought to bear on practice. This was the issue that *Re-theorising the Recognition of Prior Learning* (Andersson and Harris, 2006) addressed by drawing attention to research that moved beyond taken-for-granted adult and experiential learning theory. As an applied field of practice, RPL is very amenable to reflecting multiple theoretical perspectives. For example, Andersson's chapter illustrates how Swedish researchers are using assessment theory, organisational theory and concepts from Foucault's work. South African researchers draw on Basil Bernstein's work on knowledge, curricula and pedagogy, and on post-Vygotskian cultural-historical activity theory. Researchers in Scotland use social identity theory. Actor network theory has been used in England. There are many more theoretical lenses that could be utilised; for example, the full range of learning theories, concepts to explore the gender and race dimensions of RPL, and a range of disciplinary-specific approaches. It is pleasing to note that researchers from disciplines and professions beyond education are involved in RPL and publishing their research. This raises the question of how to link 'specialist' research by health professionals, psychologists, engineers or management specialists to 'generalist' research undertaken by educationists. For example, a big challenge would be to bring social science-based research into dialogue with research based on economic theory for a discussion about the costs and benefits of RPL. Building interdisciplinary bridges and broadening perspectives would help us to build richer and more scholarly accounts of current and potential practice.

What is clear is that, internationally, we can learn a lot from each other – through comparative, practice-based research partnerships for example. Different countries have different strengths and shared interests that could form the basis for Special Interest Groups (SIG) around *applied* research issues. Indeed, the Prior Learning International Research Centre (PLIRC) has already established a SIG on the use of e-portfolios, web technology and digital media in RPL. The chapters in this volume suggest further possibilities, *inter alia*: RPL and workforce development (involving Australia, Canada, Scotland and OECD researchers); RPL and labour mobility including the recognition of overseas professional qualifications (involving Canada, European Union and OECD researchers); RPL in the context of national qualifications frameworks (involving Scotland, Australia, South Africa, EU); RPL and working with refugees (involving England, Scotland, Sweden); and RPL in different educational sectors (higher education

[North American countries], the professions [Canada, England], vocational education and training [Sweden, Australia], senior secondary level [Scotland, OECD researchers]).

What the above implies is greater segmentation (but not fragmentation!) of our applied research. This is already happening in Scotland with research into formative and summative types of RPL and the Sweden chapter distinguishes between work- and education-focused RPL. Chapters also suggest differentiation *within* work-focused RPL – that is: RPL at the level of national workforce development strategy; within employment sectors; with individual professional and regulatory bodies; in particular industries; and in relation to specific employers and workplaces. Within education, we need to continue to think about disciplines and RPL, RPL in particular professions and occupations, and RPL in relation to a range of programme and course design strategies.

In terms of research that is primarily *theoretical and academic*, the chapter reviews lead us to suggest that the time has come to accept that RPL is complex and contested. It is clear that in many instances practice has not lived up to policy and rhetorical expectations and claims. This phenomenon has tended to be addressed via enquiries into 'barriers to implementation'. Perhaps we now need to delve more deeply than this and examine the concept of RPL itself. This is where we would move into the exciting realm of 'new theorising', as Michael Young challenged us to do in the 'Endword' of *Re-theorising the Recognition of Prior Learning* (Andersson and Harris, 2006). In education, it is where we would begin to research the institutional, curricular, pedagogic conditions under which RPL is most likely to succeed, and be able to articulate the reasons why (and why not). For example, why does RPL seem to work best in higher level vocational education and training in Australia and at postgraduate levels in England and Scotland? Similar analyses and accompanying business arguments are required in relation to economic, employment, labour market and workplace conditions, and the ways in which these inhibit or enable RPL. Furthermore, our concern is 'prior learning', but we have not yet developed theorised ways to understand the nuances of prior learning and the meaning of 'practice'.

Issues not addressed in the chapters

What has not been covered in the chapters? As RPL and related concepts and procedures spread around the world, there may well be an increasing

11

need for practices capable of operating on a large scale, especially in relation to rapidly developing countries such as China, and much to learn from the type of development work undertaken in such contexts. A corollary is the need to address the role of RPL in contexts characterised by vast structural inequalities. This is the situation that South Africa has had to face in the post-apartheid era, and that countries such as Australia and Canada are still grappling with in relation to Indigenous and First Nations people. RPL practices have been developed in the context of particular cultural heritages, education systems and work practices; how much flexibility is there for working within different cultural paradigms? Language issues also come to the fore – how is the interface between language competence and other forms of competence to be mediated, especially in multilingual contexts?

Conclusion

The chapters in this book make it clear that the field of RPL is emerging as a distinct area of research, with its own body of scholarly literature. Our challenge now is to nurture that growth. If we are to research and articulate a professional, theoretical and critical base for RPL, there is an urgent need to attract and support more researchers and graduate students. The Prior Learning International Research Centre (PLIRC) has the goal of stimulating innovative, provocative and rigorous research into RPL. The scholars who contributed to this book share this vision. In that spirit, we offer this volume, in the hope that it will serve as a foundation for the future development of scholarship and research in the field.

References

Andersson, P. and Harris, J. (eds) (2006) *Re-theorising the Recognition of Prior Learning*. Leicester: National Institute for Adult Continuing Education (NIACE).

Morrissey, M., Myers, D., Bélanger, P., Robitaille, M., Davison, P., Van Kleef, J. and Williams, R. (2008) *Achieving our Potential: An Action Plan for Prior Learning and Recognition (PLAR) in Canada*. Ottawa: Canadian Council on Learning.

Thomas, A. (2000) 'Prior Learning Assessment: The quiet revolution', in A. Wilson and E. Hayes (eds) *Handbook of Adult and Continuing Education*. San Francisco: Jossey-Bass.

Young, M. (2006) 'Endword', in P. Anderson and J. Harris (eds) *Re-theorising the Recognition of Prior Learning*. Leicester: National Institute for Adult Continuing Education (NIACE).

CHAPTER TWO

Australia: An overview of 20 years of research into the Recognition of Prior Learning (RPL)

Roslyn Cameron

Abstract

Australia introduced the Recognition of Prior Learning (RPL) as part of a national training reform agenda that included the introduction of a competency-based vocational education and training system, a national qualification system and training packages. RPL is now a standard and requirement of any offering of accredited training that is embedded in the Australian Qualifications Framework (AQF). As time has progressed, and RPL policy and practice has evolved, it has become more central to the vocational education and training (VET) sector than any other post-compulsory educational sector. RPL is also a growing activity outside the education sector, impacting on human capital and workforce development policy and initiatives. The Australian Government's current policies related to reforms in higher education, the social inclusion agenda (specifically in relation to education) and workforce development (including skilled migration) may see even greater impetus for RPL activity across educational sectors and within workplaces.

In terms of research, there is a body of literature reporting on policy and implementation issues (drivers, benefits and barriers), case studies and a smaller sub-set of literature related to workplace skills recognition. New areas of research interest are emerging regarding building RPL practitioner capabilities and using Web 2.0 technologies and digital media. The RPL research community is small and very little of the RPL literature engages critically with the theoretical underpinnings of

RPL. Nonetheless, a small number of commentators/researchers have identified gaps and directions for future research.

Introduction

The chapter begins with a brief contextual overview of the history of the Recognition of Prior Learning (RPL), framing policies, ongoing conceptual and definitional confusion, and the extent of implementation. The main body explores Australian RPL research, with particular reference to the vocational education and training (VET) and higher education (HE) sectors. Major government-funded and commissioned research on RPL is presented with a summary of methodological approaches. Next, themes within the research literature are identified and discussed. The chapter concludes with a discussion of gaps in research and future research opportunities, calling for a widening of the RPL research agenda, more theoretical and critical perspectives, and greater diversity in terms of lines of inquiry and methodological approaches.

Although 86 pieces of literature have been reviewed, the chapter cannot claim to have covered all the RPL research in Australia during the period from 1990 to April 2010. A broad definition of research has been adopted, to include single-method studies (qualitative or quantitative), mixed-method studies and non-empirical conceptual work.

Contextual overview of RPL in Australia

History and policy

The Recognition of Prior Learning is a relatively new concept and practice in Australian education and training. Officially introduced in the early 1990s as part of a larger national training reform agenda that included the introduction of a competency-based vocational education and training system, training packages and an Australian Qualification Framework (AQF), its first formal location was within the National Framework for the Recognition of Training (NFROT).

However, the VET sector had shown interest in RPL before this, with growing demand from unions and employers for practices and procedures to recognise workplace learning. The first project to respond to this demand (in 1987) was the Ford/TAFE (technical and further education) 'Articulation Project', a tripartite strategy between the Victorian

Government, the Ford car manufacturing company and Broadmeadows College of TAFE in Victoria. Similar projects in other states followed (South Australia, Western Australia and New South Wales). The report from the Ford/TAFE project (Broadmeadows College of TAFE, 1990) greatly influenced the speed and direction of policy thereafter, with mixed effects and outcomes. Smith (2008) argues that the introduction of RPL was premature:

> *the incorporation of RPL into the national VET system happened too quickly for anyone to truly know what they were dealing with. RPL was national policy long before it could have become widely understood as an educational process, and before the implications of its incorporation into (an inarticulate) VET pedagogy were clear. Exploration of alternative practice models was effectively foreclosed at the end of 1993, and the VET system has since invested in refining RPL policies, evaluating current practice, and defining the accounting for RPL in national data collections (ibid., p. 7).*

Indeed, research in the 1990s that began to engage in critical theoretical analysis and discussion of the pedagogic practice of RPL was soon submerged by a stream of research and literature that focused primarily on issues of implementation.

RPL is now standard and a requirement of any accredited training within the Australian Qualifications Framework (AQF). The AQF locates school, work-based and academic qualifications at all levels (from secondary school to doctorate) in a single framework that is recognised across Australia and internationally. Every qualification is categorised according to the educational sector responsible for its accreditation. The sectors are senior secondary schools, adult and community education (ACE), vocational education and training (VET) and higher education.[1]

In June 2004, the AQF Advisory Board (AQFAB) endorsed *National Principles and Operational Guidelines for Recognition of Prior Learning (RPL)*, designed to assist all post-compulsory education and training providers in developing consistent policies and procedures. A major shift happened in May 2009, when the government adopted the *AQF National Policy and*

---

[1] In Australia, VET is the overarching term for technical and further education (TAFE) colleges, private colleges and community-based provision.

Guidelines on Credit Arrangements (AQFC, 2009).[2] This incorporated and replaced existing policies on RPL, credit transfer and articulation. Within this new framework, RPL is reconceptualised as an assessment and credit process, although approaches taking a more developmental approach continue to exist in small pockets of activity, particularly in relation to Indigenous Australians. It is too early to comment on the level of acceptance and implementation of this new policy within the VET and HE sectors. As with previous RPL-related policy and principles/guidelines, actual adoption and enactment will be influenced by the context.

Conceptual and definitional confusion

A number of authors have noted conceptual confusion in and around the policy and practice of RPL (Doddrell, 2002; Bateman and Knight, 2003; Wheelahan *et al.*, 2003a; Cameron, 2004; Smith, 2004; Hargreaves, 2006; Smith, 2008). This is mainly attributable to the differential historical development of RPL in territories, states and sectors; for example, differing sectoral missions, funding frameworks, policies, governance and accreditation systems. Smith (2004) identifies narrow and broad conceptualisations of RPL:

> *Views vary from quite tightly defined notions of RPL as access to a training program or qualification, through to conceptions of RPL as a reflective process that can directly impact on the nature of learning and the process of training (ibid., p. 5).*

Policy definitions also vary, and much time and effort has been devoted to unpacking the relationships between RPL (for access or advanced standing) and credit transfer. The issue of prior learning derived from formal education and training has also been addressed in different ways.

As outlined, RPL is now subsumed under the overarching term of 'credit', defined and positioned as one of several 'credit processes' (see Figure 2.1). 'Credit' becomes the principal overarching concept for recognising learning, supported by 'credit inputs', 'forms of credit' and 'credit

---

[2] Further refinement may take place following the outcomes of the AQF *'Pathways Project'*, commissioned by the Deputy Prime Minister in March 2009 to improve VET/HE articulation and enable competency-based and merit-based systems to become more student-focused. However, at the time of writing, the report was not publicly available.

Figure 2.1 Credit terminology framework

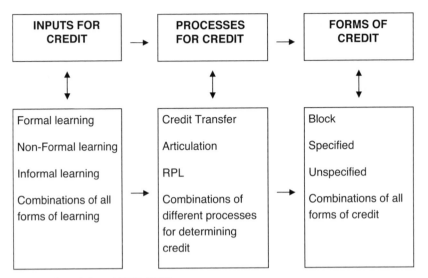

Source: Adapted from AQFC (2009)

processes'. 'Credit inputs' provide the basis for credit through the different forms of learning that can be recognised. 'Forms of credit' are the different credit options and outcomes. 'Credit processes' are utilised by education and training providers to determine credit decisions (AQFC, 2009, p. 9). In this way, RPL is reconceptualised and repositioned as one type of assessment-oriented credit process along with credit transfer and programme articulation arrangements. All of the concepts and definitions in Figure 2.1 are unpacked further in Appendix 2.1.

Bowman *et al.* (2003) undertook a study commissioned by ANTA (the Australian National Training Authority) and published by the National Centre for Vocational Education Research (NCVER) using the AVETMISS data referred to above. They found that RPL grew from 2.4 per cent in 1995 to 4 per cent in 2001. Age was an important factor, with RPL greatest for students in the 25–39 age range (5.1 per cent in 2000). Students in the 40–65 age range were the next highest, and those up to 19 years of age had the lowest RPL rates (2.6 per cent in 2000). In terms of equity groups, the uptake of RPL was mixed and in many cases lower than students overall. According to Hargreaves (2006), a partial reason for this is that equity group members are more likely to participate in training than to seek recognition of existing skills (even when eligible)

Table 2.1 Summary of VET sector RPL statistics (2001)

AQF level	Rate of RPL (%)
Diploma Higher	10
Cert I & II	2
Non award	< 1
Age range	**Rate of RPL (%)**
Up to 19	2.1
20–24	4.6
25–39	5.0
40–64	4.3
Other	1.4
All ages	4.0
Equity groups	**Rate of RPL (%)**
Aboriginal and Torres Strait Islanders (ATSI)	2.1
Reported disability	3.1
Non-English speaking backgrounds (NESB)	3.9
Within the VET sector	**RPL activity (%)**
TAFE	4.7
Private providers	3.0
Community-based providers	0.6

Source: Adapted from Bowman *et al.* (2003)

because the learning process provides benefits in and of itself. Table 2.1 summarises this data.

Bateman and Knight (2003) researched the take-up of RPL in VET in relation to equity groups (funded by the NCVER). Their results regarding disability echoed those above, finding that VET students with a disability were slightly less likely to obtain RPL (3.5 per cent in 1999) than non-English speaking students, but about equally likely in 2000. Similarly, they found Indigenous students much less likely to obtain RPL (2.1 per cent in 2000).

Using both of the above datasets, a cross-sector study of post-compulsory RPL commissioned by AQFAB (Wheelahan *et al.*, 2003a, pp. 18–20) reported an RPL rate of 8 per cent in the VET sector and 5 per cent in higher education (see below). Echoing Bowman *et al.* (2003), the report found most RPL in relation to higher-level qualifications in both the VET and HE sectors. RPL rates were slightly higher for equity group students with a disability and students from regional areas were more likely to receive RPL than metropolis-based students. Students from non-English speaking backgrounds (NESB) were far less likely to receive RPL than students from English-speaking backgrounds, and Indigenous students received about half the RPL compared to non-Indigenous counterparts. Hargreaves (2006) refers to more recent RPL data for the VET sector and reports a slight decline in RPL in 2004 at 3.6 per cent, followed by a return to 4 per cent in 2006.

It is abundantly clear that despite widespread support for RPL, uptake remains low and has not reached expectations. This is in spite of it being mandatory for the VET sector to offer RPL to any student enrolling on an accredited course, and despite government funding to increase RPL activity. These formal arrangements for RPL also apply in the ACE sector if courses are nationally accredited. However, it is difficult to obtain a completely accurate picture due to the limitations of secondary datasets and the fact that only 'up front' enrolment-recorded RPL is counted. RPL in the form of early progression, accelerated learning or challenge testing *after* enrolment is not captured by existing datasets (Bowman *et al.*, 2003; Bateman, 2006; Hargreaves, 2006). It is noted that these 'hidden' forms of RPL are often seen as more effective than the 'traditional methodology of RPL assessment conducted up-front and prior to training' (Bowman *et al.*, 2003, p. 47).

RPL has not been universally embraced by the higher education sector. Various reasons for this are advanced. In a master's thesis, Doddrell (2002) identified the following factors: lack of inclusion of the HE sector in the national training reform agenda; the autonomous nature of HE providers in terms of how they define RPL; the association of RPL with competency-based training and assessment; and a general suspicion of unaccredited learning. Wheelahan *et al.* (2003a) drew attention to the ways in which universities develop their own policies and practices in relation to RPL. In addition, Pitman (2009) summarised the following factors:

- The hierarchical organisation of knowledge in higher education and a frequently associated view that knowledge acquired within universities is superior to knowledge acquired elsewhere.
- A perspective that RPL has a detrimental effect on academic standards.
- A connection between RPL and what is seen as the minimalistic and over-specific outcomes approach in competency-based education and training.

- The view that a formal educational environment imparts certain skills and attributes missing in students that receive significant amounts of RPL.

Pitman (2009) examined the university RPL policy environment by undertaking a content analysis of a sample of 38 university websites. He found that 29 universities accepted RPL. A previous study by Childs *et al.* (2002) had identified 13 universities that mentioned RPL by name. Pitman (2009, pp. 236–7) concludes that there is 'significant evidence that the profile of RPL in Australian universities is increasing insofar as it can be measured in formal policy positions and documents including their online accessibility'. He points out that most universities offer a 'blanket' RPL policy rather than anything more specific. However, three-quarters of his sample of universities indicate that they accept RPL, the vast majority (90 per cent) providing extra resources:

> … *a publicly available document outlining their institutional policies, processes and guidelines on RPL. More than half of the policies deal with RPL either exclusively or in a significant manner, including precise definitions, institutional aims and guidelines on how informal learning should be measured.*

Nonetheless, many of the policies favour and are weighted towards credit transfer. Pitman (2009, p. 228) concludes that 'universities remain unwilling to facilitate a process for which they feel no ownership and are not being provided with leadership'. He further qualifies his findings by pointing out that there is often a discrepancy between what is stated and what is implemented and enacted on the ground, and that further research is needed to investigate this correlation.

Government-funded/commissioned research into RPL policy and practice

The research on RPL policy and practice in Australia is anchored around four major government-commissioned studies. Most of these have been referred to above and are summarised here:

1. In 2001, the Australian Qualifications Framework Advisory Board (AQFAB) commissioned Ryan and Watson to review the cross-sectoral research and to scope a future research agenda. The report,

     published in 2001, was entitled: *RPL in Australia: Recent Literature and Directions for Future Research.*

2.   This led to the AQFAB-commissioned research into the policy and practice of RPL across all four sectors of post-compulsory education (ACE, VET, HE and secondary schools). The report, by Wheelahan *et al.* (2003a), was entitled: *Recognition of Prior Learning: Policy and Practice in Australia.* It paved the way for the development of the *National Principles and Operational Guidelines for Recognition of Prior Learning* (AQFAB, 2004).

3.   The Australian National Training Authority (ANTA) commissioned research to identify and analyse drivers of and barriers to effective implementation of RPL within the VET sector. This report, prepared by the NCVER, was entitled: *Recognition of Prior Learning in the Vocational Education and Training Sector* (Bowman *et al.*, 2003).

4.   ANTA commissioned a further study into RPL and credit transfer. The report, published by the NCVER, was entitled: *Giving Credit: A Review of RPL and Credit Transfer in the Vocational Education and Training Sector, 1995 to 2001* (Bateman and Knight, 2003).

As Cameron (2008, p. 9) notes, three major national reports appeared in 2003, marking a watershed in the literature by drawing 'the accumulated literature together to create a solid basis for further developments in policy, practice and research in the area'.

    Since 2003, there has been a slow stream of RPL research and academic literature, mostly in relation to the VET sector, with a focus on the recognition of workplace skills. In 2005, the International Labour Office (ILO) Skills and Employability Department commissioned a comparative study of workplace skills recognition practices in Australia, New Zealand, Canada, the United States and South Africa. Research questions included: What are the purposes of RPL in each of the countries? What factors, including institutional factors, influence its use, especially in the workplace? How do the structure and the qualifications base of the TVET/VET (technical/vocational education and training) sector influence the concept, policies and practice? What are the main barriers to RPL, especially in the workplace (Dyson and Keating, 2005)?

    In 2007, in the context of the Organisation for Economic Co-operation and Development (OECD) thematic reviews, the NCVER published a report on behalf of the Department of Education, Science and Training (DEST), entitled: *Recognition of Non-Formal and*

Informal Learning in Australia: Country Background Report (Misko *et al.*, 2007).

In 2009, the Australian National Quality Council (NQC) instigated an exploration and analysis of frameworks for recognising workplace learning to inform broader policy on skills recognition. This research drew on international case studies and models from Scotland, Mexico, Ireland and the United Kingdom, along with five approaches already utilised in Australia: i) provider-based workplace assessment services; ii) industry-based assessment systems; iii) the assessment of trade skills; iv) the use of enterprise business processes to meet VET assessment requirements; v) the credit-rating of workplace learning. The final report, entitled *Alternative Frameworks for the Recognition of Workplace Training*, was published by the NQC in July 2009.

Table 2.2 shows the research methodologies used within the above government-funded/commissioned studies. These are categorised as quantitative, qualitative mixed methods (i.e. a combination of quantitative and qualitative) and/or conceptual (i.e. non-empirical). Four of these seven reports took a qualitative approach to data collection and analysis, whilst the remaining three employed mixed methods. No conceptual research was conducted.

Most of the research presented above has been sponsored by government departments and agencies, and as a result tends to reflect these stakeholders' agendas. During the initial stages of the introduction of RPL in Australia many researchers focused upon the benefits RPL would bring. Approximately 15 years down the line, research has tended to focus on whether intended benefits have borne fruit (Cameron, 2004; Cameron and Miller, 2004b; Smith, 2004; Catts and Chamings, 2005; Cleary and Down, 2005; Hargreaves, 2006; McKenna and Mitchell, 2006; Wagner and Childs, 2006; Wagner, 2007).

Summary

Smith (2008) reminds us how small the Australian RPL research community is. She also notes the dominance of certain research questions. These, she argues, assume RPL to be a 'given' part of the (particularly VET) landscape in an unproblematic way. Research methods tend to flow from this, predominantly involving 'identifying stakeholder needs; collecting statistical and case study data on current practice; mapping available resources; charting issues; summarising critical success factors and making recommendations for improvement'. Through this research a

Table 2.2 Main government-funded/commissioned research and methodologies

Researchers	Funding body and purpose	Methodology
Ryan and Watson, 2001	AQFAB To scope a future research agenda	**QUALITATIVE** **Scoping paper** **Literature review**
Wheelahan *et al.*, 2003a	AQFAB The policy and practice of RPL across all four sectors of post-compulsory education	**MIXED METHOD** **Online questionnaire** **Interviews** **Consultations** **Secondary data statistical analysis**
Bowman *et al.*, 2003	ANTA Drivers of and barriers to effective implementation of RPL within the VET sector	**MIXED METHOD** **(predominantly** **QUALITATIVE)** **Literature review/ environmental scan** **Secondary data statistical analysis** **Structured interviews** **Focus groups** **National forum**
Bateman and Knight, 2003	ANTA Study into RPL and credit transfer from 1995 to 2001	**MIXED METHOD** **Literature review (1995–2001)** **Secondary data statistical analysis**
Dyson and Keating, 2005	ILO Recognition for skills acquired in the workplace	**QUALITATIVE** **International comparative** **Consultations** **Field visits** **Interviews**
Misko *et al.*, 2007	DEST OECD thematic review	**QUALITATIVE** **Literature review** **Telephone and face-to-face interviews** **Series of case studies**
National Quality Council, 2009	NQC Exploration and analysis of frameworks for recognising workplace learning	**QUALITATIVE** **Environmental scan** **Desktop review** **Consultations**

wealth of data on RPL sites and procedures has been amassed. However, none of the methods have led us to question the place of RPL as a 'fixture' (*ibid.*, p. 3).

Themes in the Australian RPL research literature (1990–2010)

Benefits and drivers of RPL

Much research focuses on the perceived *benefits* of RPL. Misko *et al.* (2007, pp. 111–14) categorise these broadly as economic, educational, social and personal benefits. Doddrell (2002) found a set of 'assumptions' about the benefits of RPL: that it lays the foundation for lifelong learning; that it is particularly relevant for mature-age learners and an assumption of social justice in education alongside economic and efficiency imperatives. Smith and Clayton (2009, p. 11) summarise similar multiple benefits: 'recognition has been presented as a key plank in lifelong learning, a critical strategy for enhancing skill development and addressing skill shortages, and a mechanism for promoting equity and social inclusion'.

Albrecht (2001, p. 10) quantifies the economic and social benefits of skills recognition. Drawing on *Brain Gain: The Economic Benefits of Recognizing Learning and Learning Credentials in Canada* (Bloom and Grant, 2001), she compares skills recognition in Australia with Canada and finds that based on the Canadian study, which estimates 2.17 per cent of the adult Canadian population are unrecognised learners (over half a million), Australia has approximately 325,000 unrecognised learners. The studies formulate a 'recognition dividend' in monetary terms to calculate the social benefits of recognition to individuals and the economy.

Research tends to address the *drivers* of RPL in terms of categories of stakeholder; for example, registered training organisations (RTOs), educational sectors, industry and individuals/students. According to Bowman *et al.* (2003, p. 13), the major driver of RPL for RTOs is compliance with the Australian Quality Training Framework, followed by customer service imperatives such as access and equity obligations, demands from clients, efficiency concerns, and student and industry demands. Hargreaves (2006, p. 3) found a further driver of RPL for RTOs: 'genuine and valuable learning outcomes … regardless of whether recognition is awarded'.

The key drivers for RPL in VET and ACE relate to human capital policy that attempts to address rates of workforce participation, an ageing workforce and economic competitiveness within a global economy, as well as policy related to social inclusion. For the higher education sector, drivers have centred on the three principles of quality, efficiency and equity (Cohen *et al.*, 1994).

For industry, research notes drivers such as the need for up-skilling; the recognition of skills and skill gaps for human resource development; and management and enterprise bargaining requirements (Bowman *et al.*, 2003, p. 13). Hargreaves (2006) found that the fast-tracking of qualifications and the fostering of a learning culture built confidence and motivation in employees for further development, with spin-offs for industry. Wilson and Lilly (1996, p. 14) add the driver of staff having to spend less time away from the workplace compared to traditional training.

Research identifies a wide range of drivers for individuals/students. These include the options of:

- gaining a qualification either for its own sake or for work requirements, and not having to repeat skills and knowledge training (Bowman *et al.*, 2003, p. 13);
- being assessed in the workplace for recruitment and promotion purposes, or as part of training needs analysis (Toop and Burleigh, 1993);
- fast-tracking qualifications (Hargreaves, 2006, p. 2; Miller, 2009);
- rapid access to better paid jobs (Wilson and Lilly, 1996, p. 14);
- gaining assistance with career planning (Smith, 2004; Cameron and Miller, 2008; Cameron, 2009).

Barriers to RPL

Consideration of barriers to successful policy and practice is a common form of research in RPL. Dyson and Keating's (2005) comparative study of RPL for *workplace learning* across five nations (Australia, Canada, New Zealand, South Africa and the United States) noted barriers in all nations at the systems level, the organisational level and the individual level.

Barriers at the systems level tend to revolve around funding and financing. Difficulties occur because awarding rules and practices and assessment procedures tend to be institutionally specific, and because general and vocational qualifications originate within different domains of learning. Organisational barriers to RPL operate at management, department and practitioner levels. Dyson and Keating (*ibid.*, p. 62) found: 'a lack of faith on the part of teachers in the process, overly rigorous assessment processes, processes where there is not enough rigour, lack of infrastructure to support RPL'. At the individual level, barriers included level of educational attainment – individuals with lower levels of educational attainment were less likely to apply for RPL. Hargreaves (2006, p. 5) noted that formal training acts as a form of 'insurance [for employers] that their employees have the required skills'. This is the case in a range of occupations and professions where safety is paramount. Maher *et al.* (2010) endorse this in their recent review of RPL research and literature undertaken as a scoping exercise for developing a skills recognition framework for the Australian rail industry.

A range of barriers impact upon RPL in *educational contexts*, including:

- low levels of awareness and understanding (Bowman *et al.*, 2003; Smith and Clayton, 2009);
- how RPL is funded, resourced and costed (Napier and Scott, 1995; Wilson and Lilly, 1996; Gibson, 1997; Mattner, 1997; Bowman *et al.*, 2003; Wheelahan *et al.*, 2003a; Hargreaves, 2006);
- how time consuming, complex and bureaucratic the process is (Napier and Scott, 1995; Mattner, 1997; Bowman *et al.*, 2003; Wheelahan *et al.*, 2003a, 2003b; Hargreaves, 2006; Smith and Clayton, 2009);
- confusing language (Bowman *et al.*, 2003; Wheelahan *et al.*, 2003b; Smith, 2004);
- problems with perceptions of equivalence (Davison, 1996; Gibson, 1997; Hager, 1998);
- the lack of high-quality RPL information and support for candidates (Smith and Clayton, 2009);
- devaluing of RPL by educational institutions and practitioners (Smith and Clayton, 2009);
- reticence of VET practitioners to engage in RPL (Hewson, 2008); and
- lack of confidence in the outcomes of RPL and inconsistencies in assessments (Kenyon *et al.*, 1996; Wheelahan *et al.*, 2003a; Hargreaves, 2006).

Access and social inclusion

The potential contribution of RPL to access and social inclusion is another recurring theme in the research literature. RPL is seen as having a strong social justice element, which includes access to and equity in formal education (Gibson, 1997; Mattner, 1997; Bowman *et al.*, 2003). However, some research findings question this, arguing that RPL benefits individuals who are 'mid-career, established in the workforce, older, work full-time, and in associate professional, professional or managerial occupations' (Wheelahan *et al.*, 2003a, p. 20). The conclusion drawn from this and subsequent studies is that RPL serves those from socio-economic backgrounds who already have experience of, and success in, post-compulsory education and training. As Cameron (2006, p. 119) puts it, it is those with 'significant accumulated educational capital who are familiar with formal learning systems and the associated discourse who are more likely to utilise the RPL process'. In their scoping exercise for RPL in the rail industry, Maher *et al.* (2010) identified little research on equity issues and equity groups (Indigenous, non-English speaking background, women returning to the workforce), and echo earlier research findings showing that these candidates are less likely to access and complete RPL than other groups. Moreover, the dominant model of RPL in Australia is the credentialing model (Butterworth, 1992), and Cameron (2004) found that this approach is neither relevant nor appropriate to the needs of disadvantaged and disengaged groups of learners.[3]

Recognition of workplace learning

The reports by Dyson and Keating (2005) and the National Quality Council (2009) represent major pieces of research on the recognition of skills acquired in the workplace. In addition, Blom *et al.* (2004) researched RPL in enterprise-based RTOs, and Cleary and Down (2005) researched models of RPL within seven enterprises in terms of success factors, inhibitors and the potential for partnership-working with VET providers. Maher *et al.* (2010) conducted preliminary research into the skill recognition practices of three rail industry organisations. In addition to these studies are numerous case studies exploring RPL at the interface of VET and industry (Broadmeadows College of TAFE, 1990; Wilson and Lilly, 1996; Smith, 2004; Catts and Chamings, 2005; McKenna and Mitchell, 2006; Perry, 2009).

From a human capital framework, Shah and Long (2004) and Shah *et al.* (2007) explored skills recognition and labour mobility, focusing on

---

[3] See Pokorny in this volume, who cites research that found the opposite.

labour mobility across borders, comparing the Australian situation and the European Union with particular reference to the 'Trans-Tasman Mutual Recognition Arrangement' between Australia and New Zealand.

Use of ICT and Web 2.0 technologies for RPL (e-portfolios)

Technological innovation in RPL is a new area of research interest. The locus of activity for the VET sector is the Australian Flexible Learning Framework (Department of Education, Employment and Workplace Relations) focusing on learning in VET, with particular reference to skill shortage areas. Although they found limited use of new technologies with respect to RPL, they did discover the growing adoption of e-portfolios. The use of online assessment tools was noted in Western Australia, Queensland, Victoria and New South Wales.

In an international study on the use of e-portfolios for gaining recognition or credit towards a formal VET qualification, Miller (2009) refers to the types of technology that can be used for evidence gathering – accessible mobile devices (digital and video cameras), MP3 recorders, smart mobile phones and point-of-view devices. She argues that e-portfolios can assist with managing 'digitally rich assets and artefacts' (*ibid.*, p. 5).

Perry (2009, p. 17) explored the use of e-portfolios to support RPL and found examples in a range of contexts:

- recognising the business and administration skills of rural women by the TAFE New South Wales (NSW) Western Institute;
- supporting assessment in fabrication and welding (with a strong focus on photo and image evidence) at TAFE NSW Illawarra;
- the use of *Moodle* as an e-portfolio with Lifeline volunteers in Hobart; and
- the *WebCT/Blackboard* platform for e-portfolios with students of Aviation Safety at Swinbourne TAFE.

Research suggests that Indigenous learners transfer knowledge through oral processes including story telling, speech, song and dance. Eagles *et al.* (2005) utilised online voice technologies to enable culturally relevant and sensitive oral evidence to be recorded as evidence for RPL with Indigenous learners/workers. Boyle (2009) researched the use of e-portfolios for skills recognition with Indigenous art workers in central

Australia (Charles Darwin University and 'Desart', the Association of Central Australian Aboriginal Art and Craft Centres), using *Skillsbook* to upload MP3 files, videos, photos and a range of text documents.

The use of e-portfolios in higher education is being addressed in the Australian ePortfolio Project, funded by the Australian Learning and Teaching Council. The project has conducted two symposiums covering topics such as discipline-specific initiatives and e-portfolios to capture and present professional standards, graduate attributes and students' reflective skills.

Researching and building RPL practitioner capability

Practitioner-based and practitioner-oriented research has been stimulated by the Council of Australian Governments' (COAG) 'RPL Initiative' (2006–09), which supported a wide range of projects aiming to improve the take-up of RPL in VET.

McKenna and Mitchell (2006) utilised appreciative inquiry to undertake national research with 325 RPL practitioners in VET RPL practitioner forums. Funded through the Department of Education, Science and Training (DEST) 'Reframing the Future' programme, the resulting report contains 'think pieces' and a series of case studies of RPL 'done well'.

Hewson (2008) noted the reticence of VET practitioners to engage in RPL and organised a colloquium for 100 TAFE practitioners in New South Wales to explore and exchange ideas about increasing RPL provision. Using a grounded theory approach, participants were invited to 'share insights from their experiences and understandings and provide an overarching environmental awareness and contextualisation of issues affecting RPL' (*ibid.*, p. 3). In this way it was hoped to find exemplary practice in RPL process, pedagogy and outcomes.

Mitchell and Gronold (2009) reported on a work-based action learning research project designed to increase the confidence of 14 Queensland-based RPL assessors in their professional judgements. Entitled 'Compliance to Creativity', the project focused on the concept of 'advanced practice' and the attributes and characteristics of 'advanced' RPL practitioners. Results showed a shift in consciousness amongst assessors:

> *Over the course of the project they moved from a humble position – that they*
> *were not worthy to be called advanced practitioners – to a position at the end*

of the project where they not only identified their own strengths as advanced practitioners (particularly in their case studies) but committed to using these strengths to assist their colleagues (ibid., p. 1).

Theoretical and conceptual discussions and critique

Although the preceding research themes include applied theoretical discussion and some critical analysis, this final and separate theme identifies researchers and studies where critique is central.

As noted, the RPL research community in Australia is small and this is reflected in the amount of critical literature. Recent engagements in critical theoretical discussion (Bateman, 2003; Wheelahan, 2003; Wheelahan *et al.*, 2003b; Cameron and Miller, 2004a, 2004b, 2004c; Fox, 2005; Cameron, 2005b, 2006, 2008; Wagner and Childs, 2006; Smith, 2008; Hamer, 2010) have built on the critiques that emerged in the 1990s, before the post-2003 watershed. For example, Hager (1998, p. 533), who looked at the differences between informal learning and formal education from a philosophical perspective which he summarised as follows:

- informal learning is typically of a different kind from the learning prescribed by the content of formal education courses;
- informal learning does not fit very well with the narrow view of knowledge that is usually taken for granted in formal education;
- learners themselves, influenced by prevailing assumptions about education and knowledge, are often unaware of the significance, range and depth of their informal learning;
- informal learning is highly contextual in contrast to the generality that is privileged in formal education.

Critical writers in the 1990s also drew attention to problems with the 'equivalence' of unaccredited learning and formal education, and to the related issue of 'translating' learning (Davison, 1996; Gibson, 1997; Hager, 1998).

Continuous attention has been drawn to the disjuncture between policy-based promises and rhetoric, and the actual reality of RPL in Australia (Mattner, 1997; Pithers, 1999; Wheelahan *et al.*, 2003b; Cameron and Miller, 2004b). Over the years, a range of authors have conceptualised alternative models of RPL (Jones and Martin, 1997; Wheelahan *et al.*,

2003b; Cameron and Miller, 2004c; Cameron, 2006; Wheelahan, 2006). Cameron and Miller (2004c) drew attention to the limitations of perceiving RPL as a form of assessment. Mention has already been made of how RPL in Australia lacks relevance to certain groups such as Indigenous learners. Wagner and Childs (2006) researched the exclusionary narratives at play in RPL processes for skilled migrants in Australia and the relationship of these narratives to 'subterranean' forms of racism. Fox (2005, p. 367) critiques RPL in the HE sector in terms of its value, usefulness, relevance and viability for adult learners, referring to it as a 'white elephant'.

Hamer's empirical research (2010) focuses on operations of power in the assessor-candidate relationship and questions the assumption that RPL is a benign activity. She recommends greater awareness amongst RPL practitioners regarding operations of power in practices and identities. Drawing on the philosophy of recognition, she concludes that more complex and sophisticated skills recognition systems are needed.

All in all, few theoretical and conceptual resources have been brought to bear on RPL in Australia: Cameron (2005a, 2008) and Hamer (2010) draw on insights from postmodernism; Wheelahan *et al.* (2003b) and Cameron (2006) deploy some of Bernstein's theory related to knowledge and pedagogy, and Cameron (2008) uses Bourdieu's concept of cultural capital and transitional learning theory. In general, the view is that more theoretical frameworks and research are needed in order to address the 'ambiguity', 'uncertainty' and 'unexamined assumptions' that characterise the RPL 'discursive space' (Smith, 2008, p. 1).

Gaps and future directions for RPL research

Table 2.3 summarises the research literature addressed in this chapter in terms of contextual focus and methodological approach. This forms the basis for a discussion about research gaps and directions. Six pieces of literature could not be categorised in terms of methodological approach; for example, references made to policies in order to illuminate the terrain more generally. This explains the difference in total numbers for contextual focus (n=86) and methodological approach (n=80).

Just under half of the research literature on RPL in Australia (1990–April 2010) has focused on the VET sector (n=40, 47 per cent). This is followed by cross-sectoral focus (n=12, 14 per cent) and research pertaining to specific target groups (n=10, 12 per cent). The ACE sector

Table 2.3 Summary of Australian RPL research literature (1990 to April 2010)

Contextual Focus	Frequency	%
VET	40	47
Cross–sectoral	12	14
Specific target groups	10	12
HE	9	11
ACE	8	8
Workplace/industry	7	8
TOTAL	86	100

Methodological Approach	Frequency	%
QUALITATIVE	31	39
CONCEPTUAL	27	34
MIXED METHODS	12	15
QUANTITATIVE	5	6
OTHER: applied field research, implementation trials	5	6
TOTAL	80	100

and the workplace are the least-researched areas. In terms of methodological approaches, qualitative research dominates (n=31, 39 per cent), followed by conceptual (n=27, 34 per cent) and mixed methods (n=12, 15 per cent). Quantitative research is the least-favoured approach.

The following excerpts identify several areas needing further research and analysis:

- Bateman and Knight (2003, p. 13) note that much of the research literature relates to implementation and related processes rather than to *the concept* of RPL itself.
- Bateman (2003, p. 5) identifies a lack of research and critical analysis of *macro influences* on RPL.
- Blom *et al.* (2004, p. 9) assert that the majority of RPL research has 'focused on its application in education and training sectors and there is a lack of literature on *skills recognition within industrial settings*', or within enterprise-based training environments.
- Hargreaves (2006) highlights the effect of a lack of *statistical collection of data* on the uptake of RPL. He notes the absence of a comprehensive national dataset and reports that the most recent attempts to document the uptake of RPL were in 2003.

- Misko *et al.* (2007, p. 4) refer to the lack of *quantitative and longitudinal research* into RPL.
- Smith (2008, pp. 9–10) argues for research into *how* RPL works, including viewing it *as embodied practice* and undertaking *ethnographic studies* located in the 'micro-worlds of particular RPL enactments'.
- Maher *et al.* (2010, p. 5) point to a need for research directed at *company or RTO level*, taking account of context-specific demands and constraints, the *retrospective experiences* of those who have experienced the process, and to *understandings of knowledge* within RPL.

This section of the chapter concludes by bringing together the positional stances of three authors in order to begin to develop an argument for future RPL research in Australia. Tara Fenwick is a noted researcher and scholar in the fields of adult education and organisational theory, Peter Freebody is a qualitative educational research methodologist, and Judy Harris is an internationally recognised scholar in RPL. Their perspectives and foci for future RPL research reflect their differing theoretical perspectives and the multiple contexts in which RPL is operationalised in Australia.

Given the recent focus in Australia on building RPL practitioner capability and the growing use of skill recognition systems and frameworks within workplaces, Tara Fenwick's (2004) argument for critical human resource development (HRD) is pertinent. She draws from critical management theory and critical pedagogy to propose critical HRD which links adult education's focus on learning to training and development, career development and organisational development. She argues that critical HRD would 'support a space *within* HRD to nurture critical questions about power, interests, and equity and to articulate critical challenges of oppressive organizational structures and knowledge legitimation' (*ibid.*, p. 193). An interesting aspect of her thesis is the creation of a 'middle space' where 'critical adult educators might find fruitful alliances with their HRD colleagues towards just, equitable, life-giving and sustainable work' (*ibid.*, pp. 193–4).

Freebody (2003) proposes four roles that educational research must endeavour to achieve. These can also be applied to RPL research:

1. more powerful theoretical accounts of education practice;
2. more refined and empirically justifiable methodological approaches to the conduct of research;

3. more effective, inclusive and equitable daily practices in homes, schools, colleges, universities and workplaces; and
4. more effective, inclusive and equitable public policies for the conduct of education (*ibid.*, pp. 212–13).

In the editorial introduction to *Re-theorising the Recognition of Prior Learning*, Harris (2006, p. 9) identifies three overarching reasons for re-theorising and re-examining RPL:

1. RPL offers a generative site in which to research changing socio-economic conditions and their effects on education.
2. RPL offers a site in which to research the complexity of the issues involved in opening a path from informal, experience-based learning into formal learning situations.
3. RPL links to an ever-expanding range of initiatives in widening participation in education and training (e.g. work-based learning). As such there is likely to be relevance beyond those practices 'named' RPL.

Together these three perspectives and positions combine to present a strong argument for future directions in RPL research in Australia. Given the many sites of RPL in terms of educational sectors, workplaces and industry, a need for empirically rigorous interdisciplinary inquiry is paramount, as is diversity in terms of research questions and methodological approaches that engage and generate more critical, theoretically powerful and inclusive research.

Conclusion

Research in Australia from 1990 to April 2010 has been reviewed. The 1990s produced a small amount of research and literature which, in the main, engaged in critical analysis of RPL policy, practice and pedagogy. In 2003, three major government-funded reports marked a watershed in RPL research, literature and practice. Research conducted in the aftermath of these reports has focused predominantly on implementation. Despite the multiple sites of RPL in contemporary Australia, it remains strongly embedded in the education system, overwhelmingly in the VET sector. Careful note must be taken of the marked under-utilisation and unenthusiastic adoption of RPL in the HE sector. Thematic analysis of the RPL research literature in Australia identified several major themes, including an emerging area of research into the use of ICT and Web 2.0 technologies.

Gaps were also identified and an argument for future research directions presented. The gaps centre around a lack of research that focuses on: macro-contextual forces and influences on RPL; micro-level analysis through examination of the experiences of RPL applicants; critical perspectives that acknowledge aspects of power and identity; forms of knowledge and the values assigned to different forms of learning; critical perspectives on and innovations in skill recognition within enterprises and workplaces; RPL pedagogy and practice especially within the HE sector; the role of organisations and practitioners as gatekeepers to formal learning systems; and alternative models of RPL, including arguments for RPL as something other than assessment prior to enrolment.

The lack of ethnographic, longitudinal and quantitative studies, and the need for interdisciplinary perspectives which utilise diverse and innovative research methodologies to explore RPL in differing contexts and at different levels or even multiple levels of analysis, has been identified. It is hoped that research which accommodates these findings will provide greater theoretical depth and foster greater insight into RPL.

References

Albrecht, J. (2001) 'Skills recognition in the post-compulsory sector: An international comparison, towards a recognition dividend'. Paper presented at the AARE Conference, Fremantle 2001. Available at: http://www.aare.edu.au/01pap/alb01291.htm.

Australian Qualifications Framework Advisory Board (AQFAB) (2004) *National Principles and Operational Guidelines for Recognition of Prior Learning*. Canberra: AQF. Available at: http://www.aqf.edu.au/rplnatprin.htm# (Accessed 2 October 2005).

Australian Qualifications Framework Council (2009) *AQF National Policy and Guidelines on Credit Arrangements, Final Draft May 2009*. Canberra: AQF Council, Canberra. Available at: http://www.aqf.edu.au/Portals/0/Documents/Credit%20Transfer%20Project%20-%20Final%20draft%20policy.pdf (Accessed 5 June 2009).

Bateman, A. (2003) 'Has RPL served its purpose?' *Proceedings of the 6th Australian VET Research Association Conference: The Changing Face of VET*. Sydney: Australian Vocational Education and Training Research Association (AVETRA).

Bateman, A. (2006) 'Yes, we are there! Think piece', in S. McKenna and J. Mitchell (eds) *RPL Done Well in VET: Resources Generated for the 'Reframing the Future' National Forums*. Elizabeth, South Australia: Reframing the Future. Available at: http://www.reframingthefuture.net/docs/2007/Publications/3EVP_RPL_Done_Well_1mar07.pdf (Accessed 28 March 2009).

Bateman, A. and Knight, B. (2003) *Giving Credit: A Review of RPL and Credit Transfer in the Vocational Education and Training Sector, 1995 to 2001*. Adelaide: National Centre for Vocational and Educational Research (NCVER).

Blom, K., Clayton, B., Bateman, A., Bedggood, M. and Hughes, E. (2004) 'RPL in enterprise-based RTOs: How does it work?' *Proceedings of the 7th Australian Vocational Education and Training Research Association Conference: Learner and Practitioner – the Heart of the Matter*. Canberra: AVETRA.

Bloom, M. and Grant, M. (2001) *Brain Gain: The Economic Benefits of Recognizing Learning and Learning Credentials in Canada*. Ottawa: Conference Board of Canada. Available at: http://www.conference-board.ca/education/pdf/Brain_Gain_Detailed_Findings.pdf.

Bowman, K., Clayton, B., Bateman, A., Knight, B., Thomson, P., Hargreaves, J., Blom, K. and Enders, M. (2003) *Recognition of Prior Learning in the Vocational Education and Training Sector*. Adelaide: National Centre for Vocational and Educational Research (NCVER).

Boyle, A. (2009) 'E-nabling E-portfolios for Skills Recognition of Aboriginal Artworkers in Central Australia'. Paper presented at the *12th Australian Vocational Education and Training Research Association Conference*, Sydney, Australia.

Broadmeadows College of TAFE (1990) *Recognition of Prior Learning – Ford/TAFE Articulation Project Principal Report*, Broadmeadows COT.

Butterworth, C. (1992) 'More than one bite at the APEL', *Journal of Further and Higher Education*, Vol. 16, No 3, pp. 39–51.

Callan, V. and Fergusson, A. (2009) 'How training organisations are using e-learning to support national training initiatives around apprenticeships and RPL'. Paper presented at the *12th Australian Vocational Education and Training Research Association Conference*, Sydney.

Cameron, R. (2004) 'RPL and mature-age job seekers', *Adult Learning Australia*. Available at: http://www.ala.asn.au/research/index.html.

Cameron, R. (2005a) 'The mature-aged in transition: Innovative practice for re-engagement'. Paper presented at the *8th Annual Australian*

Vocational Education and Training Research Association Conference, Brisbane.

Cameron, R. (2005b) 'Trajectories, transitions and transformations'. *Proceedings of the 13th Annual International Conference on Post-Compulsory Education and Training.* Griffith University, Gold Coast, December.

Cameron, R. (2006) 'RPL and the disengaged learner: The need for new starting points'. In P. Andersson and J. Harris (eds) *Re-theorising the Recognition of Prior Learning.* Leicester: National Institute of Adult Continuing Education (NIACE).

Cameron, R. (2008) 'Adult Learning and career transitions: Development of a lifelong learning model for engagement, recognition and transitions'. PhD Thesis, Southern Cross University, Lismore, Australia.

Cameron, R. (2009) 'A career and learning transitions model for those experiencing labour market disadvantage', *Australian Journal of Career Development*, Vol. 18, No 1, pp. 17–25.

Cameron, R. and Miller, P. (2004a) 'Recipes for recognition and lifelong learning: Community-based approaches to fostering learning transitions'. *Proceedings of Making Connections: Transition to University.* Brisbane: QUT, Carseldine.

Cameron, R. and Miller, P. (2004b) 'RPL: Why has it failed to act as a mechanism for social change?' *Proceedings of Social Change in the 21st Century Conference.* Brisbane: Queensland University of Technology, Centre for Social Change.

Cameron, R. and Miller, P. (2004c) 'A transitional model of recognition'. *Proceedings of International Conference on Post Compulsory Education and Training.* Surfers Paradise: Griffith University, Centre for Learning Research.

Cameron, R. and Miller, P. (2008) 'A transitional model to assist those experiencing labour market disadvantage'. Paper presented at the *17th Annual Australian Association of Career Counsellors (AACC) Conference*, Hobart, 26–28 March. Available at: http://epubs.scu.edu.au/cgi/viewcontent.cgi?article=1078&context=comm_pubs.

Catts, R. and Chamings, D. (2005) 'RPL and social capital: The training of volunteers for emergency service organisations'. *Proceedings of 4th International Conference on Researching Work and Learning*, P. Hager and G. Hawke (eds). Sydney: University of Technology, Australian Centre for Organisational, Vocational and Adult Learning (OVAL Research), Broadway.

Childs, M., Ingham, V. and Wagner, R. (2002) 'Recognition of Prior learning on the web – a case of Australian universities', *Australian Journal of Adult Learning*, Vol. 42, No 1, pp. 39–56.

Cleary, M. and Down, C. (2005) *Enterprise RPL Project*. Brisbane: Australian National Training Authority (ANTA).

Cohen, R., Flowers, R., McDonald, R. and Schaafsma, H. (1994) 'Learning from experience counts: Recognition of Prior Learning in Australian universities', in *Recognition of Prior Learning in Australian Universities*, Australian Vice-Chancellors' Committee on Credit Transfer Project. Canberra: Australian Government Publishing Service.

Davison, T. (1996) '"Equivalence" and the Recognition of Prior Learning (RPL)', *Australian Vocational Education Review*, Vol. 3, No 2, pp. 11–18.

Doddrell, E. (2002) *The Evolution of RPL in Australia: From its Origins to Future Possibilities*, Master's Thesis, Murdoch University, Melbourne.

Dyson, C. and Keating, J. (2005) *Skills, Knowledge and Employability-Recognition of Prior Learning Policy and Practice for Skills Learned at Work*, Skills Working Paper No 21. Geneva: International Labour Office (ILO).

Eagles, D., Woodward, P. and Pope, M. (2005) 'Indigenous learners in the digital age: Recognising skills and knowledge'. *Proceedings of the 8th Australian Vocational Education and Training Research Association Conference: Emerging Futures – Recent, Responsive and Relevant Research*, Brisbane.

Fenwick, T. (2004) 'Toward a critical HRD in theory and practice', *Adult Education Quarterly*, Vol. 54, No 3, pp. 193–209.

Fox, T. (2005) 'Adult learning and the Recognition of Prior Learning: The "white elephant" in Australian universities', *Australian Journal of Adult Learning*, Vol. 45, No 3, pp. 352–70.

Freebody, P. (2003) *Qualitative Research in Education Interaction and Practice*. London: SAGE Publications.

Gibson, T. (1997) 'Report on the implementation of RPL principles and models in the Victorian State Training System'. Melbourne: Office of Training and Further Education.

Hager, P. (1998) 'Recognition of informal learning: Challenges and issues', *Journal of Vocational Education and Training*, Vol. 50, No 4, pp. 521–35.

Hamer, J. (2010) 'Recognition of Prior Learning: Normative assessment or co-construction of preferred identities?', *Australian Journal of Adult Learning*, Vol. 50, No 1, pp. 100–15.

Hargreaves, J. (2006) *Recognition of Prior Learning: At a Glance*. Adelaide: National Centre for Vocational and Educational Research (NCVER).

Harris, J. (2006) 'Introduction and overview of chapters', in P. Andersson and J. Harris (eds) *Re-theorising the Recognition of Prior Learning*. Leicester: National Institute of Adult Continuing Education (NIACE).

Hewson, J. (2008) 'RPL policy to practice: Why the reticence of practitioners to engage?' Paper presented at the *11th Australian Vocational Education and Training Research Association Conference*, Adelaide. Available at: http://www.avetra.org.au/AVETRA%20Work%2017.04.08/CS6.1%20-%20Janet%20Hewson.pdf.

Jones, M. and Martin, J. (1997) 'A new paradigm for Recognition of Prior Learning (RPL)', in W. Fleet (ed.) *Issues in Recognition of Prior Learning: A Collection of Papers*. Melbourne: Victorian RPL Network.

Kenyon, R., Saunders, J. and Gibb, J. (1996) *Improving RPL: A Training Providers' Perspective*. Adelaide: National Centre for Vocational and Educational Research (NCVER).

Maher, K., Davies, L., Harris, R. and Short, T. (2010) *Scoping the Potential of Skills Recognition in Rail, Final Report March 2010*. Brisbane: CRC for Rail Innovation, Education and Training Programme.

Mattner, S. (1997) 'RPL: Between policy and practice', *Australian Vocational Education Review*, Vol. 4, No 1, pp. 16–23.

McKenna, S. and Mitchell, J. (eds) (2006) *RPL Done Well in VET: Resources Generated for the 'Reframing the Future' National Forums*. Elizabeth, South Australia: Reframing the Future. Available at: http://www.reframingthefuture.net/docs/2007/Publications/3EVP_RPL_Done_Well_1mar07.pdf (Accessed 28 March 2009).

Miller, A. (2009) 'The world of e-portfolio'. *The Knowledge Tree*, Edition 18. Available at: http://kt.flexiblelearning.net.au/tkt2009/ ?page_id=18 (Accessed 19 February 2010).

Misko, J., Beddie, F. and Smith, L. (2007) *The Recognition of Non-formal and Informal Learning in Australia: Country Background Report*. Canberra: Commonwealth of Australia.

Mitchell, J. and Gronold, J. (2009) 'Increasing the confidence of advanced RPL assessors'. Paper presented at the *12th Australian Vocational Education and Training Research Association Conference*, Sydney. Available at: http://www.avetra.org.au/papers-2009/papers/35.00.pdf> (Accessed 29 May 2009).

Napier, R. and Scott, M. (1995) 'Methodologies for Recognition of Prior Learning in agricultural education', *Australian Journal of Adult and Community Education*, Vol. 35, No 1, pp. 33–42.

National Quality Council (NQC) (2009) *Alternative Frameworks for the Recognition of Workplace Training, Final Report July 2009.* Canberra: Department of Education, Employment and Workplace Relations (DEEWR). Available at: http://www.nqc.tvetaustralia.com.au/__data/assets/pdf_file/0003/49764/Workplace_Training_Report.pdf.

Perry, W. (2009) *E-portfolios for RPL Assessment: Key Findings on Current Engagement in the VET sector, Final Report.* Canberra: Australian Flexible Learning Framework, Department of Education, Employment and Workplace Relations (DEEWR). Available at: http://pre2005.flexiblelearning.net.au/newsandevents/E-portfolios_for_RPL_Assessment_Final_190309.pdf (Accessed 30 March 2009).

Pithers, R. (1999) 'Recognition of prior learning: Promises and emerging reality', *Australian Vocational Education Review*, Vol. 6, No 1, pp. 10–16.

Pitman, T. (2009) 'Recognition of Prior Learning: The accelerated rate of change in Australian universities', *Higher Education Research and Development*, Vol. 28, No 2, pp. 227–40.

Ryan, C. and Watson, L. (2001) *RPL in Australia: Recent Literature and Directions for Future Research.* Report prepared for the Australian Qualifications Framework Advisory Board (AQFAB), RPL Working Party, Lifelong Learning Network, Canberra.

Shah, C. and Long, M. (2004) *Global Labour Mobility and Mutual Recognition of Skills and Qualifications: European Union and Australia/New Zealand Perspectives.* Working Paper 56. Victoria: Monash University, ACER/CEET.

Shah, C., Long, M. and Windle, J. (2007) *Recognition of Skills and Qualifications: Labour Mobility and Trade in Services.* Victoria: Monash University, CEET.

Smith, H. (2008) 'RPL in Australian VET: What do we know (about it)? Paper presented at the *11th Australian Vocational Education and Training Research Association Conference*, Adelaide.

Smith, L. (2004) *Valuing Recognition of Prior Learning: Selected Case Studies of Australian Private Providers of Training.* Adelaide: National Centre for Vocational and Educational Research (NCVER).

Smith, L. and Clayton, B. (2009) *Recognising Non-formal and Informal Learning: Participant Insights and Perspectives.* Adelaide: National Centre for Vocational and Educational Research (NCVER).

Toop, L. and Burleigh, J. (1993) *Arrangements for the Recognition of Prior Learning in Australian Vocational Education.* Employment and Training Advisory Committee, Vocational Education Employment & Training Advisory Committee (VEETAC), Department of Education Employment and Training (DEET), Canberra.

Wagner, R. (2007) 'So doctors become taxi drivers: Tackling professional skills recognition in Australia', *The International Journal of Interdisciplinary Social Sciences,* Vol. 1, No 1, pp. 155–62.

Wagner, R. and Childs, M. (2006) 'Exclusionary narratives as barriers to the recognition of qualifications, skills and experience: A case of skilled migrants in Australia', *Studies in Continuing Education,* Vol. 28, No 1, pp. 49–62.

Wheelahan, L. (2003) 'Recognition of prior learning and the problem of "graduateness"'. Paper presented at the *6th Annual Australian Vocational Education and Training Research Association Conference,* Sydney.

Wheelahan, L. (2006) 'Vocations, "graduateness" and the Recognition of Prior Learning', in P. Andersson and J. Harris (eds) *Re-theorising the Recognition of Prior Learning.* Leicester: National Institute of Adult Continuing Education (NIACE), pp. 241–60.

Wheelahan, L., Dennis, N., Firth, J., Miller, P., Newton, D., Pascoe, S. with support from Brightman, R. (2003a) *Recognition of Prior Learning: Policy and Practice in Australia.* Commissioned by the Australian Qualifications Framework Advisory Board (AQFAB).

Wheelahan, L., Newton, D. and Miller, P. (2003b) 'Recognition of Prior Learning: Why is it so difficult to accredit learning that has occurred outside the academy towards the award of a qualification? A report from Australia'. *Proceedings of the 'Researching Learning outside the Academy' International Conference.* Glasgow Caledonian University and University of Stirling: Centre for Research in Lifelong Learning (CRLL), 27–29 June.

Wilson, J. and Lilly, M. (1996) *Recognition of Prior Learning.* Adelaide: National Centre for Vocational and Educational Research (NCVER).

Appendix 2.1 Credit Terminology Framework Definitions

Term	Definition
Inputs for credit	
Formal learning	Learning that takes place through a structured programme of learning and assessment that leads to the full or partial attainment of a recognised AQF qualification, or other formally recognised qualification.
Non-formal learning	Learning that takes place through a structured programme of learning, but does not lead to a formally recognised qualification.
Informal learning	Learning gained through work-related, social, family, hobby or leisure activities and experiences. Unlike formal and non-formal learning, informal learning is not organised or externally structured in terms of objectives, time or learning support.
Processes for credit	
Articulation	A process that enables students to progress from one completed qualification to another with credit in a defined pathway.
Credit transfer	A process that provides students with agreed and consistent credit outcomes based on equivalence in content, and learning outcomes between matched qualifications.
Recognition of Prior Learning (RPL)	An assessment process that involves assessment of the individual's relevant prior learning to determine the credit outcomes of an individual application for credit.
Forms of credit	
Block credit	Credit granted towards whole stages or components of a qualification.
Specified credit	Credit granted towards particular or specific components in a qualification.
Unspecified credit	Credit granted towards elective components in a qualification.

Source: Adapted from AQFC (2009, p. 8)

CHAPTER THREE

Canada: A typology of Prior Learning Assessment and Recognition (PLAR) research in context

Joy Van Kleef

Abstract

Prior Learning Assessment and Recognition (PLAR) emerged in Canada through government initiatives to increase and improve the quality of Canadian labour supply through further and accelerated education. From the outset, these initiatives reflected a paradigm that ensured organisational control over what knowledge would be considered to have value. Research into PLAR has for the most part been applied, frequently deploying descriptive and exploratory qualitative studies to inform implementation. This chapter explores research on PLAR outside Québec over the past 16 years (1995–2010 inclusive). The first section presents several broad contextual forces that have impacted on the development of PLAR practice. Public policy and competitive dynamics relating to post-secondary education that have helped to shape PLAR's research context are identified. Next, a typology is presented that frames Canadian research to date and draws attention to the types of research conducted, who participates and whose interests have been served. Finally, the ideas are brought together to consider gaps and what the future of research in PLAR might hold.

Introduction

It was 1989, and the boardroom table was set with briefing packages for each ministry's senior officers. At one end were a pile of statistical reports and a PowerPoint presentation at the ready in case further information was required. As I began my briefing to the Minister on our research into Prior Learning Assessment and Recognition (PLAR), I scanned the faces of my audience for clues of their initial response. I detected genuine support, curiosity, lack of interest, and resistance. Little did I know that these reactions foreshadowed most responses to PLAR over the forthcoming two decades. Nor could I have anticipated the path PLAR would take before becoming part of the way we look at learning.

Prior Learning Assessment and Recognition in Canada is slowly evolving. Its progress has been influenced by interrelated contextual factors – demographic/economic, political, social and pedagogical – that have both supported and impeded its development. This chapter explores PLAR in nine provinces and three territories in Canada over the past 16 years (1995–2010 inclusive). The impact of long-term labour force demographics, government public policy and competitive tensions relating to post-secondary education are examined for their role in shaping PLAR and the research that has been generated. A typology is presented that frames our research to date and draws attention to what has been accomplished, who conducts research, and whose interests are served. Finally, the ideas discussed in preceding sections are brought together to consider what the future of PLAR and its research might hold.

To understand how PLAR and its research reached their current status, we need to examine not only relevant chronological events and the forces that helped generate them, but also the rationale provided to those whose cooperation was necessary to undertake those events (Keeton, 1997). Canada's ten provinces and three territories each address PLAR differently, presenting a challenging context in which to make general statements about PLAR nationwide in Canada. In order to keep this review manageable, I have chosen to reference PLAR developments at the federal level, and in five provinces: British Columbia, Manitoba, Nova Scotia, Ontario and Saskatchewan. These jurisdictions were early leaders in PLAR, they reflect diverse sets of PLAR arrangements, and they continue to provide most of the PLAR services in the country. They also share certain demographic characteristics that have created positive conditions for recognising prior learning. A sixth province, Québec, has the longest history of development in PLAR and is perhaps the most developed. It is not included in this review due to the unavailability of detailed information in English and the author's monolingual status. However, Rachel Bélisle's chapter in this book provides a valuable overview of scholarly research in Québec since 2002.

A brief review of Canada's demographics helps set the context for the evolution of PLAR.

Troubling labour force demographics

Demographic projections for Canada's population and skilled labour force over the past few years have been consistent and troubling. Like many developed nations, Canada's general and labour force populations are rapidly ageing, lifespans among older adults are increasing, the birth rate is falling. Data from the 2006 census revealed that 15.3 per cent of the total labour force was aged 55 and older, compared to 11.7 per cent five years earlier (Statistics Canada, 2008). Morrissey *et al.* (2008) report that as the retirement of older workers increasingly outpaces the inflow of younger entrants, labour supply problems will become more critical. They also describe a labour market that is increasingly subject to 'churning' as workers move across sectors, occupations and regions in response to large-scale shifts in economic conditions. As traditional sectors of employment such as manufacturing decline and technological advances change work requirements, skill gaps add to the pressure on educational institutions to prepare new entrants to the labour force and upgrade or re-skill the existing workforce.

One strategy used to increase Canada's workforce has been immigration. Current estimates are that, by 2011, 100 per cent of Canada's net labour force growth will be from immigration and, by 2030, immigrants will account for 100 per cent of the country's population growth (Statistics Canada, 2007). Yet despite an immigrant population that is better educated than Canada's domestic population, Canada has not capitalised on the talents of its immigrant labour supply (Bloom and Grant, 2001; Reitz, 2001).[1] Lack of adequate credential assessment and prior learning assessment are identified as causes of slow economic and social integration (Human Resources and Skills Development Canada, 2002; Standing Committee on Human Resources, Social Development and the Status of Persons with Disabilities, 2008), and a contributing factor to other costly social problems (Brouwer, 1999; Bloom and Grant, 2001).

---

[1] Statistics Canada report that both recent and established immigrants have higher levels of educational attainment than people born in Canada (Galarneau and Morrisette, 2008).

Although immigrant workers are important sources of future labour, they are not enough to solve Canada's labour shortage problems (Morrissey *et al.*, 2008). Their numbers are insufficient; they share many of the same skill-related challenges experienced by Canadian-born workers; and they face additional cultural, language and financial barriers to employment and education. Other strategies are necessary to strengthen our labour supply and retention of older workers, improving labour force access for under-represented groups, and facilitating adults' opportunities for relevant education and training are some of the measures being investigated (Morrissey *et al.*, 2008). Proponents of recognising prior learning argue that PLAR could help to improve Canada's labour supply by providing a mechanism to support all of these additional strategies.

A multifaceted national public policy agenda

The federal government encouraged the use of PLAR as a labour force development tool throughout the 1990s. Reports produced from 1994 to 1998 reveal that federal support for PLAR arose in the context of a failure to recognise and take account of immigrants' knowledge and skills, resulting in a major barrier to the practice of their professions and trades in Canada. Associated restrictions on social and employment integration contradicted demographic, economic and social public policy objectives, which taken together formed much of the basis of Canada's vision for future prosperity. Economic public policy recognised the important role that immigrants were destined to play as investors, workers and consumers. For prosperity to be peaceful, our long-standing national policy of multiculturalism called for full and equitable participation of individuals and communities of all origins in the evolution and shaping of Canadian society (Government of Canada, 1988).

Federal/provincial relations in Canada have historically been characterised by undulating tension over who should set public policies on human capital development. The provinces have exclusive constitutional jurisdiction over education but, until a decade ago, they shared responsibility for labour force development with the federal government. The natural overlaps between these areas of responsibility have been a source of competitive tension whenever the federal government has embarked on initiatives which were viewed by the provinces as matters of education. Responsibility for most areas of labour force development have since been devolved from the federal government to the provinces through negoti-ated labour force agreements, but in 1994 when PLAR was emerging, the federal government signalled its support by initiating federal policy development and funding the first of several national conferences. These conferences, which attracted a range of stakeholder groups, primarily focused on networking, implementation discussions, pilot project presen-tations and professional development – providing a unifying environment for budding PLAR practitioners in post-secondary education, employ-ment preparation and immigrant integration. Federal support for PLAR was expressed in other ways as well. Throughout the 1990s, the federally funded, multi-stakeholder-based Canadian Labour Force Development Board (CLFDB) included PLAR as part of a proposed employment tran-sition system for Canada and conducted national consultations on the potential for national PLAR standards. In 1999, the Board proposed a national action plan for PLAR for foreign-trained Canadians (Training and Development Associates, 1999), but its agenda was cut short by the dissolution of the CLFDB later that year and with it a key pan-Canadian policy-making structure supporting PLAR.

Despite constitutional limitations on the extent to which the federal government could provide leadership in education, it continued to find ways to influence the education and training of adults under the auspices of national labour force development. In 2002, Human Resources and Skills Development Canada (HRSDC) led the development of a national 'Innovation Strategy' which set out the government's position on skills and learning. The Strategy stated that Canada's learning system must be strengthened to meet the skills and labour force demands of the coming decades. The Strategy also noted that insufficient PLAR capacity was an important gap in Canada's learning infrastructure and that increased recognition of prior learning would motivate more adults to gain addi-tional skills, and remove a significant barrier to full participation and mobility in the labour market.

However, the federal government's policies with regard to PLAR did not extend beyond what Thomas (2000) called 'benign and enabling' – extending support through rhetoric and project funding, but never estab-lishing requirements or linking PLAR to ongoing federal financing for stakeholders. In 2005, the federal government did not fund the national conference on PLAR, and in 2006, along with the final stages of devolution of labour force development to the provinces, federal funding was perma-nently terminated. In 2008, alternative public and private sector sources were found to fund the continuation of national PLAR conferences led by the Canadian Association for Prior Learning Assessment (CAPLA), but the loss of federal funding was a blow to pan-Canadian efforts to expand organisational awareness, understanding and participation in PLAR.

Implementation of PLAR in the provinces

Throughout the 1990s, PLAR was also emerging as a policy issue for provincial governments. Canada's provinces differ from one another in many respects, including economic base, population size and balance of urban to rural residents, cultural composition and political leanings. Yet their approaches to PLAR had some commonalities. In this section, I focus on these commonalities as a way of examining evolutional factors from a pan-Canadian perspective. In doing so, I have relied on several key reports such as Morrissey *et al.* (2008), as well as historical documents and consultative interviews with key informants who were active in PLAR in the early 1990s. Characteristics that the provinces have most in common include the following:

1. In each province, the initial introduction of PLAR can be traced to Canadian adult educators, many of whom, quite independently from one another, became acquainted with the work of the Council for Adult and Experiential Learning (CAEL) in the United States and began to promote exploration of the application of PLAR in Canadian post-secondary education.
2. Heavily influenced by demographics and economic projections, public policy-makers were quick to identify the potential of PLAR as a social and economic development tool, and began to encourage its integration into existing education systems and employment preparation programmes.
3. Shortly after its introduction, the direction of PLAR diverged. One development was assessment for academic credit primarily at the college level of education.[2] The second, but to a lesser degree, was assessment of prior learning for personal development, training needs assessment and employment. In both cases, organisations seeking

---

[2] Colleges are similar to VET or FET institutions in other countries. Until recently, they offered certificate and diploma programmes rather than degrees.

government support for early PLAR initiatives framed their intentions primarily in terms of economic development.

4. The primary focus of PLAR initiatives has been on implementation within existing systems of education, professional regulation and employment. These initiatives have not challenged the systems themselves or their control over the value given to non-formal and informal learning (Butterworth and Bloor, 1994). Organisational decision-makers have firmly controlled the criteria against which prior learning is judged, the quality standards used to conduct assessments, the amount of 'say' a PLAR candidate has in how they might demonstrate their learning, the type of 'value' assigned to assessment results and the transferability of assessment outcomes.

5. PLAR is present in most of Canada's public colleges which use a relatively consistent 'credit exchange' (Butterworth, 1992) form of PLAR. Developmental models are more prevalent in PLAR services for employment preparation.[3]

6. Although there are exceptions in each province, most universities do not conduct PLAR and are reported to be resistant (Blinkhorn, 1999; Nesbit *et al.*, 2007; Peruniak, 2007). In a 2006 survey, the Association of Universities and Colleges of Canada reported that out of 40 university respondents, 11 reported using PLAR (AUCC, 2006). A 2009 survey referencing 115 institutions by the Canadian Institute for Recognizing Learning found no change, with assessments conducted by only 11 universities (Van Kleef, 2009). Sources of resistance included concerns about the quality of prior learning (Ferguson, 1998; Bloom and Watt, 2001; Shandro, 2006), the purpose of a university education (Blinkhorn, 1999; Nesbit *et al.*, 2007) and relinquishing control over what learning should 'count' towards an academic credential (Thomas, 2000). Particular exceptions were found in British Columbia and Nova Scotia, where a number of university-colleges active in PLAR have recently become universities and at least for the time being have continued to offer PLAR.

7. Parallel to PLAR has been a movement supporting an approach to assessment and the use of learning outcomes as criteria against which all learning, including prior learning, should be judged in academic

---

[3] Butterworth's (1992) work is discussed in other chapters in this volume (see, for example, Pokorny).

settings. Learning outcomes are generally viewed as statements that integrate knowledge and skills (and sometimes attitudes), expressed in terms of performance. They are established for courses, course clusters and in some cases programmes. The term 'competency' is used in some academic settings, but it can also refer to criteria against which prior learning is judged in regulated occupations.

8. Unlike other countries where the development of national qualifications systems has been a driver of PLAR, no Canadian provincial (or national) qualifications systems exist. Competencies associated with employment in unregulated occupations are not organised; PLAR has proved difficult to implement in the absence of a common understanding of basic occupational functions. Some employment sector councils are working towards establishing competencies and assessment processes for employers within their individual sectors, but to date these have not become standard practice. Initial employer interest and curiosity can succumb to concerns about capacity, time, cost and poaching.

9. Most regulated professions are familiar with PLAR, but levels of interest, support and engagement vary. Pressures to implement and improve current assessment measures are increasing as fairness legislation is passed.[4]

10. Workers in community-based organisations have a history of experimentation with PLAR, but have been negatively impacted by financial constraints and the limitations of early PLAR designs. Nevertheless, some of Canada's most creative and innovative PLAR initiatives, particularly the use of portfolio-based assessment, have been developed by these organisations.

In summary, PLAR has developed a public policy and institutional presence in Canada, particularly as a labour force development tool. It has demonstrated slow growth in a patchwork of organisationally-driven services for adult students, workers and professionals through both traditional and innovative means of assessment.

---

[4] Fairness legislation has now been passed in three provinces; it requires regulators to ensure that their licensing processes treat immigrant professionals equitably.

PLAR and adult educators[5]

In examining the historical development of PLAR, the question arises: 'Who has been responsible for sustaining PLAR throughout its rather arduous evolution?' There has been no research conducted on the characteristics or motivations of PLAR design and delivery agents, so we cannot answer the question definitively; but there are indicators that point to individual adult educators at the local level as among those most responsible.[6]

Links between PLAR and adult educators make sense.[7] They both engage with all spheres of adult learning – in formal institutional contexts, in workplace training programmes, in trade unions and in community-based initiatives. They both encourage the development of knowledge and skills within a framework of lifelong learning. Adult educators have been prominent participants at national PLAR conferences and have led a number of key professional development initiatives: for example, the national conference sponsored by Human Resources Development Canada in 1997; practitioner training sponsored by the Ontario Council of Regents in 1996; professional development sessions at national forums coordinated by the Canadian Association for Prior Learning Assessment in 2003, 2006, 2008 and 2010; training sessions conducted within First Nations Technical Institute conferences between 1995 and 2006; and practitioner training at Red River College in 2009. They are institutional practitioners, community-based practitioners and academic researchers.

Early institutional practitioners, whose task it was to find ways to expand their numbers and implement PLAR in their institutions in the early and mid-1990s, emerged as key facilitators of PLAR in formal educational settings. College-based practitioners dominated the field, developing training resources that used the works of Knowles (1970), Brundage and Mackeracher (1980), Bloom (1984), Kolb (1984), Simosko

---

[5] See Wihak and Wong in this volume for a detailed study of adult educators, Adult Education and PLAR.

[6] This is unlike countries such as Australia and New Zealand, where PLAR often takes place in the workplace by formally accredited assessment agencies established by comprehensive national PLAR policy; or France, where PLAR takes place under national legislation in mainstream university programmes; or in Norway or Portugal, where specifically mandated assessment centres conduct assessments.

[7] This relationship is explored in some depth in Wihak and Wong's contribution to this volume.

(1989) and Keeton (1997) to introduce principles of adult learning to the uninitiated. Many of these practitioners exhibited an uncommon enthusiasm for their work – a trait that has been admired by some and belittled by others. The emphasis has been on implementation, influenced by pressures of temporary, limited and targeted funding, short government-mandated project deadlines, and policy priorities focused on economic rather than educational drivers.

Community-based PLAR practitioners are a more eclectic group comprising community-based educators and researchers scattered across the country, who engage with adult learners interested in PLAR for personal, career development and employment purposes. The PLA Centre, Halifax is an example of a community-oriented organisation led by adult education activists that has contributed to sustainable PLAR practices in its region. Perhaps its most notable study is *Achieving Our Potential: An Action Plan for Prior Learning Assessment and Recognition in Canada* (Morrissey *et al.*, 2008), which documents dozens of community-based PLAR pilot and research projects across Canada, and presents a cogent argument for using PLAR to reduce the participation gap between people in marginalised circumstances and opportunities for employment, education, and community and civic involvement.

Academic researchers who have taken an interest in PLAR are mainly university faculty and graduate students. Today, their numbers are small. Their research has been quantitative and qualitative; their commentaries represent a range of theoretical perspectives from transformative learning theories (e.g. Wong, 2000, 2009) to complexity theory (e.g. Fenwick, 2006).

These three groups of adult educators – institutional practitioners, community-based practitioners and academic researchers – have been primary sources of PLAR research in Canada, carving over time a research agenda shaped by their own interests and by the stipulations of government funding initiatives. In order to understand what has been accomplished over the past 16 years, we need a sense of the types of research that have been conducted. For this purpose, a typology is presented in the following section.

Framing PLAR research in Canada

A typology to frame PLAR research methods in Canada serves several purposes. It illuminates the types of research that have been conducted, how deeply issues have been examined and how thoroughly available means of investigating PLAR have been used. It can identify long-term research trends and, in so doing, help to identify priorities for future research. Where certain types of research appear dominant, the typology can support the need for training in specific research methods, and it can play a role in developing common PLAR research terminology. The analysis and observations that follow the presentation of the typology may also contribute to our understanding of why, after two decades, PLAR continues to have an uncertain future.

Identifying PLAR research

The following definition of research used by the University Research Council at Nipissing University (2008) was adopted:

> *Research is any original and* systematic investigation *[emphasis added] undertaken in order to increase knowledge and understanding and to establish facts and principles. It comprises the creation of ideas and generation of knowledge that lead to new and substantial improved insights and/or the development of new materials, devices, products and processes. It should have the potential to produce results that are sufficiently relevant to increase knowledge. Good reflective inquiry produces theories and hypotheses and benefits any intellectual attempt to analyse facts and phenomena.*

> *In applied fields of study, research ... takes the form of systematic investigation into phenomena of concern to the field of study using a range of quantitative and qualitative approaches, the results of which add to, confirm, or reject what is already known. It is also a reflective investigation of the dynamic interaction between theory and practice in a field of study. From this investigation new understandings are developed as practices are explored in relation to peer review concepts, principles and theories. The maintenance of practice competency and the advancement of practice knowledge are critical components of research.*

A strength of this definition is that it permits the characterisation of PLAR as an applied field of practice that can reflect more than one theoretical perspective. For the purpose of this chapter, *systematic investigation* refers to a research study which has, at a minimum, a clearly stated purpose and methodology, formal findings, and a written report (if the research is not ongoing). Reflective commentaries not directly linked to research were reviewed but not included in the typology (e.g. Thomas, 1998; Conrad, 2008; Spencer, 2008). These important contributions to the literature often draw the field's attention to links between theory and practice, and examine practice from a range of philosophical perspectives that introduce new research questions and challenge current practice, but nevertheless do not conform to the above definition of research.

Although this definition is vulnerable to criticism; for example, from those who use peer-reviewed publication as a defining characteristic, it does allow us to include much of the practical research (Richardson, 1994) that has been used to improve real-world PLAR practices and develop organisational policies. On the basis of this definition, a systematic search for all available PLAR-related reports, journal articles, books, theses, conference presentations, and working papers published between 1995 and 2010, was conducted. The following sources and documents met the criteria of containing systematic investigations of PLAR phenomena, and of drawing conclusions from the evidence presented:

- Achieving *Our Potential: An Action Plan for Prior Learning Assessment and Recognition in Canada* (Morrissey *et al.*, 2008).
- *Canada's Portfolio* (Canadian Association for Prior Learning Assessment, 2009).
- *Canadian Journal for Studies in Adult Education.*
- *Canadian Journal of University Continuing Education.*
- *New Approaches to Lifelong Learning Annotated Bibliography* (Vanstone, 1999).
- Projects and studies reported in proceedings of national recognising learning conferences and workshops in 2003, 2004, 2005, 2006, 2007, 2008 and 2009.
- *ProQuest* – UMI Dissertation Publishing.
- *RPL Practitioner Resource List* (Saskatchewan Institute for Applied Science and Technology, 2007).
- *State of the Field Review: Prior Learning Assessment and Recognition* (Wihak, 2006).
- *Work and Lifelong Learning Resource Base* (WALL) (Centre for the Study of Education and Work, 2009).

Systematic investigation of other resources may produce additional sources of research that could be added to those included in this chapter. A total of 78 items which cover most Canadian studies were identified. Only research in which PLAR was a primary topic of examination was included. Only studies for which research reports were available for review were included (which excluded summaries, encapsulations and presentation materials alone).

A typology for PLAR research

The typology presented here builds on a two-dimensional classification structure for non-experimental, quantitative research developed by Johnson (2001). A number of other research classification systems were considered, including Krathwohl (1998) and Marshall and Rosman (2006), and a helpful synthesis of qualitative research types provided by Merriam (2009). In the end, Johnson's typology was adopted as a starting point for several reasons. First, his focus on the primary objective of research as the defining factor showed potential for better understanding the scope of past PLAR research methods. Further, the use of 'time' as a second dimension in his typology offered promise for delineating future research needs, and his claim of simplicity, exclusivity of categories and exhaustiveness pledged clarity and ease of use. Finally, I was particularly interested in exploring whether Johnson's framework could be extended to include experimental, qualitative and mixed-method research in PLAR.

Accordingly, the typology presented in Table 3.1 can be used to classify four types of PLAR research. The following is a description of each type beginning with the presentation of their two main dimensions – research objective and time. The number of Canadian studies belonging to each research type and sub-type is reported in brackets in each section of the typology.

Four types of research

The four main types of PLAR research – experimental quantitative research, non-experimental quantitative research, qualitative research and mixed-method research – are presented sequentially and cross-referenced with the three time dimensions – retrospective, cross-sectional and prospective research. Experimental research and non-experimental research each have three possible sub-types: descriptive, explanatory and predictive. An additional 'exploratory' sub-type has been allocated to

56

Table 3.1 Types of PLAR research (1995–2010)

Research Objective		Time Dimension	
	Retrospective	Cross-Sectional	Prospective
Experimental Quantitative Research (0)			
Controlled testing to understand causal processes	Retrospective, Experimental (0)	Cross-sectional, Experimental (0)	Prospective, Experimental (0)
Non-experimental Quantitative Research (16)			
1. Descriptive (13)	Retrospective, Descriptive (1)	Cross-sectional, Descriptive (12)	Prospective, Descriptive (0)
2. Explanatory (0)	Retrospective, Explanatory (0)	Cross-sectional, Explanatory (0)	Prospective, Explanatory (0)
3. Predictive (3)	Retrospective, Predictive (1)	Cross-sectional, Predictive (2)	Prospective, Predictive (0)
Qualitative Research (52)			
1. Descriptive (33)	Retrospective, Descriptive (6)	Cross-sectional, Descriptive (27)	Prospective, Descriptive (0)
2. Explanatory (incl. theory generation) (0)	Retrospective, Explanatory (0)	Cross-sectional, Explanatory (0)	Prospective, Explanatory (0)
3. Predictive (0)	Retrospective, Predictive (0)	Cross-sectional, Predictive (0)	Prospective, Predictive (0)
4. Exploratory (19)	Retrospective, Exploratory (0)	Cross-sectional, Exploratory (9)	Prospective, Exploratory (10)
Mixed-method Research (Qualitative and Quantitative) (10)			
1. Non-experimental, descriptive; Qualitative, Descriptive (10)	Retrospective (2)	Cross-sectional (8)	Prospective (0)
2. Non-experimental, descriptive; Qualitative, Exploratory (0)	Retrospective (0)	Cross-sectional (0)	Prospective (0)

qualitative research.[8] Mixed-method research is not explored in any depth and requires further investigation; but since it has played an important role thus far in PLAR research in Canada it is included in the typology.

Experimental quantitative research is characterised by randomised testing of phenomena controlled for one or more independent variables. It is not a strong feature of the typology at the present time largely because there has been no experimental research in PLAR in Canada to date, and thus no data with which to test the typology's strengths and weaknesses. However, it is possible that future research will be carried out on experimental bases and thus could still be accommodated in this typology. It is acknowledged, however, that the number and variety of independent variables in social science research lend themselves less to experimentation than to controlled non-experimental inquiry (Kerlinger, 1986).

Non-experimental quantitative research is often conducted when experimentation is not possible or feasible, but where relations between variables can be examined. Johnson (2001) suggests that there are many strategies that can be used to establish evidence for causality in non-experimental research, but that conclusions must be tempered and grounded; for example, by consistency that is found across multiple studies. Non-experimental, quantitative research generally reflects a positivist approach to research (Merriam, 2009).

Qualitative research is more commonly found in educational research and, regardless of sub-type, aims to increase understanding by revealing the perspectives of those engaged in or affected by a phenomenon. Qualitative research is usually rooted in philosophies that emphasise experience and meaning-making (e.g. constructivism) and employs inductive processes of data collection using the researcher as the primary instrument and rich narrative descriptions as the end product (Merriam, 2009). There are several types of qualitative research, but they all tend to share a quest for understanding phenomena in their 'natural' or everyday context.

Two methods used to qualitatively increase our understanding are: a) inductive analysis of documentary data; and b) the perspectives of research subjects through direct interaction such as interviews. Both methods have their strengths and weaknesses. Documents provide stable evidence and some resistance to investigator influence (Merriam, 2009). Direct interaction, on the other hand, provides more flexible, fluid opportunities to

---

[8] I would like to thank Dr Johnson for his assistance with this aspect of the typology.

reach beneath the surface of initial expressions in order to deepen the researcher's understanding of perspectives on a phenomenon, but is more vulnerable to researcher bias. Based on these considerations, and building on Johnson's (2001) typology, I have included both methods as part of qualitative research.

Mixed-method research has been a valuable type of PLAR research, combining both quantitative and qualitative methods of inquiry. The *Slice of the Iceberg* (Aarts *et al.*, 1999) study on PLAR was descriptive, non-experimental research involving statistical data collection and analysis of learner performance; it also included descriptive, qualitative research in the form of semi-structured focus groups with learners and assessors. The data gleaned from both methods were used to support the study's findings, and have been used by PLAR proponents across Canada and internationally.

Four research sub-types
Table 3.1 illustrates how the four types of research have been assigned sub-types which identify their primary objectives as: description, explanation, exploration or prediction. Only one objective is assigned as primary to each research study:

- 'Descriptive research'. In this group are non-experimental and descriptive studies which have the primary objective of increasing our understanding by identifying characteristics of a phenomenon. Data may also be gathered from narratives provided by participants. An example of this is: *PLAR: An Investigation of Non-sponsored Learning for College Credit* (Blinkhorn, 1999), which describes the 'lived experience' of adult college students engaged in portfolio assessment. A researcher engaged in this form of research would ask the question 'what are participants' perspectives on the phenomenon?' and may hypothesise about variables, but would not correlate or claim cause and effect.
- 'Explanatory research' presents possible explanations for phenomena; it may establish correlations between variables to identify causal factors that produce change. Researchers may adopt a positivist orientation and consider such questions as 'why does a phenomenon operate as it does?' or 'what are the dynamics involved in the phenomenon's operation?' Johnson (2001) reminds us that generalisations should not be made from evidence stemming from a single non-experimental study. An example of explanatory, non-experimental

research in PLAR would be a series of studies that seek possible correlation between PLAR and accelerated graduation rates. Incorporating one or more control techniques and testing alternative hypotheses are two ways to help establish evidence for causality.

Explanatory *qualitative* research can be conducted from many different paradigms; for example, constructivist or critical theory. The intention of a qualitative researcher is to become intimately familiar with the unique perspectives of participants from close range and to make findings in the form of insights gained from analysis of large volumes of narrative data. These insights are vulnerable to a host of challenges such as data load and bias, but there are strategies that some theorists propose to enhance pattern identification and recognition of coherence and divergence in data so that generalisations might be considered. Myers (2000) suggests that partial generalisations may be possible for similar populations and that the aggregation of single studies may allow for generalisations produced through theory building. Stake (1978) offers the concept of naturalistic generalisation – a partial intuitive process arrived at by recognising the similarities of objects and issues in and out of context. This form of analysis depends on rich description so that readers may recognise essential similarities in order to establish the basis for naturalistic generalisations.

Explanatory qualitative research has a role in expanding our understanding of PLAR. For example, a series of investigations that have as their objective the establishment of a relationship between portfolio development and levels of preparation in employment transition could include in-depth interviews to explain the role that developmental PLAR plays in preparing workers for the job search process.

- 'Exploratory research'. Exploratory qualitative research generally addresses new areas of activity or problems that require solutions. PLAR has been rich in exploratory research in Canada, primarily through pilot research projects that investigate the use of new assessment policies, procedures, methods and tools. An example is York University's recently initiated PLAR project with internationally educated nurses, in which immigrant nurses will undergo a pilot PLAR process for provincial registration with the College of Nurses of Ontario.
- 'Predictive research'. Predictive, non-experimental research is conducted when a researcher's objective is to predict or forecast some future event or phenomenon (without linking cause and effect)

60

(Johnson, 2001). An example is *Profiling Prior Learning Assessment Candidates and Policy Implications at the University of Guelph* (Smith, 1999), where the results of a survey were used to forecast whether PLAR would encourage adult student participation in a new blended learning bachelor of commerce programme.

The capacity of qualitative research to predict is the subject of philosophical and political debate. It may be the weakest type of research, since the data gleaned from the narratives of participants are highly individual and exact replication is impossible. However, it can be classed as predictive if the researcher's primary objective is to use qualitative data to forecast some phenomenon in the future. In this sense, some PLAR pilot research projects are predictive when they are used to forecast the success of permanent implementation. Johnson's (2001) strategies for non-experimental research results can also be used to strengthen the contribution that qualitative research can make to prediction, such as the use of multiple sites, using results of previous experimental studies and collecting longitudinal data. PLAR pilot research studies that have collectively shown a positive impact of PLAR on participants' self-confidence, following assessment or over time, could be used to forecast improved self-confidence, particularly if similar populations and conditions apply.

Three time frames
This component of the typology has three time frames – retrospective, cross-sectional and prospective (Johnson, 2001). I have deviated from Johnson's model by substituting the term 'prospective' for his term 'longitudinal' in order to acknowledge that retrospective and prospective research may also be longitudinal (examining a phenomenon over an extended period of time):

• Retrospective research studies collect and analyse data on phenomena that occurred over a period of time in the past (Johnson, 2001). *Slice of the Iceberg* (1999) is an example of retrospective research.
• Cross-sectional research studies collect data, and may compare sections or samples across a population at a single point in time or during a single, relatively brief time period (Johnson, 2001). Stowe (2000) reported on a cross-sectional study of PLAR at Canadian universities. Thomas *et al.* (2001) conducted a cross-sectional study of student perceptions of PLAR.

- A prospective research study collects data at multiple points in real time about the same group of people. A study that follows a group of adult students throughout their PLAR experience or until they graduated or obtained employment would be a prospective research study. In 2008, the Upper Canada Leger Centre for Education and Training conducted a prospective study on the assessment and recognition of young at-risk adults.

Applying the typology

Examining PLAR research using this typology provides an opportunity to review the types of studies conducted and who has participated, and to comment on the research gaps and whose interests have been served. An expanded form of the typology, including citations, target groups and researcher affiliations, is provided as Appendix 3.1.

Types of studies

I began this chapter with a historical overview positioning PLAR primarily as a tool endorsed by governments to serve public economic policy on labour force development, by improving immigrant integration through accelerated post-secondary education. Shortly after implementation, this initial focus was extended to all adults, and the objective of education was extended to employability and employment. Following the tenet that 'those who hold the gold make the rules', one would expect to see PLAR research follow a funding trail that would explore its potential and success in these areas. Analysis bears this out. Most research studies are descriptive and cross-sectional, meaning that for the most part Canadian researchers have been describing PLAR-related phenomena at singular points in time.

With few exceptions, studies are relatively small-scale, qualitative investigations that are rich in data and insights regarding issues of implementation. A primary focus of the non-experimental quantitative and mixed-method research has been on describing local practices by educational institutions, and individual learner or faculty perspectives. Exploratory research has centred on the practical applications of PLAR in short-term pilot studies of mechanisms, designed to move individuals along specific paths towards educational and economic advancement. Two large-scale, mixed-method studies have been completed; both in the college sector (Aarts *et al.*, 1999; Aarts *et al.*, 2003). All research studies make findings in support of recognising prior learning, and most offer recommendations on how to increase or improve practice.

Of the 78 studies in the typology, none were experimental, 16 were non-experimental quantitative, 52 were qualitative and ten were mixed-method; 56 studies were descriptive, 19 were exploratory, three were predictive and none were explanatory; 58 studies were cross-sectional, ten were prospective and ten were retrospective.

The researchers and the researched

In addition to tracking the objectives of Canadian research in PLAR, research target groups and researcher affiliations were also identified (see Appendix 3.1). In the 78 studies examined, research target groups are scattered across sectors and stakeholder groups, including adults in the general community, students, immigrants, at-risk young adults, colleges, universities, school boards, workers, apprentices, unemployed and under-employed persons, researchers, and multi-stakeholder groups.

Researchers and their affiliations include university faculty and researchers, graduate students, colleges, community-based organisations, occupational bodies, multi-stakeholder groups and quasi-governmental organisations.

A striking finding is that 36 studies were led by university-based researchers and 16 of these examined PLAR in a university context. They include 25 descriptive, five exploratory and three predictive studies; there are three mixed-method studies. There are no university-led explanatory studies. Twenty-nine of the university-led studies are cross-sectional, six are retrospective and one is prospective.

The number of research studies involving publication of research findings through a peer review process is low (e.g. Belanger and Mount, 1998; Peruniak and Welch, 2000; Spencer *et al.*, 2003; Livingstone *et al.*, 2005; Van Kleef, 2006; Lordly, 2007; Peruniak, 2007; Wihak, 2007).

These data on research participants suggest that although the wide range of target groups demonstrates the variety of contexts in which PLAR may be applied, its scattered, tentative and cross-sectional character has provided 'thin ice' upon which to rest our confidence in the long-term validity and reliability of PLAR for many target groups. The data also suggest that PLAR researchers have been preoccupied with implementation. University-based research on PLAR is perhaps more plentiful than previously perceived, but it has been dominated by a small number of educators/researchers at a few institutions. A review of past PLAR research reveals both topic/content and methodological gaps. It also exposes some of the dominant interests that have been served during the evolution of PLAR in Canada.

Research gaps

Several gaps in Canadian research on PLAR are documented by Wihak (2006) in her synopsis of empirical research up to 2005. The typology here strengthens those findings and also suggests that several of the gaps could be addressed by adjusting current research strategies. For example, exploratory and descriptive qualitative research can be valuable forerunners to experimental research, but qualitative PLAR studies have not been used as building blocks for quantitative research. There are no quantitative studies examining the impact of PLAR on the length of participants' academic programmes or the size of their study workloads, even though there are repeated claims and qualitative findings that PLAR reduces both. Further, qualitative studies with similar objectives have not been synthesised, or systematically analysed for divergence or commonalities upon which to begin building generalisations.

Additionally, the typology reveals that no experimental research has been carried out. No explanatory research with specific objectives of correlation or causation has been attempted, and little predictive research has been conducted. Although research methods should always be determined by the nature of the research question, these methodological gaps suggest that we could benefit from a consolidation of what we already know, and a re-direction of PLAR research using under-utilised methods to explore neglected contexts and new issues and strengthen our current understandings.

Public policy-makers' interests in PLAR as a labour force development tool could be investigated by quantitative research; for example, by using experimental or controlled non-experimental research to assess PLAR's impact on employment, its effect on post-secondary enrolment, and its links to organisational costs and savings. Other gaps such as university faculty, and administration attitudes and awareness of PLAR, concerns about quality, and other drivers of resistance to PLAR, could be addressed through greater use of mixed-method research strategies.

Most studies examine the potential or current utility of PLAR within existing social structures that have pre-existing concrete value systems for recognising learning. For example, pilot research on using PLAR to identify occupation-related knowledge and skills uses competencies created by occupational bodies as assessment criteria. Research on PLAR at colleges and universities shows that institutionally established programme and course learning outcomes are used as assessment criteria. Researchers that examine PLAR for personal development or employment preparation, and even action research, tend to engage individual participants more fully in the design and development of assessment processes, but they too eventually present the value of prior learning in terms of criteria set by other authorities (e.g. employer expectations, federal employability skills).

Blyler (1998) characterises research from a critical perspective as that which aims to empower and emancipate by re-interpreting the relationship between researcher and participants as one of collaboration, where participants define research questions, and social action and change are the desired results. Internationally, PLAR theorists draw attention to the degree to which formal recognition of prior learning has been controlled by dominant societal structures (educational institutions, employers) whose self-interest limits access to educational and civic engagement by marginalised groups (Michelson, 1997; Harris, 1999). The effect, these critics contend, is the rejection of valuable knowledge and skills and the people who hold them.

The historical evolution and current modes of practice of PLAR in Canada are vulnerable to this critique. Given the emphasis on PLAR as an organisationally controlled tool for economic development, it should be no surprise that research into PLAR's theoretical underpinnings, emancipatory potential, or pedagogical strengths and weaknesses, has received little targeted attention. There are only three publications that examine PLAR and its current applications from a critical perspective (Spencer et al., 2003; Peruniak, 2007; Moss, 2008). A fourth study proposes the advancement of PLAR to support the economic and social integration of marginalised populations through large-scale changes to existing social structures and ways of thinking about learning (Morrissey et al., 2008). Currently, these studies constitute at best whispers in the hallways of institutions and governments that for the most part continue to respond with the same mix of reactions that I witnessed in that boardroom 20 years ago – support, curiosity, lack of interest and resistance.

Limitations of this review

The studies examined for this chapter do not reflect all of the Canadian PLAR research conducted since 1995. In particular, they do not include research conducted in Québec, or initiatives that remained internal to PLAR development within organisations and were not publicly reported. An additional limitation is the exclusion of research on PLAR in bridging programmes for immigrants, if PLAR was not a major component of the programme. A number of public reports were unavailable, such as a series of research pilot reports conducted in Ontario in 1994 and 1995 that pursued faculty professional development, and student portfolio development (Blinkhorn, 1999). A few initiatives produced no reports and some did not have sufficient information on methods to meet the definition of research used in this chapter.

In establishing the typology and assigning research studies to each category, no judgement was made on the quality of the research beyond the criteria set in the definition.

A limitation of the historical synthesis at the beginning of this chapter is the focus on only five of Canada's 13 provinces and territories. Bélisle helps to fill this important gap on Québec in the next chapter.

A limitation of the typology's design is that it only allows for the selection of one primary methodological objective. In instances where PLAR studies had more than one methodological objective, a judgement was made about which was primary, thereby introducing the possibility of researcher subjectivity into the classification process. A second weakness of the typology is that it contains 36 sub-categories which many would not consider simple, thus falling short of my ambition of meeting Johnson's (2001) criterion of simplicity – although it does, however, appear to meet his criteria of exclusivity and exhaustiveness. Finally, the typology subsumes several sub-types of research which may be better made explicit. For example, comparative research can be a form of explanatory research, and several forms of critical inquiry (Merriam, 2009) are not delineated.

The future of PLAR research in Canada

The story of PLAR research in Canada is part of the larger story of the general evolution of PLAR. In her chapter in this book, Wong supports the need to further engage Canada's universities in PLAR services and research. The typology suggests that there are under-utilised types of research that could move us forward from small-scale, descriptive and exploratory qualitative studies to quantitative research that builds on the richness of the understandings we have developed to date. We need to synthesise where possible, experiment where we need to, and discover the long-term impacts of PLAR.

The research gaps identified present many opportunities for future inquiry. But they also raise disturbing questions about how tradition can discourage innovation. If PLAR is appropriately situated in the field of adult learning, why is it that no faculties of education in Canadian universities have formal PLAR policies? (See Wihak and Wong, in this volume.) Why is it not in the curriculum of every adult education faculty? Why is there so little critical research in PLAR? Why is it that after 20 years we still know so little about the validity of PLAR methods and their long-term impact? With reference to competency-based education, Jones (1999) contends that implementation in the vocational sector provides no time or opportunity to participate in or gain access to university-based academic debates, so it is not surprising that there are gaps between the questions being asked in academic papers and issues arising from or in practice. A similar observation can be made of the disjuncture that exists between implementation and research in PLAR. Those who offer PLAR services conduct little or no theoretically-based research; those who conduct theoretical research do not offer PLAR services, thus creating a gap between those who ask the practical and the theoretical questions and little opportunity for dialogue. The stories in the other chapters of this book allude to similar dichotomies, tensions and historical forces that have affected PLAR in other countries. Perhaps we will find some of the answers to our questions in the collective rather than the experience of any single nation.

References

Aarts, S., Blower, D., Burke, R., Conlin, E., Ebner Howarth, C., Howell, B., Lamarre, G. and Van Kleef, J. (1999) *A Slice of the Iceberg: Cross-Canada Study of Prior Learning Assessment and Recognition*. Toronto: Cross-Canada Partnership on PLAR.

Aarts, S., Blower, D., Burke, R., Conlin, E., Lamarre, G., McCrossan, W. and Van Kleef, J. (2003) *Feedback from Learners: Cross-Canada Study of Prior Learning Assessment and Recognition*. Kitchener: Cross-Canada Partnership on PLAR.

Association of Universities and Colleges of Canada (AUCC) (2006) 'Mapping Canadian university capacity, expertise and key issues related to foreign credential recognition for internationally-educated professionals: Final report'. Ottawa: Association of Universities and Colleges of Canada.

Belanger, C. and Mount, J. (1998) 'Prior Learning Assessment and Recognition (PLAR) in Canadian universities', *Canadian Journal of Higher Education*, Vol. 28, No 2, pp. 99–120.

Blinkhorn, K. (1999) 'Prior learning assessment and recognition: An investigation of non-sponsored learning for college credits', PhD Thesis. Ontario Institute for Studies in Higher Education, Toronto, Ontario.

Bloom, B. (1984) *Taxonomy of Educational Objectives*. Boston: Pearson Education.

Bloom, M. and Grant, M. (2001) *Brain Gain: The Economic Benefits of Recognizing Learning Credentials in Canada*. Ottawa: Conference Board of Canada.

Bloom, M. and Watt, D. (2001) *Exploring the Learning Recognition Gap in Canada. Phase 1 Report*. Ottawa: Conference Board of Canada.

Blyler, N. (1998) 'Taking a political turn: The critical perspective and research in professional communication', *Technical Communication Quarterly*, Vol. 7, No 1, pp. 33–52.

Brouwer, A. (1999) 'Immigrants need not apply'. Toronto: Caledon Institute of Social Policy.

Brundage, D. and Mackeracher, D. (1980) *Adult Learning Principles and their Application to Planning*. Toronto: Ministry of Education.

Butterworth, C. (1992) 'More than one bite of the APEL: Contrasting models of accrediting prior learning', *Journal of Further and Higher Education*, Vol. 16, No 3, pp. 39–51.

Butterworth, C. and Bloor, M. (1994) 'The professional development model of APEL – some problems of assessment and validity', in P. Armstrong, B. Bright and M. Zukas (eds) *Reflecting on Changing Practices, Contexts and Identities: Proceedings of the Annual Meeting of the Standing Conference on University Teaching and Research in the Education of Adults – SCUTREA*. Hull, England, 12–14 July.

Canadian Association for Prior Learning Assessment (CAPLA) (2009) *Canada's Portfolio*. Ottawa: Canadian Association for Prior Learning Assessment. Available at: http://www.canadasportfolio.ca (Accessed 20 November 2009).

Centre for the Study of Education and Work (2009) *Work and Lifelong Learning Resource Base*. Toronto: University of Toronto. Available at: http://www.learningwork.ca/node/184 (Accessed 20 November 2009).

Conrad, D. (2008) 'Revisiting the recognition of prior learning: A reflective inquiry into RPL practice in Canada', *Canadian Journal of University Continuing Education*, Vol. 2, No 34, 89–110.

Fenwick, T. (2006) 'Reconfiguring RPL and its assumptions: A complexified view', in P. Andersson and J. Harris (eds) *Re-theorizing the Recognition of Prior Learning*. Leicester, England: National Institute of Adult Continuing Education (NIACE).

Ferguson, F. (1998) 'Prior learning assessment in health and human service programs in British Columbia'. Vancouver: Centre for Curriculum, Transfer and Technology.

Galarneau, D. and Morrisette, R. (2008) 'Immigrants' education and required job skills', *Perspectives*. Catalogue No 75-001-X. Ottawa: Statistics Canada.

Government of Canada (1988) *Canadian Multiculturalism Act*. R.S., 1985, c. 24 (4th Supp.), C-18.7.

Harris, J. (1999) 'Ways of seeing the recognition of prior learning (RPL): What contribution can such practices make to social inclusion?' *Studies in the Education of Adults*, Vol. 31, No 2, pp. 124–39.

Human Resources and Skills Development Canada (2002) *Knowledge Matters: Skills and Learning for Canadians*. Ottawa, ON.

Johnson, B. (2001) 'Towards a new classification of non-experimental quantitative research', *Educational Researcher*, Vol. 30, No 2, pp. 3–13.

Jones, A. (1999) 'The place of judgment in competency-based assessment', *Journal of Vocational Education and Training*, Vol. 51, No 1, pp. 145–60.

Keeton, M. (1997) 'Historical forces shaping the Prior Learning Assessment movement', *Journal of the National Institute on the Assessment of Experiential Learning*, 4–9.

Kerlinger, F. (1986) *Foundations of Behavioural Research*. New York: Holt, Rinehart and Winston.

Knowles, M. (1970) *The Modern Practice of Adult Education: Andragogy versus Pedagogy*. New York: Association Press.

Kolb, D. (1984) *Experiential Learning*. Englewood Cliffs, NJ: Prentice Hall.

Krathwohl, D. (1998) '*Methods of Educational and Social Science Research: An Integrated Approach*'. Available at: http://www.cclc.ca (Accessed 20 June 2009).

Livingstone, D., Raykov, M. and Turner, C. (2005) *Canadian Adults' Interest in Prior Learning Assessment and Recognition: A 2004 National Survey.* Toronto: Centre for the Study of Education and Work, University of Toronto.

Lordly, D. (2007) 'Dietetic Prior Learning Assessment: Student and faculty experiences', *Canadian Journal of Dietetic Practice and Research*, Vol. 68, No 4, pp. 207–12.

Marshall, C. and Rosman, G. (2006) *Designing Qualitative Research.* Thousand Oaks: Sage Publications.

Merriam, S. (2009) *Qualitative Research: A Guide to Design and Implementation.* San Francisco: Jossey-Bass.

Michelson, E. (1997) 'The politics of memory: The recognition of experiential learning', in S. Walters (ed.) *Globalization, Adult Education and Training: Impacts and Issues.* Cape Town, South Africa: Zed Books, pp. 141–53.

Morrissey, M., Myers, D., Bélanger, P., Robitaille, M., Davison, P., Van Kleef, J. and Williams, R. (2008) *Achieving our Potential: An Action Plan for Prior Learning and Recognition (PLAR) in Canada.* Ottawa: Canadian Council on Learning.

Moss, L. (2008) 'Prior Learning Assessment and Recognition (PLAR) and the impact of globalization: A Canadian case study'. PhD Thesis, McGill University, Montreal, Quebec.

Myers, M. (2000) 'Qualitative research and the generalizability question: Standing firm with Proteus', *The Qualitative Report*, Vol. 4, Nos 3–4. Available at: http://www.nova.edu/ssss/QR/QR4-3/myers.html.

Nesbit, T., Dunlop, C. and Gibson, L. (2007) 'Lifelong learning in institutions of higher education', *Canadian Journal of University Continuing Education.* Vol. 33, No 1, pp. 35–60.

Nipissing University (2008) 'Definition of research used by the university research council'. North Bay: Nipissing University. Available at: http://www.nipissingu.ca/research/downloads/DefnofResearchforwebsite.pdf (Accessed 20 November 2009).

Peruniak, G. (2007) 'Back eddies of learning in the Recognition of Prior Learning', *Canadian Journal of University Continuing Education*, Vol. 33, No 1, pp. 88–106.

Peruniak, G. and Welch, D. (2000) 'The twinning of potential: Toward an integration of Prior Learning Assessment with career development', *Canadian Journal of Counselling*, Vol. 34, No 3, pp. 232–45.

Reitz, J. (2001) 'Immigrant skill utilization in the Canadian labour market: Implications of human capital research, *Journal of International Migration and Integration*, Vol. 2, No 3, pp. 347–78.

Richardson, V. (1994) 'Conducting research on practice', *Educational Practice*, Vol. 23, No 5, pp. 5–10.

Shandro, G. (2006) *Prior Learning Assessment and Recognition Framework for Nurse Practitioner Education and Regulation in Canada*. Ottawa: Canadian Nurses Association.

Simosko, S. (1989) *Assessing Learning: A CAEL Handbook for Faculty*. Columbia, OH: Council for Adult and Experiential Learning.

Smith, G. (1999) 'Profiling Prior Learning Assessment candidates and policy implications at the University of Guelph'. Unpublished Report. Guelph: University of Guelph.

Spencer, B. (2008) 'Have we got an adult education model for PLAR?' *Proceedings of the Canadian Association for the Study of Adult Education (CASAE) Annual Conference*. Available at: http://www.oise.utoronto.ca/CASAE/cnf2008/OnlineProceedings-2008/CAS2008%20Proceedings.html (Accessed 27 July 2010).

Spencer, B., Briton, D. and Gereluk, W. (2003) 'The case for Prior Learning Assessment and Recognition for labour education in Canada', *Just Labour: A Canadian Journal of Work and Society*, Vol. 2, Spring 2003, pp. 45–53.

Stake, R. (1978) 'The case study method in social inquiry', *Educational Researcher*, Vol. 7, No 2, pp. 5–8.

Standing Committee on Human Resources, Social Development and the Status of Persons with Disabilities (2008) *Employability in Canada: Preparing for the Future*. Ottawa: Communications Canada.

Statistics Canada (2007) *Portrait of the Canadian Population in 2006, 2006 Census* (Catalogue no. 97-550-XIE). Ottawa: Minister of Industry.

Statistics Canada (2008) *The Daily*, 4 March. Ottawa: Statistics Canada.

Stowe, S. (2000) *Prior Learning Assessment*. Toronto: York University.

Thomas, A. (1998) 'The tolerable contradictions of Prior Learning Assessment', in S. Scott, B. Spencer and A. Thomas (eds) *Learning for Life: Canadian Readings in Adult Education*. Toronto: Thompson Educational Publishing, Inc.

Thomas, A. (2000) 'Prior Learning Assessment: The quiet revolution', in A. Wilson and E. Hayes (eds) *Handbook of Adult and Continuing Education*. San Francisco: Jossey-Bass.

Thomas, A., Collins, M. and Plett, L. (2001) *Dimensions of the Experience of Prior Learning Assessment and Recognition*. Toronto: University of Toronto.

Training and Development Associates (1999) *Reaching our Full Potential: Prior Learning Assessment and Recognition for Foreign-trained Canadians*. Ottawa: Canadian Labour Force Development Board.

Van Kleef, J. (2006) 'Strengthening PLAR: Integrating theory and practice in post-secondary education', *Journal of Applied Research on Learning*, Vol. 2, No 1, pp. 1–22.

Van Kleef, J. (2009) *Taking Account: A Report on the Number of PLAR Assessments Conducted by Public Post-secondary Institutions in Canada*. Ottawa: Canadian Council on Learning.

Vanstone, S. (ed.) (1999) *Publications and Resources on Prior Learning Assessment and Recognition*. Bibliography compiled for Research Network for New Approaches to Lifelong Learning (NALL), Toronto: Ontario Institute for Studies in Education. Available at: www.eric.ed.gov/ERICWebPortal/recordDetail?accno=ED430116 (Last updated 29 February 2000).

Wihak, C. (2006) *State of the Field Review: Prior Learning Assessment and Recognition (PLAR)*. Ottawa: Canadian Council on Learning.

Wihak, C. (2007) 'Prior Learning Assessment and Recognition in Canadian universities: View from the web', *Canadian Journal of Higher Education*, Vol. 37, No 1, pp. 95–112.

Wong, A. (2000) *University-level Prior Learning Assessment and Recognition: Building Capacity for an Institutional Response*. Saskatoon: University of Saskatchewan.

Wong, A. (2009) *Community-engaged experiential learning in higher education: Implications for students, faculty, institutions, and communities: The Role of Prior Learning Assessment and Recognition (PLAR)*. Paper presented at the Canadian Society for the Study of Higher Education Conference, Ottawa, Ontario.

Appendix 3.1 Canadian Research In PLAR

Research report / Lead author	Research type	Time dimension	Target sector	Researcher affiliation
1995				
1. Evans, S. (1995) *A study of the knowledge, perceptions, and benefits of prior learning assessment for awarding college credit at Cabot College.* Master's thesis. Memorial University, St John's, NF.	Non-experimental, Descriptive	Cross-sectional	Faculty and management	Graduate student
1996				
2. Brawn, B. (1996) *Assessment of equivalent learning: Survey of assessed students, Spring 1996.* New Westminster: Douglas College.	Non-experimental, Descriptive	Cross-sectional	Adult students	College
3. Council of Ontario Universities (1996). *Prior learning assessment: Issues and opportunities for Ontario universities.* Toronto.	Qualitative, Descriptive	Cross-sectional	Universities	Universities
4. Wong, A. (1996) *Prior learning assessment: A guide for university faculty and administrators.* Saskatoon: University of Saskatchewan, University Extension Press.	Qualitative, Descriptive	Cross-sectional	Faculty and admin.	University
1998				
5. Belanger, C. and Mount, J. (1998) Prior learning assessment and recognition (PLAR) in Canadian universities. *The Canadian Journal of Higher Education,* 28(2), 99–120.	Non-experimental, Descriptive	Cross-sectional	Universities	University
6. Ferguson, F. (1998) *Prior learning assessment in health and human service programs in British Columbia.* Vancouver: Centre for Curriculum, Transfer and Technology.	Qualitative, Descriptive Non-experimental, Descriptive (both)	Cross-sectional	Colleges and universities	Colleges and universities

Appendix 3.1 continued

Research report Lead author	Research type	Time dimension	Target sector	Researcher affiliation
1999				
7. Aarts, S., Blower, D., Burke, R., Conlin, E., Ebner Howarth, C., Howell, B., Lamarre, G. and Van Kleef, J. (1999) *A slice of the iceberg: Cross-Canada study of prior learning assessment and recognition.* Toronto: Cross-Canada Partnership on PLAR.	Qualitative, Descriptive Non-experimental, Descriptive (both)	Retrospective	Adult students (college)	Colleges
8. Barker, K. and Belanger, C. (1999) *The status of PLA/ PLAR in professional programs in Ontario universities.* Toronto: Council of Ontario Universities and Ontario Ministry of Citizenship, Culture and Recreation.	Qualitative, Descriptive Non-experimental, Descriptive (both)	Cross-sectional	Universities	Universities
9. Blinkhorn, K. (1999) *Prior learning assessment and recognition: An investigation of non-sponsored learning for college credits.* Doctoral thesis. Ontario Institute for Studies in Higher Education, Toronto, Ontario.	Qualitative, Exploratory	Cross-sectional	Adult students	Graduate student
10. Goldberg, M. and Corson, D. (1999) *Immigrant and aboriginal first language as prior learning qualifications for formal employment in the business, government and education sectors.* NALL Working Paper 03–199. Toronto: Ontario Institute for Studies in Education.	Non-experimental, Descriptive	Cross-sectional	Immigrant and Aboriginal workers	University
11. Smith, G. (1999). *Profiling prior learning assessment candidates and policy implications at the University of Guelph.* Unpublished report. Guelph: University of Guelph.	Non-experimental, Predictive	Cross-sectional	Adult students	University
12. Training and Development Associates (1999) *Reaching our full potential: Prior learning assessment and recognition for foreign-trained Canadians.* Ottawa: Canadian Labour Force Development Board.	Qualitative, Descriptive Non-experimental, Descriptive (both)	Cross-sectional	Immigrants	Multi-stakeholder

Reference	Methodology	Design	Population	Setting
13. Vanstone, S. (ed.) (1999, July) *Publications and resources on prior learning assessment and recognition.* [Online]. Bibliography compiled for Research Network for New Approaches to Lifelong Learning (NALL). [2000, 29 February]. Available at: http://www.plar.com /publications/database.	Qualitative, Descriptive	Retrospective	Researchers	University
2000				
14. Day, M. (2000) *Developing benchmarks for prior learning assessment and recognition: Practitioner perspectives* Belleville, ON: Canadian Association for Prior Learning Assessment.	Qualitative, Descriptive Non-experimental, Descriptive (both)	Cross-sectional	PLAR practitioners	Community-based
15. Lennox, J. and Philip, L. (2000) *A comparative analysis of the academic performance of graduate students admitted under the special-case provisions at York University.* Unpublished report. Toronto: York University, Faculty of Graduate Studies.	Non-experimental, Predictive	Retrospective	Adult students	University
16. Office of Institutional Research (2000) *The learners' perspectives on prior learning assessment: Results of a provincial survey of PLA students.* New Westminster, BC: Centre for Curriculum, Transfer and Technology.	Non-experimental, Descriptive	Cross-sectional	Adult students	Colleges and universities
17. Peruniak, G. and Welch, D. (2000) The twinning of potential: Toward an integration of prior learning assessment with career development. *Canadian Journal of Counselling,* 34(3), 232–44.	Qualitative, Descriptive	Cross-sectional	Career counsellors	University
18. Riffell, M. and Wilson, B. (2000) *MTD-PLAR project: Progress report.* Winnipeg: Prior Learning Assessment Centre.	Qualitative, Exploratory	Cross-sectional	Adult students	College and community-based
19. Stowe, S. (2000) *Prior learning assessment.* Toronto: York University.	Qualitative, Descriptive	Cross-sectional	Universities	University

Appendix 3.1 continued

Research report Lead author	Research type	Time dimension	Target sector	Researcher affiliation
20. Wong, A. (2000) *Assessment and recognition of experiential learning in higher education: Impact of government policy, institutional innovation, and information technology.* Saskatoon: University of Saskatchewan.	Qualitative, Descriptive	Cross-sectional	University students	Universities
21. Wong, A. (2000) *University-level prior learning assessment and recognition: Building capacity for an institutional response.* Saskatoon: University of Saskatchewan.	Qualitative, Descriptive	Cross-sectional	Universities	University
2001				
22. Barker, K. (2001) *Sustaining prior learning assessment in British Columbia: Discussion paper.* Victoria: Ministry of Advanced Education and Centre for Curriculum, Transfer and Technology.	Qualitative, Descriptive	Cross-sectional	Colleges and universities	Government
23. Bloom, M. and Grant, M. (2001) *Brain Gain: The economic benefits of recognizing learning credentials in Canada.* Ottawa: Conference Board of Canada.	Non-experimental, Descriptive	Cross-sectional	Adults in community	Multi-stakeholder
24. Castle, D. (2001) *A profile of prior learning assessment candidates and its implications for PLA policy and procedures at the University of Guelph.* Unpublished report. Guelph, ON: University of Guelph.	Non-experimental, Predictive	Cross-sectional	Adults in community	University
25. Centre for Curriculum, Transfer and Technology (2001) *Prior learning assessment practices in British Columbia: 2000/2001 PLA survey.* Vancouver: Centre for Curriculum, Transfer and Technology.	Non-experimental, Descriptive	Cross-sectional	PLAR practitioners	Colleges and universities

No. / Reference	Methodology	Design	Population	Setting
26. Gereluk, W. (2001) *A report from learning labour: A prior learning assessment and recognition project.* Athabasca, AB: Athabasca University.	Qualitative, Descriptive	Cross-sectional	Unionised workers	University
27. Hall, G. (2001) *Program-based prior learning assessment and recognition project: Final report.* Winnipeg: Manitoba Tourism Education Council in partnership with Red River College.	Qualitative, Exploratory	Prospective	College students	College
28. Lior, K., Martin, D. and Morais, A. (2001) *Tacit skills, informal knowledge and reflective practice.* NALL Working Paper 24 – 2001. Toronto: Ontario Institute for Studies in Education.	Qualitative, Descriptive	Cross-sectional	Workers	Multi-stakeholder
29. Thomas, A., Collins, M. and Plett, L. (2001) *Dimensions of the experience of prior learning assessment & recognition.* Toronto: University of Toronto.	Qualitative, Descriptive	Cross-sectional	Multi-sector	Multi-stakeholder
2002				
30. Smith, K. (2002) *A phenomenological study conducted to further develop the base of knowledge related to post-secondary student experiences with prior learning assessment and recognition.* Master's thesis, Memorial University, St John's, NF	Qualitative, Descriptive	Cross-sectional	Adult students	Graduate student
31. Williams, R. (2002) *Impact evaluation of the PLA centre learning portfolio programs.* Bedford, NS: Praxis Research & Consulting.	Qualitative, Descriptive	Cross-sectional	Adults in community	Community-based
2003				
32. Aarts, S., Blower, D., Burke, R.., Conlin, E., Lamarre, G., McCrossan, W. and Van Kleef, J. (2003) *Feedback from learners: Cross-Canada study of prior learning assessment and recognition.* Kitchener, ON: Cross-Canada Partnership on PLAR.	Qualitative, Descriptive Non-experimental, Descriptive (both)	Cross-sectional	Adult students (college)	Colleges

Appendix 3.1 continued

Research report Lead author	Research type	Time dimension	Target sector	Researcher affiliation
33. Austin, Z., Galli, M. and Diamantouros, A. (2003) Development of a prior learning assessment for pharmacists seeking licensure in Canada. *Pharmacy Education, 3(2)*, 87–97.	Qualitative, Exploratory	Cross-sectional	Immigrant pharmacists	University
34. Graham, K. (2003) *Developing a prior learning assessment and recognition process for northern nurse practitioner students.* Master's thesis. St Francis Xavier University, Antigonish, NS.	Qualitative, Exploratory	Cross-sectional	Nurses	Graduate student
35. Kennedy, B. (2003) *A spring snapshot: The current status of prior learning assessment and recognition (PLAR) in Canada's public postsecondary institutions.* Ottawa: Council of Ministers of Education Canada.	Qualitative, Descriptive Non-experimental, Descriptive (both)	Cross-sectional	Colleges and universities	Multi-stakeholder
36. Pankhurst, K. (2003) *Learning by experience during work.* Doctoral thesis. University of Toronto.	Qualitative, Descriptive	Retrospective	Workers	Graduate student
37. Shmyr, Z. (2003) *Recognition of prior learning (RPL) within the newcomer community: A needs assessment. Final Report.* Regina: Saskatchewan Association of Immigrant Settlement and Integration Agencies (SAISA).	Non-experimental, Descriptive	Cross-sectional	Immigrants and refugees	Community-based
38. University of Waterloo. (2003) *Looking forward … towards optometric practice in Canada.* Waterloo: University of Waterloo.	Qualitative, Exploratory	Cross-sectional	Immigrant professionals (optometrists)	University
2004				
39. Darville, R., Coombs, D. and Baker-McDonald, N. (2004) *It really gets you thinking: Prior learning assessment for young at-risk adults 18–29.* Ottawa: Human Resources and Skills Development Canada.	Qualitative, Descriptive	Cross-sectional	Adults at risk	School Board

Reference	Methodology	Design	Population	Conducted by
40. McGuire, M. (2004) *A report on issues, barriers and best practices related to PLAR and the advancement of internationally educated nurses and practical nurses into professional nursing education, registered nurse licensure and employment.* Calgary: Mount Royal College.	Qualitative, Descriptive Non-experimental, Descriptive (both)	Cross-sectional	Professionals (internationally educated nurses)	University
41. OARS Training Inc. (2004) *PLAR as a workforce development tool: Linking the partners.* Winnipeg: Manitoba Workplace Prior Learning Assessment and Recognition Committee.	Qualitative, Exploratory	Cross-sectional	Adults in community	Multi-stakeholder group
42. Riffell, M. (2004) *PLAR in Canadian apprenticeship systems: Development, benefits, issues and concerns.* Master's thesis. University of Manitoba, Winnipeg, MAN.	Non-experimental, Descriptive	Cross-sectional	Apprenticeship systems	Graduate student
2005				
43. Barrington Research Group (2005) *Best practices in prior learning assessment and recognition (PLAR): Final report.* Edmonton, Alberta: Alberta Council on Admissions and Transfer.	Qualitative, Descriptive	Cross-sectional	Adults in community	Multi-stakeholder group
44. Livingstone, D., Raykov, M. and Turner, C. (2005) *Canadian adults' interest in prior learning assessment and recognition (PLAR): A 2004 national survey.* Toronto: OISE.	Non-experimental, Descriptive	Cross-sectional	Adults in community	University
2006				
45. Canadian Institute for Recognizing Learning (2006) *PLAR report and recommendations: A prior learning assessment and recognition (PLAR) model for nursing baccalaureate equivalency.* Toronto: College of Nurses of Ontario.	Qualitative, Exploratory	Cross-sectional	Immigrant professionals (nurses)	Regulatory body
46. College of Extended Learning (2006) *Review of prior learning assessment at the University of New Brunswick from 1998–2004.* Fredericton: University of New Brunswick.	Qualitative, Descriptive Non-experimental, Descriptive (both)	Retrospective	Adult students	University

Appendix 3.1 continued

Research report Lead author	Research type	Time dimension	Target sector	Researcher affiliation
47. Haley, B. and Simosko, S. (2006) *Prior learning assessment and internationally trained medical laboratory technologists: Capstone report.* Nanaimo, BC: Susan Simosko Associates Inc.	Qualitative, Descriptive	Cross-sectional	Immigrant professionals (laboratory technologists)	Regulatory body
48. Miller, R. and Gill, M. (2006) *Workers in transition: prior learning assessment and recognition. Final report.* Winnipeg: Centre for Education and Work.	Qualitative, Exploratory	Prospective	Adults in community	Multi-stakeholder
49. PLA Centre (2006) *Nova Scotia Employment Assistance Services Prior Learning and Assessment Research and Demonstration Project.* Halifax.	Qualitative, Exploratory	Prospective	Unemployed adults	Community-based
50. PLA Centre (2006) *Portfolio learning development in the federal correctional institutions of the Atlantic region 2003–2006. Final report.* Halifax.	Qualitative, Exploratory	Prospective	Inmates and correctional workers	Community-based
51. Riffell, M. (2006) *Recognizing prior learning of immigrants to Canada: Moving towards consistency and excellence.* Ottawa: CAPLA.	Non-experimental, Descriptive	Cross-sectional	Immigrant professionals	Community-based org.
52. Robinson, M. (2006) *Exploring flexible admissions at the graduate school level.* Master's thesis. Royal Roads University, Victoria, BC.	Qualitative, Descriptive	Cross-sectional	Adult students	Graduate student
53. Shandro, G. (2006) *Prior learning assessment and recognition framework for nurse practitioner education and regulation in Canada.* Ottawa: Canadian Nurses Association.	Qualitative, Descriptive Non-experimental, Descriptive (both)	Cross-sectional	Institutions Regulators	Professional body CNA

Reference	Method	Design	Population	Setting
54. Van Kleef, J. (2006) Strengthening PLAR: Integrating theory and practice in post-secondary education. *Journal of Applied Research on Learning*, 2(1), 1–22.	Qualitative, Descriptive	Retrospective	Colleges and universities	Graduate student
55. Wihak, C. (2006). *State of the field review: Prior learning assessment and recognition (PLAR).* Ottawa: Canadian Council on Learning.	Qualitative, Descriptive	Cross-sectional	All sectors	University
2007				
56. Arscott, J., Crowther, I., Young, M. and Ungarian, L. (2007) *Producing results in prior learning: A report from the gateways project.* Edmonton: Athabasca University.	Qualitative, Exploratory	Prospective	Adult students	University and colleges
57. Baskwill, A. and Dryen, T. (2007) *Improving access for internationally educated massage therapists in Ontario: The development of a new assessment process and bridging programme.* Toronto: College of Massage Therapists of Ontario.	Qualitative, Exploratory	Prospective	Immigrant professionals (massage therapists)	Regulator
58. Lordly, D. (2007) Dietetic prior learning assessment: Student and faculty experiences. *Canadian Journal of Dietetic Practice and Research*, 68(4), 207–12.	Qualitative, Descriptive	Retrospective	University	University
59. Morin, L. (2007) *Prior learning assessment and recognition (PLAR): Access and retention of adult learners.* Master's thesis. Athabasca University, Athabasca, Alberta.	Qualitative, Descriptive	Cross-sectional	Adult learners	University
60. Olsen, R. (2007) *PLAR processes for human resource professionals at Manitoba Hydro – Five years later.* Winnipeg: Dynamic Resource Management.	Qualitative, Exploratory	Prospective	Employees	Multi-stakeholder
61. Peruniak, G. (2007) Back eddies of learning in the recognition of prior learning. *Canadian Journal of University Continuing Education*, 33(1), 88–106.	Qualitative, Descriptive	Cross-sectional	Adult students	University

Appendix 3.1 continued

Research report / Lead author	Research type	Time dimension	Target sector	Researcher affiliation
62. Van Kleef, J., Amichand, S., Ireland, M., Orynik, K. and Potter, J. (2007) *Quality assurance in PLAR: Issues and strategies for post-secondary institutions – Volume I.* Ottawa: Canadian Council on Learning.	Qualitative, Descriptive	Cross-sectional	Colleges and universities	Colleges and universities
63. Van Kleef, J., Amichand, S., Ireland, M., Orynik, K. and Potter, J. (2007) *Quality assurance in PLAR: Annotated bibliography – Volume III.* Ottawa: Canadian Council on Learning.	Qualitative, Descriptive	Retrospective	Researchers	Colleges and universities
64. Wihak, C. (2007) Prior learning assessment and recognition in Canadian universities: View from the web. *Canadian Journal of Higher Education, 37,* 95–112.	Qualitative, Descriptive	Cross-sectional	Universities	University
2008				
65. Folinsbee, S. (2008) *Prior learning assessment and recognition: Options for the workplace and the workforce. A literature review.* Winnipeg: Manitoba Workplace PLAR Committee.	Qualitative, Descriptive	Retrospective	Adults in community	Private consultant for multi-stakeholders
66. Hall, G. (2008) Buyer Beware: Report on PLAR policies and procedures of post-secondary educational institutions in Canada. Ottawa: Canadian Tourism Human Resource Council.	Qualitative, Descriptive	Cross-sectional	Universities	Multi-stakeholders
67. McLaren, J. (2008) *Prior learning assessment and recognition with young at risk adults: Final report.* Cornwall, ON: Upper Canada Leger Centre for Education and Training.	Qualitative, Exploratory	Prospective	At-risk young adults	Community-based

Reference				
68. Morrissey, M., Myers, D., Bélanger, P. and Robitaille, M., Davison, P., Van Kleef, J. and Williams, R. (2008) *Achieving our potential: An action plan for prior learning and recognition (PLAR) in Canada*. Ottawa: Canadian Council on Learning.	Qualitative, Descriptive	Cross-sectional	Adults in community	Community-based
69. Moss, L. (2008) *Prior learning assessment and recognition (PLAR) and the impact of globalization: A Canadian case study*. Doctoral thesis, McGill University, Montreal.	Qualitative, Descriptive	Cross-sectional	Adult students	Graduate student
70. Pederson, A. (2008) *Seduction and abandonment or wooing and support? Mentoring to facilitate transition of internationally educated midwives*. Master's thesis. Royal Roads University, Victoria.	Qualitative, Descriptive	Cross-sectional	Immigrant professionals (midwives)	Graduate student
2009				
71. Conrad, D. (2009) *Exploring the contribution of mentoring to knowledge building in PLAR practice*. Athabasca: Athabasca University. Accessible from: http://hdl.handle.net/2149/2249	Qualitative, Descriptive	Cross-sectional	Adult students in post-secondary institutions	University
72. Gill, M. (2009) *The use of workplace skills-based prior learning assessment and recognition: Strategies for persons with acquired physical disabilities in employment transition*. Winnipeg: Centre for Education and Work.	Qualitative, Exploratory	Cross-sectional	Adults with disabilities	Multi-stakeholder
73. Nunavut Arctic College. (2009) *Portfolio development at Nunavut arctic college: 2009–10*. Iqaluit, NU: Nunavut Arctic College.	Qualitative, Exploratory	Prospective	Adult students	College
74. Amichand, S. (2009) *Quality assurance assessment report: An in-depth review of methods and processes*. Saskatoon: SIAST.	Non-experimental, Descriptive	Cross-sectional	Faculty, students, employers	College

Appendix 3.1 continued

Research report Lead author	Research type	Time dimension	Target sector	Researcher affiliation
75. Van Kleef, J. (2009) *Taking account: A report on the number of PLAR assessments conducted by public post-secondary institutions in Canada*. Ottawa: Canadian Council on Learning.	Non-experimental, Descriptive	Retrospective	Colleges and universities	Multi-stakeholder
76. VETASSESS (2009) *Multiple assessment pathways project: Evaluation report*. Vancouver: Industry Training Authority.	Qualitative, Exploratory	Cross-sectional	Skilled trades	Regulator
77. Faculty of Nursing. (——) *Prior learning assessment and recognition for internationally educated nurses*. Toronto: York University (in progress).	Qualitative, Exploratory	Prospective	Immigrant professionals (nurses)	University
2010				
78. Morrissey, M. (2010) *RPL in Nova Scotia: An environmental scan*. Halifax: PLA Centre.	Qualitative, Descriptive	Cross-sectional	All sectors	Community-based

NOTE:
The following items were reviewed but excluded:

- Documents with little or no information on method and analysis
- Published articles reflecting commentary or opinion only
- Initiatives in which PLAR is not a major element

CHAPTER FOUR

Québec: An overview of RAC/RPLC research since 2002[1]

RACHEL BÉLISLE

Abstract

This chapter provides an overview of scholarly research in the Recognition of Prior Learning undertaken since 2002 in Québec, Canada. That date corresponds to the adoption of a Québec government policy and action plan encouraging the development of official recognition practices in three systems: the education system at secondary and post-secondary levels; the public employment system; and the professional system which comprises 46 'professional orders'. In Québec, recognition practices are designated 'reconnaissance des acquis et des compétences' (RAC) (Recognition of Prior Learning and Competencies [RPLC] in English). The chapter begins with some historical background on RAC/RPLC and delimits the field of study. It then provides a general picture of research published since 2002,

[1] This chapter is an adaptation of a presentation made at the workshop 'Prior Learning Assessment and Recognition: Emergence of a Canadian community of scholars', organised by Christine Wihak in Ottawa, November 2010, with financial support from the Social Science and Humanities Research Council of Canada (SSHRC). I want to thank Judy Harris and Christine Wihak for inviting me to the workshop and for accepting a chapter for this book, which is close to my verbal presentation. I also want to thank Françoise McNeill, who translated my presentation from French to English and gave me some linguistic coaching before the workshop; Tanis Moreland (Research assistant at l'Équipe de recherche sur les transitions et l'apprentissage (ÉRTA), Université de Sherbrooke) for her work on the manuscript; and Leah Moss, from McGill University, Montreal, who was generous enough to help me with the English adaptation of this chapter in a very tight time-frame.

scholars involved in the field, available funding in recent years and the development of public policy. It concludes with a brief introduction to related research in France and links with developments in Québec.

Introduction

Although Québec is part of the Canadian federation, it has a strong Francophone identity and is considered by many to be a distinct society or nation.[2] Education, employment and work are Québec jurisdictions, and as a result are significantly different in character from other parts of Canada. The same applies to official policies, legislation and practices in reconnaissance des acquis et des compétences (RAC).

RAC research is influenced by its specific context and also by the fact that postgraduate research programmes in the social sciences in Québec Francophone universities draw largely on research literature from France. Even though Québec education scholars read publications in English pertaining to research in Anglo-Saxon countries, many work with conceptual frameworks that are influenced by French sociology, psychology of work, ergonomics or psychoanalysis. There is a tradition of collaboration amongst Francophone education scholars and a deep conviction that if we want to reduce the gap between research, practice and policy, we need to publish in French first. This is also true for RAC research.

To provide a backdrop for the RAC research in Québec, I first present some historical milestones and delimit the field of study. Thereafter, I provide a picture of the published research since 2002 and the scholars involved. After an overview of sources of funding in recent years, I present a brief analysis of the role of research in the development of public policy in the field. The chapter ends with a perspective on the Québec-France collaboration.

---

[2] French is the official language of Québec and the first language of the majority of the population; however, the Anglophone minority has the right to services in English. That is why many official documents are in both languages. In this chapter, I refer to English documents if they exist.

Delimiting the field

Recognition of prior learning became well known in the adult education sector in Québec at the beginning of the 1980s thanks to the work of the Commission Jean (Commission d'étude sur la formation des adultes, 1982) and Marthe Sansregret's publications (e.g. Sansregret, 1983, 1984). Greatly inspired by initiatives in the United States, her work has influenced the practices of several Québec institutions in significant ways. A little later, the Institut canadien d'éducation des adultes (ICÉA) launched a series of research projects to document some specific issues and develop material to support structured recognition processes (Bélisle, 1997, 2004a; Institut canadien d'éducation des adultes, 1999). Research in RAC was also supported by the Centre d'information et de recherche en reconnaissance des acquis (CIRRAC). Housed at the Université de Sherbrooke, this Centre had members from across the province until it was disbanded in the 1990s. One legacy of CIRRAC is a chapter in an edited book (Chaput and Meyer, 1997), published seven years after the 1989 Fontevraud conference (France). The book represents an important marker in the Québec-France collaboration in the field of recognition of prior learning, establishing links between Québec and French recognition practices and the work of the Council for Adult and Experiential Learning (CAEL) in the United States.

In the late 1980s and the 1990s, the term 'prior learning recognition' was used in educational establishments in Québec, while 'recognition of skills' or 'recognition of competencies' was used in public employment agency and community-based organisations concerned with occupational integration. The term 'reconnaissance des acquis et des compétences' was adopted by organisations such as the ICÉA (1999) because of a concern with policies and practices across all sectors. That term was enshrined in the *Government Policy on Adult Education and Continuing Education and Training* (Gouvernement du Québec, 2002a) and in the accompanying *Action Plan* (Gouvernement du Québec, 2002b).

Even so, a range of terms remain in use within sectors. The Québec Ministry of Education uses the term 'recognition of acquired competencies' (RAC) in vocational and technical training (to be consistent with the French acronym, RAC). The term 'reconnaissance des acquis extrascolaires' (out-of-school learning) is still in use in basic adult general education at the secondary level, while universities refer to the 'recognition of prior learning'. In the world of work, the public employment agency, sectoral labour force committees, regulated professions and trades,[3] and community-based organisations, the term 'reconnaissance des compétences' (recognition of competencies) is frequently used.

All of these terminological differences reflect different emphases within recognition activities. Some processes lead to official ratification, with assessment results entered into state records or into the records of state-mandated organisations; for example, diplomas, professional titles and certain professional certifications. I refer to this as 'official recognition'. Educational institutions, the world of work and community-based organisations often have structured non-formal recognition processes that lead to other forms of accreditation (e.g. a documented professional project that provides access to financial help for specific training).

From here on, I use the acronym RAC/RPLC to designate all recognition policies or practices in Québec. They are all included in RPL as a general field. This is in keeping with ICÉA (1999), the Conseil supérieur de l'éducation (CSE) (2000) and other scholars (e.g. Pineau *et al.*, 1997). If non-formal recognition was common in the 1990s, the Québec government in 2002 took 'aggressive action toward the official recognition of adults' prior learning and competencies' (Gouvernement du Québec, 2002b, p. 25). The government *Action Plan* set out eight priority measures that had to be implemented across three systems and their specific sectors: the education system (including secondary and post-secondary levels, general adult education, vocational and technical sectors); the public employment system (including Québec employment agency and partners from different sectors); and the professional system (including the 46 professional orders). It should be noted that none of these eight priority measures included explicit research activities.

In this chapter, RAC/RPLC activities are considered which share the above historical background and have the same main phases: 1) information; 2) the identification and formalisation of prior learning, knowledge, competencies or skills; 3) evaluation; and 4) some form of accreditation (Bélisle, 2004a, 2006).

---

[3] In Québec, 51 professions (engineering, medicine, vocational guidance counselling, for example) are regulated by 'professional orders' – bodies authorised by the government to set standards for admission to the profession and practice standards within the profession. There are, at the end of 2010, 46 professional orders in Québec (some orders regulate more than one profession). Admission to, and practise of, skilled trades (such as electrician) are also regulated by government-authorised bodies.

Research overview

I have focused my own inquiry for this chapter on research with RAC/RPLC as a central component undertaken by Québec researchers since 2002. To be included, research needed to be structured and rigorous; that is, consist of clearly articulated research problems, notions or concepts, methods and modes of analyses, with findings that have been or will be published.[4] Documentary analyses, and speculative or empirical research (quantitative and qualitative), have been included; for example, study trips abroad to help inform the development of services in Québec. There is an emphasis on research conducted by scholars or supervised by scholars. The research overview that follows is divided into four parts: papers published since 2002; scholars with RAC/RPLC as a research interest; sources of funding; and the role of research in the development of public policy.

Publications[5]

As mentioned, three systems are involved in 'official recognition' in Québec. Many of the publications which directly refer to RAC/RPLC are concerned with only one system or sector. However, some research does address policies, practices or adults' experiences in more than one system or sector. Other work focuses specifically on non-formal recognition practices.

Only three papers have been published in scholarly, peer-reviewed journals. One documents a pedagogical innovation by university practitioners to recognise prior learning in a college-level programme for teachers. The article concerned presents materials developed during the project as well as participants' evaluations (St-Pierre *et al.*, 2010). The

---

[4] I have included some research that is 'borderline' in terms of the use of scientific concepts and explicit methodology.

[5] My search methodology involved the use of the Érudit database, using French or English search terms such as 'reconnaissance des acquis' or 'reconnaissance de compétences'. Érudit is the Québec platform for the publication and dissemination of research in the social sciences and humanities in Canada. I consulted the CVs of known researchers (see next section), searched the Bibliothèque et Archives Canada and used my own database on RAC/RPLC that I have constructed in the course of my extensive work in the field.

second publication addresses the use of the *bilan de compétences*[6] or 'competencies audit' in vocational guidance (Michaud *et al.*, 2007). It includes a literature review of the French vocational guidance competencies audit and an analysis of secondary data from a competencies audit service in Québec. It is clear that the audits have a positive effect on candidates' self-recognition. Drawing on the work of a French scholar in vocational guidance, the authors assert that in Anglo-Saxon countries there is no equivalent of the French *bilan de compétences* used in vocational guidance (Lemoine, 1998, in Michaud *et al.*, 2007, p. 174). The third journal article is a literature review addressing the demand for recognition from adults without a secondary diploma (Bélisle, 2004b).

To my knowledge, the only edited book on RPL published in Québec since 2002 is the one that I co-edited with a French colleague, Jean-Pierre Boutinet. This is a peer-reviewed collection from Québec, France and Switzerland, with two Québec-specific chapters. One uses Axel Honneth's concept of recognition to analyse two structured initiatives with adults not in possession of diplomas (Garon and Bélisle, 2009); the second explores the inclusion of experience from the private sphere in RAC/RPLC (Solar and Bélisle, 2009). Both chapters are based on speculative design with reference to some public documents on RAC/RPLC.

Another edited collection was published in 2006 by the Association pour le développement des méthodologies d'évaluation en éducation (ADMEE), an international association active in RPL assessment, with a European arm (which has Québec members). This collection includes a research paper on the Québec 'Record of Learning in basic general education', a type of non-formal recognition at the secondary level that is used in adult education centres (Goyer *et al.*, 2006). In a similar category, a paper published online in a peer-reviewed collection (Bélisle *et al.*, 2008) presents a short description of a research problem and the conceptual framework that was used at the beginning of a project.

What is more common is the production and subsequent online publication of research reports. This group of publications consists of reports written by scholars, supervised by senior researchers, or by scholars working on projects with advisory committees. These are not

---

[6] This expression is translated in a number of ways. In this chapter, I use 'competencies audit' but in other contexts it is referred to as 'competency profile', 'skills assessment' and 'personalised skills audit'.

anonymously reviewed. With the aim of documenting the development of RAC/RPLC services, many of them examine official documentation (public or not), and in some cases present findings from interviews or questionnaires. Because services are growing rapidly, these reports have a short shelf-life, especially those that are weaker on conceptual and methodological aspects.

A report by Geneviève Talbot (2005) attempts to give an overall picture of the implementation of RAC/RPLC in Québec; although its methodology is not explicit, the report covers a very large spectrum of activities including information that was very hard to obtain at the time, especially concerning general education at the secondary level. For example, the 2002 *Action Plan* announced the introduction of the General Educational Development (GED) test at the secondary level, and Talbot's report was for a time the only source of information on this issue. A recent report (Bélisle *et al.*, 2010) goes further regarding the implementation of the GED in Québec school boards. Based on official documentation and interviews, it charts the development of RAC/RPLC services in general education at the secondary level, in vocational and technical training, and for people with degrees and professional experience from other countries. Vocational guidance practitioners in these domains have many questions and require training, especially in those three sectors.

Two civil society organisations have published research reports on RAC/RPLC in their specific areas (ACDEAULF, 2006; COCDMO, 2007).[7] One of the important findings from the Association canadienne d'éducation des adultes des universités de langue française's report (based on administrative data and questionnaires to gather quantitative and qualitative data) is that experience is a '*bête noire*' (ACDEAULF, 2006, p. 16) in Québec universities because they do not yet know how to assess it.[8] Using documentary analysis, questionnaires and group interviews, the Coalition des organismes communautaires de développement de la main-d'œuvre's report shows that many community-based organisations are involved in RPLC, but do not identify their activities as such (COCDMO, 2007). This echoes a finding by Bélisle (2006), who surveyed and conducted focus group interviews with vocational guidance counsellors.

[7] ACDEAUFL is the Canadian Association for the Education of Adults in French-speaking Universities and COCDMO is the Coalition of Community-based Organisations for Workforce Development.

[8] In this context, '*bête noire*' refers to a weak element in RPL in Québec universities for which no sustainable solution has yet been found.

Michel Lejeune's report (2008) is an international comparison (France, United States and England) to inform the development of services to recognise workers' competencies in Québec. Its conceptual framework examines three phases of implementation and refers to four institutional models: a model regulated by the market; a model driven by the government; a model driven by social partners; and a community-based model.

Contrary to the priorities set out in the 2002 *Action Plan* (e.g. on basic education), there are not many *online* RAC/RPLC publications on research (in the sense used here) by the Ministry of Education. An exception is the work referred to above regarding the Record of Learning in basic general education (Bélisle, 2004a; Goyer and Grimard, 2005). Another exception is an online research report where two Québec scholars, Paul Bélanger and Magali Robitaille, introduce official documentation and institutional discourses regarding RAC/RPLC (Morrissey *et al.*, 2008). Some online research reports in work-related training or adult education consider recognition of competencies as a secondary topic (D'Ortun *et al.*, 2005; Bélanger and Robitaille, 2008; Solar and Tremblay, 2008). Online publications also include student papers on specific aspects of RAC/RPLC (Boutin, 2006; Solar-Pelletier, 2006; Noël, 2010).

As noted, research reports are not always available online. This is true of a report published in 2010 by the association of professional bodies of Québec, the Conseil interprofessionnel du Québec (CIQ) in the context of the implementation of the 'Québec-France Understanding' (Ministère des relations internationales, 2010). France Fontaine, in collaboration with Huguette Bernard, both specialists in assessment and evaluation at Université de Montréal (research development design), put forward a method for the development of a benchmark or standard (*référentiel*) for each professional body (Fontaine, 2010). To the best of my knowledge, the only relevant doctoral thesis defended with success to date in Québec is by Leah Moss at McGill University in Montreal (Moss, 2007) – a case study of RPL at the Royal Military College of Canada in Kingston, Ontario. That there is only one thesis, and that it is on practices in another province, demonstrates how young the field is in Québec.[9]

---

[9] The thesis is available online via Proquest.

Scholars involved in research

Interest in RAC/RPLC research can be ascertained through scholars' CVs, papers and reports on the subject, and by searches of specialised databases. Academic events can also help to identify people with an interest in the field, although very few conference presentations on RAC/RPLC make their way into peer-reviewed publications or form the basis of substantial research reports.

In 2004, 112 researchers from Québec and French Canada took part in a survey conducted by two scholars from Université du Québec à Montréal, in collaboration with the Centre de documentation sur l'éducation des adultes et la condition féminine (CDEACF) (Documentation Centre on Adult Education and the Status of Women) (Bélanger and Doray, 2004). In their report, the two researchers included RPL in career guidance or educational engineering research. Three years later, two Université de Montréal scholars (also in collaboration with the CDEACF) reviewed Canadian French-language research publications on adult learning between 1997 and 2007 (Solar and Tremblay, 2008). They classified RPL as a separate topic, noting that of the 227 texts included in their sample only 3 per cent explored RPL (*ibid.*, p. 56).

In 2009, the Conseil de la science et de la technologie (CST), a Québec government agency, published a research and knowledge transfer strategy in adult education and training. In preparation, the Conseil put together a list of scholars, and found that (as at 2008) 90 scholars in Québec were 'specialists of adult education and continuing education and training' (CST, 2009, p. 9). However, only 5 per cent of that number was reported as having expertise in RAC/RPLC.

A search in the Research Directory (Expertise recherche Québec, 2008), using 'recognition' and 'prior learning' or 'competencies' as keywords, generated nine individuals with research interests in official RAC/RPLC. A search using 'portfolio' or 'audit' (*bilan*) and 'competencies' resulted in two additional names. The majority of these 11 scholars are working in university faculties of education. A search of CVs posted on university websites showed very few research projects or publications specifically on RAC/RPLC, except for Bélisle, D'Ortun, Houle and Michaud. However, maintaining directories and CVs is a big challenge for scholars, and it is likely that the number of academics focusing on RAC/RPLC research is increasing. Table 4.1 presents Québec's scholars who are listed for their interest in RAC/RPLC research.

Table 4.1 Researchers identified as researchers in RAC/RPLC

	Bélanger and Doray, 2004	Solar and Tremblay, 2008	Conseil de la science et de la technologie, 2009	Expertise recherche Québec, 2008
RPLC	RAC/RPLC included in career guidance or educational engineering	RAC/RPLC is a separate topic	RAC/RPLC is a separate topic	RAC/RPLC is a separate topic
Number of researchers	3	3	< 4 (5% of 90)	9
Names of researchers	Bélisle (UdeS); Gagnon (Laval); Gobeil (CSE)	Bélisle(UdeS); Talbot (CSQ); Solar-Pelletier (HEC)	n.d.	Bélisle (UdeS); Boudreault (UQAM); Coulombe (UQAC); D'Ortun (UCO); Guilbert (Laval); Houle (UdeM); Lacourse (UdeS); Voyer (UQAM); Zourhlal (UQAC); Côté (UCO); Michaud (UdeS)

UdeS: Université de Sherbrooke; Laval: Université Laval (Québec City); CSE: Conseil supérieur de l'éducation; CSQ: Centrale des syndicats du Québec; HEC: Montréal, Business school (Hautes études commerciales); UQAM: Université du Québec à Montréal; UQAC: Université du Québec à Chicoutimi; UdeM: Université de Montréal; UCO: Université du Québec en Outaouais (Gatineau–Hull).

Developing and funding RAC/RPLC research in Québec

There is no research without money, and funding has a huge impact on interest in a research field. The publications outlined above have received funding from a range of agencies and sources:

- The Canadian Council on Learning (CCL) has funded three previously mentioned research initiatives involving other provinces (Bélanger and Robitaille, 2008; Morrissey *et al.*, 2008; Solar and Tremblay, 2008).
- The Commission des partenaires du marché du travail (labour market partners) funded two research projects through its Programme de subventions à la recherche appliquée (PSRA) (Applied Research Programme) (D'Ortun *et al.*, 2005; Lejeune, 2008).
- The Ministry of Education established two research contracts (Bélisle, 2004a; Goyer and Grimard, 2005; Goyer *et al.*, 2006).
- Internal funds at Université de Sherbrooke allowed two pieces of research (Bélisle, 2006; Bélisle *et al.*, 2010).
- Other civil society organisations have funded four research programmes (Talbot, 2005; ACDEAULF, 2006; COCDMO, 2007; Fontaine, 2010).

Official RAC/RPLC is the focus of one grant from the Social Science and Humanities Research Council of Canada (SSHRC) (Bélisle *et al.*, 2008).[10] This research team is studying the learning spaces of Québec adults who have received official RAC/RPLC at secondary level. The project is constituted as a case study to map the territory of adults' learning spaces, with the RAC/RPLC process as one of the learning spaces. Included in the data are RAC/RPLC application files and interviews with 42 adults and about half a dozen practitioners. The conceptual framework is based on the triad of formal, non-formal and informal modes of learning and on barriers to participation in adult education. Adults' literacy practices (Bélisle and Bourdon, 2006) outside and inside the RAC/RPLC process are also considered. The team is interested in how the work of French sociologist Bernard Lahire (1998; forthcoming) and the New Literacy Studies (Barton and Papen, 2010) can help to

---

[10] SSHRC grants are very prestigious in academic circles in Canada.

document plurality and learning in informal and non-formal settings. The first results of this research project are expected to be published in 2011.[11]

To the best of my knowledge, three other projects have received funding from the Programme de subventions à la recherche appliquée (PSRA) (Applied Research Programme):

1. A team from Université Laval (Lucie Héon, Liette Goyer and Jacques Blanchet) is studying RAC/RPLC in the road transport sector.
2. A team from the National Institute of Scientific Research (INRS) (Frédéric Lesemann, Michel Lejeune and Jean-Luc Bédard) is researching a concerted approach to the development and recognition of competencies.
3. A professor from the Université du Québec en Outaouais (Francine d'Ortun) is exploring self-directed learning in relation to the recognition of competencies (CPMT, 2010).

My colleague from l'Équipe de recherche sur les transitions et l'apprentissage (ÉRTA), Guylaine Michaud, was awarded a grant from the Fonds québécois de recherche sur la société et la culture (FQRSC) for a research project on the competencies audit. She is also the Principal Investigator of three other projects concerned with competencies audit and different research populations (funded by Human Resources and Skills Development Canada [HRSDC]). Finally, some RAC/RPLC scholarly work is located on the boundary between practice and research; for example, in the areas of continuing education or pedagogical innovation. Grants are available from funds dedicated to pedagogical issues for this work; for example, for Lise St-Pierre and her team (St-Pierre *et al.*, 2010).

The role of research in the development of public policy in RAC/RPLC

The development of public policy can be defined in terms of five stages (Bouchard, 2001; Bélisle, 2006, 2009; Lemieux, 2009; Bélisle *et al.*, 2010). These stages help to understand the development of RAC/RPLC in Québec and the role that researchers can play in the field. The five stages

---

[11] For more information, see www.erta.ca. RPLC is also a secondary topic in other ÉRTA projects; for example, in community-based organisations (Michaud, Bélisle, Bourdon and Garon).

are: 1) problem identification and agenda setting; 2) looking at alternatives; 3) formulation and adoption; 4) implementation; and 5) evaluation. As is well documented, these stages are not linear, and the examples that follow show how actors step back to a preceding stage or step over a stage.

Even though government policy was adopted in 2002, some RAC/RPLC research projects looking at alternatives in other countries (i.e. stage 2) began *after* 2002 and were published between 2004 and 2008 (Bélisle, 2004a; Solar-Pelletier, 2006; Lejeune, 2008). Documentation of implementation began in 2005 (Talbot, 2005; Goyer *et al.*, 2006; Bélisle *et al.*, 2008; Morrissey *et al.*, 2008; Bélisle *et al.*, 2010; Fontaine, 2010; St-Pierre *et al.*, 2010), and recent PSRA and SSHRC research funding has been directed to implementation in specific contexts, using data from more established practice and experience. There are also a large number of research projects concerned with the agenda-setting phase (Bélisle, 2006; COCDMO, 2007; Michaud *et al.*, 2007; Garon and Bélisle, 2009; Solar and Bélisle, 2009; Bélisle *et al.*, 2010). Research initiatives relating to non-official RAC/PLRC, or to aspects of official RAC/RPLC that were not taken into account in the 2002 policy (e.g. the link with vocational guidance), can contribute to later analysis and/or updates policy. Research to develop conceptual tools or to document particular problems (Bélisle, 2006; Michaud *et al.*, 2007) can also be used to design other research projects at the implementation stage.

Québec–France collaboration

The language issue has played a key role in international collaboration in the field. Although the CVs of Québec scholars working on RAC/RPLC in various university faculties of education indicate that very few of them deliver conference or seminar presentations in English, they do travel overseas to present their work in French. As previously mentioned, the relationship between Québec and France regarding RPL has been important since the late 1980s. Indeed, many of the documents reviewed for this chapter cite sources from France; for example, research problems that have been documented and/or contributions to conceptual frameworks.

However, the development of RPL in France differs in several important ways from RAC/RPLC in Québec. For example, France has legislation with laws on *bilan de compétences* (1991), *validation des acquis professionnels* (VAP) (1992) and *validation des acquis de l'expérience* (VAE) (2002). The 2002 law places obligations on education institutions to

97

provide VAE. These obligations have had an effect on research because many scholars have been involved in the implementation of VAE in their institutions. Furthermore, scholars were invited to undertake contractual research for ministries or social partners in order to monitor implementation. Another important difference is the institutional research focus in France on the practices of VAE panels (*jury*) and VAE counsellors/VAE guides (*accompagnateurs*). Interest in those professional practices has surfaced only recently in Québec and remains marginal (Bélisle *et al.*, 2010).

In France, hundreds of papers and scores of books on VAE are available online, in academic databases or in libraries. Among the many French scholars who have published in the VAE area are: Gilles Pinte (2003, 2009), Marie-Christine Presse (2004, 2009), Patrick Mayen (2007), Bernard Prot (2007, 2009), Isabelle Astier (2008), Patricia Champy-Remoussenard (2009) and Isabelle Cherqui-Houot (2009). Peer-reviewed journals *Éducation permanente* and *Savoirs* frequently publish articles on RPL. It is also possible to find special editions of peer-reviewed journals focusing on VAE; for example, in *L'orientation scolaire et professionnelle* (Clot and Prot, 2003). Books edited by scholars are also available (e.g. Neyrat, 2007; Boutinet, 2009).

Conclusion

This was a brief review of RAC/RPLC research in Québec and a short introduction to research in France. Although some documents, people or establishments may have been missed, the picture that emerges from Québec, in 2010, is dominated by applied research. Quick results and dissemination to stakeholders are central preoccupations, explaining, for example, the popularity of online reports. Publications stemming from fundamental research or applied research with solid conceptual frameworks are still very much in the minority.

In the strategy put forward by the Conseil de la science et de la technologie (Science and Technology Council) (CST, 2009), it was deemed necessary to strengthen RAC/RPLC research. This recommendation is still salient and projects due to be completed in 2011–12 prefigure new kinds of results based on observations and more complex methodologies.

References

ACDEAULF (2006) *La reconnaissance des acquis dans les universités québécoises: état de la situation.* Montréal: Association canadienne d'éducation des adultes des universités de langue française. Available at: http://www.acdeaulf.ca/pdf/rapport_reconnaissance_acquis.pdf.

Astier, I. (2008) 'Écriture de soi, une injonction réflexive. L'exemple de la validation des acquis de l'expérience', *Sociologie et sociétés*, Vol. 40, No 2, pp. 51–68.

Barton, D. and Papen, U. (2010) (eds) *The Anthropology of Writing. Understanding Textually-mediated Worlds.* London: Continuum International Publishing Group.

Bélanger, P. and Doray, P. (2004) *Un portrait de la recherche en éducation et formation des adultes: ses artisanes et artisans.* Montréal: CIRDEP/UQAM. Available at: http://bv.cdeacf.ca/EA_PDF/81640.pdf.

Bélanger, P. and Robitaille, M. (2008) *A Portrait of Work-related Learning in Québec.* Ottawa: Work and Learning Knowledge Centre. Available at: http://www.nald.ca/library/research/ccl/quebec/quebec.pdf.

Bélisle, R. (1997) 'Question de compétences. The Competence Issue: A tool for women. Working together on links between past and future', in W. Mauch and U. Papen (eds) *Making a difference: Innovations in adult education.* Frankfurt am Main: UNESCO Institute for Education, German Foundation for International Development and Peter Lang, pp. 62–81. Available at: http://www.eric.ed.gov/ERICWebPortal/search/detailmini.jsp?_nfpb=true&_&ERICExtSearch_SearchValue_0=ED424356&ERICExtSearch_SearchType_0=no&accno=ED424356.

Bélisle, R. (2004a) *Bilan des acquis d'adultes non diplômés: place à l'innovation. Rapport préparé dans le cadre d'un contrat entre l'Université de Sherbrooke et la Direction de la formation générale des adultes du ministère de l'Éducation du Québec* (collaboration J. Guillette, P. Dionne et M. Leclerc). Sherbrooke/Québec: Équipe de recherche sur les transitions et l'apprentissage (ÉRTA)/Ministère de l'éducation. Available at: http://www.mels.gouv.qc.ca/dfga/politique/reconnaissance/colloque2005/pjdata/Act_12e.pdf.

Bélisle, R. (2004b) 'Valoriser les acquis des adultes non diplômés', *Cahiers scientifiques de l'Association francophone pour le savoir-ACFAS*, Vol. 100, pp. 128–41.

Bélisle, R. (2006) *Relance de la reconnaissance des acquis et des compétences au Québec: la place des conseillères et des conseillers d'orientation* (collaboration Daniel Touchette). Sherbrooke: Équipe de recherche sur les transitions et l'apprentissage. Available at: http://www.erta.ca/media/publications/rapport%20RACCO.pdf.

Bélisle, R. (2009) 'Can public policy support career development in a complex, compartmentalized and harsh world?' Opening keynote address, Pan-Canadian Symposium on Career Development and Public Policy. Winnipeg: Career Development Services Working Group (CDSWG) of the Forum of Labour Market Ministers (FLMM). Available at: http://www.flmm-cds.ca/CMFiles/Belisle_Ouverture%20FMMT%202009_%20finale_English.pdf.

Bélisle, R. and Bourdon, S. (2006) 'Variété, diversité et pluralité des pratiques et de l'apprentissage de l'écrit – Introduction', in R. Bélisle and S. Bourdon (eds) *Pratiques et apprentissage de l'écrit dans les sociétés éducatives*). Québec: Presses de l'Université Laval, pp. 1–27.

Bélisle, R., Gosselin, M. and Michaud, G. (2010) *La formation des intervenantes et des intervenants en reconnaissance des acquis et des compétences: un enjeu pour le développement des services. Rapport de recherche pour soutenir la réflexion collective*. Sherbrooke: Équipe de recherche sur les transitions et l'apprentissage. Available at: http://erta.ca/media/publications/belisle_gosselin_michaud_pefrac_rapport2010.pdf.

Bélisle, R., Michaud, G., Bourdon, S., Garon, S. and Chanoux, P. (2008) 'Favoriser la lisibilité des espaces d'apprentissage non formel et informel fréquentés par les adultes sans diplôme'. Articles proposés *1er Forum mondial de l'éducation et de la formation tout au long de la vie*. Paris: Comité mondial pour l'éducation et la formation tout au long de la vie (CMEF) en collaboration avec le Centre INFFO, le Conseil régional d'Île-de-France et l'UNESCO. Available at: http://www.centre-inffo.fr/forum-mondial/spip.php?article 97.

Bouchard, C. (2001) 'Inspirer, soutenir et rénover les politiques sociales', in F. Dufort and J. Guay (eds) *Agir au coeur des communautés. La psychologie communautaire et le changement social*. Québec: Presses de l'Université Laval, pp. 343–65.

Boutin, M. (2006) 'Les perceptions vis-à-vis de la reconnaissance des acquis et des compétences de personnes formées en pharmacie à l'étranger'. Essai de maitrise en orientation (Med Thesis), Faculté d'éducation, Université de Sherbrooke, Sherbrooke. Available at:

http://www.erta.ca/publications.html?controller=publications&task=show&id=276Itemid%3D8.

Boutinet, J-P. (2009) (ed.) *L'ABC de la VAE*. Toulouse: érès.

Champy-Remoussenard, P. (2009) 'Caractéristiques et fonctions de l'écriture sur l'activité professionnelle: l'éclairage des pratiques de VAE en France', in F. Cros, L. Lafortune and M. Morisse (eds) *Les écritures en situations professionnelles*. Québec: Presses de l'Université Laval, pp. 73–94.

Chaput, M. and Meyer, N. (1997) 'Reconnaissance des acquis dans les universités', in G. Pineau, B. Liétard and M. Chaput (eds) *Reconnaître les acquis. Démarches d'exploration personnalisée*. Paris: L'Harmattan, pp. 147–54.

Cherqui-Houot, I. (2009) 'Actes de validation à l'université: un modèle entre l'être et le savoir, la personne et le collectif', in R. Bélisle and J-P. Boutinet (eds) *Demandes de reconnaissance et validation des acquis de l'expérience. Pour qui? Pour quoi?* Québec: Presses de l'Université Laval, pp. 71–102.

Clot, Y. and Prot, B. (2003) 'Expérience et diplôme: une discordance créatrice', *L'Orientation scolaire et professionnelle*, Vol. 32, No 2, pp. 183–201.

COCDMO (2007) *Reconnaissance des compétences génériques pour les personnes en démarche d'insertion et peu scolarisées. Inventaire des outils des organismes communautaires œuvrant au développement de la main-d'œuvre.* Montréal: Coalition des organismes communautaires pour le développement de la main-d'œuvre. Available at: http://www.cocdmo.qc.ca/pdf/COCDMO%20RCG_Rapport%20final_Octobre2007.pdf.

Commission d'étude sur la formation des adultes (1982) *Apprendre: une action volontaire et responsable. Énoncé d'une politique globale de l'éducation des adultes dans une perspective d'éducation permanente.* Montréal: Gouvernement du Québec.

Conseil de la science et de la technologie (CST) (2009) *Défi formation. Stratégie de recherche et de transfert de connaissances pour favoriser le développement de l'éducation et de la formation des adultes.* Québec: CST. Available at: http://www.cst.gouv.qc.ca/IMG/pdf/Strategie_Formation_VF.pdf.

Conseil supérieur de l'éducation (CSE) (2000) *La reconnaissance des acquis, une responsabilité politique et sociale. Avis au ministre de l'éducation.* Québec: Les publications du Québec. Available at: http://www.cse.gouv.qc.ca/pdfs/acquis.pdf.

CPMT (2010) *Programme de subventions à la recherche appliquée (PSRA).* Available at: http://www.cpmt.gouv.qc.ca/recherches/index.asp (Accessed 7 October 2010).

D'Ortun, F., Dolbec, A. and Savoie-Zajc, L. (2005) *La qualification professionnelle de la main-d'œuvre, des pratiques à géométrie variable. Inventaire et documentation in situ des dispositifs nationaux de qualification professionnelle initiés par les partenaires sociaux de différents pays occidentaux.* Hull: Université du Québec en Outaouais. Available at: http://www.cpmt.gouv.qc.ca/publications/pdf/RECHERCHES_T9_appels_Dolbec_rapport.pdf.

L'Équipe de recherche sur les transitions et l'apprentissage (ÉRTA) (2009) *L'écrit dans l'apprentissage informel et non formel à l'âge adulte, 77e Congrès de l'Association francophone pour le savoir (ACFAS).* Ottawa: Équipe de recherche sur les transitions et l'apprentissage. Available at: http://erta.ca/media/publications/programme_colloque611acfas_erta%20_3%20mai2009.pdf.

Expertise recherche Québec (2008) *Répertoire des chercheurs.* Québec: Ministère du Développement économique, Innovation et Exportation. Available at: http://www.researchersdirectory.ca ifd/ ?locale=fr.

Fontaine, F. (2010) *Reconnaissance des compétences développées par l'expérience professionnelle. Document de soutien à la réflexion des ordres professionnels* (collaboration de H. Bernard). Montréal: Conseil interprofessionnel du Québec.

Garon, S. and Bélisle, R. (2009) 'La valorisation des acquis d'adultes sans diplôme du secondaire: entre proposition de reconnaissance et risque de mépris', in R. Bélisle and J-P. Boutinet (eds) *Demandes de reconnaissance et validation des acquis de l'expérience. Pour qui? Pour quoi?* Québec: Presses de l'Université Laval, pp. 103–31.

Gouvernement du Québec (2002a) *Government Policy on Adult Education and Continuing Education and Training: Learning throughout Life.* Québec: Ministère de l'Éducation. Available at: http://www.mels.gouv.qc.ca/REFORME/formation_con/Politique/politique_a.pdf.

Gouvernement du Québec (2002b) *Action plan for adult education and continuing education and training. Learning throughout life.* Québec: Ministère de l'Éducation. Available at: http://www.mels.gouv.qc.ca/REFORME/formation_con/Plan/plan_a.pdf.

Goyer, L. and Grimard, D. (2005) *Synthèse de trois recherches portant sur le prototype de la démarche personnalisée du bilan des acquis relatifs à la formation générale de base (Volet A).* Québec: DFGA, Ministère de l'Éducation, du

Loisir et du Sport. Available at: http://www.mels.gouv.qc.ca/dfga/ politique/reconnaissance/colloque2005/pjdata/Act_12a.pdf.

Goyer, L., Landry, C. and Leclerc, C. (2006) 'Regard sur une expérimentation du bilan des acquis relatifs à la formation de base en éducation des adultes au Québec', in G. Figari, P. Rodrigues, M. Alves and P. Valois (eds) *Évaluation des compétences et apprentissages expérientiels. Savoirs, modèles et méthodes.* Lisbonne: Educa-Formaçao, pp. 61–73.

Institut canadien d'éducation des adultes (ICÉA) (1999) 'Overview of research trends in Adult Education in Canada', in W. Mauch (ed.) *World Trends in Adult Education Research. Report on the International Seminar, Montréal, September 06–09, 1994.* Hamburg: UNESCO Institute for Education, pp. 188–232. Available at: http://www. unesco.org/education/uie/online/468rep.pdf.

Lahire, B. (1998) *L'homme pluriel. Les ressorts de l'action.* Paris: Nathan.

Lahire, B. (forthcoming) *The Plural Actor.* London: Polity Press.

Lejeune, M. (2008) *Pertinence pour le Québec des instruments de reconnaissance des acquis de l'expérience en France, aux États-Unis et au Royaume-Uni* (sous la direction de F. Lesemann). Montréal: TRANSPOL. Available at: http://www.cpmt.gouv.qc.ca/publications/pdf/RECHERCHE _Pertinence_pour_le_Quebec_des_instruments.pdf.

Lemieux, V. (2009) *L'étude des politiques publiques. Les acteurs et leur pouvoir* (third edition). Québec: Les Presses de l'Université Laval.

Mayen, P. (2007) 'Conseiller en Point Relais Conseil, une activité inédite dans le champ de l'information/orientation/conseil', *Éducation permanente*, No 171, pp. 183–200.

Michaud, G., Dionne, P. and Beaulieu, G. (2007) 'L'efficacité du bilan de compétences', *Revue canadienne de counseling*, Vol. 41, No 3, pp. 173–85. Available at: http://cjc-rcc.ucalgary.ca/cjc/index.php/rcc/article/ view/337/181.

Ministère des relations internationales (2010) *Detailed Information about the Understanding.* Available at: http://www.mri.gouv.qc.ca/en/ grands_dossiers/qualifications_professionnelles/en_details.asp (Accessed 5 December 2010).

Morrissey, M., Myers, D., Bélanger, P., Robitaille, M., Davison, P., Van Kleef, J. and Williams, R. (2008) *Achieving our Potential: An Action Plan for Prior Learning and Recognition (PLAR) in Canada.* Ottawa: Canadian Council on Learning.

Moss, L. (2007) 'Prior Learning Assessment and Recognition (PLAR) and the impact of globalization: A Canadian case study'. PhD Thesis,

Department of Integrated Studies in Education, McGill University, Montréal.

Neyrat, F. (2007) *La validation des acquis de l'expérience: la reconnaissance d'un nouveau droit.* Broissieux: Éditions du croquant.

Noël, C. (2010) *Retour aux études universitaires et acquis expérientiels: perceptions d'acteurs du communautaire.* Mémoire de maitrise en orientation (MSc), Faculté d'éducation, Université de Sherbrooke, Sherbrooke. Available at: http://www.erta.ca/media/publications/MEMOIRE%20CNoel%20MAI%202010.pdf.

Pineau, G., Liétard, B. and Chaput, M. (1997) (eds) *Reconnaître les acquis. Démarches d'exploration personnalisée.* Paris: L'Harmattan.

Pinte, G. (2003) 'La validation des acquis de l'expérience (VAE) à l'intersection de la formation professionnelle continue et de l'éducation permanente', *Esprit Critique*, Vol. 5, No 1. Available at: http://194.214.232.113/0501/esp0501article06.html.

Pinte, G. (2009) 'Le conseiller VAE: Nouveau métier de la formation des adultes?', *Savoirs*, No 21, pp. 96–112.

Presse, M-C. (2004) 'Entre intention et réalité, les obstacles à la validation des acquis', *Éducation permanente*, No 158, pp. 141–51.

Presse, M-C. (2009) 'La validation des acquis de l'expérience en France: entre promotion et reproduction sociales', in R. Bélisle and J-P. Boutinet (eds) *Demandes de reconnaissance et validation des acquis de l'expérience. Pour qui? Pour quoi?* Québec: Presses de l'Université Laval, pp. 133–59.

Prot, B. (2007) 'Pour sortir des idées fixes sur l'évaluation', *La revue de l'IRES*, Vol. 3, No 55, pp. 101–22.

Prot, B. (2009) 'La double vie du collectif dans les acquis individuels', in R. Bélisle and J-P. Boutinet (eds) *Demandes de reconnaissance et validation des acquis de l'expérience. Pour qui? Pour quoi?* Québec: Presses de l'Université Laval, pp. 15–41.

Sansregret, M. (1983) *La reconnaissance des acquis expérientiels des femmes aux États-Unis.* Montréal: Collège John Abbott.

Sansregret, M. (1984) *Projet de reconnaissance des acquis expérientiels.* Montréal: Collège John Abbott.

Solar, C. and Bélisle, R. (2009) 'La reconnaissance des acquis: une histoire qui a du genre', in R. Bélisle and J-P. Boutinet (eds) *Demandes de reconnaissance et validation des acquis de l'expérience. Pour qui? Pour quoi?* Québec: Presses de l'Université Laval, pp. 43–69.

Solar, C. and Tremblay, N. (2008) *Bilan des recherches en français au Canada sur l'apprentissage des adultes: 1997–2007. En collaboration avec le CDÉACF.* Fredericton, NB: Conseil canadien sur l'apprentissage/centre du savoir sur l'apprentissage chez les adultes. Available at: http://www.ccl-cca.ca/pdfs/AdLKC/reports08/Bilandesrecherches CDEACFfinal.pdf.

St-Pierre, L., Martel, L., Ruel, F. and Lauzon, M. (2010) 'Expérimentation d'une démarche et d'instruments de reconnaissance des acquis expérientiels en enseignement collégial au Québec', *Revue des sciences de l'éducation*, Vol. 36, No 1, pp. 117–47.

Solar-Pelletier, L. (2006) *La reconnaissance des acquis en France et au Québec, éléments de comparaison.* Maitrise en sciences de la gestion (MSc Thesis), HEC Montréal, Montréal. Available at: http://bv.cdeacf.ca/documents/PDF/horscollection/103029.pdf.

Talbot, G. (2005) *La reconnaissance des acquis et des compétences au Québec: à l'aube d'une relance: synthèse des principaux écrits.* Québec: Centrale des syndicats du Québec. Available at: http://www.education.csq.qc.net/sites/1673/documents/publications/D11593.pdf.

CHAPTER FIVE

England: Accreditation of Prior Experiential Learning (APEL) research in higher education

HELEN POKORNY

Abstract

The Assessment of Prior Experiential Learning (APEL) emerged in English higher education in the late 1980s as a means of extending access to those who had not followed a traditional educational route. Influenced by theories and models of experiential and reflective learning (Kolb, 1984; Schön, 1987), APEL was introduced by a small number of institutions through projects that aimed to widen participation. In the late 1990s, APEL gained increased momentum through its profile in national policy as part of debates around lifelong learning (Fryer, 1997) and, around the same time, more targeted developments took place in response to professional body requirements, particularly in nursing and midwifery.

More recently, APEL has been promoted as part of the drive to ensure that universities place greater emphasis on employability and links with industry. This has given rise to new higher education programmes such as foundation degrees, which place specific emphasis on work-based learning and to a number of APEL development projects funded through the Higher Education Funding Council for England (HEFCE) 'Workforce Development Programme'. Despite its history and policy profile, APEL remains a marginal activity in English higher education.

Introduction

This chapter considers the way in which Assessment of Prior Experiential Learning (APEL) practices have developed in response to drivers of social inclusion and employability, examines some of the research literature and outlines some potentially fruitful research directions for the future. The first section focuses on the historical context; the latter section addresses more contemporary developments.

In England the term APEL is used to denote the inclusion of learning from experience as a basis for credit exemption towards an HE award. The acronym AP(E)L is sometimes used to signify and emphasise the option of prior learning being experiential. The process of awarding credit for prior learning is the subject of guidelines produced by the Quality Assurance Agency for Higher Education, *Guidelines on the Accreditation of Prior Learning* (QAA, 2004a). These guidelines do not address entry to the initial stage of a higher education (HE) award via APEL because this battle has already been won. Admission to the entry level of a programme can be on the basis of a matriculation qualification, equivalent qualifications designed for adult returners, some vocational awards, or through various forms of APEL including tests and/or interviews. Thus APEL research and literature in England is predominantly concerned with the processes of gaining credits towards an HE award. This process is formalised within quality assurance systems as opposed to the less formalised and less systematic processes of making academic judgements in relation to admitting students to the entry level of courses. Some writers suggest that this formalisation has led to a decrease in APEL activity (Colley *et al.*, 2003; Peters, 2005).

The historical context

Harris (2006, p. 2) notes: 'As with all educational interventions, the idea and practice of [APEL] have been formed and shaped by the inter-relations of historical, cultural, economic and political forces in different social contexts.' In England, the development of APEL derives largely from two sets of social conditions. The first of these, from the 1980s onward, was the adult education movement and concerns about social justice and widening participation for adults, including the development of 'Access to Higher Education'[1] courses and feminist-inspired courses for women

---

[1] Access to higher education courses were referred to as 'Access with a capital A', as opposed to other measures to widen access – 'access with a small a'.

(Colley *et al.*, 2003). This work predominantly focused on recognising learning from diverse social contexts including the community and family. The second set of social conditions relates to the economic skills agenda with its drivers of globalisation and marketisation, which has focused predominantly on the accreditation of learning from work-based contexts. However, the complexities and tensions around these potentially competing social goals of APEL are often rendered invisible in rhetoric, which simply presents it as a process of 'recognising the significant knowledge, skills and understanding which can be developed as a result of learning opportunities found at work, both paid and unpaid, and through individual activities and interests' (QAA 2004a, p. 1).

Early APEL practice was embedded in the then polytechnic sector through the Council for National Academic Awards (CNAA).[2] Prior to 1992, the CNAA was the awarding body for academic qualifications in polytechnics. In 1986, through the establishment of a credit accumulation and transfer scheme (CATS) to promote articulation and student mobility, the CNAA legitimised the use of APEL at both undergraduate and postgraduate level, for admission purposes. At that time the CNAA awarded over half of the undergraduate degrees in the United Kingdom (UK) (Evans, 1994), thereby firmly establishing APEL as a feature of the higher education landscape.

However, this form of learning posed a challenge to the privileging of knowledge developed by and through the academy, and was met with resistance from academics who were concerned about threats APEL posed to academic standards. In an attempt to address these concerns, the CNAA proposed a framework which tied APEL into traditional academic practices. Additionally, Evans (*ibid.*) was particularly keen to separate the APEL assessor and advisor roles to reassure sceptics that decision making rested within academic staff. It could be argued that separating these roles resulted in confusion and a mismatch around assessment expectations. So, although this principle was taken on board in many APEL processes and still appears within some university policies, it no longer pertains within the *Guidelines on the Accreditation of Prior Learning* (QAA, 2004a). Rather, current thinking stresses the importance of promoting a shared understanding about standards and criteria between students and assessors, and between groups of assessors (Price, 2005). The CNAA (through Evans) was also keen to stress the rigour of the assessment process demonstrated

---

[2] Polytechnics were vocational tertiary education teaching institutions before 1992.

primarily by its complexity and level of difficulty for the candidate: 'A considerable amount of work is required of APEL candidates to gain academic credit and it is often more demanding than the work completed by students on formal courses' (Evans, 1994, p. 77). Academic concerns meant that APEL evolved with an emphasis on demonstrating equivalence with learning in the taught curriculum, rather than on exploring the equivalence and/or value of learning from experience more broadly. This was noted in the outcome of a pilot project undertaken from 1989 to 1991:

> *when staff do move on to consider APEL for credit they tend to look only to award credit where prior learning corresponds exactly with the course elements: there is a reluctance to recognise mature intellectual attainment in itself as credit-worthy (Evans and Turner, 1993, p. 28).*

Early forms of APEL did not focus solely on the assessment of individual applications for credit, but also included the accreditation of employers' in-house training and development programmes. This type of process appeared to be incorporated relatively quickly and easily into higher education: 'By the end of the 1980s some 50 employing organisations and professions, covering most occupations ... had negotiated credit rating agreements with a rapidly increasing number of institutions' (Evans, 1994, p. 17). Indeed, the accreditation of work-based learning (WBL)continues to be a key feature of APEL today.

The profile of APEL in England increased and also shifted in the mid- to late-1990s as part of policy debates around lifelong learning (Fryer, 1997; Wailey, 2002). A number of credit consortia were established in different parts of the country, all of which promoted APEL as part of credit-based curricula. The South East England Consortium for Credit Accumulation and Transfer (SEEC) established an APEL network which published practitioner accounts of APEL practice at undergraduate and postgraduate level (Storan, 1993; Croker *et al.*, 1998; Wailey, 2002), along with the *Code of Practice for the Assessment of Prior (Experiential) Learning* (SEEC, 1995), *A Quality Code for AP(E)L* (Croker, 1998) and a review of quality assurance processes (Johnson, 2002).

In 1997, the English National Board (ENB) for Nursing, Midwifery and Health Visiting commissioned SEEC to undertake an investigation into the reliability and validity of assessment strategies for accrediting prior learning. Health faculties in 83 institutions were surveyed, resulting in 47 usable responses which were mapped against the *Code of Practice for the*

Assessment of Prior (Experiential) Learning (SEEC, 1995). From the sample of responses received, ten detailed follow-up case studies were undertaken including interviews with staff and students, and an activity involving the assessment of two pre-circulated APEL accounts. 'Account A' described the work undertaken by a nurse to research and produce a health education package on the theme of healthy eating. 'Account B' was a report of a nurse's experience of facilitating groups including a reminiscence group for the elderly. This was in a more traditional academic format, and compared her approach to the academic and formal literature on group work. The ten case studies were used as a basis for discussion about APEL institutional guidance and assessment processes. Eight of the case study respondents rated account A as worthy of a higher level of credit than account B, which was described as 'descriptive, learning implicit rather than explicit, theoretical, an academic essay, insufficiently focused, fragmented, insufficient and not sufficiently applied to practice' (Skinner *et al.*, 1997, p. 85). Surprisingly, at least 95 per cent of the 47 survey respondents offered APEL. The report noted that this was because the ENB, through the introduction of a 'framework for continuing education' leading to the Higher Award (which stipulated an APEL route), had:

> *almost overnight introduced the concept and practice of credit transfer on a large scale into nursing and midwifery education ... on the assumption that the use of AP(E)L in HE was uniform, widespread and unproblematic (ibid., pp. 93–94).*

This assumption was erroneous, and schools of nursing and health studies thus found themselves unexpectedly leading APEL developments with varying levels of support and interest from the higher education institutions, within which they were located. This does not appear to have been a straightforward process. The report noted: 'There is evidence that staff had real difficulty in developing a professional model of education, which is practice-based, to fit into a "pure" academic model of AP(E)L' (*ibid.*, p. 87). In analysing the judgements made about prior learning, the researchers found that:

> *Learning from professional experience is differentiated and appears to be valued differently. Three types of learning in practice are identified: (i) the student's ability to apply theory to practice; (ii) the student's ability to change own practice; or (iii) the student's ability to bring about change in the field of practice as a result of learning. This 'value added' approach is reflected in the level and volume of credit that could be given (Skinner et al., 1997, p. 87).*

110

However, the research did find high levels of internal consistency in APEL assessments with a consensus of decision making in response to the pre-circulated APEL accounts. It was also noted that applying the traditional model of academic assessment to the APEL process could leave the APEL student disadvantaged in terms of time and effort vis-à-vis students on a taught route:

> *AP(E)L assessment strategies are thorough and often very complex. They are based on the usual HE assessment model. There is an assumption in HE that its assessment model is valid. It can be argued that this is therefore a legitimate model for AP(E)L. The AP(E)L assessment strategies appear to be consistently applied and in some instances seem over-zealous to the point of treating AP(E)L students very differently to others (ibid., p. 91).*

Several studies of nursing schemes undertaken earlier had similarly reported that the preparation of the APEL claim was indeed more onerous and time-consuming than actually taking a taught course (Arkin, 1991; Thorne, 1991; Howard, 1993; Houston et al., 1997). The systems underpinning APEL were also reported as being complex and including many different stages and people/personnel (Skinner et al., 1997; Heath, 2001). Students seemed confused about the requirements of the process. Furthermore, Houston et al. (1997) in their study noted that:

> *a further difficulty encountered was the students' inability to value their clinical experiences. They repeatedly focussed on presenting evidence from previous educational experiences, and failed to draw on their clinical experiences (ibid., p. 189).*

However, Skinner et al. (1997) observed that as practitioners gained experience of APEL they were more able to adapt their practice:

> *AP(E)L is developing quickly. Those in the field of AP(E)L are at the cutting edge of practice, learning from experience and making changes. As AP(E)L staff gain confidence and respect from colleagues so they feel freer to take risks and to account for their decisions. All this must happen if AP(E)L is to remain vibrant and responsive to the needs of nursing and midwifery practitioners (ibid., p. 89).*

The English National Board (ENB) continued to be a key driver in the development of APEL in HE (Bond and Wilson, 2003), and nurse education remains an area of higher education where APEL has thrived and where a specialist research literature has developed (Clarke and Warr, 1997; Scott, 2007, 2010a).

Exploring the development of APEL practice more broadly across the English HE sector, Merrifield *et al.* (2000) found policies in a high proportion of universities, but very little evidence that students were accessing the process itself. This research provides the most comprehensive understanding to date of how limited the take-up of APEL in English higher education has been. The research surveyed 107 of 133 English higher education institutions and conducted ten detailed case studies where institutions claimed to have promoted APEL internally. They found that even though universities were likely to have APEL policies in place, practice was uneven across the institutions, with the majority of activity in nursing and social care, professional development and management courses.

Research into approaches to APEL assessment and their social consequence

A range of APEL literature and research deals with approaches to assessment. Butterworth (1992) conceptualised two dominant models of APEL: 'credit-exchange' and 'developmental'. She analysed the origins and contrasting philosophies of the two models, and gave the government-led National Vocational Qualifications (NVQ) framework and the development of competence-based vocational education as an example of the credit-exchange model. The NVQ framework was informed by employers and embraced APEL as a means by which experienced workers could demonstrate their competence against established standards of performance, reducing or obviating the need for training. The focus of this approach, she suggested, was the foregrounding of evidence of performance, followed by credentialing against detailed pre-determined standards. Specific qualifications for APEL assessors were also established within the NVQ framework. One of the criticisms levelled at this approach is that it reduces APEL to a performance-related activity linked to specific occupational standards, tied to an economic model and a labour market orientation (Butterworth 1992). That said, the NVQ framework did much to promote APEL at the pre-degree level in vocational education. It also opened up potential APEL-based pathways to higher education through higher level NVQs. However, take-up of this level of NVQ qualification by higher education has been minimal (Garnett *et al.*, 2004).

Butterworth described the developmental model of APEL as student-centred and liberal in its approach, mirroring practices in many educational and professional contexts where reflection is a key pedagogy and where the work of Kolb (1984) and Schön (1987) is drawn upon. The model requires APEL candidates to re-visit and re-evaluate their experience, and emphasises the *process* of learning rather than (or as much as) the products of learning. Butterworth (1992, p. 41) argued that:

> *whilst the principles behind the two models were described in published guide-lines produced by the then two most important bodies influencing practice in the field: the Council for National Vocational Qualifications (1989) and the Council for National Academic Awards (1986) … the differences between the two approaches are not yet sufficiently realised nor articulated.*

In both approaches assessment is generally via a portfolio of evidence. Butterworth's further criticism of the credit-exchange model is that it encourages a reductionist and fragmented view of an individual's skills and knowledge, and is therefore unsuitable for evidencing learning in complex jobs and professional contexts. Interestingly and somewhat paradoxically, given that the APEL process is about assessing *prior* learning, her criticism of the credit-exchange process model is that:

> *the individual may feel understandably pleased to be given credit, and perhaps have more confidence as a result of this recognition, but in one very important respect they are no different after assessment than before: their understanding of their competence will not have been altered by the assessment process, for it has not been explored. Putting it simply, they have not learned anything they did not know before (ibid., p. 45).*

In her own practice, Butterworth favoured the development-oriented model. This approach, operationalised as a written reflective narrative, has been very influential in the development of APEL (Mulholland and Leith, 1999). In practice, it operates on a continuum with the credit-exchange approach – providing evidence of learning through a portfolio mapped to learning outcomes and supported by a reflective narrative. Butterworth (1992, p. 50) argues that completing the portfolio provides 'significant personal and professional development for the individual'. However, a number of authors investigating their own APEL practice and providing a student perspective have concluded that the emphasis given to the principles of reflective practice and experiential learning in the developmental APEL model is problematic for candidates, and distorts their learning. Very often, rather than being encouraged to foreground the situated context of their learning, candidates are required to embed their learning within an academic context. Likewise, assessors often reject the legitimacy of learning acquired outside of the university environment until it is translated into an academic language with which they are familiar (Trowler, 1996). Indeed, one of the key criteria for Butterworth (1992, p. 48) in judging an APEL claim was that: 'the concepts, explanations and analyses offered should be similar to those used by established authorities in the field'.

Trowler (1996), in his analysis of Butterworth's two approaches, notes that the emphasis placed on reflection in developmental APEL has meant that the practice has found favour with some academics because it 'does not require academic staff to accredit a different form of knowledge from that normally accredited in higher education' (*ibid.*, p. 21). On the basis of 40 semi-structured interviews with academics, he claimed that although there was an appreciation of adult learners, there was an unwillingness to accredit knowledge and abilities gained from experience. He quoted one respondent who emphasised the importance of disciplinary knowledge over and above experiential 'views':

> *most people at the beginning of the course have views ... which are over simplistic ... the [domain] requires an understanding of [discipline x and discipline y] and familiarity with the literature (ibid., p. 22).*

Interestingly, Trowler found academics in disciplines in the natural sciences, engineering, technology and design for whom the credit-exchange approach created no difficulties for them as assessors: as one interviewee put it: 'it's very easy to do with us ... because we can easily see what they [i.e. the candidates] have done' (*ibid.*). Trowler concluded that whilst any claim for credit may legitimately contain elements of both approaches to varying degrees, the developmental approach can act as a barrier to widening participation and social inclusion because it requires traditional HE skills and 'capital':

> *going through the process of assisted reflection requires personal qualities such as confidence, facility in language use and in conceptual thought, all aspects of the cultural capital important to educational success as that concept is currently defined ... exactly the sort of (socially derived) qualities which have ensured*

114

that under-represented groups remain under-represented in higher education (ibid., p. 28).

Although Butterworth and Trowler wrote more than a decade ago, the requirement for the translation of learning from experience into a form of learning more commonly accredited in higher education continues to be widely promoted through both the requirement for 'reflection' and the emphasis placed in English APEL on matching experience against established HE learning outcomes.

Trowler (1996) further argues that the developmental approach to APEL can distort learning because of 'the alienation of the learner from his or her experience through its objectification' (*ibid.*, p. 24). This is echoed by Fenwick (cited in Pokorny, 2006, p. 266), who argues that: 'what becomes emphasised are the conceptual lessons gained from their experience, which are quickly stripped of their location and embeddedness'. Indeed, this discussion can be traced back to Usher (1989), who argued that matching to syllabus learning outcomes renders the APEL process one of techniques and mechanisation: 'reducing experience to a raw material that can be transformed into a commodity – assessed experiential learning – which can then be exchanged for entrance and advanced standing' (*ibid.*, p. 74). He argued that focusing on *operationalising* such procedures avoids confronting questions such as who controls the actions, who makes the decisions about what is required, and what constitutes satisfactory evidence.

Ambivalence around the status of prior learning in the higher education curriculum is one of Trowler's key concerns. He notes that where there is ambiguity about 'the relative status of academic and personal understanding ... the implications for students can be serious ... and ... a common response to uncertainty and insecurity is to erect barriers, in this case bureaucratic procedures, in an attempt to ensure that standards are maintained' (Trowler, 1996, p. 26). An alternative epistemological perspective is offered by Lave and Wenger's (1993) communities of practice, and by Brown and Duguid (2000) who argue that knowledge is the product of the interaction of social, economic, historic, cultural and physical networks encompassing community, tools and activities:

From this perspective learning takes place within activities and experiences and not from reflection upon them ... This suggests we need to consider approaches to APEL that focus on exploration of this complex experience, with the assessor

> *learning from the candidates' experiences and considering candidates' learning within an inclusive set of criteria for defining what counts as equivalent (Pokorny, 2006, p. 267).*

Colley *et al.* (2003) were commissioned by the then Learning and Skills Development Agency (a quasi-governmental body) to research and map the conceptual terrain around non-formal and informal learning. Their work included consideration of how APEL has developed as an educational practice. They examine the formalisation of APEL as a process of auditing and re-packaging prior learning to fit the reference points of the traditional HE course, and conclude that:

> *by increasing such formalising attributes, the nature of learning is changed in ways that may run counter to the intentions of those introducing these approaches, and which raise more substantial questions of unequal power relations in learning (ibid., p. 66).*

Peters (2006) analysed the role of learning outcomes in APEL. She takes issue with Betts and Smith's (1998) view that learning outcomes are central to APEL because they are 'sufficiently transparent for the student to be able to put the case and prove the outcomes have been met' (*ibid.*, p. 90). Her research shows that students find the language of learning outcomes impenetrable and alienating, and a barrier to 'capturing the nature of their knowledge and identities in a meaningful way' (Peters, 2006, p. 179). She argues that the emphasis becomes not recognising learning from outside the institution, but proving academic ability through the use of the forms developed by the academy for the purpose, namely the learning outcomes. In earlier work, Peters (2005) used critical discourse analysis as a method to analyse texts arising from her own institutional APEL processes and to demonstrate how APEL served to 'reassure academics that controls are in place' whilst also ensuring 'that knowledge outside of the institution continues to be devalued and hinders attempts by students to gain recognition for alternative forms of learning are thwarted' (*ibid.*, p. 283). This echoes earlier work by Fraser (1995), who in analysing her experience of implementing APEL noted that students seemed increasingly unconvinced by the APEL process and cynical about the need to 'play the game'.

Colley *et al.* (2003) analyse what happens to prior learning when the workplace is the source of the experiential learning. They argue that for women this can 'transform the apparently emancipatory recognition of such learning into a further source of oppression' (*ibid.*, p. 60). Focusing predominantly on workplace learning reinforces gender divisions of labour, rendering invisible the significant experiences of many women.

Whilst there are some reports of APEL processes undertaken with groups such as refugees and asylum-seekers (Peters, 2000; Clarke, 2005), and from non-work related social contexts (Peters and Pokorny, 2003; Peters *et al.*, 2004), nevertheless a central research conclusion is that APEL in England has thus far failed to achieve its potential of bringing diverse sites of knowledge production into the mainstream academy (Merrifield *et al.*, 2000). Pokorny (2006) examined APEL practices using actor-network-theory (ANT) to illuminate how it is that these practices maintain barriers to accrediting prior learning despite national policies around lifelong learning and the endeavours of APEL advocates over the years.

Although research undertaken in the context of English higher education has largely involved small-scale investigations of practice, it does yield consistent messages over time about the way in which complex APEL practices that require mapping to existing curricular learning outcomes and the framing of learning in an academic format have failed to open up the academy to prior learning.

Current APEL priorities and practices

The global economic agenda has influenced lifelong learning policy and higher education in England, as in the rest of the developed world:

> *This general phenomenon of giving education an economic orientation is not a uniquely British affair ... There is a strong Eurocentric dimension to this ... with key documentation produced by the European Union (EU) and the Organisation for Economic Cooperation and Development (OECD) framing much of the conceptualisation of lifelong learning policy globally (Warren and Webb, 2007, p. 5).*

Institutions of higher and further education in England are encouraged to demonstrate a greater willingness to engage with and respond to the specific skill demands and needs of employers – this means providing more flexible, accessible and tailored courses designed (wherever possible) with employers to equip students for the workplace. The launch of the two-year foundation degree (FD) qualification in 2000 was one government response to this agenda. The initial FD framework included APEL as a specific part of the curriculum, along with work-based learning (WBL). The FD was expected to be both a means of opening access for mature students without formal qualifications and of accelerating progression for experienced students – this alongside developing work-based competence and employability. Nevertheless, an evaluation of FDs by the Quality Assurance Agency (QAA, 2003) found little evidence of the use of APEL, and the APEL focus in the 2004 FD benchmark statement (QAA, 2004b) was subsequently muted and couched in terms of 'alternative entry' to the start of a course – a much more restricted definition.

In recent years, the concept and practice of APEL appears to have been more successfully integrated into the accreditation of employment-based learning by higher education. This sidesteps some of the issues of individual APEL assessment by awarding credits to roles/grades and training programmes. This enables employers to provide academic credit for their employment-based programmes which may also link to a higher academic award. Although barriers remain (Scott, 2010b), it does appear that it is in the field of WBL higher education degrees that APEL is thriving and pushing boundaries. These degree programmes usually have more generic learning outcomes than traditional degrees, plus a high level of negotiation around the practice-based content of the programme, which can make them more amenable to APEL. Indeed, Prince (2003), Chisholm and Davis (2007) and Lester (2007) offer conceptual and practice-based arguments for removing the conventional 50 per cent ceiling on the award of APEL in postgraduate programmes to allow for the award of work-based degrees on the basis of 100 per cent APEL. Haldane and Wallace (2009) describe how technology can assist with APEL guidance in WBL programmes (which successfully recruit around 1,000 students per year). APEL is also more financially attractive to institutions if embedded within a WBL programme because guidance and assessment can be delivered within the curriculum. This is because the Higher Education Funding Council for England (HEFCE) does not fund pre-enrolment APEL processes (Gallacher and Feutrie, 2003). Thus what might previously have been identified as APEL may become subsumed under WBL or the accreditation of employment-based learning and training. However, English Higher Education is undergoing dramatic changes in funding which from 2012 will see HEFCE funding withdrawn from postgraduate study, and all undergraduate subjects by 2012 with the exception of Science, Technology, Engineering and Mathematics. Universities will be able to increase their fees considerably to compensate for this loss of funding. Undergraduate students will be expected to pay these increased course fees through a state-funded deferred payment loan which for the first time will be available to part-time as well as full-time students. Postgraduate courses will be under pressure to demonstrate demand and financial sustainability. Within such a context, through enabling experienced students to study at an accelerated rate, APEL could provide a means for universities to attract and retain experienced students many of whom may have become unemployed due to the global economic downturn.

In 2007, HEFCE declared APEL a national priority area in the context of provision developed with employers and employer bodies (HEFCE, 2007). Through the 'Workforce Development Programme', funding was provided to help further and higher education institutions develop the infrastructure to engage with employers and co-deliver and co-fund programmes. This included resourcing brokerage arrangements between employers, training providers and educational institutions. Although the initial evaluation of these co-funded programmes expresses cautious optimism about the development of provision for employers within higher education, there is no specific reference to the use of APEL (Dickinson, 2008).

Although, as Armsby et al. (2006) point out, WBL may have certain features that can support APEL, a WBL degree does not of itself resolve 'concerns about what and how high level knowledge gained outside of universities is recognised and legitimised' (ibid., p. 370). The researchers gathered the perspectives of five HE WBL tutors undertaking APEL assessment in WBL degrees. These are offered as vignettes with three short case studies of APEL claims where there was disagreement about the outcome of the claim. It is argued that what counts as valid learning is still firmly in the control of individual academics. Moreover, the researchers found that some tutors assessing prior experiential learning within WBL degrees were influenced by their own disciplinary subject positioning and:

> assess experiential learning as if it were packaged within university modules
> … Some assessors find it difficult to envisage what their theoretical subject
> knowledge looks like in practice (ibid., p. 374).

Armsby et al. also found that some assessors responded negatively to the more personal style of writing of APEL candidates. It seems that APEL in WBL may generate some of the same academic resistance as APEL in conventional taught courses. They argue that: if APEL is to develop in HE it will need to include practices which:

> *are likely to involve holistic, integrative interpretations … the valuing of con-*
> *text-bound knowledge; and the articulation of values and judgments of assessors*
> *(Armsby et al., 2006, p. 381).*

This view reflects a growing consensus in the wider APEL literature (Feutrie, 2000; Starr-Glass, 2002; Peters, 2005; Pokorny, 2006). Cleary *et al.* (2002) point out that in France the APEL process focuses on:

> *the learner's ability to engage in problem solving and critical thinking*
> *rather than establishing the equivalence between the outcomes of experiential*
> *learning and the required outcomes of the element of the academic programme*
> *against which the learner is seeking credit (ibid., p. 9).*

Similarly, Pouget and Osborne (2004), in their analysis of the French and UK systems of APEL, draw on writers like Eraut (1994) and notions of capability rather than competence, central to which is the concept of 'potentiality'. They point out that a capable student may be able to demonstrate the potential to succeed in a specific employment context, but fail to meet a narrow subset of curricula learning outcomes. In a similar vein, research by Peters (2006, p. 180) concluded that assessors need to be 'trained to value the unfamiliar – learning from sources never imagined, represented in unfamiliar ways'. Gallacher and Feutrie (2003, p. 80) agree that if APEL is to develop, 'HE staff need to be more prepared to reconsider their approach and procedures'. This, they suggest, goes beyond technical issues, though these are important, and highlights the importance of considering the social context within which assessment takes place.

Starr-Glass (2002), in his case study analysis, questions:

> *whether validity [of APEL claims] should be seen as essentially concurrent or*
> *predictive. Concurrent validity looks for similarity between [APEL claims]*
> *and … presently enrolled students … which tends to make the practice of*
> *APEL an exercise in mapping and confirming the familiar (ibid., p. 223).*

He goes on to suggest that if APEL was viewed as a process that had predictive validity then, as facilitators, we might wish to examine: 'A much broader correlation between the ways in which knowledge is acquired, processed and utilised by those who prove long term to be successful or well adapted' (*ibid.*).

Conclusions and research directions

APEL practices are very much influenced by the values and interests driving the process, and as such tend to be socially reproductive in character. Although some adult educators originally saw potential in APEL to open up higher levels of learning beyond the traditional values and interests of academic institutions, governments, professions and employer organisations, this has largely been unrealised in English higher education. Over four decades, the traditional tool for APEL assessment remains the portfolio linked to articulated and explicit learning outcomes. The fact that assessment conducted under the rubric of APEL is still seen as a threat to traditional standards is perhaps reinforced by the recent production of national *Guidelines on the Accreditation of Prior Learning* (QAA, 2004a).

However, APEL does thrive in some parts of higher education, in the new universities, in certain types of professional higher education (particularly health and social care, management and education studies) and increasingly in the context of WBL programmes. Several potential areas for fruitful research can be proposed:

1   Analysing the social context within which APEL assessment takes place and its impact upon participants and their learning.
2   Examining why and how APEL has been successful in certain professional education programmes linking to Starr-Glass's (2002) notion of the 'predictive validity' of APEL; that is, the conditions under which it is most likely to succeed.
3   Mapping the extent to which APEL forms part of WBL and professional programmes such as nursing at higher education level and the forms it takes.
4   Exploring the concepts of 'capability' and potential rather than competence (following Pouget and Osborne, 2004); that is, moving beyond the portfolio linked to articulated and explicit learning outcomes modelled on traditional higher education curricula.

References

Arkin, A. (1991) 'Giving credit to prior learning', *Personnel Management*, Vol. 23, No 4, pp. 41–3.

Armsby, P., Costley, C. and Garnett, J. (2006) 'The legitimisation of knowledge: A work-based learning perspective of APEL', *International Journal of Lifelong Education*, Vol. 25, No 4, pp. 369–83.

Betts, M. and Smith, R. (1998) *Developing the Credit-based Modular Curriculum in Higher Education*. London: Falmer.

Bond, C. and Wilson, V. (2003) 'Bridging the academic and vocational divide – A case study on work-based learning in the UK NHS', *Innovations in Education and Training International*, Vol. 37, No 2, pp. 134–44.

Brown, J. and Duguid, P. (2000) *The Social Life of Information*. Boston, MA: Harvard Business School Press.

Butterworth, C. (1992) 'More than one bite at the APEL', *Journal of Further and Higher Education*, Vol. 16, No 3, pp. 39–51.

Chisholm, C. and Davis, M. (2007) 'Analysis and evaluation of factors relating to accrediting 100% of prior experiential learning in UK work-based awards', *Assessment and Evaluation in Higher Education*, Vol. 32, No 1, pp. 45–59.

Clarke, A. (2005) 'Using Assessment of Prior Experiential Learning (APEL) to support refugee access into higher education and employment', *Investigations in University Teaching and Learning*, Vol. 3, No 1, pp. 84–93.

Clarke, J. and Warr, J. (1997) 'Academic validation of prior and experiential learning: evaluation of the process', *Journal of Advanced Nursing*, Vol. 26, No 6, pp. 1235–42.

Cleary, P., Whittaker, R., Gallacher, J., Merrill, B., Jokinen, L. and Carette, M. (2002) *Social Inclusion through APEL: The Learners' Perspective – Comparative Report*. Centre for Social and Educational Research, European Commission/Socrates.

Colley, H., Hodkinson, P. and Malcolm, J. (2003) *Informality and Formality in Learning: A Report for the Learning and Skills Research Centre*. London: Learning and Skills Research Centre, Learning and Skills Development Agency.

Council for National Academic Awards (1984) *Access to Higher Education: Non Standard Entry to CNAA First Degree and Diploma of Higher Education Courses*. London: CNAA.

Croker, D. (1995) *APEL: A Quality Code for AP(E)L: Issues for Managers and Practitioners*. Proceedings of the South East England Consortium (SEEC) National Conference, December.

Croker, D., Ellis, D., Hill, Y., Storan, J. and Turner, I. (eds.) (1998) *APEL: Beyond Graduateness*. London: Southern England Consortium for Credit Accumulation and Transfer, SEEC.

Dickinson, P. (2008) *Formative Evaluation of the Higher Level Skills Pathfinders*. London: Higher Education Funding Council for England (HEFCE). Available at: http://www.hefce.ac.uk/pubs/rdreports/2008/rd14_08/.

Eraut, M. (1994) *Developing Professional Knowledge and Competence*. London: Falmer Press.

Evans, N. (1994) *Experiential Learning for All*. London: Cassell Education.

Evans, N. and Turner, A. (1993) *The Potential of the Assessment of Experiential Learning in Universities*. London: HMSO.

Feutrie, M. (2000) 'France: The story of La Validation des Acquis (Recognition of Experiential Learning)', in N. Evans (ed.) *Experiential Learning Around the World: Employability and the Global Economy*. London: Jessica Kingsley.

Fraser, W. (1995) *Learning from Experience: Empowerment or Incorporation?* Leicester: National Institute of Adult Continuing Education (NIACE).

Fryer, R. (1997) *Learning for the Twenty-first Century: First Report of the National Advisory Group for Continuing Education and Lifelong Learning*. London: HMSO.

Gallacher, J. and Feutrie, M. (2003) 'Recognising and accrediting informal and non-formal learning in higher education: An analysis of the issues emerging from a study of France and Scotland', *European Journal of Education*, Vol. 38, No 1, pp. 71–83.

Garnett, J., Portwood, D. and Costley, C. (2004) *Bridging Rhetoric and Reality: Accreditation of Prior Experiential Learning (APEL) in the UK*. Bolton: University Vocational Awards Council (UVAC).

Haldane, A. and Wallace, J. (2009) 'Using technology to facilitate the accreditation of prior and experiential learning in developing personalised work-based learning programmes: A case study involving the University of Derby, UK', *European Journal of Education*, Vol. 44, No 3, Part 1, pp. 369–83.

Harris, J. (2006) 'Introduction and overview of chapters', in P. Andersson and J. Harris (eds) *Re-theorising the Recognition of Prior Learning*. Leicester: National Institute of Adult Continuing Education (NIACE).

Heath, V. (2001) 'Accreditation of prior (experiential) learning: Making the difference', *Nurse Education Today*, Vol. 21, No 2, pp. 496–500.

Higher Education Funding Council for England (HEFCE) (2007) *Circular Letter Number 03/2007*. Available at: http://www.hefce.ac.uk/Pubs/circlets/2007/cl03_07/ (Accessed 26 November 2009).

Houston, L. Y., Hoover, J. and Beer, E. (1997) 'Accreditation of Prior Learning: Is it worth it? An evaluation of a pilot scheme', *Nurse Education Today*, Vol. 17, No 3, pp. 184–91.

Howard, S. (1993) 'Accreditation of prior learning: Andragogy in action or a "cut price" approach to education?', *Journal of Advanced Nursing*, Vol. 18, No 11, pp. 1817–24.

Johnson, B. (2002) *Models of APEL and Quality Assurance*. London: Southern England Consortium for Credit Accumulation and Transfer, SEEC.

Kolb, D. (1984) *Experiential Learning: Experience as the Source of Learning and Development*. New Jersey: Prentice-Hall.

Lave, J. and Wenger, E. (1993) *Situated Learning: Legitimate Peripheral Participation*. Cambridge: Cambridge University Press.

Lester, S. (2007) 'Professional practice projects: APEL or development?', *Journal of Workplace Learning*, Vol. 19, No 3, pp. 188–202.

Merrifield, J., McIntyre, D. and Osaigbovo, R. (2000) *Changing but not Changed: Mapping APEL in English Higher Education*. London: Learning from Experience Trust.

Mulholland, J. and Leith, H. (1999) 'The development of a system for accrediting prior learning of nurses', *Nurse Education Today*, Vol. 19, No 3, pp. 199–206.

Murphy, A. (2003) 'Is the university sector in Ireland ready to publicly assess and accredit personal learning from outside the academy?', *European Journal of Education*, Vol. 38, No 4, pp. 401–11.

Peters, H. (2000) 'Working towards AP(E)L with refugees and asylum seekers', in S. Bailie, C. O'Hagan and A. Mason (eds) *APEL and Lifelong Learning*. Belfast: University of Ulster, pp. 68–71.

Peters, H. (2005) 'Contested discourses: Assessing the outcomes of learning from experience for the award of credit in higher education', *Assessment and Evaluation in Higher Education*, Vol. 30, No 3, pp. 273–85.

Peters, H. (2006) 'Using critical discourse analysis to illuminate power and knowledge in RPL', in P. Andersson and J. Harris (eds) *Re-theorising the Recognition of Prior Learning*. Leicester: NIACE.

Peters, H. and Pokorny, H. (2003) 'A runaway horse: Attempting to harness prior learning in the academic context'. Paper presented at the Centre for Research in Lifelong Learning (CRLL) International Conference, Researching Learning outside the Academy, Glasgow, June.

Peters, H., Pokorny, H. and Johnson, L. (2004) 'Cracking the code: The assessment of prior experiential learning at London Metropolitan University', in E. Michelson and A. Mandell (eds) *Portfolio Development and the Assessment of Prior Learning*, Virginia, USA: Sylus Publishing.

Pokorny, H. (2006) 'Recognising prior learning: What do *we* know?', in P. Andersson and J. Harris (eds) *Re-theorising the Recognition of Prior Learning*. Leicester: NIACE.

Pouget, M. and Osborne, M. (2004) 'Accreditation or *validation* of prior experiential learning: Knowledge and *savoirs* in France – a different perspective?', *Studies in Continuing Education*, Vol. 26, No 1, pp. 45–65.

Price, M. (2005) 'Assessment standards: The role of communities of practice and the scholarship of assessment', *Assessment and Evaluation in Higher Education*, Vol. 30, No 3, pp. 215–30.

Prince, C. (2003) 'University accreditation and the corporate learning agenda', *Journal of Management Development*, Vol. 23, No 3, pp. 256–69.

Quality Assurance Agency for Higher Education (QAA) (2003) *Overview Report on Foundation Degree Reviews*. London: QAA. Available at: http://www.qaa.ac.uk/reviews/foundationDegree/overview/Founda tionoverviewMar04.pdf.

Quality Assurance Agency for Higher Education (QAA) (2004a) *Guidelines on the Accreditation of Prior Learning*. London: QAA. Available at: http://www.qaa.ac.uk/academicinfrastructure/apl/APL.pdf.

Quality Assurance Agency for Higher Education (QAA) (2004b) *Foundation Degree Qualification Benchmark*. London: QAA. Available at: http://www.qaa.ac.uk/reviews/foundationdegree/benchmark/fdqb.asp.

South East England Consortium (SEEC) (1995) *Code of Practice for the Assessment of Prior (Experiential) Learning*. London: Southern England Consortium for Credit Accumulation and Transfer, SEEC.

Schön, D. (1987) *Educating the Reflective Practitioner*. San Francisco: Jossey-Bass.

Scott, I. (2007) 'Accreditation of prior learning in pre-registration nursing programmes: Throwing the baby out with the bath water?', *Nurse Education Today*, Vol. 27, No 4, pp. 348–56.

Scott, I. (2010a) 'Accreditation of prior learning in pre-registration nursing programmes 2: The influence of prior qualifications on perceived learning during the foundation year', *Nurse Education Today*, Vol. 30, No 5, pp. 438–42.

Scott. I. (2010b) '"But I know that already": Rhetoric or reality, the accreditation of prior experiential learning in the context of work-based learning', *Research in Post-Compulsory Education*, Vol. 15, No 1, pp. 19–31.

Skinner, J., Nganasurian, W., Pike, S. and Hilton, A. (1997) 'An investigation into the reliability and validity of assessment strategies for the Accreditation of Prior Learning of nurses, midwives and health visitors: A report for the English National Board for nursing, midwifery and health visiting'. London: South East England Consortium for Credit Accumulation and Transfer, SEEC.

Starr-Glass, D. (2002) 'Metaphor and totem: exploring and evaluating prior experiential learning', *Assessment and Evaluation in Higher Education*, Vol. 27, No 3, pp. 222–31.

Storan, J. (1993) *Getting to the Core of APEL: Assessment of Prior Experiential Learning: Issues and Practice*. London: Southern England Consortium for Credit Accumulation and Transfer, SEEC.

Thorne, P. (1991) 'Assessment of Prior Experiential Learning', *Nursing Standard*, Vol. 6, No 10, pp. 32–4.

Trowler, P. (1996) 'Angels in marble? Accrediting prior experiential learning in higher education', *Studies in Higher Education*, Vol. 21, No 1, pp. 17–29.

Usher, R. (1989) 'Qualifications, paradigms and experiential learning in higher education', in O. Fulton (ed.) *Access and Institutional Change*. Buckingham: SRHE and Open University Press.

Wailey, T. (2002) *How to do AP(E)L*. London: Southern England Consortium for Credit Accumulation and Transfer, SEEC.

Warren, S. and Webb, S. (2007) 'Challenging lifelong learning policy discourse: Where is structure and agency in narrative-based research?', *Studies in the Education of Adults*, Vol. 39, No 1, pp. 5–21.

CHAPTER SIX

European Union: Research and system building in the Validation of Non-formal and Informal Learning (VNFIL)

Judy Harris

Abstract

In a context where education is increasingly conceptualised as a key part of economic and social policy, the European Commission is driving forward a strong policy focus on the Validation of Non-formal and Informal Learning (VNFIL), along with life-long learning, credit systems, the European Qualification Framework and the development of learning outcomes. Even so, there does not seem to be an agreed definition of VNFIL. Terminology varies and this has led to some difficulties in ascertaining the extent of practice, although research accounts suggest that patterns of take-up are 'strongly differentiated' and generally low (Bjørnåvold, 2007; Adam, 2008; Werquin, 2010).

This chapter is an overview of VNFIL research in the European Union, starting with the most prevalent: research via inventories and comparative studies; research via collaboration and networks; project-based and implementation-oriented research and development; doctoral research; and critical academic research re policy and practice.

The research picture is polarised between a wealth of policy-related inventories, projects and comparative studies on the one hand and a small amount of doctoral work on the other. In the main, there is little attention to scholarly research. There are not many research-based articles in peer-reviewed journals (although more in the field of assessment than in other fields). Rigorous critical engagement with policy and aspects of practice is conspicuous by its absence. The research field is therefore wide open with ample opportunities to build upon the practical, systems-building work and information gathering that has been privileged to date, and to deploy different methodologies and theoretical insights to illuminate and develop particular aspects of policy and practice.

Introduction

In European Union (EU) policy circles, the assessment and recognition of prior learning is increasingly referred to as the Validation of Non-formal and Informal Learning (VNFIL) – Validation for short. However, other terms have been used historically and in particular sectors, and continue to be used. In this chapter, I use the terms that writers or researchers use rather than attempt to standardise terminology. This is because there are usually reasons (ideological, political, theoretical and so on) for the choice of a particular term; to standardise would run the risk of obfuscating arguments that are made. Where I am referring to practices in general terms, or where no particular term is prefigured, I use 'Validation'.

The chapter begins with a discussion of how I have determined what counts as 'research' and the boundaries around that. The methodology I have used as the researcher-writer to identify 'research' to be included for review and discussion in the chapter is then presented. This is followed by some contextual background – a brief introduction to the European Union and an outline of the key policies and decisions that have influenced the development and direction of VNFIL. The main body of the chapter is organised according to types of research, starting with the most prevalent: research via inventories and comparative studies; research via collaboration and networks; project-based and implementation-oriented research and development; doctoral research and critical academic research re policy and practice. The chapter ends with a general discussion about the nature of the research in the EU and makes some recommendations.

What counts as 'research'?

The definition of research and the boundaries around what counts as research for this chapter have been arrived at with the nature of the EU context in mind. Basically, broad parameters are drawn. Along with Van

128

Kleef (in this volume, who draws on the University Research Council at Nipissing University [2008]), research is understood as any:

> *original and systematic investigation undertaken in order to increase knowledge and understanding and to establish facts and principles. It comprises the creation of ideas and generation of knowledge that lead to new and substantial improved insights and/or the development of new products, practices and processes.*

In concrete terms, this definition allows consideration of:

- Empirical research – both qualitative and quantitative – using a range of methods including documentary analysis and literature reviews, surveys, case studies, interviews. Some of this research may bring a particular and explicit theoretical lens or set of concepts to the interpretation of the data; other research may be guided by the theory of the methodology – for example, forms of discourse analysis or general qualitative analysis.
- Non-empirical research – theoretically and conceptually driven engagements with the phenomenon of concern, including reflective inquiry and the development of ideas.
- Research and development – where a period of research such as a scoping exercise precedes a developmental activity; for example, piloting a particular model of practice or process. There may or may not be a period of evaluation thereafter.

Methodology used to identify and include research

There were systematic and less systematic aspects to this. The systematic process involved:

- Searching official websites for policy-specific research; for example, the EU, the Organisation for Economic Co-operation and Development (OECD) and UNESCO.[1]
- Searching databases for broader (and more academic) research; for example, VOCED, Theses in English, British Education Index,

---

[1] www.europa.eu; http://www.oecd.org; http://www.unesco.org; http://www.adam-europe.eu/adam/project/view.htm?prj=3678; http://www.lifelonglearningprogramme.org.uk.

EBSCO online research databases, Science Direct, DART-Europe e-theses portal, the Education-*line* database, Educational Research Abstracts Online, the European Reference Index for the Humanities and the Universal Index of Doctoral Dissertations in Progress.

• Searching key journals since 2000, especially those with explicit European coverage: European Journal of Education, Lifelong Learning in Europe, European Education Research Journal, Assessment and Evaluation, and European Journal of Educational Studies.

The less systematic process included taking account of research and literature that was recommended to me informally. Searching was iterative in that citations in articles, reports, theses and so on were followed up, leading to fresh cycles of review. Given my relative outsider status in relation to EU policy development, the services of an expert were sought to assist with the section on the EU policy context.[2] The review is constrained by my monolingual status (although help was sought to gain insight into some of the academic literature in French).

This chapter is an *overview* of Validation research and development in the EU. As such, it steers clear of EU countries that are the subject of other chapters in this volume (namely Scotland, England and Sweden). As well as the 27 EU member states, the chapter includes candidate countries and countries with 'associated' status in relation to the EU (see section below). Because of the policy-oriented nature of the EU context, some of the research that is discussed is 'grey' literature; that is, not published. For example, a report may be included because of its significance to the field. Because of the fast-moving nature of policy development, I have focused on research and activities since 2000, except when consciously wanting to draw attention to historical developments. The overall aim of the chapter is to give a flavour of the activities being undertaken; it does not and cannot claim to be exhaustive.

---

[2] I am indebted to Professor John Konrad, of Konrad Associates International, for input into the background of European Commission policy and related developments. Drawing on his professional expertise in educational sciences as applied to vocational education and training, Professor Konrad has worked for the European Commission as an expert in lifelong learning since 2000.

Contextual background

A brief introduction to the European Union

The European Union is an economic and political union of 27 member states.[3] Committed to regional integration, the Union was established by the Treaty of Maastricht on 1 November 1993, thereby superseding the former 'European Community'. Before being admitted to the European Union, a country must fulfil the economic and political conditions generally known as the 'Copenhagen criteria'. These require a candidate country to have a stable democracy that guarantees the rule of law, human rights and the protection of minorities. It must also have a functioning market economy and a civil service capable of applying and enforcing EU laws. Enlargement of the EU is conditional upon the agreement of each member state, as well as the approval of the European Parliament.

Bulgaria and Romania were the most recent countries to accede (in 2007). There are four official candidate countries at the time of writing: Croatia, Iceland, Macedonia and Turkey. Albania, Bosnia and Herzegovina, Montenegro and Serbia are officially recognised as potential candidates. Kosovo is also a potential candidate, but the European Commission[4] does not list it as an independent country because not all member states recognise it as separate from Serbia. Four Western European countries have chosen not to join the Union but have partly committed to its economy and regulations: Iceland (which is also a candidate country); Liechtenstein and Norway (which are a part of the single market through the European Economic Area); and Switzerland (which has similar ties through bilateral treaties).

An outline of the key policies and decisions that have influenced the development and direction of VNFIL

Interest, investigation and early Validation practices began in the United Kingdom (UK) and France well before the formal establishment of the

---

[3] Belgium, France, Germany, Luxembourg, the Netherlands, Italy, Ireland, Denmark, the United Kingdom, Greece, Portugal, Spain, Austria, Cyprus, Malta, Sweden, Finland, Hungary, Poland, Romania, Slovakia, Latvia, Estonia, Lithuania, Bulgaria, the Czech Republic and Slovenia.

[4] The mission of the European Commission is to promote the general interest of the European Union.

EU. Most other EU countries have become involved as a result of the emergence of Validation as a policy issue. Table 6.1 shows the *key political landmark texts and decisions*[5] as they pertain to higher education, and vocational education and training. It is clear that Validation is linked to the lifelong learning agenda and to an intention to value learning more broadly than hitherto (Colardyn and Bjørnåvold, 2004, 2005).

The overarching EU vision is for Europe to develop as 'the world's most dynamic knowledge-based economy'.[6] To achieve this, education is increasingly conceptualised as an integral part of economic and social policy (although this is not without criticism; see below). The 'Bologna process' was established in 1999 (Bologna, 1999) to oversee the realisation of a European Higher Education Area (EHEA) by 2010 and subsequently to establish priorities into the next decade.[7] With the broad aims of harmonisation and mobility, the Bologna process has exerted far-reaching changes to the structure, content and conduct of higher education (Adam, 2008) and professional recognition. The Copenhagen Declaration brought the then slower-moving European vocational education and training sectors into the same political agenda, thereby fusing the Lisbon Strategy which was set up by the European Council in March 2000 (at the Lisbon Summit) with the Bologna Process: 'The development of high quality vocational education and training is a crucial and integral part of this strategy, notably in terms of promoting social inclusion, cohesion, mobility, employability and competitiveness' (European Commission, 2002).

Alongside the above political commitments, a wide range of developmental activities have been undertaken, most of which have a research dimension (as defined in the opening section of this chapter).

---

[5] Bologna documents have been adopted by the ministers responsible for higher education in participating countries. They are not legally-binding documents (as international treaties usually are); it is up to each country and its higher-education community to endorse or reject the Bologna principles, although the effect of 'international peer pressure' should not be underestimated.

[6] See Lisbon European Council, Presidency Conclusions, 23–24 March 2000; http://www.europarl.europa.eu/summits/lis1_en.htm.

[7] Bologna is an unusual process in that it is loosely structured, driven by participating countries in cooperation with a number of international organisations, including the Council of Europe. For this reason, citations are attributed to 'Bologna'.

Table 6.1 Key political landmark texts and decisions

Landmark text	Landmark development
Teaching and Learning: Towards the Learning Society, European White Paper (European Commission, 1995)	Identified 'skills recognition' as an important component of the acquisition of new knowledge
Towards the European Higher Education Area: The *Prague Communiqué* (Bologna, 2001)	Following the Bologna Declaration, the *Prague Communiqué* identified lifelong learning as an 'essential element' of the European Higher Education Area (EHEA)
Making a European Area of Lifelong Learning a Reality (European Commission, 2001)	'A comprehensive new European approach to valuing learning is seen as a pre-requisite for the area of lifelong learning … Proposals focus on the identification, assessment and recognition of non-formal and informal learning as well as on the transfer and mutual recognition of formal certificates and diplomas' (*ibid.*, p. 4)
	'Valuing and rewarding learning, especially non-formal and informal learning in all sectors, thereby recognising its intrinsic worth. Rewarding learning can also encourage those who are most alienated to return to learning' (*ibid.*, p. 14)
The *Copenhagen Declaration on Enhanced European Cooperation in Vocational Education and Training* (Bologna, 2002)	This Declaration launched developments based on enhanced voluntary cooperation between member states and candidate countries. The approach that was advocated was a bottom-up 'open method of coordination' to 'promote mutual trust, transparency and recognition of competencies and qualifications and thereby establishing a basis for increasing mobility and facilitating access to lifelong learning'
The *Helsinki Communiqué* (European Commission, 2006)	Re-emphasised the importance of 'promoting the recognition of non-formal and informal learning to support career development and lifelong learning' as one of the means of 'improving the attractiveness and quality of vocational education and training'
The *Berlin Communiqué* (Bologna, 2003); the *Bergen Communiqué* (Bologna, 2005); the *London Communiqué* (Bologna, 2007); the *Leuven and Louvain-la-Neuve Communiqué* (Bologna, 2009)	All of these communiqués stress the contribution that the 'Recognition of Prior Learning' can make to lifelong learning at higher education level within the Bologna Process, the EHEA and (after the *Bergen Communiqué*) within national qualifications frameworks linked to an overarching and comprehensive European Qualifications Framework (encompassing all education from school to doctorate)

133

Types of research

Research via inventories

Inventories are a very common feature on the VNFIL landscape of the EU (and beyond).[8] They are valued because they set a context and baseline for developments by gathering information about (usually national) states of play across several dimensions: policy, definitions, rationales, practices, and so on. Methodologically, they tend to consist of 'progressive focusing' from country studies to more in-depth case studies, concluding with a synthesis report or some sort of 'snapshot' document. A common format is for each country to produce the first report via questionnaires, desk research, policy analysis and statistical analysis. Synthesis reports are generated through cross-analysis of the country reports using a 'common analytical framework'.

The first EU inventory was produced in 2000 by Jens Bjørnåvold under the auspices of the European Centre for the Development of Vocational Training (CEDEFOP[9]) and published as: *Making Learning Visible: Identification, Assessment and Recognition of Non-formal Learning in Europe*. The initiative offered an opportunity for member states to exchange experiences on the character and stage of their national policies and practices. The final report listed practices in 15 European countries and identified five models: Austro-German, Mediterranean, Nordic, National Vocational Qualifications-oriented and Franco-Belgian.

The following year (2001) the European Commission and CEDEFOP agreed to formally establish a European inventory of approaches to VNFIL, the objective of which was to catalogue policies, practices and methodologies, and to analyse converging and diverging trends. The main beneficiaries were envisaged as being policy- and decision-makers. A second inventory (for 2004), also prepared by Colardyn and Bjørnåvold, was published in 2005 as *The Learning Continuity: European Inventory on Validating Non-formal and Informal Learning*. It involved 14 established member states, and summary information on eight new member states and two candidate countries.

---

[8] Although not discussed in this chapter, an inventory involving 38 countries was carried out by the UNESCO Institute for Lifelong Learning in 2005 in the context of the United Nations Decade – Education for Sustainable Development (Singh, 2009).

[9] CEDEFOP is the European Union's reference and information centre for vocational education and training.

ECOTEC Research and Consulting was commissioned by the Directorate General of Education and Culture of the European Commission to undertake the next inventory, building on and updating the previous one. The number of countries surveyed increased to 30, and the scope was broadened to report on Validation practices in the public, private and voluntary sectors. Ten case studies of good practice and several synthesis chapters were also included. As the inventory process extended and became formalised, more attention was given to methodological aspects. ECOTEC both participated in and supervised the research, which involved a participatory approach (engaging all stakeholders) and a 'comprehensive' and 'multidimensional' methodology, making use of primary and secondary and qualitative and quantitative data. The initial collection and updating of information was undertaken by country correspondents through literature reviews, web searches and telephone, and face-to-face interviews. The case studies involved gathering additional primary and secondary data. These and the synthesis chapters were undertaken by ECOTEC (Otero *et al.*, 2005).

A 2007 update was also undertaken by ECOTEC (Otero *et al.*, 2008). Additional desk research was conducted with a focus on the development of Validation in higher education. The research methodology was made more explicit and included:

- Systematic web and literature review to obtain information on recent developments and further information on already identified initiatives – for example, new research and policy papers, policy evaluations and data on take-up. Over 100 abstracts were produced derived from VNFIL sources external to the inventory, classified according to document type, country coverage and keywords in order to be accessible to a wide audience.
- Stakeholder interviews with over 90 stakeholders either by email, telephone or face-to-face.
- A quality-assurance procedure whereby each draft chapter was reviewed internally and externally (involving over 60 reviewers).
- Case studies: six initiatives were selected as in-depth case studies; further desk research was undertaken plus up to four interviews in each case study site.

A 'snapshot' document was produced in 2008 by CEDEFOP to capture some emerging trends. A further ECOTEC inventory was due to be published towards the end of 2010; at the time of writing, country reports are not available. In future years, the EU inventory will be handled by GHK Consulting Limited.

The OECD is involved in similar work and more than half of the countries surveyed by that organisation are also EU countries. The OECD's inventories on the Recognition of Non-formal and Informal Learning (RNFIL) emanated from an agreement amongst education ministers in 1996 to develop strategies for 'lifelong learning for all'. The research methodologies are similar to those deployed within the EU inventories. Typically, a country report is produced in/by the country concerned. The OECD then conducts fact-finding review visits of approximately four days per country, which inform a second country report compiled by the review team called a 'thematic review'. The results of the latest OECD survey have recently been published: *Recognising Non-Formal and Informal Learning: Outcomes, Policies and Practices* (Werquin, 2010).

Key findings from the inventories

Some of the key observations from the most recent inventories are now presented to give a flavour of the state of play in EU countries. The snapshot document (CEDEFOP, 2008) refers to the 'multi-speed' character of developments and classified countries accordingly. The report also highlights the role of national qualifications frameworks, and shifts to learning outcomes as catalysts for the development of Validation policy and practice. A distinction between Validation processes with predominantly formative dimensions (with support and guidance for individuals), and those that are more summative and oriented to certification, is formalised in this document.[10]

European countries are classified into three main groups. First, those countries where Validation has become a practical reality for individual citizens; that is, it has moved from the level of general policy to tangible practice. Countries like Belgium, Denmark, Estonia, Finland, France, Ireland, the Netherlands, Norway, Portugal, Slovenia, Romania, Spain and the UK fall into this category (*ibid.*, p. 24). Second, those countries where (as at December 2007) Validation is *emerging* as a practical reality, but where practices still have to be put in place to ensure that individuals can access

---

[10] See Whittaker in this volume for detailed discussion of formative and summative approaches.

services on a systemic and systematic basis. Although countries like Austria, the Czech Republic, Iceland, Italy, Germany, Hungary, Lithuania, Luxembourg, Malta, Poland and Sweden belong to this category, levels of activity vary considerably within the group (*ibid.*, p. 27). The third category comprises countries where activity is low or non-existent; mainly because the idea is new and has not yet found a place on policy agendas, perhaps because it is seen as 'controversial'. This group includes Bulgaria, Croatia, Cyprus, Greece, Latvia, Lichtenstein, Slovakia and Turkey (*ibid.*, p. 31).

Given the nature of the organisation, the findings of the 2010 OECD survey are framed by economic perspectives (see Werquin and Wihak, in this volume). As mentioned, some of the issues covered are the same as those covered by the EU inventory process. Moreover, a representative number of European Union countries form part of the OECD study, namely: Austria, Belgium, the Czech Republic, Denmark, Finland, France, Germany, Greece, Hungary, Iceland, Ireland, Italy, Luxembourg, the Netherlands, Norway, Poland, Portugal, Slovakia, Spain, Sweden, Switzerland, Turkey and the United Kingdom. Given that EU countries comprise 16 of the 30 OECD sample, the survey findings can be taken to be fairly representative of the state of play re Validation in Europe (although the report uses the term 'recognition').[11] A central observation is that, despite governments' support, 'Recognition processes are often marginal, small-scale and not yet sustainable' (Werquin, 2010, p. 3). Correspondingly, take-up is low. Moreover, legitimacy and credibility issues remain, and VNFIL cannot be seen as a cheap option compared to

---

[11] Other writers and commentators have made different classifications regarding stages and type of development, according to *inter alia:* regulatory frameworks (from intention to enshrined in law); the top-down or bottom-up nature of processes (often depending on the learning culture of the country concerned); whether development is sector-specific or across most/all sectors, institution-specific or across most/all institutions; the outcomes of validation (access, exemptions, credits etc.); what is assessed (experiential learning/knowledge, skills, learning outcomes, capacities etc.); the tools that are used (portfolios, dossiers, observations, tests and exams); where the main authority lies (government, sector, organisation, institution, at programme level); whether there is a national qualifications framework or not; whether higher education is involved or not; whether it is possible to acquire a full qualification via Validation or not; type of application (school certificate, entry to higher education, exemptions from formal programmes, labour competence certification, discrete applications such as the involvement of professional bodies) and so on. It seems as if the data provided by the inventories allows many different comparisons to be drawn.

the provision of formal education and training. Werquin (2010) refers to 'islands of good practice' and the need to develop research activity – points that are taken up later in this chapter.

Comparative studies

Gallacher and Feurie (2003) undertook an exploration of issues associated with introducing the *Validation d'Acquis de l'Expérience* (VAE) in France, and what was then the Accreditation of Prior Experiential Learning (APEL) in Scotland. Analysing similarities and differences, they concluded that there are 'problems of complexity and formality' in both countries; also 'problems associated with accrediting different kinds of knowledge'. Overall, despite efforts, 'achievements have been limited'.

In 2004, Pouget and Osborne undertook an in-depth study into the process of *Validation des Acquis Professionnels* (VAP), comparing concepts and their implementation in France with their Anglo-Saxon counterparts. They noted 'subtle but essential cultural differences' and concluded that the VAP process in France adopts a different ('third way') position in terms of the relationships between different forms of knowledge, which they claim is more successful in giving parity of esteem to professional and vocational knowledge.[12]

In a follow-up to Evans (2000), Corradi *et al*'s. (2006) *Recognising Experiential Learning: Practices in European universities* offer a structured, descriptive and comparative overview of practices, finding what they term a 'motley palette of practices: a rich, varied, highly promising and often incomparable mix of divergent experiences, provisions and regulations' (*ibid.*, p. 8). Case studies of aspects of practices in seven countries relevant to this chapter are offered (France, Estonia, Italy, Holland, Lapland, Norway and Ireland).[13]

Research via collaboration and networks

Research to develop principles and guidelines
In May 2004, the Council of the European Union adopted *Common European Principles for the Identification and Validation of Non-formal and*

---

[12] This approach is reported on by Pokorny in this volume.
[13] See also Valk (2009) for an overview of the recognition of prior experiential learning in European universities.

Informal Learning to ensure greater comparability between approaches in different countries and at different levels. This initiative was greatly facilitated by inventory processes. Methodologically, the development took a bottom-up approach; that is, it was an inductive process where principles were abstracted and distilled from existing practices. Addressing the purpose of VNFIL, individual entitlements, the obligations of stakeholders, confidence and trust issues, credibility and legitimacy, the principles are designed to operate at a meta-level, and to allow countries and contexts to infuse their own values and practices as well as to learn from each other. It is noteworthy that the Principles also enshrine a distinction between 'identification' and 'validation' – similar to 'formative' and 'summative': [14]

> *Identification records and makes visible the individual's learning outcomes. This does not result in a formal certificate or diploma, but it may provide the basis for such formal recognition. Validation is based on the assessment of the individual's learning outcomes and may result in a certificate or diploma (Council of the European Union, 2004, p. 2).*

Building on the Principles, the *European Guidelines for Validating Non-formal and Informal Learning* (CEDEFOP, 2009a)[15] are the result of a collaborative process within the 'cluster on recognition of learning outcomes' (see below). They are intended to be a practical voluntary resource for policy-makers and practitioners, including enterprises, employment sectors and non-governmental organisations. They contain detailed strategies to support the further development of Validation at European, national and local levels.

The Guidelines emphasise inclusiveness, in that there are two Validation routes: one that moves straight to assessment (i.e. is more summative); and one that allows for guidance and the gathering of evidence (i.e. is more formative):

> *Learning achieved through non-formal or informal means is only distinguishable from learning achieved through formal programmes by the context of learning. The tools for assessing learning are essentially the same, though some adaptation of the tools – as well as possible combination of different tools – is necessary to take account of contextual differences, such as the timescale over*

---

[14] See http://www.ecotec.com/europeaninventory/principles.html.

[15] See http://www.cedefop.europa.eu/EN/publications/5059.aspx.

> *which the learning took place. This is important, as the outcomes of validation of non-formal and informal learning are sometimes perceived as inferior to validation applied to the formal situation because different assessment tools are used or they are applied differently.*

Indeed, this is a growing theme in the research and development literature.[16] Commentators are generally agreed that there is a need to promote practices that include guidance, reflection and self-assessment, and that there is a place for both formative and summative approaches in policy. Many countries have begun to frame their practices in this way (Scotland, the Netherlands, Finland and Estonia, for example).

The Guidelines also stress the importance of considering the type of learning that is to be assessed, before an assessment method is selected. Criteria are offered to indicate necessary considerations: breadth of knowledge, skills and competences to be assessed; depth of learning required; how current or recent are the knowledge, skills and competence; sufficiency of information for an assessor to make a judgement; authenticity of the evidence. Having determined the type of learning, it is possible to examine the fitness for purpose of different assessment methods. The following criteria need to be considered:

- Validity – the tool must measure what it is intended to measure.
- Reliability – the extent to which identical results would be achieved every time a candidate is assessed under the same conditions.
- Fairness – the extent to which an assessment decision is free from bias (context dependency, culture and assessor bias).
- Cognitive range – does the tool enable assessors to judge the breadth and depth of the candidate's learning?[17]

These criteria are summarised in a set of checklists.[18] Although the design process appears (and is) democratic, reaching agreements between more than 25 countries has not always been easy. Indeed, the 2009 version of the Guidelines is currently being revised and (re)evaluated in a series of stages up to November 2011.

---

[16] See Whittaker (in this volume) for a discussion of how these orientations have developed in Scotland.

[17] CEDEFOP (2009) A range of methods are described and analysed on pp. 59–65.

[18] *Ibid.* Annex 2, pp. 78–85.

Clusters and peer-learning activities
The period 2006–09 saw specific partnerships – 'clusters' and peer-learning activities. The above-mentioned 'cluster on recognition of learning outcomes' brought together roughly 25 countries with a particular interest in Validation, augmented by financial, organisational and analytical support from CEDEFOP. The cluster took responsibility for taking forward a broad range of issues related to adopting learning outcomes in education and training policy and practice, and organised three peer learning activities.[19] The French community of Belgium hosted the activity in February 2007, and a series of national case studies and workshops were offered in order to develop a deeper understanding of quality assurance procedures in the Recognition of Non-formal and Informal Learning.[20] It was these deliberations that led CEDEFOP (2009b) to define the recognition/validation of learning outcomes as inclusive of formal, non-formal and informal learning:

> *The confirmation by a competent body that learning outcomes (knowledge, skills and/or competences) acquired by an individual in a formal, non-formal or informal setting have been assessed against predefined criteria and are compliant with the requirements of a validation standard. Validation typically leads to certification.*

The 'cluster on recognition of learning outcomes' has been successful and congruent enough with the European Commission agenda to have been made into a sub-group of the EQF Advisory Group, the aim of which is to promote the exchange of ideas among policy-makers.

Networks
Established in 2003, the CEDEFOP open-access 'virtual community' supports the development and implementation of methods and systems for Validation. It is intended as a meeting place for policy-makers, practitioners, researchers and others, and as a way to continue to support the development, dissemination and uptake of EU transnational projects.

Following the Leuven Communiqué (Bologna, 2009), Scotland, Ireland and the Netherlands hosted an event (in February 2010) to share practice in the area of Recognition of Prior Learning (RPL). Workshops

---

[19] See http://www.kslll.net/PeerLearningClusters/clusterDetails.cfm?id=13.
[20] See http://www.kslll.net/PeerLearningActivities/PlaDetails.cfm?id=74.

were sought which addressed: lifelong learning, widening participation and access; flexible learning paths; engaging employers and workforce development; RPL processes and procedures; student experiences; and building assessment capacity. It has since been agreed to establish a European RPL Network and the inaugural meeting took place on 5 November 2010 in Scotland.[21] Expressions of interest have been extended to all Bologna countries, consultative members and practitioner representatives to:

- Help promote and inform the effective use and practice of RPL across participating countries.
- Provide a means for member countries to share and learn from policies and practice across Europe.
- Build links between European countries at various stages of RPL development.

A possible research strand is also mentioned in the European RPL Network brief: as in undertake 'research into the use and impact of RPL' (this type of development would link directly to the Prior Learning International Research Centre [PLIRC]). The brief also characterised the take-up of Validation in higher education as 'patchy', with some institutions being 'quite dynamic' in their approaches, especially vocationally-oriented higher education institutions such as the Hogeschool van Amsterdam (a university of applied sciences where programmes are practice-focused and tailored to individual needs).

Project-based and implementation-oriented research and development

All countries (including candidate countries and those with special relationships to the EU) are able to participate in and benefit from the European Commission's 'Lifelong Learning Programme' (LLP). This is a funding programme for all stages of lifelong learning – school, college, university, workplace and community. There are several sub-programmes within it: *Erasmus* supports the mobility of HE students and staff across Europe for both work placement and study purposes; *Leonardo* provides

---

[21] See Whittaker in this volume for more detail.

opportunities for vocational education and training; *Grundtvig* funds training opportunities for adult education organisations, staff and learners; *Comenius* supports project-based partnerships, in-service opportunities and assistantships for all levels of school and further education; and *transversal study visits* give learning professionals opportunities to exchange expertise with European colleagues. The budget of the Lifelong Learning Programme for 2007–13 is seven billion euros. Projects concerned with Validation are most likely to be funded through Leonardo or Grundtvig. A search for 'prior learning' on the ADAM portal (for Leonardo projects) indicated over a thousand projects in receipt of funding. Four projects have been selected to schematically illustrate the type of research and development activities that are under way.

The Recognition of Prior Learning Outcomes (RPLO) 2008–10[22]
This project is a partnership of nine organisations from six countries: the UK (including Cambridge Assessment [a department of the University of Cambridge]; and Konrad Associates International [a lifelong learning research and development centre]); Italy (the Fondazione Politecnico di Milano – a specialist institution in engineering, architecture and industrial design); the Netherlands (the Hogeschool INHOLLAND University of Applied Sciences); Finland (the Satakunta Vocational Adult Education Centre); Sweden (Municipality of Södertälje); and Switzerland (ECAP – an adult education and research organisation with strong trade union links).

The RPLO project builds on CEDEFOP (2007) research into validating the non-formal and informal learning of vocational education and training (VET) teachers and trainers as a means of enhancing qualification levels and professionalising their role. That study provided a comparative overview of the approaches and methodologies that countries were using. The RPLO project seeks to improve the attractiveness, status and effectiveness of VET teaching by piloting the European Guidelines in relation to initial teacher, training and continuing professional development for educators in lifelong learning. The partner countries will collaborate and ensure that developments align with the EQF and the European Credit System for VET (ECVET). In essence, the

---

[22] Details about this project are available from http://www.adam-europe.eu/adam/project/view.htm?prj=3937.

project is concerned to embed RPL into learning, assessment and certification systems in order to make existing credit-based qualifications 'RPLO-friendly'. The project outputs can be used in relation to any practitioner involved in learner support and progression – in teaching, assessment, quality assurance, leadership and management, information-advice-guidance, mentoring, moderation or inspection. The project has developed:

- A validated methodology for RPLO with new tools, methods and support materials.
- Units of learning and assessment which relate to national standards; for example, a Level 5, 15-credit unit/module called 'The Principles and Practice of RPL' (complete with indicative content) that can be embedded into a wide range of teacher training qualifications at undergraduate and postgraduate levels.
- Comprehensive assessment and verification guidance, including reference to rules of combination and demonstrations of the ways in which quality assurance can enhance the reliability and validity of RPLO.

Transparency and Mobility through Accreditation of Vocational Learning Outcomes (CREDIVOC) 2007–09[23]

This Leonardo project was coordinated by the University of Bremen, and involved partner universities in France, Germany, Austria, Finland and Ireland. Each core partner was supported by a national and/or regional consortium of VET institutions and other social partners. Within the context of the EQF and the ECVET, the project aimed to identify, test and transfer innovative instruments to recognise and accredit learning outcomes from initial and continuing vocational education and training in relation to higher levels of education. The focus was on selected occupational fields in the 'engineering in technology' sector.

In the first stage of the project (2007–08), a survey of 'accreditation of prior learning' systems, strategies, instruments and procedures was undertaken using/developing a 'common analytical framework', based on

---

[23] Project outputs are available from http://lspace6.via-on line.de/oldenburg/cv.nsf/ AusgabeNews?OpenForm.

'type of accreditation – blanket/individual'[24] and 'the methodology of the assessment tools or instruments used'. This led to a state-of-the-art report published as an online book.[25] In the second stage of the project (2008–09), selected case studies were examined in depth and piloting activities undertaken to study the level, workload and equivalence of learning outcomes. This culminated in a second online book, with chapters presenting empirical evidence regarding the efficacy of the selected cases-procedures. Thereafter, implications and ideas for the further development and cross-sector and cross-national transfer are discussed. The project concluded on a sober note, referring to the fact that the issue of 'equivalence' remains unresolved: 'despite a great variety of strategies all countries lack a developed and established concept in one particular field, namely, the equivalence assessment of learning outcomes from vocational and higher education programmes' (Tutschner *et al.*, 2009, p. 128).

OBSERVAL 2007–09[26]

Led by the European University Continuing Education Network (EUCEN), with partner teams in 24 EU countries representing higher education, VET and adult education, OBSERVAL is a planned response to expressed concerns regarding the lack of availability of information on Validation. Through a process of collaboration and information sharing, a database has been created to inform and support decision makers, social partners, human resource managers, and those in charge of Validation. Regularly updated and internet accessible, it houses documents and 'grey' literature which may be hard to find outside of the country of production. It is also a place to house particularly relevant and important Lifelong Learning Project outputs. The sourcing, selecting, preparation and uploading of information are managed by a steering group of experts. This online platform was launched in October 2010. Four categories of data are available:

---

[24] Individual recognition operates on a case-by-case basis; blanket recognition refers to comparison of education and training programmes (i.e. more like credit-rating).

[25] See http://lspace6.via-on-line.de/Oldenburg/cv.nsf/Alles/B631A3A8BAC081 E0C1257602003F4D50/$file/00010612.pdf.

[26] See http://observal.org/observal/homepage.

1. Formal documents: official texts from partner countries, tools used by institutions implementing Validation (standards, dossiers, portfolios, grids of interviews), statistics, reports on results. These documents are presented in the originating language with a brief comment in English explaining content and key points.

2. National reports: including debates and discussions, updates on the articulation of Validation with other European initiatives (the EQF, the introduction of credit systems, learning outcomes, individual pathways, the 2008–10 Action Plan on adult education, and so on).

3. Case studies: presenting interesting or innovatory initiatives and experiments, including difficulties experienced. Cases will include videos, reports of interviews with members of juries, portraits of candidates, and so on.

4. Reviews of publications: an annual annotated bibliographical review of reports, books and articles.

Putting Informal Learning into Practice 2008-10[27]

This project is oriented to informal learning in workplaces. It began as a collaboration between Dutch organisations, including Philips Electronics Nederland (development, production and marketing); Kenniscentrum EVC (a knowledge centre for the Accreditation of Prior Learning); Liftgroup (a knowledge centre for the textile, carpet, fashion and retail industry); and Hogeschool Arnhem en Nijmegen. The focus of the collaboration is to share information on informal learning in order to bridge the gap between theory and the factory floor.

The Putting Informal Learning into Practice project extended collaboration to partner with organisations in the United Kingdom, Belgium, Greece and Lithuania – universities, knowledge centres, small- and medium-sized companies – and multinational companies – in order to:

1. Gather existing theoretical knowledge about informal learning.

2. Identify existing knowledge and experience of informal learning in various European countries.

3. Adapt theoretical knowledge and practical experience to the Dutch situation.

4. Transform this knowledge and experience into practical tools to promote, facilitate and validate informal learning in organisations, with

---

[27] See http://www.adam-europe.eu/adam/project/view.htm?prj=5012.

particular attention to lower-skilled workers in production environments in manufacturing, health and social work, the wholesale and retail trades, and motor vehicle and motorcycle repair.

As the above four cameos of Lifelong Learning Projects show, these generously funded research and development projects are overwhelmingly practical and implementation-oriented. Working within a framework of largely uncritical acceptance of VNFIL, they usually benefit from high-level collaborative partnerships between sectors and countries. Often beginning with scoping exercises or surveys, and continuing through piloting and testing, they aim to produce useable resources for the field.

Doctoral research

Validation and motivation to study further (Gomez)
Research is under way in relation to the Portuguese National System for Recognising, Validating and Certifying Competencies (RVCC). Created for adults in 2001, this is an ambitious system to certify experiential learning. The main driver was the large number of adults who were competent in their jobs, but who lacked formal school-leaving certification. According to the National Institute of Statistics, in 2000 more than three million labour-market-active adults had not completed nine years of basic schooling.[28] The RVCC process has targeted some of the most deprived communities in Portugal. The main assessment framework is a set of national key competencies at a range of levels, divided into four areas: language and communication; mathematics for life; citizenship and employability; and information and communication technologies. Adults who wish to have their competence certified can register in centres that have been established for this purpose. With the help of facilitators, people are able to demonstrate that they have the competencies stated in the framework. This can lead to full certification (up to academic grade 12 or vocational level III).

Research in the Faculty of Psychology and Education at the University of Porto explores the effects of programmes of recognition, validation and certification of prior learning on adults with low levels of formal qualifications (Gomez *et al.*, 2008). Both qualitative and quantitative methodologies

---

[28] See http://www.guni-rmies.net/observatory/bp.php?id=109.

are used to capture and attempt to isolate the relationship between adult education and training, and 'psychological empowerment'. Although this doctoral work (by Isabel Gomez) is still in progress, early conference presentations suggest a correlation in that there is a 'consistent pattern of positive opinions across time' and 'increasing motivation for further participation in education and training'. This leads Gomez *et al.* (*ibid.*, p. 6) to propose that Validation programmes 'might in fact be contributing to the engagement of these low-qualified adults in the lifelong learning paradigm'.

Validating the competencies of high-skilled immigrants (Scholten)
Scholten (2007) researched the identification, assessment and recognition of the competencies of high-skilled immigrants in Holland. A series of five pilot projects were undertaken in the early 2000s as part of a Nuffic project on international credit evaluation (Nuffic is the Netherlands Organization for International Cooperation in Higher Education and Research). International credit evaluation had traditionally been undertaken in relation to formal qualifications only. The pilot projects aimed to extend this approach by taking into account the non-formal and informal learning of the professionals concerned (teachers, medical doctors and refugees from a range of professional backgrounds). Portfolios were the preferred means 'to make the prior learning of highly skilled immigrants visible' to 'recognition bodies (higher education institutions, ministries and employers)' (*ibid.*, p. 315).

Scholten's doctoral study reflects on the five pilot projects using a 'reconstructive multiple case study' aiming to 'derive more general design principles' (p. 318) from the earlier work. A series of theoretical building blocks were developed drawing on analyses of the literature, and theories of competence, portfolio development processes and assessment. A complex set of typologies emerged which Scholten used to revisit the empirical data from the pilot projects. For example, distinctions are made between competency-based learning and content-based learning; between 'conservation' and 'extension' orientations to knowledge; between four different types of portfolio (dossier, reflective, personal development, training), and their respective functions, impact, structure and content, standards and evidence; the formative and/or summative nature of the assessment, and so on. Complex mappings were undertaken of the intentions of and interactions within each pilot.

Some interesting findings emerged. For example, the teachers' pilot took place in a competency-based environment with trained portfolio assessors. The process involved a formative process which would identify competencies that would be assessed further using other methods. A few problems were identified, one of which was that the candidates–teachers were unfamiliar with 'the assessment culture and the cognitive processes that play an important role in portfolio development' (*ibid.*, p. 321). They therefore needed a longer orientation period with advisor support.

The medical doctors came from a 'problem-based learning' training background with elements of competency-based and content-based learning. The pilot was oriented towards the 'dossier-information' type of portfolio in order to provide insight into prior learning. This worked well, except for the need for assessors and advisers to be well-versed in their roles, for the candidates to understand the cyclical nature of portfolio development, and for there to be more guidance pertaining to the format and structure of the final portfolio. The pilot with refugees from varying professional backgrounds took a 'development-oriented' approach which also worked well. However, the same issue emerged; that is, the importance of training in portfolio development for candidates, irrespective of their level of prior learning. Without such training and adviser support, portfolios exhibited a tendency to be descriptive.

The Assessment of Prior Learning (APL) in distance education computer science and educational science programmes at undergraduate level (Joosten-ten Brinke)[29]

Joosten-ten Brinke (2008) researched five questions for her doctoral thesis at the Open University of the Netherlands:

1. How are APL characteristics elaborated in the literature, and what relationships exist between APL and quality frameworks?
2. Is self-assessment – a key component of portfolios – a suitable tool to support candidates in gathering evidence for university APL?

---

[29] Joosten-ten Brinke is an assessment specialist. Several articles have been published from this thesis. See, for example, Joosten-ten Brinke *et al.* (2009) and Joosten-ten Brinke *et al.* (2010).

3. How do APL candidates, assessors and tutors perceive the quality of APL instruments?
4. What are the assessors' approaches to portfolio assessment?
5. What forms of support in APL have the highest value and efficiency?

The study, involving mixed method empirical research, found that self-assessment *was* a suitable method for APL, although candidates lacked confidence in the university level of their prior learning; APL was viewed positively in both computer science and educational science, but significantly so by the tutors, assessors and candidates in educational science (one possible explanation advanced for this was 'the familiarity with APL and portfolio development that is inherent in Educational Science' [*ibid.*, p. 104]); the two domains valued different skills and knowledge in APL tutors (in computer science 'domain knowledge' was most highly valued, whereas in educational science 'judgement and evaluation skills' were deemed to be most important); all assessors viewed the portfolio approach as 'relevant, fair and useful' (*ibid.*, p. 105), although they interpreted the approach and the general assessment criteria differently in the two domains. The overall finding was that 'support is most needed in the … evidence-gathering phase' and that that support needs to be domain-specific.

The thesis makes far-reaching recommendations for APL procedures at the information and evidence-gathering stages, and a range of recommendations for future research (commenting: 'The literature on APL is mainly descriptive and as yet has hardly any scientific basis' [*ibid.*, p. 110]). The proposed research agenda consists of:

*   More experimental research designs, so that more objective and conclusive comparisons can be made between different APL procedures.
*   Experimental research, where assessors using different approaches to assessment assess the same portfolios.
*   Longitudinal research into the long-term effects of APL: 'Do learners admitted to educational programmes in the traditional way … differ in their knowledge, skills and competencies after certification from learners admitted by way of APL?' (*ibid.*, pp. 110–11).[30]

---

[30] Compare with Cantwell and Scevak's (2004) research in Australia, which found that 'while students had developed a positive learning profile, a continued belief in the structural simplicity of knowledge appeared to have a significant diminishing effect on the quality of adjustment and on the quality of learning outcomes' (Abstract). See also Travers in this volume.

- The impact of APL in the workplace; specifically on 'learner development in the professional context' (*ibid.*, p. 111).
- Research into ICT support for APL candidates such as interactive learning environments, semantically enhanced content and social software (e.g. wikis, weblogs, ePortfolios, social bookmarks, and social networks like YouTube, Facebook and Flickr). Could these techniques 'stimulate and support individuals in recognising their competencies' (*ibid.*, p. 111)?

Academic research re: policy and practice, including critique

As a relative outsider to the EU debates and developments regarding Validation. I have been awed by the sheer volume of information and studies that are available, and the very real progress that is being made to develop systems that are resource-efficient, quality-assured and flexible. However, my searches have revealed very little critical academic research into policy and practices (except for the work in Sweden, Scotland and England that is reported on in other chapters in this volume).[31] Perhaps this is because of the nature of the funding for research and development.

Pires (2007) interrogates Validation from a theoretical perspective informed by 'learning approaches and adult education', and surface tensions, contradictions and lack of research evidence. Questions of the validity and reliability of VNFIL judgements have been raised since 1998 (Bjørnåvold, 1998; Andersson and Fejes, in this volume). As discussed above, some doctoral work is also raising critical questions in this regard. In a recently published article, Peters *et al.* (2010) draw critical attention to the same issues in terms of 'identity, methodology, and strategic and socio-political matters'. On a slightly tangential but nonetheless relevant note, Straka (2004) undertook a comprehensive conceptual mapping of the literature on informal learning, focusing on the individual and his/her socio-culturally shaped environment. The conclusion drawn was that informal learning is a 'metaphor with a severe problem, namely the lack of systematically and empirically grounded valid evidence on why, when, how and what is learned under "informal conditions"'.

---

[31] There may be some work in French that I have missed.

An edited collection of papers on Validation (Bélisle and Boutinet, 2009) draws attention to some of the theoretical work that has been undertaken by French-speaking university academics. In that collection, Prot (2009) deploys Vygotskian concepts of 'everyday' and 'scientific' knowledge to unpack Validation processes. Schurmans (2009) suggests that Validation oriented to formal qualifications enjoys more social value and status than formative processes and/or practices that are not so directly qualification-related. Drawing on empirical work, Presse (2009) argues that Validation in France, despite their innovative departures from practices elsewhere, tends to reproduce rather than challenge existing social inequalities in education and training systems. These chapters are interesting in that they show how a growing range of philosophical and social theories can be brought to bear on this applied field.[32]

In contrast, there is a wider range of theoretically and conceptually driven engagement with the discourses of lifelong learning; that is, the discourses that drive Validation, usually premised on the need for economic competitiveness in a knowledge economy to be achieved through better management of human resources. Ideas and arguments in this vein are developed using mainly Foucauldian concepts and discourse analysis.[33] For example, in a large-scale Economic and Social Research Council (ESRC)-funded project, Grek (2010) argues that 'Europeanisation' is a 'conduit' of globalisation whereby national governments have 'seemingly ceded some of their autonomy in education policy development to international organisations'. In this way, notions such as 'skills' and 'competencies' have been 'normalised' along with the 'construction of [associated] policy problems'. Other writers draw attention to the 'totalisation' of learning that lifelong learning implies, wherein *all* learning becomes subject to public scrutiny in the name of 'inclusivity'. This, it is argued, means that 'governmentality' is inscribed into practices such as Validation: learners are encouraged to become individualistic, self-regulating and entrepreneurial individuals – essentially compliant and self-governing through processes that feel empowering (Tuschling and Engemann, 2006). Moving outwards are theoretically informed critiques of policy borrowing and lending (e.g. Chakroun, 2010), and cautionary tales about learning outcomes, national qualifications frameworks and the EQF (Young, 2008; Allais *et al.*, 2009).

---

[32] I am indebted to Dr Patrick Werquin for translating the French for me.

[33] See Andersson and Fejes in this volume, where this work is covered in detail, so not revisited here.

General discussion about the nature of the VNFIL research in the EU

The European Commission is driving forward a strong policy focus on VNFIL in the context of a skills agenda and a yoking of education to human capital development. Under these conditions, the time is right for Validation. It sits comfortably as part of the development of (economic understandings of) lifelong learning, credit systems, the EQF and the development of learning outcomes. Even so, there does not seem to be an agreed definition across Europe. Terminology varies and this has led to some difficulties in gauging the extent of practice, although research accounts suggest that patterns of take-up are 'strongly differentiated' and generally low (Bjørnåvold, 2007; Adams, 2008; Werquin, 2010) despite literally thousands of well-resourced research and development projects. Moreover, terminological slippage all too often disguises the range of social projects that are in fact being advanced through the Validation agenda (most particularly, potential conflict between practices driven by economic imperatives, and those driven by widening participation and social inclusion principles). Basically, progress is being made, but slowly, and more in relation to policy than practice.[34]

The research picture is somewhat polarised between a wealth of policy-related inventories, projects and comparative studies on the one hand, and a small amount of doctoral work on the other. The policy-related research has produced comprehensive mapping of the states of play in different countries and across the EU; lots of development- and implementation-led projects have tested Validation approaches, methods and instruments, and there has been some elaboration of what quality and quality assurance might mean in relation to them. Doctoral research has begun to theorise VNFIL in more exacting ways, and suggests that cognisance be taken of profession and programme specificities.

In the main, however, little attention has been given to scholarly research. Indeed, there is scant scholarly evidence, apart from the outcomes of development projects, to support particular approaches to Validation. There are not many research-based articles in peer-reviewed journals (although more in the field of assessment than in other fields). Rigorous critical engagement with policy and aspects of practice is

---

[34] The adoption of the term 'validation' is itself worthy of deconstruction and analysis. Is it more instrumental than the term 'recognition', for example?

conspicuous by its absence. Inquiry could be undertaken into the role of lifelong learning and Validation in relation to the loss of jobs and increased longevity. Research into the relationship between language and Validation also seems to be lacking, especially in multilingual contexts. Learning outcomes, although gaining in popularity, remain problematic in some quarters – is the yoking of non-formal and informal learning to learning outcomes the only way to go?[35] It may be that the very concept of Validation is still requiring of theorisation. The research field is therefore wide open, with ample opportunities to build upon the practical, systems-building work and information gathering that has been privileged to date, and to deploy different methodologies and theoretical insights to illuminate particular aspects of policy and practice.

The most recent OECD study (Werquin, 2010, pp. 84–5) made some pointed recommendations in this regard highlighting the need for cost-benefit analyses; evaluations of interventions based on clearly identified objectives; the need for longitudinal, quantitative data from which to develop criteria and conditions of success to enhance the predictive validity of Validation; and research to identify groups of people with 'existing human capital reserves' – that is, groups of the population or individuals who are highly skilled but unqualified (without certification).

A range of other research opportunities also emerge from the ground covered in this chapter. Generally speaking, the field would benefit from more experimental research, carefully constructed to measure specific aspects of Validation. Echoing the point made earlier, there is a real need to establish longitudinal studies so that the impact of Validation in

---

[35] See the following quote from the otherwise supportive CEDEFOP report (2009b) *The Shift to Learning Outcomes*:

> *However, more and more stakeholders warn that the learning outcomes perspective can easily be reduced to mere rhetoric having little effect on education, training and learning practices. Some go even further stating that uncritical use of the learning outcomes perspective may prove harmful and represent a distraction. A key question asked in the study is whether increased attention to learning outcomes will make any difference at local level and to individual learners? While the learning outcomes perspective is a visible part of the overarching education and training objectives, it is not always clear how this perspective influences definition of standards and curricula, teaching and assessment practices and – eventually – individual learning conditions.*

http://www.cedefop.europa.eu/etv/Upload/Information_resources/Bookshop/494/4079_en.pdf.

relation to individuals, institutions and workplace can be measured; for example, how many people have participated, what qualifications/credits they have achieved, how they have fared over time etc. Case studies of where Validation works particularly well could be analysed in terms of the conditions of their success, and lessons learned for future activity. Evidence to date suggests that different professions and programmes are inscribed with particular predispositions and cultural practices, which suggest some approaches to Validation will work better than others. This could be further explored. Overall, there is a need for more theorising, especially in relation to some of the ambiguities that surround Validation and that remain glossed over by policy discourse. For example, the fact that the question of 'equivalence' has not been fully addressed seems to suggest that Validation practices straddle complexities that may not actually cohere readily and that are still not well understood.[36]

To return to Werquin's (2010) 'islands of good practice' and the need for them to be conjoined; he argues that VNFIL is a strong option under certain sets of labour market and educational policy conditions. As an example, he suggests that 'a context characterised by [economic] stability if not affluence is highly conducive to recognition' and that this may remain the case even in a recessionary climate. It may also be the case that Validation works better at different levels of the skill and education chain, perhaps at the lower and higher ends? What is clear is that it works 'for some people under some circumstances', and it is those social and economic conditions that we need to research as fully as possible to match practice outcomes with policy aspirations.

References

Adam, S. (2008) 'Why is the Recognition of Prior Experiential Learning important and what are the national and institutional implications of this for lifelong learning?', *New Challenges in Recognition: Council of Europe Higher Education Series.* No 10, pp. 27–48.

Allais, S., Young, M. and Raffe, D. (2009) (eds) *Learning from the First Qualifications Frameworks.* ILO Working Paper Employment Series. Geneva: ILO.

---

[36] See, for example, Breier in this volume, who outlines how the knowledge question has been so much a part of RPL debates in South Africa.

Bélisle, R. and Boutinet, J-P. (eds) (2009) *Demandes de Reconnaissance et Validation d'Acquis de l'Expérience*. Quebec: Les Presses de l'Université Laval.

Bjørnåvold, J. (1998) *Validation and Recognition of Non-formal Learning: The questions of validity, reliability and legitimacy*. Vocational Research and Training: The European Research Field. Background Report, Vol. 2, pp. 215–33.

Bjørnåvold, J. (2007) *Validation of Non-formal and Informal Learning in Europe: A Snapshot*. Thessaloniki: CEDEFOP.

Bologna (1999) *The European Higher Education Area: Joint Declaration of the European Ministers of Education Convened in Bologna*, 19 June 1999. Available at: http://www.ntb.ch/SEFI/bolognadec.html.

Bologna (2001) *Towards the European Higher Education Area: The Prague Communiqué*. Available at: http://www.bologna-berlin2003.de/pdf/Prague_communiquTheta.pdf.

Bologna (2002) *The Copenhagen Declaration on Enhanced European Cooperation in Vocational Education and Training*, 29–30 November. Available at: http://ec.europa.eu/education/lifelong-learning-policy/doc/policy/copenhagen_en.pdf.

Bologna (2003) *Realising the European Higher Education Area: The Berlin Communiqué*. Available at: http://www.bologna-bergen2005.no/Docs/00-Main_doc/030919Berlin_Communique.PDF.

Bologna (2005) *The European Higher Education Area: Achieving the goals: The Bergen Communiqué*. Available at: http://www.bologna-bergen 2005.no/Docs/00-Main_doc/050520_Bergen_Communiqu.pdf.

Bologna (2007) *Towards the European Higher Education Area: Responding to Challenges in a Globalised World: The London Communiqué*. Available at: http://www.cepes.ro/services/inf_sources/on_line/2007LondonCo mmunique.en.pdf.

Bologna (2009) *The Bologna Process 2020: The European Higher Education Area in the New Decade: The Leuven and Louvain-la-Neuve Communiqué*. Available at: http://www.ond.vlaanderen.be/hogeronderwijs/bologna/conference/documents/leuven_louvain-la-neuve_communiqu%C3%A9_april_2009.pdf.

Cantwell, R. and Scevak, J. (2004) 'Engaging university learning: The experiences of students entering university via recognition of prior industrial experience', *Higher Education Research and Development*, Vol. 23, No 2, pp. 131–45.

CEDEFOP (2007) *Recognition and Validation of Non-formal and Informal Learning for VET teachers and trainers in the EU Member States.* Cedefop Panorama series; 147. Luxembourg: Office for Official Publications of the European Communities.

CEDEFOP (2008) *Validation of Non-formal and Informal Learning in Europe: A Snapshot 2007.* Luxembourg: Office for Official Publications of the European Communities.

CEDEFOP (2009a) *European Guidelines for Validating Non-formal and Informal Learning.* Luxembourg: Office for Official Publications of the European Communities.

CEDEFOP (2009b) *The Shift to Learning Outcomes: Policies and Practices in Europe.* Luxembourg: Office for Official Publications of the European Communities.

Chakroun, B. (2010) 'National Qualifications Frameworks: From policy borrowing to policy learning', *European Journal of Education.* Special Issue: Human and social capital development for innovation and change, Vol. 45, No 2, pp. 199–216.

Colardyn, D. and Bjørnåvold, J. (2004) 'Validation of formal, non-formal and informal learning, Policy and practices in EU member states', *European Journal of Education.* Vol. 39, No 1, pp. 69–89.

Colardyn, D. and Bjørnåvold, J. (2005) *The Learning Continuity: European Inventory on Validating Non-formal and Informal Learning, National Policies and Practices in Validating Non-formal and Informal Learning.* CEDEFOP Panorama series; 117. Luxembourg: Office for Official Publications of the European Communities. Available at: http://www.cedefop. europa.eu/EN/Files5164_en.pdf.

Corradi, C., Evans, N. and Valk, A. (2006) *Recognising Experiential Learning: Practices in European Universities.* Tartu: Tartu University Press.

Council of the European Union (2004) *Common European Principles for the Identification and Validation of Informal and Non-formal Learning.* Brussels: European Commission. Available at: http://www.ecotec.com/ europeaninventory/principles.html.

European Commission (1995) *Teaching and Learning: Towards the Learning Society.* European White Paper. Brussels: Commission of the European Communities.

European Commission (2001) *Making a European Area of Lifelong Learning a Reality.* Communication from the Commission. Brussels: Commission of the European Communities. Available at: http:// www.bologna-berlin2003.de/pdf/MitteilungEng.pdf.

European Commission (2002) *The Copenhagen Declaration on Enhanced European Cooperation in Vocational Education and Training*. Available at: http://ec.europa.eu/education/lifelong-learning-policy/doc/policy/copenhagen_en.pdf.

European Commission (2006) *The Helsinki Communiqué on Enhanced European Cooperation in Vocational Education and Training*. Brussels: Commission of the European Communities.

Evans, N. (2000) *Experiential Learning Around the World: Employability and the Global Economy*. London: Jessica Kingsley.

Gallacher, J. and Feurie, M. (2003) 'Recognising and accrediting informal and non-formal learning in higher education: An analysis of the issues emerging from a study of France and Scotland', *European Journal of Education*, Vol. 38, No 1, pp. 71–83.

Gomez, I., Coimbra, J. and Menezes, I. (2008) 'Recognition, validation and certification of competences: the low-qualified and the learning paradigm in Portugal'. Paper presented at the 38th Annual SCUTREA Conference, University of Edinburgh, 2–4 July.

Grek, S. (2010) 'International organisations and the shared construction of policy "problems": Problematisation and change in education governance in Europe', *European Educational Research Journal*, Vol. 9, No 3, pp. 396–406.

Joosten-ten Brinke, D. (2008) 'Assessment of Prior Learning'. PhD thesis, Open University of the Netherlands.

Joosten-ten Brinke, D., Sluijsmans, D. and Jochems, W. (2009) 'Quality of Assessment of Prior Learning (APL) in university programmes: Perceptions of candidates, tutors and assessors', *Studies in Continuing Education*, Vol. 1, No 1, pp. 61–76.

Joosten-ten Brinke, D., Sluijsmans, D. and Jochems, W. (2010) 'Assessors' approaches to portfolio assessment in Assessment of Prior Learning procedures', *Assessment and Evaluation in Higher Education*, Vol. 35, No 1, pp. 55–70.

Otero, M., McCoshan, A. and Junge, K. (2005) (eds) *European Inventory on Validation of Non-formal and Informal Learning*. Final Report to DG Education and Culture of the European Commission. Birmingham: ECOTEC Research and Consulting Limited. Available at: http://www.ecotec.com/europeaninventory/publications/inventory/european_inventory_2005_final_report.pdf.

Otero, M., Hawley, J. and Nevala, A-M. (2008) (eds) *European Inventory on Validation of Informal and Non-formal Learning: 2007 Update*. Final

Report to DG Education and Culture of the European Commission. Birmingham: ECOTEC Research and Consulting Limited. Available at: http://www.ecotec.com/europeaninventory/publications/inventory/EuropeanInventory.pdf.

Peters, S., Mahieu, C., Salmon, A., Danse, C. and de Viron, F. (2010) 'Recognition and Validation of Non-formal and Informal Learning in French-speaking Belgium: Discourses and practices', *Lifelong Learning in Europe*, Vol. 15, No 2, pp. 119–28.

Pires, A-L. (2007) 'Recognition and Validation of Experiential Learning: An education problem', *Educational Sciences Journal*, No 2, pp. 5–19.

Pouget, M. and Osborne, M. 'Accreditation or *Validation* of prior experiential learning: Knowledge and *savoirs* in France – a different perspective?', *Studies in Continuing Education*, Vol. 26, No 1, pp. 45–66.

Presse, M-C. (2009) 'La validation des acquis de l'expérience en France: entre promotion et reproduction sociales', in R. Bélisle and J-P. Boutinet (eds) *Demandes de Reconnaissance et Validation d'Acquis de l'Expérience*. Quebec: Les Presses de l'Université Laval, pp. 133–40.

Prot, B. (2009) 'La double vie en collectif dans les acquis individuels', in R. Bélisle and J-P. Boutinet (eds) *Demandes de Reconnaissance et Validation d'Acquis de l'Expérience*. Quebec: Les Presses de l'Université Laval, pp. 15–37.

Scholten, A. (2007) 'Exploration of portfolio characteristics for the Recognition of Prior Learning: The identification, assessment and recognition of actual competencies of highly skilled immigrants'. PhD Thesis, University of Twente.

Schurmans, M-N. (2009) 'La construction sociale des jugements d'excellence et son rapport avec la validation des acquis', in R. Bélisle and J-P. Boutinet (eds) *Demandes de Reconnaissance et Validation d'Acquis de l'Expérience*. Quebec: Les Presses de l'Université Laval, pp. 161–84.

Singh, M. (2009) 'Recognition, validation and accreditation of non-formal and informal learning and experience: Results of an international study', in *International Handbook of Education for the Changing World of Work*. Part VIII, Section 15. Paris: UNESCO, pp. 2597–613.

Straka, G. (2004) Informal Learning: Genealogy, concepts, antagonisms and questions. University of Bremen.

Tuschling, A. and Engemann, C. (2006) 'From education to lifelong learning: The emerging regime of learning in the European Union', *Educational Philosophy and Theory*, Vol. 8, No 4, pp. 451–69.

Tutschner, R., Wittig, W. and Rami, J. (2009) (eds) *Accreditation of Vocational Learning Outcomes: Perspectives for a European Transfer*. Bremen: Institut Technik und Bildung and Universitat Bremen. Available at: http://lspace6.via-on-line.de/oldenburg/cv.nsf.

Valk, A. (2009) 'Recognition of prior experiential learning in European universities', *Assessment in Education: Principles, Policy and Practice*, Vol. 16, No 1, pp. 83–95.

Werquin, P. (2010) *Recognition of Non-formal and Informal Learning: Country Practices*. Paris: OECD. Available at: http://www.oecd.org/document/29/0,3343,en_2649_39263294_44870941_1_1_1_1,00.html.

Young, M. (2008) *Bringing Knowledge Back In: From Social Constructivism to Social Realism in the Sociology of Knowledge*. London: Routledge.

CHAPTER SEVEN

Organisation for Economic Co-operation and Development (OECD): Research reveals 'islands of good practice'

Patrick Werquin and Christine Wihak

Abstract

This chapter is a brief overview and discussion of the work of the Organisation for Economic Co-operation and Development (OECD) in relation to the Recognition of Non-formal and Informal Learning (RNFIL). Studies of the state of play regarding RNFIL in OECD countries are conducted periodically. They provide a vast amount of information and data on RNFIL policy, practices and procedures around the world.

While the official OECD final reports focus on the analysis of policy options, this brief discussion paper highlights some of the ways the data could be examined to yield broader insights. At this time, the OECD studies remain a very rich and still largely un-mined source of information for further research on RNFIL policy and implementation.

Introduction

This chapter is a brief overview and discussion of the Organisation for Economic Co-operation and Development (OECD) work in relation to the Recognition of Non-formal and Informal Learning (RNFIL). The OECD was founded in 1961 to assist member countries to achieve economic prosperity and stability. Through a continual monitoring process, the OECD collects and analyses economically relevant information that is used to support policy discussions and decisions among the members. At present, 34 countries across six continents comprise the membership, each sharing a democratic form of government and a strong commitment to the market economy. Because over two-thirds of the OECD countries are European, the OECD also collaborates closely with the European Commission. Readers are advised to consult the OECD website and the chapter *European Union: Research and system building in the Validation of Non-formal and Informal Learning (VNFIL)* in this volume for further details.

Education is an area of concern for the OECD, with specific interests and focuses on higher education and adult learning; education, economy and society; human capital; and research and knowledge management. Given these interests, it is imperative that the OECD has a substantial knowledge base concerning RNFIL, which is seen as intimately linked to the promotion of policies on lifelong learning. Consequently, the OECD conducted studies of RNFIL policy and practice in 22 countries.[1] Commencing in 2006, the research was designed to answer the following questions about RNFIL activity in each country:

- What is it?
- How do you measure it?
- How do you assess it?
- Who does it?
- Does it work?
- What does it give to people?
- Is it accepted?

The research method for their investigations involved documentary review and field research. Participating countries first prepared a *Country Report* summarising existing data and policy documents using a common reporting mechanism. These reports provided background on relevant contextual factors (e.g. demographics, internationalisation, technology, social change, economic activity, labour force issues). They also described

---

[1] Participating countries are South Africa, Germany, Australia, Austria, Belgium (Flemish Community), Canada, Chile, Korea, Denmark, Spain, Greece, Hungary, Iceland, Ireland, Italy, Mexico, Norway, the Netherlands, the Czech Republic, the United Kingdom, Slovenia and Switzerland.

the role of government (national and/or state) in RNFIL, political and legal considerations, and institutional organisation for RNFIL delivery. Technical issues, such as qualifications, credit arrangements and assessment practices, were highlighted. Consideration of stakeholder behaviour, combined with in-depth case studies, concluded each report.[2]

After the country reports were completed, the OECD research team visited a selection of the participating countries to probe the reported information. Through discussions and the collection of additional information, these 'Thematic Review' visits advanced 'understanding of stakeholder behaviour, to investigate what is working and not working with current practice, and to capture innovative case studies and unintended policy outcomes' (OECD, 2010).

The most recent OECD report (Werquin, 2010a) analyses and summarises information drawn from the Country Reports and Thematic Review visits. The report offers a series of policy recommendations concerning RNFIL implementation. In addition, the OECD published a shorter report highlighting best practices (Werquin, 2010b).[3]

Overview of the implementation of the Recognition of Non-formal and Informal Learning (RNFIL)

At the inaugural meeting of the Prior Learning International Research Centre (PLIRC), Werquin (2009) provided an overview of the implementation of RNFIL within the 22 participating countries, drawing on data from the OECD study. His summary highlighted key comparisons amongst the countries in a format not presented in the published OECD reports (Werquin, 2010a, 2010b), using a classification scheme for categorising countries in terms of the status of RNFIL development. Looking at the OECD results this way, it becomes apparent that every country in the study has made at least some initial efforts at implementation. On the other hand, no country has a fully developed system. The different categories and associated descriptions that Werquin used to classify countries

---

[2] Country Reports are available from: http://www.oecd.org/document/63/0,3343,en_2649_39263238_37141759_1_1_1_1,00.html.

[3] The full report is available from: http://www.oecd.org/document/29/0,3343,en_2649_39263294_44870941_1_1_1_1,00.html. The report *Recognition of Non-formal and Informal Learning: Country Practices* is available from: http://www.oecd.org/document/25/0,3343,en_2649_39263238_37136921_1_1_1_1,00.html.

are shown in Table 7.1, while Table 7.2 shows how the countries were ranked according to this classification scheme.

Table 7.1 Models and their characteristics

Model	Characteristics
System	Inclusive policy, a vision, a *culture* of RNFIL and a global system. In detail: legal framework or political consensus, practice, all groups or individuals, financial provision, quality assurance, all levels and sectors of education and training, significant participation, high level of acceptance by the society, evaluation of the system (data, research…).
Quasi-system	Inclusive policy, a vision and a global system. In detail: legal framework or political consensus, practice, all groups or individuals, financial provision, quality assurance, all levels and sectors of education and training.
Consistent set of practices	Vision. In detail: many practices, access for most individual profiles, some financing available, not all levels or educational sectors.
Fragmented set of practices	Clear objectives. In detail: practices, target groups, some financing, few levels or educational sectors.
Some practices	Some convincing attempts in very specific fields, sectors or institutions.
Initial stage	Some interest in the RNFIL concept. Some attempts in very narrow fields, sectors or institutions on a small scale. Some rhetoric in the context of lifelong learning. Some broad documents. A lot of inertia.
Nothing	No practice, no policy orientation documents, no rhetoric, no interest whatsoever in the concept of RNFIL.

Table 7.2 Models, status and country

RNFIL status	Country
System	
Quasi-system	Ireland, Netherlands, Denmark, Norway
Consistent set of practices	Australia, Canada, South Africa, UK, Belgium (Flanders)
Fragmented set of practices	Germany, Spain, Italy, Korea, Mexico, Iceland, Switzerland
Some practices	Austria, Chile, Slovenia
Initial stage	Hungary, Greece, Czech Republic
Nothing	

This classification raises interesting directions for future research. For example, could the classification scheme be improved or critiqued? How could it be usefully applied to RNFIL developments in countries *not* included in the OECD study? Most importantly, can different levels of RNFIL development be systematically linked to socio-economic factors within a country?

Werquin's presentation (2009) also singled out specific aspects of RNFIL implementation as a basis for cross-country comparison. One very important consideration for RNFIL is whether full credentials can be obtained through this mechanism alone, or whether RNFIL needs to be combined with some kind of formal education or formal vocational training. Table 7.3 summarises how the different countries fare on this dimension. At this point, only Ireland offers the possibility, whilst it is absolutely not possible in ten of the countries.

The OECD study (Werquin, 2010a) also found that countries were highly variable in terms of the use of RNFIL in relation to the formal education system. Table 7.4 identifies exemplar countries in terms of different RNFIL practices within the formal education system.[4]

Similarly, countries differed markedly in the relationship between RNFIL and workforce development and vocational training (see Table 7.5)

Further research could be conducted to look at how countries outside the OECD study are faring on these types of specific factors. And, again, the relationship between the presence or absence of specific RNFIL applications and socio-economic context needs further exploration.

Table 7.3 Whole qualifications via RNFIL?

For all qualifications	In some instances	Not possible
Ireland	South Africa, Australia, Austria, Belgium (Flanders), Canada (British Columbia, Québec, Ontario, Saskatchewan), Denmark, Italy (Emilia Romagna), Mexico, Norway, Netherlands, UK (Scotland and England), Slovenia, Switzerland	Germany, Canada (other provinces and territories), Korea, Chile, Spain, Greece, Hungary, Iceland, Italy (Val d'Aosta, Macerata), Czech Republic

[4] Tables 4 and 5 were prepared by John West in 2008, for the 4th OECD Expert Meeting in Mexico.

Table 7.4 RNFIL and formal education

Type of application	Exemplar countries	Typical examples
Second-chance school certificate	Canada, Mexico, Norway, Chile, Spain	General Education Development (GED), *Bachillerato*, adult education referenced to school system
Entry to higher education	South Africa, UK, Belgium (Flanders), Mexico	Universities working together (CENEVAL[5]), access to higher education courses
Exemptions from formal programmes	Hungary, Chile, UK, Belgium (Flanders)	Modular higher education programmes with exemptions available, specific credits. University discretion over exemptions

Table 7.5 RNFIL, workforce development and vocational education and training

Type of application	Exemplar countries	Typical examples
Labour competence certification	Netherlands, Germany, South Africa, Belgium (Flanders)	Exceptional procedures to allow those with established competence to gain existing formal qualification.
Vocational education and training (VET) system redesign	Spain, Mexico, Hungary, Australia, UK	Creation of RNFIL-friendly qualifications
Discrete applications	Belgium (Flanders), Hungary, Canada, Greece, Germany	European Community Driving Licence, language certificates, professional bodies

Contextual factors

To begin to understand the emergence of good practices in RNFIL, we need awareness of a number of socio-economic factors that catalyse or inhibit RNFIL development and/or activity within any given country.

---

[5] CENEVAL is the Centro Nacional de Evaluatión para la Educatión Superior (the National Centre for Assessment in Higher Education) in Mexico.

As extracted from Werquin (2010b), these factors include, *inter alia*:

- Demographic profile and changes
- Labour market factors (integration, labour mobility, labour supply, productivity, skills shortages, regulation)
- Unemployment rates (short- and long-term)
- Political systems (governance, national policies and legal frameworks, national, provincial, regional governments – division of powers)
- Immigration policy and practice
- Policies on human capital development
- Income distribution (rich–poor, rural–urban, regional disparities)
- Formal education and training systems
- National Qualifications Frameworks – presence or absence
- Collective agreements and wage restraints in the employment sector
- Development patterns in industry
- Social inclusion issues (immigrants, minorities, women etc.)

Werquin (2010b, p. 5) observes that the countries participating in the OECD study reflected a 'very mixed sample' in terms of economic context and level of economic development. This variability makes it challenging to demonstrate any systematic relationship between socio-economic factors and RNFIL. For example, development of National Qualifications Frameworks has been closely associated with RNFIL in countries as diverse as South Africa, the UK and Australia. But several countries with developed RNFIL systems, such as Canada, Korea and the United States, do not have NQFs. Because of the apparent lack of consistency, Werquin (*ibid.*, p. 12) concluded that a national qualifications framework may facilitate the recognition of non-formal and informal learning, but 'is neither a necessary nor sufficient condition for it to occur'.

Determining what strong, consistent influences stem from socio-economic context is research that remains to be done. If any generalisations are possible at this point, they would be that RNFIL tends to receive the most attention in the face of demographic decline and related skills shortages in developed countries (e.g. Australia, European Union countries, Canada), and, alternatively, in the face of the need to increase the general supply of skilled labour in countries with large, unskilled workforces (Mexico, South Africa). In addition, the attitude of the existing formal education system towards RNFIL would appear to be a critical and potentially inhibiting factor in terms of successful implementation.

Costs and benefits of RNFIL

Any analysis of how contextual factors affect RNFIL development and implementation could obviously be extended to a consideration of how these same factors affect the relative costs and benefits of RNFIL in different countries and under different circumstances. Werquin (2007) hypothesised that a model could be used to assess this question.

As Figure 7.1 shows, economies of scale are not as easy to achieve in RNFIL as in mainstream training programmes because the marginal cost of RNFIL (i.e. the additional cost of providing the service to more than one individual) declines as the system becomes more efficient, but then climbs again as individuals with skills that are more difficult to assess enter the system. The marginal cost of training, in contrast, is assumed to be high at first because training programmes/systems are expensive to implement, but to decline as more individuals participate. The model makes it clear that, depending on actual costs, RNFIL may be more efficient in some circumstances, whilst in others training may be more cost-effective. Individuals with large, easily assessable skill bases are served more cheaply through RNFIL, while those with small, difficult to assess skill bases are served more cheaply through training. The challenge for policy and implementation is to identify the point at which the marginal costs of RNFIL and training intersect.

Werquin's (2007) model has yet to be tested empirically. Possibly, data collected from the OECD study could be used to further explore the validity of the model. When Werquin presented the model to researchers attending the inaugural meeting of the Prior Learning International Research Centre (PLIRC) in 2009, interest was expressed in whether the model could account for the longer-term effects of RNFIL. For example, a recent study conducted under the auspices of the Council for Adult and Experiential Learning (CAEL) in the United States (Klein-Collins, 2010) has demonstrated that adult students who had prior learning assessed for credit both engaged in more education and had higher persistence towards credential completion than those who did not have their learning assessed. Any econometric model concerning costs and benefits of RNFIL would need to reflect such phenomena in order to provide a valid estimation.

Figure 7.1 Cost of RNFIL versus training

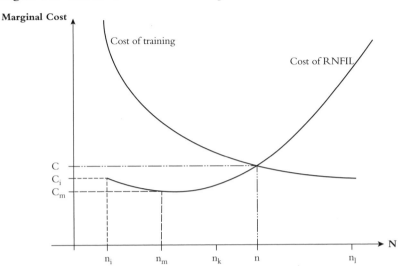

X-axis: **N**: number of individuals in training or in a recognition programme
Y-axis: **Cost** for each additional individual, going through training or through a recognition programme

Main tags on X-axis:
n_i: number of individuals when RNFIL are set in motion (initial cost)
n_m: number of individuals when cost of RNFIL is minimal (C_m, when the system is most effective)
n_k: example of a number of individuals for whom the cost of recognition is less than the cost of training
n: number of individuals where the cost of organising RNFIL is equal to the cost of sending individuals on training programmes
n_l: number of individuals where cost of RNFIL has increased dramatically because all those for whom documenting skills is easy have been through an RNFIL programme and only the difficult cases are left. At this stage, training is comparatively cheap because, if a large number of individuals are on training programmes, the marginal cost of training is low (close, but not necessarily equal to Ce)

Main tags on Y-axis:
C_i: initial marginal cost when recognition programmes are initially set in motion
C_m: minimum marginal cost for recognition of non-formal and informal learning
C: marginal cost where an additional applicant in a recognition programme costs the same as an additional trainee

This model (Werquin, 2007) could also be compared theoretically and empirically with other attempts to estimate costs and benefits of RNFIL. For example, Bloom and Grant (2001), using Canadian data based on the concept of social capital, estimated that the Canadian economy as a whole stood to gain $4.1 to $5.9 billion in annual income if prior learning was recognised. The same authors estimated that individuals stood to gain $8,000 to $12,000 per year from having their prior learning recognised. However, their estimating model was very different from Werquin's in that it did not address the costs of RNFIL, only the benefits. A comparison of the advantages and disadvantages of each approach could be very illuminating.

Summary and conclusion

The OECD study (Werquin, 2010a, 2010b) collected a vast amount of information and data on RNFIL policy, practices and procedures around the world. While the official final report focused on the analysis of policy options, this discussion paper has highlighted some of the ways the data could be examined to yield other insights. These include a system to classify RNFIL maturity in different countries, relating RNFIL development to socio-economic factors, and the emergence of models to account for the cost and benefits of RNFIL. At this time, the OECD remains a very rich and still largely un-mined source of information for further research on RNFIL policy and implementation.

References

Bloom, M. and Grant, M. (2001) *Brain Gain: The Economic Benefits of Recognizing Learning Credentials in Canada*. Ottawa: Conference Board of Canada.

Klein-Collins, R. (2010) *Fueling the Race to Post-secondary Success: A 48-institution Study of Prior Learning Assessment and Adult Student Outcomes*. Chicago: Council for Adult and Experiential Learning.

Organisation for Economic Co-operation and Development (OECD) (2010) 'Recognition of Non-Formal and Informal Learning – Methodology'. Available at: http://www.oecd.org/document/46/0,3343,en_2649_39263238_37137198_1_1_1_1,00.html (Accessed 2 December 2010).

Werquin, P. (2007) 'Moving mountains: Will qualification systems produce lifelong learning?', *European Journal of Education*, Vol. 4, No 4, pp. 459–84.

Werquin, P. (2009) *Recognition of Non-formal and Informal Learning: Emerging Issues for a Research Agenda*. Presentation to the Inaugural Meeting of the Prior Learning International Research Centre, Kamloops, BC, Canada, July.

Werquin, P. (2010a) *Recognising Non-Formal and Informal Learning: Outcomes, Policies and Practices*. Paris: OECD.

Werquin, P. (2010b) *Recognition of Non-formal and Informal Learning: Country Practices*. Paris: OECD.

CHAPTER EIGHT

Scotland: Recognition of Prior Learning (RPL) research within a national credit and qualifications framework

RUTH WHITTAKER

Abstract

Recognition of Prior Learning (RPL) activity in Scotland is policy-driven and development-based. Recent and current research focuses on national and sector-based models and approaches in order to extend the scope and accessibility of RPL. The profile of RPL has dramatically increased as a result of the Scottish Credit and Qualifications Framework (SCQF), which has generated renewed enthusiasm and momentum for RPL since 2005, increasingly driven by a workforce development agenda linked to employability and skills development.

Experience has led Scotland to differentiate between formative and summative approaches to RPL; these are separate but linked, depending on the context. Recent research has been led and funded by national and European governments. Although there is an emphasis on research and development (scoping exercises, iterative piloting and network building), this does not preclude theoretical work, and Scotland has led the way in developing practical approaches to RPL that build on social identity theory.

A current focus on the development of RPL in the European context provides an opportunity to question and critically examine policy and practice in Scotland. With the development of a European RPL Network, this opportunity can be grasped.

Introduction

Since 2003, the connecting thread and key driver of research and development in the Recognition of Prior Learning (RPL) in Scotland has been the Scottish Credit and Qualifications Framework (SCQF). Government commitment to RPL within the context of the SCQF is part of Scotland's economic strategy in relation to skills development and utilisation. In *Skills for Scotland* (Scottish Government, 2007a), learning providers and awarding bodies are challenged to 'develop a system to ensure that they recognise the value of individuals' prior learning and wider achievement by building on work already undertaken through the SCQF'.

RPL is now largely driven by the workforce development agenda as part of a wider policy trend which increasingly defines the key purpose of education as the development of skills for learning, life and work. This is illustrated by the national *Curriculum for Excellence* (3–18-year-olds); the current 'quality enhancement' theme for the higher education sector, *Graduate Attributes for the 21st Century;*[1] and the recent United Kingdom (UK) Government report *Higher Ambitions*: *The Future of Higher Education in a Knowledge Economy* (DBIS, 2009).

RPL is not new in Scotland. The Accreditation of Prior Experiential Learning (APEL) was introduced in colleges and universities, as in the rest of the UK, in the late 1980s and indeed well before this, although earlier activity was not classified as 'APEL'. Through the collaborative nature of its development in Scotland, partnership working across the sectors and links to other key developments (particularly the Scottish Credit Accumulation Transfer Scheme [SCOTCATS] in the 1980s and 1990s and now the SCQF), RPL in Scotland has developed distinctive characteristics within the broader context of developments in the UK. However, due to its resource-intensive nature and the perceived complexity of the process, it has remained a marginal activity. The main barriers to more widespread use centre on the issue of resourcing, the lack of nationally recognised tools and systems, negative perceptions of the practice of RPL, and lack of awareness of the benefits to learners, employers and learning providers.

---

[1] See www.ltscotland.org.uk/curriculumforexcellence for details of the Curriculum for Excellence for 3–18-year-olds; and www.enhancementthemes.ac.uk for outcomes and reports of all the 'quality enhancement' theme projects and activities.

Launched in 2001, SCQF has led to a renewed and critical interest in RPL as a means of facilitating learning pathways between community, workplace and formal education. The SCQF is a credit-based framework underpinned by learning outcomes. Integrating all Scotland's national academic and vocational qualifications, SCQF is a descriptive rather than a regulatory framework, which 'facilitates the awarding of credit and supports credit transfer and progression routes within the Scottish system' (SCQF, 2001). It provides a model capable of integrating learning from different contexts, both formal and informal.

At a national level, this renewed interest in RPL has been driven by government policy – *Skills for Scotland: A Lifelong Skills Strategy* (Scottish Government 2007a) and *The Government Economic Strategy* (Scottish Government, 2007b). At a sector level, in terms of education and employment, RPL has been driven by specific priorities, such as: widening participation to broaden the student recruitment base; enhancing lifelong learning opportunities for under-represented groups of learners; meeting workforce development needs to strengthen the skills base; and/or meeting legislative requirements for a qualified workforce. The opportunities presented by RPL are now being actively explored by the guidance and employment sectors, as well as by learning providers. In developing models for recognising prior informal learning in contexts and organisations other than formal learning providers, the challenge has been to embrace a range of informal and non-formal learning activities which can be linked to the SCQF as a means of promoting lifelong learning. This forms part of a wider endeavour across Europe to achieve broad acceptance of informal and non-formal learning as a normal route to qualifications within a national qualification framework (NQF). Issues which have continued to act as barriers to such mainstreaming are being explored within current RPL development work in Scotland.

After a brief review of the state of play prior to the development of national SCQF *RPL Guidelines*, this chapter will consider the outcomes of RPL research and development within three contexts: the careers guidance sector; workforce development in the social services sector; and the higher education sector – as well as cross-sector activity currently being led by the 'SCQF Partnership'. It will then address the way forward for RPL in Scotland and will highlight emerging research questions.

Review of RPL development prior to the Scottish Credit and Qualifications Framework (SCQF)

As indicated, since its introduction in the late 1980s, RPL (or APEL) has remained a marginal institutional activity within further and higher education, with the exception of some newer or 'post-1992' universities and a few professional areas such as nursing, health and social care. Prior to the development of the SCQF *RPL Guidelines* (2005) there were no nationally agreed principles for recognising and credit-rating non-formal and informal learning. Rather, RPL developments took place within the context of institutions, many of which were supported through nationally or European-funded development projects.

RPL for summative credit (Accreditation of Prior Experiential Learning – APEL)

In the late 1980s, the Scottish Qualifications Authority (SQA) (then SCOTVEC) and many higher-education institutions (HEI) developed APEL mechanisms based on the portfolio approach. This tended to be a flexible, open-ended approach to evidence gathering, highly learner-centred and therefore requiring highly individualised learner support. Such an approach was largely a result of the influence of the Council for Adult and Experiential learning (CAEL) in the United States and the Learning from Experience Trust (LET) in the UK. The process of compiling a portfolio, while a valuable learning experience in itself, is a demanding one for learners, particularly for groups such as adult returners who have been out of the educational system for some time. The assessment of portfolios, particularly those compiled without structured guidance to limit the quantity of evidence, is a lengthier process than other forms of assessment (Sharp *et al.*, 2000).

As a result, APEL *for credit* was often managed through 'assessment on demand'; that is, by undertaking the normal unit/programme assessment. APEL *for entry* into programmes of study took place during the admissions process, more often than not through an interview. The outcome was not described or recorded as an APEL process. However, the prior informal learning of applicants over the age of 21 was taken into account if they did not have the standard entry requirements. APEL-type activity was also embedded in many 'Access' and 'Return to Learn' programmes provided by colleges of further education.

As part of the development of the national SCQF *RPL Guidelines*, a review of existing activity across the different sectors was undertaken (2003–04), as well as an identification of potential areas for development (Whittaker, 2005). This review was commissioned by the SCQF development partners; that is, the Quality Assurance Agency (QAA) for Scotland, the Scottish Qualifications Authority, Universities Scotland and the Scottish Executive. The first phase involved researching the current range of RPL activities across and within each sector. European RPL research and development was also considered. The methodology included an analysis of sector policy documents and project reports (higher education, further education, community learning and development and voluntary sector, as well as workplace learning and training). The second phase involved 40 semi-structured individual and group interviews with stakeholder representatives.

The review revealed that in HEIs most activity focused on gaining credit within programmes, rather than gaining initial access or entry to a programme as an alternative to traditional entry qualifications. Moreover, most APEL/RPL in Scottish universities was at the postgraduate level due to the greater ease of equating and accrediting informal learning to the specialised, professional learning that characterises this level. Attempts to match the outcomes of informal learning to the outcomes of undergraduate subjects were often less successful. With the exception of work-based learning programmes, the outcomes of most undergraduate programmes are designed to be achieved through conventional delivery, not informal learning. Even if a match could be made, the perception of the outcomes of informal learning as lower-status knowledge was reinforced by an accreditation process which required that it be translated into a form of knowledge recognised in academia.

The review concluded that RPL activity in Scotland was limited and marginal, largely due to the complexity and time-consuming nature of processes. These issues required the development of more manageable approaches to RPL support and assessment if wider activity within the HEI and college sectors was to be encouraged. They formed a key aspect of the SCQF *RPL Guidelines* (2005) which were subsequently developed. However, lack of resources to support increased RPL provision continues to act as a barrier to further activity. A funding mechanism which encourages more flexible approaches to learning and assessment would be a major factor in enabling increased activity.

176

RPL for formative personal/career development

The review highlighted that a wide range of informal learning was being undertaken by individuals through community learning and development activities, provided by local authorities, college outreach centres, and within the voluntary sector and the workplace. This learning is highly valuable to the individual as well as to the community or employer, but is usually non-assessed and therefore not accredited. It can focus on core skills, such as communication and ICT, literacy and numeracy; context-specific skills, such as committee skills or vocational skills – as well as confidence-raising, 'Return to Learn' type provision. Many of the learners engaged in these types of activities are described as 'hard to reach'. The review indicated that external recognition of this learning within the context of the SCQF would enhance the self-confidence of these individuals as 'learners', and could facilitate the identification of further learning pathways as part of an educational and career guidance process.

It was clear that a more developmental rather than instrumentalist approach needed to be developed in order to better meet the needs of learners across a range of different contexts. The awarding of specific credit within the context of formal programmes is an important function of RPL. Equally valuable, however, is the formative role RPL can play in terms of personal growth and development.

Conceptual basis for the development of national guidelines

The development of national guidelines for RPL was an integral part of the SCQF implementation plan (SCQF, 2002). The guidelines needed to be consistent with the SCQF credit-rating guidelines, the QAA *Guidelines on the Accreditation of Prior Learning* (QAA, 2004) and the *Common European Principles for the Identification and Validation of Informal and Non-formal Learning* (Council of the European Union, 2004). The purposes of the SCQF *RPL Guidelines* were to:

• provide guidance to learning providers across all post-16 education and training sectors in Scotland on managing the process of recognising the prior informal learning of learners within the context of the SCQF;

- provide a set of core principles and key features that will enable users of the SCQF to have confidence that there is consistency in approaches to recognising prior informal learning; and
- support the practice of recognising prior learning as part of the life-long learning agenda in Scotland (Whittaker, 2005).

The development of the guidelines (in 2003–05) coincided with the European Union (EU)-funded VaLEx (Valuing Learning through Experience) project, which comprised eight European partners directed by Glasgow Caledonian University (GCU). This project endeavoured to build a coherent pedagogy for RPL which would more effectively target 'hard to reach' learners.[2] The VaLEx approach and model drew on the outcomes of an earlier EU-funded project, *APEL and Social Inclusion: The Learners' Perspective*, which was also coordinated by GCU (Cleary *et al.*, 2002). Through interviews with RPL candidates, that project had identified the transformative dimension of RPL as an important, if unanticipated, outcome of the process.

The transformative dimension involved four stages of learner redefinition as a result of engaging in RPL: a redefinition of what learning is, or can be; a redefinition of what a learner is; a redefinition of the participant's own experiences as learning experiences; and, as a result, a redefinition of the self as a learner (Whittaker *et al.*, 2006a). The processes through which RPL acts as a transformative mechanism were theorised by drawing on principles of symbolic interactionism (Mead, 1934; Blumer, 1969; Meltzer *et al.*, 1975); social identity theory (Tajfel, 1978; Turner, 1985, Ellemers *et al.*, 1999), and situated learning (McLellan, 1996; Wenger, 1998) (Whittaker *et al.*, 2006a). These theories all place the development of identity in a changeable social context, with interaction with others as the key. Whittaker *et al.* (*ibid.*) argued that participation in RPL provides the social context for the development of learner identity through interaction with and validation by peers and tutors.

The VaLEx model sought to apply this theoretical proposition by locating the RPL process within a group context, and by adopting a biographical approach with a focus on personal development planning. What transpired was a structured and supported process undertaken by an individual in discussion with peers to reflect upon their own learning/performance/achievement, with the aim of building self-confidence and

---

[2] See www.valex-apel.com.

undertaking personal, educational or career development planning. This approach highlighted the forward-looking, developmental nature of the RPL process which is reflected in RPL systems in France (*Validation des Acquis de l'Expérience* [VAE]) (Pouget, 2006). The pedagogical model was piloted by the eight European partners in different educational contexts. In Scotland it was explored in a community setting with refugees by Glasgow Caledonian University and with women returners by the University of Stirling.

The extensive review and consultation process to develop the SCQF *RPL Guidelines* was taking place simultaneously, and was informed by the VaLEx research and development. Through researching the extent and nature of existing RPL activity across post-16 education and training providers and employers in Scotland, as well as potential areas for RPL development, the need to recognise and distinguish between the formative and summative dimension of RPL became clear (Whittaker, 2005). This was reinforced during a 'national debate' on RPL which was held in 2004 as part of the development of the *RPL Guidelines* (through a range of sector workshops involving higher education, colleges, community-based learning and development, employers, and professional bodies).

The anticipated and valued outcome of APEL was either entry to, or credit within, formal programmes or qualifications. The research and consultation stage of the guidelines development, and the findings of the EU APEL projects, highlighted the value of RPL in terms of confidence-building, the development of learner identity and increased motivation for continued learning. As a result, the SCQF *RPL Guidelines* incorporated a change from the term 'accreditation' to 'recognition' of prior informal learning. This enabled broader conceptualisation of the use and outcomes of the process, and a clear distinction between the separate, but linked, processes of formative and summative recognition. The key outcomes of formative recognition are therefore explicit, rather than implicit, and centre on confidence-building, making the connections between prior learning and future learning goals and developing learner identity. The key outcomes of summative recognition continue to focus on entry to a formal programme or qualification and the award of credit.

By recognising that formative recognition can be undertaken in the community or workplace, but can help prepare individuals for further learning opportunities or indeed for a summative process of recognition, RPL can effectively provide a bridge for individuals moving from informal and non-formal learning contexts to formal provision. It was also clear that in order to tackle the 'remembered pain' of the complicated and time-consuming support and assessment processes of APEL, there was a need to move to more streamlined methods embedded within curriculum design and delivery. The process of evidence-gathering should be appropriate to the type of recognition undertaken and to its purpose. For example, a process of formative recognition, linked to personal or professional development or educational and career guidance, should not require the same level of evidence as a process of summative recognition which involves an assessment process leading to the award of credit. The SCQF *RPL Guidelines* (2005, 2009) suggest a range of support and recognition mechanisms to reflect the differing forms and goals of RPL processes across different sectors.

The application of principles to practice

Since the launch of the guidelines in 2005, RPL activity in Scotland has focused on developing models and approaches at sector level, with particular emphasis on the formative dimension, and the streamlining and integration of RPL within curriculum design and delivery. This has predominantly taken place within the community learning and development sector (Whittaker, 2007; CLD, 2008), the social services sector (in relation to workforce development), the higher education sector and the careers guidance sector. Current RPL development is also being undertaken in the health sector and recent interest has been expressed by Scotland's colleges. Research and development is closely linked to EU developments in RPL within the European Qualifications Framework (EQF), the Bologna process and the Leuven Communiqué (Bologna, 2009). This Communiqué identifies RPL as a significant area for consolidation and development within European higher education as part of the Bologna process. In response to this, the Quality Assurance Agency in Scotland has established the Scottish Universities RPL Network to share practice and research in the Scottish sector, and to raise awareness of relevant developments in the rest of the UK, Europe and internationally. The SCQF Partnership has also established a cross-sector 'RPL Network' to undertake work which will build the capacity of learning providers and organisations, and support an increase in the demand side of RPL by learners (this is discussed in more detail below).

This chapter will now explore RPL research and development within three contexts in depth: the careers guidance sector; the social services sector (in terms of workforce development); and the higher education sector. These contexts were selected because they represent different stages in the cycle of RPL development in Scotland. The first stage is characterised by innovation as broad policy is translated into practice; the second stage by reflection and consolidation through which good practice is distilled back into policy development; and the third stage, which represents the translation of new policy into effective practice at an organisational level (Sharp *et al.*, 2000).

Integrating RPL within the careers guidance sector: the innovation stage – translating policy into practice

'Skills Development Scotland', which includes 'Careers Scotland', is undertaking a range of work to integrate the SCQF into careers guidance, specifically through the use of RPL. A project to develop and evaluate an RPL profiling tool and an SCQF benchmarking guide has recently been undertaken (2008–09) (Whittaker and Anderson, 2009). This work links to other national policy and development areas such as *Curriculum for Excellence: Recognising Wider Achievement* and *More Chances, More Choices.*

The purpose of the project was to link RPL and the SCQF to careers guidance for young people in schools. The majority of participating pupils were fourth-year summer and winter leavers at risk of 'no positive destination' in terms of education, training or employment. By mapping learning and skills gained through informal learning against the appropriate level of the SCQF, the project explored whether young people could gain a better idea of the types of job they could seek, or the types of learning or training programmes they could apply for. The project investigated the extent to which RPL profiling and SCQF benchmarking could help young people in their 'career planning journey'. Pupils were selected by careers advisors in four schools in different geographical areas. Selection was based on the availability of the pupils at the time and therefore to some extent constituted a convenience sampling. RPL profiling was undertaken as an individual or a group process, to ascertain whether the peer-support dimension of a group model enhanced the experience for the participants. Three main evaluation tools were used: an online questionnaire for careers advisers; a short questionnaire for pupil participants; and a feedback session for careers advisers and managers (informed by the careers advisers' questionnaire responses).

The evaluation aimed to investigate experiences and ways in which the process could be improved and applied in other contexts. The feedback session enabled the advisors and managers to reflect on the outcomes of the questionnaires, and agree recommendations for further development and application of the profiling tool. Although the sample was small, the evaluation indicated that the process may be most effectively undertaken in small groups using shared experience as the focus for reflection. It revealed that RPL is challenging when the young person cannot identify an experience upon which to reflect and that this may lead to a negative rather than positive outcome. Gender may also impact on level of engagement. In general, the girls in the pilot group engaged in the process more positively than the boys, especially in terms of the reflective activity and discussion of experiences.

As a result of the evaluation, it was agreed that the RPL profiling tool and the SCQF benchmarking guidance be further developed to enhance the accessibility of the process from the perspectives of both young people and advisors. With funding from Skills Development Scotland, the SCQF Partnership commissioned a project to field test the model and the re-developed tools with further groups of school pupils. As a result of the project evaluation, Skills Development Scotland are now exploring the applicability of the model and tools to a wider range of client groups, including the long-term unemployed and individuals facing redundancy (Whittaker and Anderson, 2009). This now forms part of a national strategy to enable individuals to benchmark their attainments and achievements to the SCQF to facilitate participation in learning and the workforce.

Integrating RPL into workforce development within the social services sector: reflection and consolidation – new policy development through distilling good practice

The SCQF *Review of the Recognition of Prior Learning* reiterated the significance of RPL in ensuring that 'individuals' skills, learning and qualifications are used in employment to optimum effect in order to have maximum economic impact for business and for individuals living and working in Scotland' (Inspire Scotland, 2008).

Legislative requirements for the registration of staff in sectors such as social services and health, and for qualified staff in the construction industry, require the development of mechanisms that will support experienced but unqualified staff to gain the necessary qualifications in a resource-efficient way. RPL is viewed as a potential mechanism for facilitating this process. As well as building the confidence of employees, RPL can help target training or learning support more effectively. Requiring employees to repeat training which does not take into account their prior learning is both de-motivating for the employee and an inefficient use of employers' resources.

The social services sector has led the way in developing RPL to support workforce development within the context of the SCQF. This was initiated by the 'SCQF/Social Services Recognition of Prior Informal Learning (RPL) Project' (2005–08), commissioned by the Scottish Social Services Council to support the implementation of the SCQF within the sector.[3]

The project aimed to engage social service workers who lack confidence as learners and/or are reluctant to undertake formal learning, and to speed up and streamline the process of RPL for credit towards qualifications without sacrificing quality. The project also sought to review the effectiveness of RPL as a means of increasing learner self-confidence; improving the quality of the learning experience; and evaluating and enhancing practice. In addition, the integration of RPL into existing organisational systems of workforce development were explored from the recruitment and induction stage onwards, and within existing systems for Scottish Vocational Qualification (SVQ) assessment. The project therefore had formative and summative dimensions.

An SCQF RPL resource pack and profiling tools were developed, piloted and evaluated. The formative stage involved learners building their confidence, recognising the skills and knowledge they have gained through previous experience, and developing the capacity to think and write reflectively. The reflective approach which forms the basis of the model is informed by the work of Boud *et al.* (1993), Kolb (1984), Moon (2000) and Schön (1987), and underpinned by the pedagogical approach developed in the VaLEx project; that is, the development of learner identity through interaction with peers (Koivisto, 2005; Pouget, 2006; Whittaker *et al.*, 2006a). The project thus provided the opportunity to develop this pedagogical approach within a workplace, rather than community setting. The materials also supported learners through a summative process of recognition. In this case, a staged approach to

---

[3] See www.sssc.uk.com for the SCQF RPL resource pack and evaluation report.

evidence-gathering enabled assessment towards an SVQ in health and social care (the vocational qualification required for registration). All of the above activities involved consultation with an RPL working group of employers and experts in social services training and development.

The resource pack and profiling tool were piloted and evaluated in two stages. The first stage (April 2006–March 2007) was to: 1) test the usefulness and applicability of the RPL process for learners (i.e. the formative, preparatory sessions and the profiling tool); 2) check the ease of use by mentors; and 3) identify refinements to the materials. Fifteen learners across three organisations (both private and voluntary care homes) participated via group sessions facilitated by a mentor from within the organisation. These learners completed and submitted evaluation questionnaires to the project team. Mentor feedback was provided to a meeting of the RPL working group.

A refined version of the resource pack and profiling tool was produced, and further piloting took place. The second evaluation reviewed the effectiveness of the RPL process in terms of increasing learner self-confidence; accelerating the achievement of vocational qualifications; improving the quality of the learning experience; and evaluating and enhancing practice. Four pilot organisations participated at this stage; one had participated in the first stage, so tested out the revised materials with a different learner group. The organisations utilised the revised processes and materials (formative stage) as a preparation for summative assessment towards qualifications, as well as within the context of induction. Focus-group discussions with learners and mentors were conducted to explore personal and professional development, as well as impact on practice. Additionally, questionnaire responses from learners were gathered. The second evaluation stage was completed in March 2008 (Whittaker, 2008).

The value of the RPL process in terms of increasing learners' confidence and motivation to undertake further learning and development was confirmed through the project evaluation. RPL promoted a positive view of learning, based on an enhancement rather than a deficit model. The peer-group approach to developing learner self-awareness of their skills, prior to embarking on a formal programme and to the development of reflective skills and writing skills, was seen as streamlining and accelerating the process of gaining a qualification. As a result of formative RPL, learners embarked on a formal qualification with greater self-confidence and greater understanding of how they learn, and how to express and demonstrate that learning.

The usefulness of the RPL profiling tool for demystifying SVQ assessment systems and language was emphasised. The tool translates SVQ 'jargon' into everyday language, enabling learners to see how they have demonstrated the competences in their everyday life and then to transfer the same skills to their social care practice. It is also a useful means of enabling someone to take a step back from the SVQ if they are struggling by providing time and space to think about personal previous experience, and then to relate that to current work roles. Used in this way, RPL can help learners progress more quickly through the qualification. The focus group discussions with learners and mentors suggested that the self-confidence generated through the identification of strengths and skills, and understanding their relevance to current work roles, led to greater confidence within the workplace itself. Impact on service delivery was difficult to quantify. However, in qualitative terms both learners and their mentors considered that increased confidence and levels of enthusiasm, and enhanced critical evaluation of their own and others' practice, had had a positive impact on their practice.

The project highlighted the importance of the mentor role in the quality of the learner experience. Mentors need to be given sufficient time, training and continuing support to carry out this role effectively. Building in opportunities for mentors to use the role as means of achieving their own professional development goals is important, both in terms of explicitly valuing the mentor role within organisations and providing staff with the motivation to undertake it (Whittaker, 2008).

In considering ways to integrate RPL within existing recruitment, induction, training and performance interviewing systems, for example, organisations need to be convinced of its value, in terms of improved processes and improved practice, to justify investment. Following the SCQF social services RPL project, further work is being undertaken to demonstrate this value to a broader range of organisations within the sector. This involves encouraging the wider use of the RPL resources in a range of different contexts and programmes, with the support of the growing number of 'RPL Champions' that have emerged through the work of this project (*ibid.*).

Pilot evaluation and subsequent, and growing, use of the resources within organisations has indicated that RPL, supported by the resource pack, can be used within the social services sector to support every aspect of workforce development – recruitment, induction, supervision, appraisal and performance interviewing. The idea of building RPL into a process of continuous employee development is now being explored; for example, using critical incident analysis and reflective discussion as part of what the organisation does. In this way, RPL could become part of an internalised (rather than externally imposed) system of professional development, which is not just linked to the achievement of qualifications.

Although the model and materials were piloted mainly with learners who were working towards the SVQ in health and social care, their generic aspects have broad applicability within the social services sector for workers at all levels. Further development in this regard is being led by a Social Services RPL Interest Group, established in July 2010 and coordinated by the Scottish Social Services Council (SSSC). Moreover, the resources have been adapted by the SCQF Partnership as a generic resource to support the development of RPL in other sectors such as Health and Education.

The REALISE project (part of the EU Objective 3 'Managing Progress' programme 2005–07), undertaken by the University of Edinburgh, highlighted differing levels of acceptance of RPL within different workplace cultures (Ahlgren *et al.*, 2007). In the context of 14 small- to medium-sized enterprises (SMEs), relationships between organisational and individual orientations to learning were explored along an 'expansive/restrictive continuum'. An expansive learning culture includes valuing the skills and knowledge gained through informal learning. The SMEs were located across 'four geographical areas, a range of organisational sizes and structures, sectors and work and learning cultures': four were in the care sector; four in the service sector; four in the manufacturing sector; and one in trade. A literature review of workplace learning models was undertaken, followed by interviews with the owner/manager/supervisor within each SME and a number of employees before and after training, as well as participant observation of the training itself.

Three types of organisational learning culture were identified: expansive, restrictive and passive-restrictive. These appear to be closely linked to sector. The care sector, for example, is more likely to hold an expansive attitude to learning and training than production sectors. It would be interesting to explore the findings of this research further by investigating the transferability of the RPL model, developed so successfully in the social services sector within organisational learning cultures defined as more restrictive.

There are persistent difficulties in engaging employers with RPL. These difficulties centre on questions such as: Who will conduct the

RPL? Where will it be conducted? Who will pay for it? What will the actual benefits for the employer be? As well as the development of infra- structure and processes, linking RPL to career and skills development requires a huge cultural shift in employing organisations. It is clear from development work in Scotland that the RPL process needs to be inte- grated within existing workforce development systems, rather than being developed as a separate (and potentially marginal) activity.

Integrating RPL within formal learning provision – the higher education sector; the cycle continues – translating new policy into effective organisational practices

The increasing diversity of the student population and the labour force, largely as a result of demographic change, requires providers to develop more flexible forms of provision, including RPL. While the current eco- nomic downturn has led to an increase in applications to colleges and universities, this masks the longer-term demographic downturn in student recruitment. New student groups will include adult returners; 'hard to reach' learners; people in employment requiring flexible, part-time study; refugees; economic migrants; and international students.

RPL can support institutional widening participation agendas by encouraging the participation of non-traditional learners in lifelong learn- ing and by enabling people who lack formal qualifications to gain access to courses. The recent UK Government report *Higher Ambitions: The Future of Higher Education in a Knowledge Economy* (DBIS, 2009) empha- sises that 'too many people with the ability to benefit from Higher Education are still not entering the system'. The nature of higher educa- tion is changing – it is becoming more flexible to allow people to move in and out depending on personal and work circumstances. RPL will be a key part of this changing attendance pattern: pre-entry guidance incor- porating RPL will enhance learner preparedness and support informed choices about study; RPL can also support curriculum development, personal development planning and work-based learning provision (Whittaker, 2006).

As part of the 'quality enhancement' theme on 'flexible delivery' for the Scottish higher education sector, QAA Scotland commissioned a proj- ect called 'Supporting the Development of the Flexible Curriculum: Flexible entry and flexible programmes within the context of the SCQF (2005–06)'. Quality enhancement themes are part of a framework to provide an integrated approach to quality assurance across higher education (drawing on innovative practice within the UK and internationally). This project established the 'HE Coordination Group for Flexible Entry (RPL and Credit Transfer)', which comprised policy-makers and practitioners from all Scottish HEIs.

This group researched current developments and key issues across the sector through a survey of all HEIs and discussions at two Coordination Group workshops. The outcome was a staff development and resource pack for flexible entry (RPL and credit transfer), and an 'agenda for action' for the sector. Recommendations focus on the need to support the mainstreaming of flexible entry and flexible programmes across the sector. This requires explicit resourcing of the provision at national and institutional levels; recognition of diverse approaches to achieving and demonstrating learning within curriculum design; and training and support for staff, developing and operating flexible entry processes and flexible programmes (Whittaker *et al.*, 2006b).

Integrating the recognition of informal and non-formal learning within mainstream curriculum design and delivery presents difficulties to HEIs in terms of their funding system and the traditional structures of learning. In *The Edgeless University*, Bradwell (2009) argues that 'we have yet to find a model for collating learning from many different sources'. The SCQF, underpinned by the notion of learning outcomes, should provide such a model, but learning outcomes, while undoubtedly an enabler of RPL, can also present barriers. Advantages include the separation of the teaching process from the learning process; the concept of the transferability of skills, knowledge and understanding; the retrospective as well as prospective facility they offer; greater ease of comparison between different qualifications and types of learning; the definition of a 'threshold level' of learning which does not inhibit the development of additional knowledge and skills (Moon, 2002); and the capacity of outcomes to be learner-defined as well as programme-defined.

The challenges learning outcomes can present to RPL are that they are generally predicated on a formal learning model (unless part of a work-based learning programme); are often easier to demonstrate at postgraduate than undergraduate level due to the more contextualised expression of knowledge and skills in the former; and often require a direct match with the outcomes of formal learning rather than a broader comparison of competence and capacity. Moreover, there is often inconsistency regarding the extent to which all learning outcomes need to be demonstrated within an assessment process, and it can be difficult to use them to develop individualised programmes to address 'gaps' in learning.

Learning outcomes need to be defined in a way that supports a variety of different means of achieving them and flexibility in mode of assessment, without detracting from the quality of the provision (Whittaker *et al.*, 2006b). This would assist in addressing parity of esteem between different modes of learning at the curriculum design stage of programmes. It would also obviate the need for individuals to translate their knowledge into forms that are deemed appropriate for assessment and credit rating, which requires a move away from informal learning to something that is more readily understood by the 'academy'. However, this requires programme developers to enhance their understanding of the complex processes through which knowledge and expertise is acquired in the workplace, and the diverse ways in which this can be evidenced (Pokorny, 2006).

As mentioned, the Scottish Universities RPL Network was established by QAA Scotland in 2008 in response to national policy drivers relating to RPL, the current focus on RPL within the context of Bologna developments and the work of the 'quality enhancement themes'. A network was also needed to respond to an immediate request for a Scottish university sector contribution to the RPL Bologna seminar in the Netherlands in December 2009.[4] This RPL Network generated a high level of interest and membership has been expanded. It is seen as a vehicle for sharing RPL practice and research in order to assist development within the Scottish sector, and for awareness raising re relevant developments in the rest of the UK, Europe and internationally. It will link into post-Bologna activities.

QAA Scotland and the Scottish Government jointly hosted an event in Brussels in February 2010, which identified the scope of and interest in a European network to share RPL practice, research and developments. A European RPL Network was launched in November 2010 by the Bologna Follow-Up Group (BFUG). With links to the SCQF RPL Network, this new network will also raise awareness of RPL developments across different sectors in Scotland. It will engage with international developments through the Prior Learning International Research Centre (PLIRC), based at Thompson Rivers University, British Columbia, Canada.

---

[4] For more information about the Bologna Seminar, see the seminar website: http://www.dashe.nl/events/bologna/rpl.html.

Participants in the Scottish Universities RPL Network have identified key areas to be explored collaboratively with Scottish, UK and international colleagues. These include:

- Sharing approaches, resources and tools in order to streamline processes and make them more accessible to learners, including making more use of technology to support evidence-gathering.
- Sharing and highlighting evidence of success in order to shift the focus of discussion to achievements rather than barriers, including longitudinal tracking of successful RPL claimants.
- The development of a theoretical framework to underpin the RPL process that can be integrated into related pedagogical developments, such as work-based learning, personal development planning (PDP) and employability.

All of the above should help to raise awareness of the opportunities RPL provides to learners and to build an evidence base capable of inspiring more confidence about RPL amongst university staff. There is still a perception amongst many academic staff that RPL processes are insufficiently robust as indicators of student achievement and likely future performance.

Consistency and transparency remain concerns across the higher education sector. Such concerns span the awarding of specific credit within programmes; the level and type of support and guidance provided to RPL applicants; assessment and quality assurance procedures for RPL; fees charged for the process; and monitoring practices at school/faculty, department and programme levels. While institutional autonomy should be maintained, agreed core principles within which RPL provision will operate should provide a more transparent and equitable process, and facilitate mutual trust and confidence between receiving institutions. As the SCQF *RPL Guidelines* are increasingly used by institutions as a source of reference and guidance, greater consistency and transparency should be attained.

The recognition of learning gained outside the UK is also a key theme in the HE sector, particularly linked to internationalisation. As part of its goal to develop a competent and sustainable workforce for Scotland, the government commissioned a scoping study on support mechanisms to recognise the learning and skills of migrant workers and refugees (2009–10).[5] The study was undertaken by the SCQF

---

[5] See www.scqf.org.uk for this scoping study (and for other details of the SCQF's work).

Partnership (coordinator), Glasgow Caledonian University on behalf of Universities Scotland, Scotland's Colleges and Skills Development Scotland. Models from the UK, Europe and further afield were explored, after which consultation was undertaken with key Scottish stakeholders across the education, training, guidance and employment sectors. The outcome was the presentation to the Scottish Government of three sustainable recognition and support models for refugees and migrant workers, with potential transferability to other groups under-represented in education and employment (Guest and Vecchia, 2010).

Cross-sector RPL activity

Following the publication of the Scottish Government's *Skills Strategy* (2007), the SCQF Partnership commissioned a study to ascertain government expectations of RPL; the current landscape of activity and existing practice; and the views of stakeholders on where the focus for RPL activity should lie within the SCQF. This research involved a review of existing policy and project documentation, and interviews and focus group discussions, with key stakeholder representatives from across the education and training, community and workplace sectors.

The research findings highlighted the significance of RPL 'in contributing to the necessary skills upgrading in Scotland required for sustainable economic growth and competitive advantage in the global economy' (Inspire Scotland, 2008). The research report identifies some good practice, but confirms that provision is patchy across education/training providers and across the country as a whole. The report is clear that RPL is a useful tool to assist employers in recruitment, to identify workforce skills and to effectively target resources for employee development. The diversity of existing practices is highlighted, and the concurrent need to share these across sectors to increase awareness, understanding and use of RPL. It is recommended that developmental activities should focus on supply/demand and capacity building, focused particularly on workplace, community learning and development and employability sectors, in order 'to ensure employers, professional bodies and individual learners, whatever their situation, know about, understand and want to participate in RPL linked to SCQF as a means of engaging or re-engaging in lifelong learning' (Inspire Scotland, 2008).

It was a result of this report, and a preceding Organisation for Economic Co-operation and Development (OECD) review of the

Recognition of Non-formal and Informal Learning (RNFIL)[6] across Scotland and England which also highlights a number of areas for development (OECD, 2008), that the above-mentioned SCQF RPL Network was established in January 2009. It comprises representatives from the main education and training (formal and non-formal) providers, employment and government. With the aim of increasing understanding, awareness, use and take-up of RPL Network, objectives include:

- developing materials to promote RPL to stakeholders and learners, including sector-specific 'business cases' for RPL;
- sharing good practice of RPL amongst providers;
- learning from the experience of learners through the development of case studies; and
- developing standard, generic policy and procedures that can be adjusted to sector and institutional needs (development of a generic SCQF RPL toolkit through adaptation of the Scottish Social Services RPL Resource Pack).

The SCQF *RPL Guidelines* were reviewed in 2008 and are now incorporated within a revised *SCQF Handbook* (SCQF, 2009).

The way forward for Scotland

An RPL scoping exercise was commissioned by the Scottish Executive in 2006 to gain an understanding of the needs and goals of different sectors in relation to RPL (Whittaker, 2006). All of the sectors consulted as part of this scoping exercise viewed RPL as a potentially important part of broader strategies regarding widening participation, lifelong learning, employability and workforce development. This was reiterated in the *SCQF Review of RPL* (Inspire Scotland, 2008). There is, however, a need to address resourcing; to improve the perception of RPL through quality-assured, but manageable, processes; and to raise awareness of the opportunities it presents to learners, to employees, to those seeking employment and to employers. Learning providers and employers will

---

[6] This term is frequently used in Europe.

only include RPL in their organisational activity if it can explicitly help to achieve their organisational priorities. Unless a good business case can be made at an institutional or employer level, organisations will not engage in RPL (Whittaker, 2006).

Since the SCQF review of RPL (Inspire Scotland, 2008), the work of the SCQF Partnership has focused on building capacity and capability to support the mainstreaming of RPL in organisations and institutions.

The broad agenda for RPL development in Scotland includes:

- *Developing RPL 'toolkits' based on models of good practice and working case studies.* These will support staff involved in developing and implementing RPL, and encourage consistency and transparency.
- *Developing more collaborative learning partnerships* between colleges, universities, community learning and development (CLD), and the employment sector to better meet the needs of learners (in terms of personal and professional goals) and employers (in terms of workforce development).
- *Awareness-raising and marketing strategies* to highlight the benefits and opportunities of RPL to learners, employees, people not in education or employment and employers, linking to the promotion of the SCQF as the national language and currency of learning.
- *Initiatives for refugees and economic migrants,* including a model to recognise learning, skills and qualifications to help ensure their participation in the workforce at an appropriate level.
- *Support for the development of learning outcomes and curricula* to ensure they are flexible enough to take account of the different experiences, learning methods and starting points of individuals wishing to take advantage of flexible credit/access/entry arrangements.
- *Exploration of ways to secure and deploy RPL resources effectively* at national, regional and institutional levels, in order to develop provision that is cost effective, not overly bureaucratic or burdensome, and robust enough to meet appropriate quality standards.
- *Gaining commitment from institutional leaders* to put in place strategies to drive RPL developments forward and secure the investment of time, resources and collaborative effort that is required to enable the necessary systems, processes and staff development to be implemented (Whittaker, 2006; Inspire Scotland, 2008).

Concluding observations

RPL activity in Scotland is policy-driven and development-based. Recent and current research focuses on national and sector-based models and approaches, in order to extend the scope and accessibility of RPL.

The SCQF has generated enthusiasm and momentum for RPL in sectors where it is a relatively new phenomenon, and where activity is still at the early stages of the development cycle; that is, in community learning and development, in employment, and in careers guidance. Creative approaches to recognising prior informal learning within the context of the SCQF are being actively investigated and developed within these sectors.

Within the formal education sector (universities and colleges), where RPL is not new, developments are hindered by the legacy of past APEL systems and resource-intensive processes. However, as we move to an increasingly diversified higher education system, and an increasingly diverse student population, the need for flexible routes into and through further and higher education is ever more apparent. Higher education is further along the continuum of development than any other sector in Scotland and, in terms of the cycle of RPL development referred to earlier, is once again focusing its efforts on translating new policy into effective practice at institutional levels. It remains necessary to challenge assumptions of what RPL is, or could be, in order to facilitate the type of innovative curriculum development which embraces and integrates prior informal learning.

RPL in Scotland is increasingly driven by a workforce development agenda. Its perceived value is linked to its anticipated contribution to employability, skills development and broadening the recruitment base for both education and employment in response to an ageing population. Such an approach demands effective partnerships between government, employers, individuals and learning and training providers, in order to meet the priorities outlined in the *Skills for Scotland: A Lifelong Skills Strategy* (Scottish Government, 2007a). The SCQF Partnership and the SCQF RPL Network are focusing on how effective collaboration between employers, learning providers, awarding bodies and others can be developed.

Areas for further research

The current focus on the development of RPL in a European context provides the opportunity to question and critically examine policy and practice in Scotland. With the development of a 'European RPL Network', this opportunity can be grasped. Moreover, the collaborative nature of RPL development in Scotland across the different sectors provides a rich resource for reflection and debate beyond our borders.

There is scope for comparative investigations at a European and/or international level in terms of all of the key functions of RPL; that is, how it supports skills recognition and skills development; is integrated into workforce development strategies; supports workforce participation in lifelong learning; and supports participation in further and higher education by non-traditional learner groups.

There is also scope for research related to the potential and actual impact of national credit and qualification frameworks on the development of RPL; at national, sector and organisational levels, for example:

- How and to what extent can credit and qualifications frameworks be used creatively to support the development of learning cultures within employment sectors/organisations/workplaces?
- Can NQF level descriptors be used to challenge assessment practices which demand comparisons between the outcomes of informal learning and those of formal programmes, as opposed to comparisons between the capacities which the curriculum seeks to achieve, and those demonstrated through personal and professional experiences?
- Does the external recognition or 'validation' of informal learning need to be achieved through the award of credit? Can we explore further the role of benchmarking, the outcomes of informal learning against national qualifications frameworks, and the value and meaning of this process for learners, employers and educational and training providers?

A range of more general ideas for research also emerged during the course of this study:

- The permeability of boundaries between informal and formal learning for learners: Can RPL be used to demystify the language and competences of formal qualifications by contextualising them in terms of life and work experiences? How can RPL (especially form-ative RPL) best be used to support transitions between informal, non-formal and formal learning contexts?

- What capacity-building measures are required with education and training providers and employers to support the development and integration of RPL within existing systems and infrastructures?
- How can effective collaborative partnerships be formed between employers and learning and training providers, in order to support the development of RPL within the context of workforce develop-ment and/or widening participation?
- The transformative dimension of RPL: How are learner identity and empowerment shaped through the social milieu of the RPL process?
- What is the impact of RPL on an individual's practice in the work-place; for example, exploring changes in levels of confidence as a result of engaging in reflective processes that involve reviewing and questioning own and others' practice? The link between this dimen-sion of RPL and the value placed on informal learning by the organisation could also be further explored.
- The complex role of the RPL facilitator as negotiator and interpreter of academic language for learners: What tensions are created by the demands of the roles of guide, expert/peer, advocate, counsellor and assessor – and how are these managed?

References

Ahlgren, L., Riddell, S., Tett, L. and Weedon, E. (2007) *Experiences of Workplace Learning in SMEs: Lessons for Good Practice, Final Report*. Edinburgh: CREID, University of Edinburgh.

Blumer, H. (1969) *Symbolic Interactionism: Perspective and Method*. New Jersey: Prentice Hall.

Bologna (2009) *The Bologna Process 2020: The European Higher Education Area in the New Decade*, the Leuven and Louvain-la-Neuve Communiqué. Available at: http://www.ond.vlaanderen.be/hogeron-derwijs/bologna/conference/documents/leuven_louvain-la-neuve_c ommuniqu%C3%A9_april_2009.pdf.

Boud, D., Cohen, R. and Walker, D. (eds) (1993) *Using Experience for Learning*. Buckingham: SRHE and Open University Press.

Bradwell, P. (2009) *The Edgeless University: Why Higher Education must Embrace Technology*. London: DEMOS.

Cleary, P., Whittaker, R., Gallacher, J., Merrill, B., Jokinen, L., Carette, M. and members of CREA (2002) *Social Inclusion through APEL: The Learners' Perspective – Comparative Report*. Glasgow: Glasgow Caledonian University.

Community Learning and Development (CLD) Managers, Scotland (2008) *Community Learning and Development Portfolio: A Resource to Record Learning, Experiences and Achievements*. Scotland: Community Learning and Development.

Council of the European Union (2004) *Common European Principles for the Identification and Validation of Informal and Non-formal Learning*. Brussels: European Commission. Available at: http://www.ecotec.com/europeaninventory/principles.html.

Department for Business, Innovation and Skills (DBIS) (2009) *Higher Ambitions: The Future of Higher Education in a Knowledge Economy*. London: UK Government.

Ellemers, N., Kortekaas, P. and Ouwerkerk, J. (1999) 'Self-categorization, commitment to the group and group self-esteem as related but distinct aspects of social identity', *European Journal of Social Psychology*, Vol. 29, Nos 2–3, pp. 371–89.

European Commission (2009) *The Bologna Process 2020: The European Higher Education Area in the New Decade*. Communiqué of the conference of European ministers responsible for Higher Education, Leuven and Louvain-la-Neuve, 28–29 April 2009.

Guest, P. and Vecchia, M. (2010) *Scoping Study on Support Mechanisms for the Recognition of the Skills, Learning and Qualifications of Migrant Workers and Refugees, Final Report*. Scottish Credit and Qualifications Framework Partnership (SCQFP).

Inspire Scotland (2008) *A Review of the Recognition of Prior Learning. Final Report*. Scottish Credit and Qualifications Framework Partnership (SCQFP).

Koivisto, M. (2005) *VaLEx – Valuing Learning from Experience, Final Project Evaluation. Report*. University of Turku.

Kolb, D. (1984) *Experiential Learning*. Englewood Cliffs, NJ: Prentice-Hall.

McLellan, H. (1995) *Situated Learning Perspectives*. New Jersey: Educational Technology Publications.

Mead, H. (1934) *Mind, Self and Society*. Chicago: University of Chicago Press.

Meltzer, B., Petras, J. and Reynolds, L. (1975) *Symbolic Interactionism: Genesis, Varieties and Criticism*. London: Routledge Keegan Paul.

Moon, J. (2000) *Reflection in Learning and Professional Development.* London: Kogan Page.

Moon, J. (2002) *The Module and Programme Development Handbook: A Practical Resource for Linking Levels, Learning Outcomes and Assessment.* London: Kogan Page.

Organisation for Economic Co-operation and Development (OECD) (2008) *Thematic Review and Collaborative Policy Analysis Recognition of Non-formal and informal learning: Scotland and England.* Paris: OECD.

Pokorny, H. (2006) 'Recognising prior learning: What do we know?', in P. Andersson and J. Harris (eds) *Re-theorising the Recognition of Prior Learning.* Leicester: NIACE.

Pouget, M. (2006) 'Pedagogical and social aspects of APEL', in C. Corradi, N. Evans and A. Valk (eds) *Recognising Experiential Learning: Practices in European Universities.* European University Lifelong Learning Network (EULLearN). Tartu: Tartu University Press.

Quality Assurance Agency (QAA) (2004) *Guidelines on the Accreditation of Prior Learning.* London: HMSO.

Schön, D. (1987) *Educating the Reflective Practitioner: Towards a New Design for Teaching and Learning in the Professions.* San Francisco: Jossey Bass Inc.

Scottish Credit and Qualifications Framework (SCQF) (2001) *An Introduction to the Scottish Credit and Qualifications Framework*, Scottish Credit and Qualifications Framework.

Scottish Credit and Qualifications Framework (SCQF) (2002) *National Plan for Implementation of the Framework*, Scottish Credit and Qualifications Framework.

Scottish Credit and Qualifications Framework (SCQF) (2005) *RPL Guidelines.* Scottish Credit and Qualifications Framework.

Scottish Credit and Qualifications Framework (SCQF) (2008) *SCQF Review.* Scottish Credit and Qualifications Framework.

Scottish Credit and Qualifications Framework (SCQF) (2009) *SCQF Handbook.* Scottish Credit and Qualifications Framework.

Scottish Government (2007a) *Skills for Scotland: A Lifelong Skills Strategy.* Holyrood: Scottish Parliament Information Centre.

Scottish Government (2007b) *Government Economic Strategy.* Holyrood: Scottish Parliament Information Centre.

Sharp, N., Reeve, F. and Whittaker, R. (2000) 'Scotland: The Story of the Assessment of Prior Experiential Learning', in N. Evans (ed.) *Experiential Learning around the World: Employability and the Global Economy.* London and Philadelphia: Jessica Kingsley Publishers.

Tajifel, H. (1978) 'Social categorisation, social identity and social comparison', in H. Tajifel (ed.) *Differentiation between Social Groups: Studies in the Social Psychology of Intergroup Relations*. London: Academic Press.

Turner, J. (1985) 'Social categorisation and the self-concept: A social-cognitive theory of group behaviour', in E. Lawler (ed.) *Advances in Group Processes: Theory and Research*, Vol. 2, pp. 77–122. Greenwich, CT: JAI Press.

Wenger, E. (1998) *Communities of Practice: Learning, Meaning, Identity*. Cambridge: Cambridge University Press.

Whittaker, R. (2005) *Report on Consultation on SCQF RPL Guidelines*. Scottish Credit and Qualifications Framework.

Whittaker, R. (2006) *Scottish Executive Recognition of Prior informal Learning (RPL) Scoping Exercise, Final Report*. Glasgow: Scottish Executive.

Whittaker, R. (2007) *Recognising Prior Learning in Community Learning and Development using the SCQF, Report 81*. Communities Scotland.

Whittaker, R. (2008) *Scottish Credit and Qualifications Framework (SCQF) Social Services: Recognition of Prior Learning (RPL) Pilot, Evaluation Report*. Dundee: Scottish Social Services Council.

Whittaker, R. and Anderson, P. (2009) *Evaluation of RPL Profiling Tool and SCQF Mapping Guide Pilot*. Skills Development Scotland.

Whittaker, S., Whittaker, R. and Cleary, P. (2006a) 'Understanding the transformative dimension of RPL', in P. Andersson and J. Harris (eds) *Re-theorising the Recognition of Prior Learning*. Leicester: NIACE.

Whittaker, R., Mills, V. and Knox, K. (2006b) *Flexible Delivery Quality Enhancement Theme: Supporting the Development of the Flexible Curriculum, Final Report*. Glasgow: QAA Scotland.

CHAPTER NINE

South Africa: Research reflecting critically on Recognition of Prior Learning (RPL) research and practice

Mignonne Breier

Abstract

Research into the Recognition of Prior Learning (RPL) in South Africa needs to be seen in relation to the extent of educational disadvantage in the country that is the legacy of apartheid, and the vision of educational redress which drove the conceptualisation of the practice in the early post-apartheid years. This chapter categorises that research according to the following broad purposes: 1) research to develop policy; 2) research to conceptualise RPL and guide practice; 3) research to monitor and quantify implementation. It includes research on the recognition of prior experience within adult pedagogy as well as RPL prior to entry, as conventionally understood. It is argued that the research has been predominantly qualitative, mainly located in university education, and, although it appears to have made an important contribution to international theorisation of the practice, it has been too small-scale and too introspective to help extend the reach of RPL in South Africa itself.

Introduction

This chapter provides a perspective on research on the Recognition of Prior Learning (RPL) in South Africa, and argues that it has been extensive, scholarly and widely published. However, given the limited implementation of RPL in South Africa, it could also be considered out of proportion. Much of it revolves around relatively few interventions which have had limited success, and the research is largely qualitative, introspective and micro-focused.

The trends need to be seen in relation to the legacy of educational discrimination in South Africa. Millions of people received little or no formal education under apartheid and, although the idea of RPL has had great political currency, the practice of RPL has been more difficult than expected.[1] Implementation models borrowed from developed countries such as the United Kingdom, the United States, Canada, Australia and New Zealand generally assume a basic level of formal education and literacy and numeracy, which cannot be presumed in South Africa. RPL practitioners have found that implementation requires different and innovative approaches. The result has been a number of studies which seek to develop new visions and models out of problematic local interventions.

In presenting this view, I use the term RPL broadly to encompass all the different ways in which the prior experience of an adult – formal, informal, non-formal – is recognised in the workplace or education system, bearing in mind that this classification might not apply in other countries. RPL in South Africa ranges from mere acknowledgement (as in RPL for access purposes only, in which there is no assessment process) to qualified acknowledgement (as in RPL via portfolio processes) to RPL for accreditation purposes or advanced standing (which usually involves challenge tests or demonstrations). I refer to the recognition of prior experience in adult pedagogy as 'rpl' lower case, to distinguish it from the 'RPL' upper case that takes place prior to entry into an education programme.

---

[1] The 2007 *Community Survey* (Statistics South Africa, 2007) found that 10.3 per cent of the population aged 20 years and over had no formal education, 16 per cent had some primary education, 5.9 per cent had completed primary schooling, 40.9 per cent had some secondary education, 18.6 per cent had a senior certificate (the school-leaving certificate attained after 12 years of schooling) and 9.1 per cent had some higher education. In line with the patterns of discrimination under apartheid, the majority of the population that had higher education was classified as White, followed by Indians, Coloureds and Africans. Likewise, the majority with no formal education were Africans, followed by Coloureds, Indians and Whites. I use this racial terminology, not because I want to perpetuate the discrimination with which it used to be associated, but because it is necessary to monitor progress towards equity. To this end, South Africans are commonly still asked to identify themselves in terms of the four main population groups, including in the education system.

I draw on the definition of the National Research Foundation (NRF) that research is 'original investigation undertaken to gain knowledge and/or enhance understanding' (NRF, 2010, p. 10). Unlike the NRF, I recognise research which has been published in non-academic publications, usually for policy purposes, as well as research that has been published in academic books and journals. I focus on empirical research and analyses of existing research that have led to new theoretical perspectives. I include initiatives that might not normally be regarded as 'research', but were nonetheless important in the development of the practice and theorisation of RPL (such as workshops, overseas study visits etc.). Nonetheless, it will be noted that a considerable proportion of the work in this chapter can be regarded as academic research, having been published in academic journals or books. This is a feature of the RPL research trajectory in South Africa which has generally been quite scholarly.

My own position in relation to RPL in South Africa also needs to be noted. Although an outsider to the RPL community, in that I am not a practitioner, I am an insider to the research community, in that I have conducted research on RPL and will be quoting from my own work. As a full-time researcher with an interest in RPL, I have probably had more opportunities than most to conduct research on the topic (although not as many as I would have liked, given limited funding). I have tried not to give my work undue emphasis in the chapter and, after much vacillation, have reported it in the third person. Whether my contiguity to the subject matter is a limitation or strength is for the reader to decide.

Based on my reading of publications emanating from the research, I address the RPL research in terms of *three broad purposes*: 1) research to develop policy; 2) research to conceptualise RPL and guide practice; 3) research to monitor and quantify implementation. Each will be discussed in turn. Although there have been many studies, I will describe only a few in depth, choosing those which I believe to have had the most influence on policy or theory.

Research to develop policy

The earliest form of RPL in South Africa was the 'grandfather matric', a policy that allowed veterans from World War II to access higher education without the usual (matriculation or 'matric') certificate, provided they were 45 years or older. 'Mature age exemption' enabled younger (aged 30 to 44) applicants without matric to study for degrees provided they had four matric subjects. The age is currently set at 23, but the 'grandfather matric' for those without any matriculation subjects still stands at 45 (Ballim *et al.*, 2000).[2]

It is widely accepted that RPL, as a distinct practice bearing that name, became an underlying principle of education policy after 1990, largely as a result of initiatives by the trade unionists and workplace trainers associated with the various National Training Boards. However, a recent paper by Jeffy Mukora (Mukora, 2010) of the South African Qualifications Authority, who studied the National Qualifications Framework (NQF) for a PhD thesis, argues that the ideas that underlie the NQF (and so too RPL) – about vertical and horizontal mobility, integration of education and training, and lifelong learning – were proposed many years earlier, while apartheid still held sway, through the reports of an investigation into education in South Africa by the Human Sciences Research Council (HSRC) that was commissioned by the Cabinet of the day at a time of great unrest in Coloured and African schools, and complaints by business about shortages of skilled labour (HSRC, 1981).[3]

Post-1990, Mukora argues, the concept of RPL was developed in the course of negotiations between 'the trade union movement and its alliance partners about the differentiated training system and industrial training'. Ideas were borrowed from England, Scotland, Australia and New Zealand (*ibid.*, p. 22).

The research pattern was similar to that followed in other areas of policy development in South Africa and included study trips abroad, numerous local workshops, and the commissioning of selected case studies and concept papers. With the help of education researchers at the Human Sciences Research Council, the framing document, *Ways of Seeing the National Qualifications Framework*, was developed and subsequently the

---

[2] It is likely that these early provisions benefited mainly Whites. Although the veterans were not exclusively white, the higher education system was predominantly so at the time.

[3] The Commission was chaired by Professor J. P. de Lange, Rector of the pro-Nationalist university, Rand Afrikaanse Universiteit, and can be seen as part of a reformist initiative of the National Party government (see Mann, 1989, for a useful analysis). The Commission proposed a new education system in which there would be 'an integrated, flexible relationship between formal and non-formal education, between school and the world of work, in the context of lifelong continuing education' and a single Ministry of Education (HSRC, 1981, p. 194; quoted in Mukora, 2010, p.18). However, these proposals were not accepted by the government of the time and many years were to pass before they became reality, in a new democratic dispensation.

terms of the NQF itself. The document gave the following pioneering definition of RPL:

> *Granting credit on the basis of assessment of prior learning is termed recognition of prior learning. An example could be a person who has taught herself to type (i.e. has not attended a course) and now wants to have her typing skills formally assessed and accredited (HSRC, 1995, p. 18).*

It should be clear from this definition that RPL was conceptualised in terms of practical knowledge. It was also seen in the context of a modular, unit standards-based approach to education. As defined in the HSRC document, a unit standard was the 'smallest entity registered and assessed on the National Qualifications Framework' and a 'statement of the outcomes (knowledge, skills and abilities) that are to be demonstrated by an individual in order to obtain credit for the unit' (HSRC, 1995, p. 16). The system was to become very unwieldy, with standards generating bodies for 12 different educational fields generating thousands of unit standards, each with 15 different constituents. These constituents included statements of purposes, specific outcomes, assessment criteria, 'learning assumed to be in place' for each of their qualifications, range statements and a 'notes' category which would specify the 'critical cross-field outcomes' (generic skills) supported by the unit standard (SAQA, 1997, p. 9). Unit standards were time-consuming to produce, difficult to write and read, and led to fragmentation of knowledge in some disciplines. The process has since been streamlined considerably, but statements of outcomes, assessment criteria and other administrative details are still required across education and training.

RPL subsequently became one of the 13 principles of the NQF and an important principle in education policy generally. The *White Paper on Education and Training* (RSA, 1995a) presented RPL as one of the bases of an integrated approach to education and training in which:

> *the recognition of learning attainments wherever education and training are offered will open doors of opportunity for people whose academic or career paths have been needlessly blocked because their prior knowledge (acquired informally or by work experience) has not been assessed and certified, or because their qualifications have not been recognized for admission to further learning, or employment purposes (RSA, 1995a, p. 3).*

This wording echoed some of the rallying cries of the trade union move-ment which envisaged a ladder from 'sweeper to engineer'. However, the *White Paper on Higher Education* (RSA, 1997) placed greater emphasis on RPL as a means to achieve horizontal and vertical mobility within the higher education system. The discourse appeared to have changed from 'redress' to 'efficiency'.

RPL was formally introduced in 1998, when the South African Qualifications Authority (SAQA) stipulated that all qualifications may be achieved in whole or in part through RPL. This includes 'learning out-comes' achieved through 'formal, informal and non-formal learning and work experience' (RSA, 1998).

Research to conceptualise and guide practice

Since the SAQA stipulation, there have been many attempts to concep-tualise RPL for the South African context. Michelle Buchler, of the Workers in Higher Education Project based at the Joint Education Trust (JET), produced a *Report on International Models and South African Models of RPL Implementation* to contribute to the development of a SAQA policy on the implementation of RPL (Buchler, 2002). SAQA subsequently produced a policy (SAQA, 2002a) and two drafts of guidelines for pub-lic comment (SAQA, 2002b, 2003) before finalising guidelines for implementation (SAQA, 2004). American academic Elana Michelson, who came to South Africa to advise on implementation, was a powerful rhetorical influence, arguing for a vision of RPL that challenged the authority of dominant, academic forms of knowledge (e.g. Michelson 1996a, 1996b, 1997a, 1997b) and critiquing South African practice (e.g. Michelson, 1999, 2006).[4]

Local academics produced numerous articles on the subject of RPL in higher education. Some provided strong motivations in favour of it (Gawe, 1999; Kistan, 2002; Moore and van Rooyen, 2002; van Rooy, 2002), others were more cautious (e.g. Geyser, 1999, 2001; Cretchley and Castle, 2001). Osman (2004) categorised RPL and weighed the pros and cons of it (Osman and Castle, 2001). Breier wrote of difficulties associated with recognising informal knowledge in formal, particularly higher, edu-cation contexts (e.g. Breier, 1997, 1999, 2001). Hendricks and Volbrecht

---

[4] Michelson revised her earlier paper (Michelson, 1996a) in order to comment on a paper by Breier (2005) which was reprinted in the same volume.

(2003) linked RPL to African Renaissance. Khanyile (2000, 2005a, 2005b) was more practically focused and concentrated on developing a model for RPL in nursing.

One of the most influential voices was that of British educationist Judy Harris, who had experience in the UK, and who, since first coming to South Africa in the mid-1990s, has contributed extensively to the categorisation, conceptualisation and theorisation of RPL.

Harris' empirical research

Harris and Saddington (1995) provided one of the earliest conceptualisations of RPL, but Harris' most important work was undertaken as coordinator of a three-year research and development programme, funded by the Human Sciences Research Council between 1996 and 1999, entitled 'RPL in Higher Education'. This research project led to the publication of *RPL: Power, Pedagogy and Possibility: Conceptual and Implementation Guides* (Harris, 2000a), a PhD thesis (Harris, 2005) and a range of articles.

The empirical part of the research project involved the development and piloting of two approaches to RPL. This was a form of 'action research' where progress was simultaneously monitored by advisory groups. Both of the approaches to RPL were developed in relation to professional education courses: an adult educator advanced diploma in the Department of Adult Education and Extra-Mural Studies at the University of Cape Town (UCT) (where Harris was based at the time); and a professional development course for community health nurses at Peninsula Technikon (where her co-researcher, Esme Moses, was based).[5] The pilot in relation to adult educators focused on access to the programme (using portfolio development); the community nurses pilot was an investigation into the feasibility of RPL for advanced standing, and involved the development and administration of a challenge test which also aimed to capture nurses' learning that was not currently taught.

Together the studies show the complexity of both types of RPL. Out of 32 nurses who undertook the challenge test, 20 passed but 12 failed. Out of seven candidates who entered the UCT RPL process, six were successful and were admitted to the adult education diploma, but one

---

[5] Technikons were higher education institutions that specialised in technical education. They are now called Universities of Technology.

(who happened to be the only African) was not. In the nurses' case, weaknesses related to apparent inabilities to generalise and contextualise, as well as to outdated knowledge. In the UCT course, the candidate was found to have been unable to produce a sufficiently 'decontextualised' account in the dominant discourse of the diploma (Harris *et al.*, 1998, pp. 11, 29). Would the 'failures' have fared better in another kind of RPL process? Harris did not ask this question specifically, but much of her work since then seems directed at answering it.

Harris' conceptualisations of RPL

Since this study, Harris has drawn on a wide range of theorists, including Basil Bernstein and Michel Foucault, to develop conceptualisations of RPL (Harris, 1999a, 1999b, 2000a, 2005, for example). One of her major contributions was the distinction between four models of RPL:

- 'Procrustean' RPL, in which only those aspects of prior learning that 'fit' or match prescribed outcomes or standards are recognised. This form is often associated with vocational education, and human capital and technical and market-related visions of education.
- 'Learning and development' RPL, influenced by liberal and humanist discourses, in which candidates' prior learning has to be 'manipulated to conform to canonical bodies of knowledge'.
- 'Radical' RPL, in which learning and knowledge are seen as power laden, collective and emancipatory (a vision shared by those who put RPL on the trade union agenda in the early 1990s).
- 'Trojan horse' RPL, in which attempts would be made to value prior learning 'in and of itself rather than solely in terms of its degree of fit with existing standards or curricula or with the cognitive capacities deemed necessary to succeed in traditional terms' (Harris, 1999a, pp. 124–39).

The Trojan horse conceptual model was developed further in *Power, Pedagogy and Possibility: Conceptual and Implementation Guides* (Harris, 2000a, pp. 79–80). Part of the HSRC project 'RPL in Higher Education' involved commissioning case studies from a number of international contexts: RPL in further education in the UK and Australia; in higher education in the UK; and within liberal arts at the State University of New York – Empire State College. In her Conceptual Guide, Harris promotes a form of RPL that aims to be 'optimally socially inclusive', assessing against broad notions of level descriptors, generic assessment criteria and broad programme outcomes wherever possible, in addition to assessment against specific programme outcomes/requirements. The prior learning recognised would be based on broad notions of equivalence between formal knowledge and prior learning, with some direct equivalence if/as required.

Harris' most recent contribution to the theorisation of RPL has been as co-editor of the volume *Re-theorising the Recognition of Prior Learning* (Andersson and Harris, 2006). In her own chapter in the book, she takes issue with RPL theorists who downplay knowledge differences and makes greater use of the concepts of Basil Bernstein to delineate knowledge boundaries and ways to cross them. Drawing on Bernstein's terminology (predominantly his distinction between vertical and horizontal knowledge structures) she re-theorises her study of the RPL pilot in the UCT adult education department.[6] She argues that the advanced diploma in question could be seen as an example of a horizontal knowledge structure which required a particular kind of gaze and critical self-reflection and that: 'Areas of prior knowledge that fell outside of this "gaze" did not count, indeed were often not seen' by the RPL facilitators (Harris, 2006, p. 67).

The importance of Harris' re-theorisation, in my opinion, is that it reminds us that different forms of knowledge have different boundary strengths and the knowledge of some RPL candidates is more 'vertical' than others. The challenge is to know the nature and strength of the border and how to cross it.

Research to monitor and quantify implementation

Along with attempts to conceptualise RPL were a number of studies designed to monitor implementation. They reflect the patchy and often difficult implementation of the practice.

---

[6] Bernstein distinguished between two forms of knowledge – horizontal and vertical discourses – which approximate, broadly speaking, to everyday and academic knowledge. Within vertical discourse, he distinguished further between those disciplines that are structured segmentally (in a similar manner to horizontal discourses) and those structured vertically. He called these horizontal and vertical knowledge structures respectively, with sociology as an example of the former and physics of the latter.

Implementation in the workplace

Ballim *et al.* (2000) note that realising the hopes and aspirations associated with RPL in the workplace has proved to be more difficult than expected:

> *This is evident in a number of bruising experiences that adult workers have had to face in some leading pilot projects initiated in the mid-1990s, which are distinctive in their ability to discount workers' knowledge and ways of knowing whilst privileging status quo standards and assessment techniques (ibid., p. 188).*

The following projects investigate the experiences of metalworkers and mineworkers in their workplaces, and rural community workers and adult educators in higher education courses. I describe them in depth because I believe they have made a very important contribution to understanding the limited take-up of RPL, by employers and unions alike, in the workplace.

Participatory action research in two trade unions

Lugg *et al.* (1998) describe a participatory research project by the Congress of South African Trade Unions (COSATU) during 1997, which showed that, by and large, workers' expectations about RPL had not been met. The researchers monitored and analysed the results of an initiative in 1993 in the automotive industry in which employers and the National Union of Metalworkers of South Africa (NUMSA) agreed on a form of RPL through which workers would be assessed against unit standards.[7] NUMSA saw the purpose of the exercise as: 'to allow workers to progress through the grading system by demonstrating and, where necessary, increasing their skills and knowledge' (*ibid.*, p. 204). The Union hoped that the project would 'prove their members skill and identify those who were eligible for a grade and wage increase and that they could use the process to further NUMSA's demand for training' (*ibid.*). The RPL process took place over a six-month period in 1996, and workers were assessed through an oral examination and on-the-job observation. Less than 10 per cent of the workers who went through the RPL process were

---

[7] At the time the trade union movement saw the NQF as an important vehicle for worker redress and accepted its elements uncritically, including unit standards. However, the unit standard system was already criticised for being over-modularised and mechanistic in its compartmentalisation of knowledge. Unit standards were often also incomprehensible, at times, with their complicated terminology or 'SAQA-speak'.

re-graded upwards (although one plant of one company claimed over 50 per cent were re-graded upwards). None were down-graded.

The second initiative involved the National Union of Mineworkers (NUM) and a mining house, which, in 1995, implemented a pilot RPL project on a mass scale. A total of 7,591 (out of a target of up to 26,000) workers were assessed for basic language and mathematics skills against national Adult Basic Education and Training (ABET) standards. In this case, the project was initiated by management, hoping also to quality assure the ABET provision at the company mines.

In the mining study, employers at national level refused to release results, but the researchers did obtain results from one of the three mines. They were dismal. For example, at ABET (Adult Basic Education and Training) level 1, only 25 per cent of the 174 English papers received certificates and only 50 per cent of the 175 numeracy papers. At ABET level 2, only 30 per cent of the 229 English papers were successful and 22 per cent of the 172 numeracy papers. At ABET level 3, 60 per cent of the 255 English papers were certificated and 20 per cent of the 234 numeracy papers.[8]

One benefit for the NUM was that its participation in the RPL processes 'strengthened its hand for winning an industry-wide agreement on the provision of ABET at mine level. In this sense the workers benefited indirectly' (*ibid.*, p. 205).

Lugg *et al.* (1998) found the outcomes for the two unions were very similar 'in that the vast majority of the workers who went through the RPL process did not receive any direct benefit'; 'very few workers were regraded, received any pay increases or had an opportunity for training as a result of being RPL'd' (*ibid.*, p. 205).

The researchers drew out the following implications for RPL practice:

- The design and implementation of RPL must include worker representation.
- Standards must recognise experiential forms of knowledge and skill.
- Workers must receive support and guidance throughout the RPL process.

---

[8] This is not to say that the ABET examination system was exemplary or an appropriate reflection of the life and work performance of the mineworkers. See Prinsloo and Kell (1999) for a critique of the ABET system.

- RPL must be linked to accreditation and education and training opportunities.
- RPL should be voluntary and available to all (*ibid.*, pp. 210–11).

There have been further important publications on worker experience of RPL by Linda Cooper, a university adult education academic and trade union educator. Cooper (1998) provides a brief historical overview of the growth of the trade union movement in South Africa, and locates RPL within a shift in trade union education from a 'transformative' to a 'human capital' discourse (*ibid.*, p. 144) that has the potential to divide rather than unite workers. She has since developed this theme in a case study of a branch of a national, municipal trade union, reported in Cooper (2006) and her own PhD thesis (Cooper, 2005).

Implementation in higher education

Higher education institutions started to implement RPL in the late 1990s, with some reluctance. In one of the very few quantitative studies of RPL, the Education Policy Unit at the University of the Western Cape, commissioned by the Council on Higher Education, found limited recognition of informal and non-formal learning, although the practice of recognising other formal qualifications was long-standing. Only four institutions had developed written policy documents on RPL and three had drafted written policies. About 100 students had been 'RPL'd' at technikons (for advanced standing as well as access) and about 250 students in the university sector had been granted access to undergraduate programmes on an RPL basis (Breier and Osman, 2000).

In 2003, Breier, assisted by Burness, conducted a further email and telephone questionnaire survey of RPL policies and practices at the 21 universities and 14 technikons in existence at the time, and compared the results with the 2000 study (Breier and Burness, 2003). They noted that there had been many government policy and discussion documents since 2000 which affirmed the importance of RPL in higher education within the context of broadening access for non-traditional students. The 16 universities and ten technikons (75 per cent of the total) that responded to the questionnaire had taken the policy pronouncements very seriously, and there had been widespread institutionalisation of RPL policies and practices among these institutions. However, RPL was mainly for access rather than credit or advanced standing. The researchers were informed of at least 459 students who had been RPL'd into various university programmes and 680 at technikons. This excluded the many thousands of students who were beginning to be RPL'd into the National Professional Diploma in Education, a nationwide initiative to upgrade the qualifications of experienced but under-qualified teachers (this is discussed in more detail below).

Drawing on the dominant categorisations of RPL at the time,[9] Breier and Burness noted that most of the initiatives fell within the technical/market (outcomes-oriented) or liberal/humanist approaches (associated with portfolios and self-development). There was no evidence of critical radical approaches beyond certain individuals who expressed such commitment. However, there were also two more types of RPL: an 'expedient' version that focused on compliance with government policy or law and the dictates of the education bureaucracy, and another approach that was less a form of RPL than a supported educational opportunity for adults without matric to enter university. This approach was marked by a focus on preservation of academic standards combined with a concern that the university should not admit students who are unlikely to succeed. It was being called a 'responsible' approach to RPL, and is similar to the 'learning and development' model described by Harris (1999a).

Reflections on implementation in higher education
Higher education academics tasked with introducing RPL have written prolifically on their initiatives, which include:

- A pilot study in which students without Grade 12 were admitted to a certificate course in Rural Resource Management at the (then) University of Natal[10] (Luckett, 1999a, 1999b).
- Various teacher education courses within the Faculty of Education at the University of the Witwatersrand (Wits) and the former Johannesburg College of Education (now merged with Wits) (e.g. Castle and Attwood, 2001; Osman and Castle, 2001, 2002; Shalem, 2001; Castle, 2003; Osman, 2003, 2004, 2006; Shalem and Steinberg, 2006).

---

[9] There have been various categorisations of RPL that appear to stem from Butterworth (1992), including Harris (1999a, 2000a), Luckett (1999a), Breier (2003) and Osman (2004).

[10] Now the University of KwaZulu Natal.

- A pilot portfolio development initiative at the University of the Western Cape (Hendricks, 2001; Thaver *et al.*, 2002).
- RPL policy and implementation in the Faculty of Education at the University of Pretoria (Motaung, 2007, 2009; Motaung *et al.*, 2008).
- RPL policy at the University of Stellenbosch[11] (Frick *et al.*, 2007).

The overall impression from these studies was that RPL was not easy to implement in a higher education context, given the extent of educational backlog in this country. Adults with limited formal education often showed difficulties in tasks that required abstraction, generalisation and self-reflection (or at least the articulation thereof), and many had difficulties with English academic literacies, understandably as English was most often not their home language. Nonetheless there were some notable exceptions of adults who had acquired extensive academic-type knowledge in their life, work or, often, trade union context, who performed exceptionally well in the university context. For many, the process of developing a portfolio could make a major contribution to an individual's self-development. Finally, the practice of RPL, while time-consuming and often resisted, encouraged academics to reflect on their own forms of knowledge and their limitations, and to consider – and in some cases improve – what they taught.

Research on RPL in adult pedagogy: 'rpl' as opposed to 'RPL'

In a somewhat different take on RPL, Breier investigated the recruitment and recognition of prior experience in the *pedagogy* of two university courses in Labour Law as part of a PhD study; that is, 'rpl' *within* the courses rather than *prior* to entry (Breier, 2003, 2004a, 2004b, 2005, 2006). The study included observation and audio-recording of the lectures in both courses, analysis of lecture transcripts, course notes, student assignments, exam questions, exam scripts and all marks achieved, as well as semi- and unstructured interviews with selected students and lecturers. Breier drew on the theories of Basil Bernstein (1999, 2000), Dowling (1993, 1998) and aspects of systemic network analysis (including Halliday, 1973, 1978, 1990) to develop a 'language' for the description of the relationship between formal and informal knowledge in pedagogy.

---

[11] Unnamed in the article, but obvious from its reference list.

213

The study also analysed the texts in terms of the three common approaches to RPL – technical/market, liberal/humanist and critical/ radical perspectiveds – and suggested a fourth way of looking at these scenarios. This 'disciplinary' approach requires one to consider the nature and structure of the discipline or field of education concerned, the relationship between formal and informal knowledge within that discipline or field, and the extent to which the pedagogic discourse mirrors that relationship (Breier, 2005).

Research on a mass RPL initiative in a teacher upgrading programme

Research on the introduction of RPL in the National Professional Diploma in Education (NPDE) deserves considerable attention because of the scale of the intervention, the extent of research that accompanied its implementation and the new visions of RPL which it produced.

The NPDE is an ambitious attempt to upgrade the qualifications of tens of thousands of under-qualified teachers in South Africa. Launched in 2001–02, RPL was introduced into the programme with some rhetoric, but a largely bureaucratic purpose designed to address distinctions between two pay classes, even though the teachers concerned often taught at the same level.

Because of a limited budget, the national Department of Education needed to restrict the programme to a maximum of two years part-time. Instead of requiring the lower-qualified teachers to take an extra two years, it offered them credit through RPL. As the programme unfolded at the 17 institutions offering it, it became clear that the Department regarded the RPL component as little more than a bureaucratic exercise, one in which all candidates would inevitably be successful. But educators still had to put together programmes that offered at least a semblance of the practice as it is conventionally understood.

Research for the ETDP Skills Education Training Authority
In 2005, the Education, Training and Development Practitioners (ETDP) Skills Education Training Authority (SETA)[12] commissioned research at

---

[12] Sector Education Training Authorities (SETAs) were established by legislation in 1998 to replace the old training boards, and to be responsible for education and training within a defined cluster of economic activities – for example, banking, manufacturing, education – and in accordance with skills development plans.

the 17 provider institutions involving visits to all institutions, and interviews with academics, tutors and administrators. The study aimed to produce an overview of RPL and associated curriculum practices in the NPDE, and to develop and improve practices where necessary. (A drawback to the study, which has been noted by the researchers, was that there were no interviews with students and no observations.) The report notes many difficulties associated with the implementation of RPL in the NPDE, while also affirming the attempts of providers.

The dominant tendency was to locate RPL relatively late in the NPDE programme. In this way the NPDE student 'could learn about academic expectations before being subjected to summative RPL assessment' (Volbrecht et al., 2006). The researchers pointed out that this approach was an extension of the developmental model advocated in SAQA RPL policy and guideline documents in that 'the entire curriculum including RPL is geared towards allowing learners to build on their prior learning through interaction with the learning opportunities provided' (ibid., p. 68).

In this developmental model, RPL is integrated into the curriculum in such a way as to ensure that learners reflect on their prior learning and how it relates to new and future learning. The emerging model can be integrated with a transformational model in which school-based knowledge and learning can play a role in transforming the knowledge base of those providing teacher training through making them more conversant with the discourses of school-based educators (ibid., p. 68).

The final research report recommends that providers 'affirm and build on a developmental and transformational RPL model that is integrated into the NPDE curriculum, and that they theorise this model as an instance of work-based learning' (ibid., p. 67). The report also notes a 'relative neglect' of the pastoral role of the educators in the institutional learning programmes, while in narrative accounts of prior learning, the NPDE students frequently referred to learning related to this role (ibid., p. 36).[13]

---

[13] Volbrecht (2009) theorises further the concept of developmental RPL, comparing it with Harris' 'trojan horse' approach, which includes a 'spine module' that begins prior to entry and then extends afterwards into the main curriculum (Harris, 1999a, cited in ibid., p. 22).

Qualitative research on the NPDE RPL

The theme of pastoral care emerges strongly in another study on the NPDE (reported in Gardiner, 2006; Breier, 2008; Ralphs, 2009; Breier and Ralphs, 2010). This research explored the implementation of RPL in the NPDE programmes of three universities, focusing in particular on the experiences of selected students.

In the monograph that emanated from the study, Breier (2008) argues that, in the context of a teacher upgrading programme like the NPDE, RPL presents a baffling conundrum. RPL usually occurs prior to commencement of a programme and requires the candidate to demonstrate competences practically, or to show them indirectly in a portfolio in which they reflect on prior experience and their learning derived from it. This proved to be very difficult in the NPDE where providers faced the following conundrum:

- RPL is all about recognition and affirmation of knowledge and skills of value.
- The NPDE is an upgrading programme for teachers with insufficient training or who were trained under a system that is now discredited, having led to knowledge gaps and teaching practices that are now thought to be problematic.
- How then do you positively acknowledge the experience of such teachers, as is usually required in RPL?

Breier found it was not surprising that the universities were not offering conventional 'front-end' RPL, which would assess prior learning before the start of the programme in a summative way. Instead, RPL procedures were being implemented alongside the formal learning programmes, sometimes quite deep into the programmes, with varying degrees of formative purpose and varying effects.

It appeared that many of the NPDE teacher-students had difficulties with the formal knowledge requirements of the courses and, in particular, with the emphasis on reflection, usually in English, which for most was a second, if not third, language. However, from analysis of portfolios and interviews, Breier (2008) concluded that these teachers showed enormous capacity for pastoral care and were also masters of what Aristotle has called practical wisdom or *phronesis*, a form of knowledge and disposition that incorporates both abstract and particular, but emphasises the particular and enables the individual to negotiate that particular in the light of a

216

general ethical understanding. It enables the individual to discern what is good and beneficial not only for him/herself, but also for a wider community. And it is inextricably bound up with the acquisition of life experience. The monograph argues that the concept of practical wisdom should form part of any curriculum that seeks to recognise prior learning. It also affirms the concept of a developmental model of RPL, as proposed by Volbrecht *et al.* (2006) as a solution to the 'RPL conundrum'.

Research on workplace implementation

There has been some evidence of research on workplace implementation by providers that have investigated aspects of RPL practice from an employer/efficiency perspective. Deller (2007) is the most comprehensive example. I could find no evidence of substantial further research from a workers' perspective, beyond the Lugg *et al.* (1998) study. Indeed, at a recent RPL conference organised by SAQA, a poster presentation by COSATU (Congress of South African Trade Unions) and its associated education institute, the Development Institute for Training, Support and Education for Labour (DITSELA), quoted that 13-year-old study as if it were the only one available (Maboye, 2011).

Research by the Organisation for Economic Co-operation and Development (OECD)

One of the most recent contributions to RPL in South Africa is from the Organisation for Economic Co-operation and Development (OECD), which sent a three-person team to South Africa for a week as part of a broader international study on RPL. Their visit was preceded by the compilation of a *Country Background Report* by three South African researchers associated with SAQA. The OECD team visited selected educational institutions, providers and other stakeholders, and compiled a report (OECD, 2009). The report found there had not been much progress towards redress since an earlier study in 2005. They identified 'islands of good practice', but were concerned that practitioners were isolated (*ibid.*, p. 23). There were 'pressing needs':

- To provide financial support for 'new and fledgling RPL services' and to build bridges between the 'islands of practice' by setting up, with funding support, a 'national practitioners' network' (*ibid.*).

217

- To develop RPL capacity in the 'forgotten' Further Education and Training (FET) sector (*ibid.*, p. 24).
- To 'transform RPL [in South Africa] from a sleeping giant into a major force in the national education and training system' (*ibid.*, p. 26).

Current research

An important study under way at the time of writing is a SAQA-sponsored study entitled 'Specialised Pedagogy: A comparative study of RPL practices within the changing landscape of the NQF in South Africa' (Ralphs, 2009).

The project is framed within the overall pursuit of what Harris (2000) called an 'optimally inclusive' model of RPL. The proposed methodology is a qualitative, cross-sectional study of RPL practices in initiatives aimed at adult applicants to certain higher education institutions, and trade unionists and workers with various levels of education. They include the RPL programme of the University of the Western Cape, the Adult Education Programme at the University of Cape Town, the RPL Portfolio Course at the Workers' College in Durban, the curriculum that the Industrial Health Resource Group at the University of Cape Town has been developing for unions, and the Prior Learning Centre, an accredited private workplace RPL provider, which provides RPL projects on contract to private companies. At this stage, it appears that many of the researchers will be drawn from the ranks of the practitioners within the projects, making it a form of action research in which the practitioner/researcher is seeking to improve practice while also researching it.

Conclusion

This chapter has attempted to provide an overview of research on RPL in South Africa in relation to the following broad purposes: 1) research to develop policy; 2) research to conceptualise RPL and guide practice; 3) research to monitor and quantify implementation. It has included within its ambit research on the recognition of prior experience within adult pedagogy, as well as prior to entry.

The empirical research has been mostly qualitative, mainly in university education departments, and it has focused quite strongly on the challenges of implementation. At the same time, judging from the extent of international publications, it appears to have made a very important

contribution to international theorisation of the practice and the epistemological issues which RPL raises. This chapter alone covers numerous
journal articles, international as well as national; also books, book chapters, doctoral and masters dissertations, and research reports.

Nonetheless, there are important gaps which need to be filled if RPL
in South Africa is to realise its full potential. There have been no large-
scale studies to audit the nature and extent of implementation, not only
in higher education, but also in other branches of education, particularly
further education; and, most importantly, in industrial and commercial
workplaces where pre-1994 policy rhetoric delivered most strongly its
RPL promise. Indeed, there appears to have been no substantial research
from a workers' perspective since the 1998 trade union study by Lugg *et
al.* The workplace research that has been conducted in recent years is
mostly by providers whose focus is on efficiency rather than redress.

While small-scale, micro-level qualitative research will continue to
be important to monitor implementation and promote further theorisation of the practice, it will not help us to gain an overview of the full
scale of provision – or lack of it. Furthermore, we need to move away
from introverted, action research to studies of the 'other': other workplaces; other providers; other forms of RPL. In situations of difference, we
might be able to conceptualise new understandings and directions to
extend the reach of RPL in South Africa.

References

Andersson, P. and Harris, J. (eds) (2006) *Re-theorising the Recognition of Prior
Learning.* Leicester, UK: National Institute of Adult Continuing
Education (NIACE).

Ballim, Y., Omar, R. and Ralphs, A. (2000) 'Learning assessment in South
Africa', in N. Evans (ed.) *Experiential Learning around the World.* Higher
Education Policy Series, 52. London and Philadelphia: Jessica Kingsley
Publishers.

Bernstein, B. (1999) 'Vertical and horizontal discourse: An essay', *British
Journal of Sociology of Education,* Vol. 20, No 2, pp. 157–79.

Bernstein, B. (2000) *Pedagogy, Symbolic Control and Identity.* Revised
edition. Lanham, USA: Rowman and Littlefield Publishers.

Breier, M. (1997) 'Whose learning? Whose knowledge? Recognition of
Prior Learning and the National Qualifications Framework', in D.
Bensusan (ed.) *W(h)ither the University.* Cape Town: Juta.

Breier, M. (1999) 'Faint hope or false promise? The RPL principle of the NQF', in W. Morrow and K. King (eds) *Vision and Reality: Changing Education and Training in South Africa*. Cape Town: University of Cape Town Press.

Breier, M. (2001) 'How to bridge the "great divide": The dilemma for the policy and practice of Recognition of Prior Learning (RPL) in South Africa', *Perspectives in Education*, Vol. 19, No 4, pp. 89–107.

Breier, M. (2003) 'The recruitment and recognition of prior informal experience in the pedagogy of two university courses in labour law'. PhD Thesis, University of Cape Town.

Breier, M. (2004a) 'A network analysis of formal and informal knowledge in adult pedagogy', *Journal of Education*, Vol. 33, pp. 5–26.

Breier, M. (2004b) 'Horizontal and vertical discourse in law and labour law', in J. Muller, A. Morais and B. Davies (eds) *Reading Bernstein, Researching Bernstein*. London: Routledge.

Breier, M. (2005) 'A disciplinary-specific approach to the recognition of prior informal experience in adult pedagogy: "rpl" as opposed to "RPL"', *Studies in Continuing Education*, Vol. 27, No 1, pp. 51–65. Republished in Andersson and Harris (2006).

Breier, M. (2006) '"In my case" ... the recruitment and recognition of prior informal experience in adult pedagogy', *British Journal of the Sociology of Education*, Vol. 7, No 2, pp. 173–88.

Breier, M. (2008) *The RPL Conundrum: Recognition of Prior Learning in a Teacher Upgrading Programme*. Cape Town: HSRC Press.

Breier, M. and Burness, A. (2003) 'The implementation of the Recognition of Prior Learning at higher education institutions in South Africa'. Bellville: Centre for the Study of Higher Education, University of the Western Cape.

Breier, M. and Osman, R. (2000) 'Preliminary report on the Recognition of Prior Learning at higher education institutions in South Africa'. Unpublished report commissioned by the Council on Higher Education and the Joint Education Trust.

Breier, M. with Ralphs, A. (2010) 'In search of *phronesis*: Recognising practical wisdom in the Recognition (Assessment) of Prior Learning', *British Journal of Sociology of Education*, Vol. 30, No 4, pp. 479–93.

Buchler, M. (2002) 'International models and South African models of RPL implementation'. Unpublished report produced by the Workers in Higher Education Project, Joint Education Trust.

Butterworth, C. (1992) 'More than one bite at the APEL – contrasting models of accrediting prior learning', *Journal of Further and Higher Education*, Vol. 16, No 3, pp. 39–51.

Castle, J. (2003) 'The prior learning paths of mature students entering a postgraduate qualification in adult education', *Journal of Education*, Vol. 29, pp. 30–56.

Castle, J. and Attwood, G. (2001) 'Recognition of Prior Learning (RPL) for access or credit? Problematic issues in a university', *Studies in the Education of Adults*, Vol. 33, No 1, pp. 60–72.

Cooper, L. (1998) 'From "rolling mass action" to "RPL": The changing discourse of experience and learning in the South African labour movement', *Studies in Continuing Education*, Vol. 20, No 2, pp. 143–57.

Cooper, L. (2005) 'Towards a theory of pedagogy, learning and knowledge in an "everyday" context: Case study of a South African trade union'. PhD Thesis, University of Cape Town.

Cooper, L. (2006) '"Tools of Mediation"': An historical-cultural approach to RPL', in P. Andersson and J. Harris (eds) *Re-theorising the Recognition of Prior Learning*. Leicester: NIACE.

Cretchley, G. and Castle, J. (2001) 'OBE, RPL and adult education: Good bedfellows in higher education in South Africa?', *International Journal of Lifelong Education*, Vol. 20, No 6, pp. 487–501.

Deller, K. (2007) 'Towards the design of a workplace RPL implementation model for the South African insurance sector.' PhD thesis, Faculty of Human Resources Management, University of Johannesburg.

Dowling, P. (1993) 'A language for the sociological description of pedagogic texts with particular reference to the "Secondary School Mathematics Scheme SMP 11–16"'. PhD Thesis, Institute of Education, University of London.

Dowling, P. (1998) *The Sociology of Mathematics Education*. London: The Falmer Press.

Frick, B., Bitzer, E. and Leibowitz, B. (2007) 'Implications of variance in ARPL policy: A South African case study', *South African Journal of Higher Education*, Vol. 21, No 4, pp. 640–53.

Gardiner, M. (2006) 'Research in the Limpopo Province for the project on RPL in teacher education, with a focus on the NPDE'. Case study report for Teachers' Education Project, 13.

Gawe, N. (1999) 'Arming ourselves for Recognition of Prior Learning', *South African Journal of Higher Education*, Vol. 13, No 2, pp. 22–8.

Geyser, H. (1999) 'RPL policy in the making', *South African Journal of Higher Education*, Vol. 13, No 2, pp. 192–9.

Geyser, H. (2001) 'RPL: Lessons from abroad', *South African Journal of Higher Education*, Vol. 15, No 2, pp. 30–6.

Halliday, M. (1973) *Explorations in the Functions of Language*. London: Edward Arnold.

Halliday, M. (1978) *Language as Social Semiotic*. London: Edward Arnold.

Halliday, M. (1990) *Spoken and Written Language*. Oxford: Oxford University Press.

Harris, J. (1999a) 'Ways of seeing the Recognition of Prior Learning: What contribution can such practices make to social inclusion?', *Studies in the Education of Adults*, Vol. 31, No 2, pp. 124–39.

Harris, J. (1999b) 'The Recognition of Prior Learning (RPL): Introducing a conceptual framework', *South African Journal of Higher Education*, Vol. 13, No 2, pp. 38–43.

Harris, J. (2000a) *RPL: Power, Pedagogy and Possibility*. Pretoria: Human Sciences Research Council.

Harris, J. (2000b) 'Prior learning: theories of learning and the Recognition of Prior Learning – implications for South African education and training'. Report commissioned for the National Centre for Curriculum Research and Development, Department of Education, Pretoria.

Harris, J. (2005) 'The hidden curriculum of the Recognition of Prior Learning: A case study'. PhD Thesis, Open University, UK.

Harris, J. (2006) 'Questions of knowledge and curriculum in the Recognition of Prior Learning', in P. Andersson and J. Harris (eds) *Re-theorising the Recognition of Prior Learning*. Leicester, UK: NIACE.

Harris, J. and Saddington, J. (1995) *The Recognition of Prior Learning: International Models of Assessment and their impact on South African Education and Training*. Cape Town: Department of Adult Education and Extra-Mural Studies, University of Cape Town.

Harris, J., Moses, E., McMillan, J. and Small, J. (1998) '"A Tale of Two Studies": Report on the Research and Development Programme in the Recognition of Prior Learning in Higher Education'. Cape Town: HSRC, UCT and Peninsula Technikon.

Hendricks, M. N. (2001) 'The recognition of prior learning in higher education: the case of the University of the Western Cape'. Minor dissertation, Masters in Public Administration, University of the Western Cape.

Hendricks, M. N. and Volbrecht, T. (2003) 'RPL as cognitive praxis in linking higher education, the African renaissance and lifelong learning', *South African Journal of Higher Education*, Vol. 17, No 1, pp. 47–53.

Human Sciences Research Council (1981) *Report of the Main Committee of the HSRC Investigation into Education (De Lange Report)*. Pretoria: HSRC.

Human Sciences Research Council (1995) *Ways of Seeing the National Qualifications Framework*. Pretoria: HSRC.

Khanyile, T. (2000) 'Recognition of Prior Learning: Its relevance to the proposed unified model of education and training for South African nurses', *Curationis*, Vol. 23, No 2, pp. 70–5.

Khanyile, T. (2005a) 'The development of the model for Recognition of Prior Learning for nurses in South Africa: Development of the RPL guidelines by the policy makers and stakeholders of nursing', *Curationis*, Vol. 28, No 4, pp. 50–6.

Khanyile, T. (2005b) 'The development of the model for Recognition of Prior Learning for nurses in South Africa: Implementation of the RPL guidelines by three nursing education institutions', *Curationis*, Vol. 28, No 5, pp. 53–60.

Kistan, C. (2002) 'Recognition of Prior Learning: A challenge to higher education', *South African Journal of Higher Education*, Vol. 16, No 1, pp. 169–73.

Luckett, K. (1999a) 'Ways of recognising the prior learning of rural development workers', *South African Journal of Higher Education*, Vol. 13, No 2, pp. 68–81.

Luckett, K. (1999b) 'Recognition of Prior Learning Report for Phase 1 of the School of Rural Community Development Project'. Unpublished draft report, University of Natal.

Lugg, R., Mabitla, A., Louw, G. and Angelis, D. (1998) 'Workers' experiences of RPL in South Africa: Some implications for redress, equity and transformation', *Studies in Continuing Education*, Vol. 20, No 2, pp. 201–15.

Maboye, M. (2011) 'Understanding Recognition of Prior Learning (RPL) in the context of Organised Labour: Opportunities and Challenges'. Poster presented on behalf of COSATU/DITSELA at National RPL Conference, Boksburg, Johannesburg, 23–25 February 2011.

Mann, M. (1989) 'Power and knowledge: The case of contemporary South Africa', *Public Administration*, Vol. 67, pp. 223–8. Available at: http://www3.interscience.wiley.com/journal/119434555/abstract (Accessed 26 July 2010).

Michelson, E. (1996a) 'Beyond Galileo's telescope: Situated knowledge and the Assessment of Experiential learning', *Adult Education Quarterly*, Vol. 46, No 4, pp. 185–96.

Michelson, E. (1996b) 'Taxonomies of sameness: The Recognition of Prior Learning as anthropology'. Paper presented at the International Consortium on Experiential Learning Conference held at the University of Cape Town, July 1996.

Michelson, E. (1997a) 'Multicultural approaches to portfolio development', in A. Rose and M. Leahy (eds) *Multicultural Approaches in Assessing Adult Learning in Diverse Settings: Current Issues and Approaches*. San Francisco: Jossey Bass.

Michelson, E. (1997b) 'The politics of memory: the Recognition of Experiential Learning', in S. Walters (ed.) *Globalization, Adult Education and Training: Impacts and Issues*. London: Zed Books.

Michelson, E. (1999) 'Social Transformation and the Recognition of Prior Learning: Lessons for and from South Africa', *South African Journal of Higher Education*, Vol. 13, No 2, pp. 99–102.

Michelson, E. (2006) 'Beyond Galileo's telescope: situated knowledge and the recognition of prior learning', in P. Andersson and J. Harris (eds) *Re-theorising the Recognition of Prior Learning*. Leicester, UK: NIACE.

Moore, A. and van Rooyen, L. (2002) 'Recognition of Prior Learning as an integral component of competence-based assessment in South Africa', *South African Journal of Education*, Vol. 22, No 4, pp. 293–96.

Motaung, J. (2007) 'Quality assurance practice in the provisioning of RPL (Recognition of Prior Learning) in higher education'. PhD Thesis, University of Pretoria.

Motaung, J. (2009) 'The "nuts and bolts" of Prior Learning Assessment in the Faculty of Education of the University of Pretoria', *Perspectives in Education*, Vol. 27, No 1, pp. 78–84.

Motaung, J., Fraser, W. and Howie, S. (2008) 'Prior Learning Assessment and quality assurance practice: Possibilities and challenges', *South African Journal of Higher Education*, Vol. 22, No 6, pp. 149–59.

Mukora, J. (2010) 'A history of RPL in South Africa'. Proceedings of the Colloquium on Recognition of Prior Learning (RPL) in the Upgrading and Up-skilling of Teachers in South Africa, December 2008. Pretoria: SAQA and the Department of Education.

National Research Foundation (NRF) (2010) 'Guidelines for members of specialist committees for the evaluation and rating of individual researchers', March 2010. Available at: http://www.nrf.ac.za/projects.php?pid=33 (Accessed 7 June 2010).

Organisation for Economic Co-operation and Development (OECD) and South African Qualifications Authority (SAQA) (2009) *Recognition of Non-formal and Informal Learning: Country Note for South Africa*. Pretoria: SAQA.

Osman, R. (2003) 'The Recognition of Prior Learning (RPL): An emergent field of enquiry in South Africa'. PhD Thesis, University of the Witwatersrand, Johannesburg.

Osman, R. (2004) 'Access, equity and justice: Three perspectives on Recognition of Prior Learning (RPL) in higher education', *Perspectives in Education*, Vol. 22, No 4, pp. 139–45.

Osman, R. (2006) 'RPL: An emerging and contested practice in South Africa', in P. Andersson and J. Harris (eds) *Re-theorising the Recognition of Prior Learning*. Leicester, UK: NIACE.

Osman, R. and Castle, J. (2001) 'The Recognition of Prior Learning: Early lessons, challenges and promises', *South African Journal of Higher Education*, Vol. 15, No 1, pp. 54–60.

Osman, R. and Castle, J. (2002) 'Recognition of Prior Learning: A soft option in higher education in South Africa?', *South African Journal of Higher Education*, Vol. 16, No 2, pp. 63–8.

Prinsloo, M. and Kell, C. (1999) 'Fast-tracking ABET delivery in South Africa'. Response to the Deputy Minister of Education. Available at: http://web.uct.ac.za/depts/educate/download/99fasttrackingabet.pdf (Accessed 27 July 2010).

Ralphs, A. (2006) RPL in the NPDE at the Nelson Mandela Metropolitan University: Case study report based on teachers from the Bizana District in the Eastern Cape. Case study report for Teachers' Education Project, 13.

Ralphs, A. (2009) 'Specialised pedagogy: A comparative study of RPL practices within the changing landscape of the NQF in South Africa'. Research proposal submitted to the South African Qualifications Authority.

Republic of South Africa (RSA) (1995a) *White Paper on Education and Training*. Notice 196 of 1995. Available at: http://www.education.gov.za (Accessed 7 June 2010).

Republic of South Africa (RSA) (1995b) *South African Qualifications Authority Act*. Government Gazette No 1521 of 4 October 1995. Available at: http://www.saqa.org.za (Accessed 7 June 2010).

Republic of South Africa (RSA) (1997) 'A programme for the transformation of higher education in South Africa', *Education White Paper 3*. Government Gazette No 1196 of 24 July 1997. Available at: http://www.education.gov.za (Accessed 7 June 2010).

Republic of South Africa (RSA) (1998) *National Standards Bodies Regulations*. Government Gazette No 18787 of 28 March 1998. Available at: http://www.saqa.org.za (Accessed 7 June 2010).

Seepe, S. (2000) 'Higher education and Africanisation', *Perspectives in Education*, Vol. 18, No 3, pp. 52–71.

Shalem, Y. (2001) 'Recognition of Prior Learning, in and through the field of academic practice', *Perspectives in Education*, Vol. 19, No 1, pp. 53–72.

Shalem, Y. and Steinberg, C. (2006) 'Portfolio-based assessment of prior learning: A cat and mouse chase after invisible criteria', in P. Andersson and J. Harris (eds) *Re-theorising the Recognition of Prior Learning*. Leicester, UK: NIACE.

South African Qualifications Authority (SAQA) (1997) 'Proceedings and decisions of the SAQA', *SAQA Bulletin*, Vol. 1, No 1, May/June 1997, pp. 5–10.

South African Qualifications Authority (SAQA) (2002a) *The Recognition of Prior Learning in the context of the National Qualifications Framework*. Policy document. Available at: www.saqa.org.za (Accessed 13 June 2010).

South African Qualifications Authority (SAQA) (2002b) 'The development, implementation and quality assurance of RPL systems, programmes and services by ETQAs, assessors and providers'. Discussion document for public comment approved for release at the ETQA sub-committee meeting of 19 February 2002.

South African Qualifications Authority (SAQA) (2003) 'Criteria and guidelines for the implementation of Recognition of Prior Learning'. Discussion document for public comment released at SAQA EXCO, 7 May 2003. Government Notice No. 657, 16 May 2003.

South African Qualifications Authority (SAQA) (2004) *Criteria and Guidelines for the Implementation of the Recognition of Prior Learning*. Available at: www.saqa.org.za (Accessed 13 June 2010).

Statistics South Africa (StatsSA) (2007) *Community Survey 2007* (Revised Version), 24 October 2007. Available at: www.statssa.gov.za.

Thaver, B., Naidoo, D. and Breier, M. (2002) 'A study of the implementation of Recognition of Prior Learning (RPL) at the University of the Western Cape, 2002'. Bellville: Education Policy Unit.

Van Rooy (2002) 'Recognition of Prior Learning (RPL): From principle to practice in higher education', *South African Journal of Higher Education*, Vol. 16, No 2, pp. 75–82.

Volbrecht, T. (2009) 'New courses for Trojan horses: Rethinking RPL in a South African teacher education curriculum', *Studies in Continuing Education*, Vol. 31, No 1, pp. 13–27.

Volbrecht, T., Tisani, T., Hendricks, M. N. and Ralphs, A. (2006) 'Recognition of Prior Learning in the National Professional Diploma in Education'. Research report prepared for the Education, Training and Development Practitioners' SETA. Available at: http://www.uwc.ac.za/usrfiles/users/5204080804/RPL_Research_1.pdf (Accessed 14 June 2010).

CHAPTER TEN

Sweden: The developing field of validation research

Per Andersson and Andreas Fejes

Abstract

Academic research on the Recognition of Prior Learning (RPL)/validation in Sweden has developed alongside the emergence of RPL as a policy area. Although activities that fit the description of RPL have long been present in Sweden, the introduction of validation as a concept has directed stronger policy attention to the phenomenon. As a consequence, researchers have placed the concept and its associated practices under scrutiny. This chapter focuses on validation in Sweden and on research undertaken since 2000. Six main themes or areas of research have emerged, which structure the piece: historical studies of RPL; research on recognition of vocational competence; RPL, immigration and gender; theories of assessment in RPL; RPL and governance; and comparative studies of RPL.

Swedish academic RPL research has utilised various methodological approaches and theoretical perspectives. Qualitative approaches dominate thus far, but quantitative ideas have been introduced at a theoretical level, via discussions on reliability and validity. The theories and concepts that have been used to explore RPL focus on phenomena such as learning, governmentality, communication and gender. Theoretical selections relate to the disciplines that have been involved – educational research has been and is dominant, but researchers from human work science and from business administration have added new perspectives.

Introduction

Research on RPL in Sweden has developed over the last ten years as a consequence of the emergence of RPL as a policy area. The concept of RPL, in Swedish *validering* (validation in English/French; the concept was borrowed from France), was introduced as late as 1996, as part of new adult education policies. Since then, RPL, or validation, as an area of policy and practice, has increased substantially. It is defined as the identification, assessment and documentation of a person's prior learning, no matter where the learning has taken place. Even though activities that fit this description have long been part of the Swedish history (which will be shown in our historical review), the introduction of validation as a concept directed a stronger policy focus to the phenomenon. As a consequence, researchers have placed the concept, and its associated practices, under scrutiny.

This chapter focuses on the emergence of validation in Sweden and on research that is directly concerned with RPL/validation as an object of study. It addresses university-based research conducted since 2000. During that time, practices of validation or RPL have developed in different areas, which means that empirical research has taken place. Although studies have been undertaken in relation to the evaluation of policy-related developments at local levels, these are not included in this study. Six main themes or areas of research have emerged, which structure this chapter:

1. Historical studies of RPL
2. Recognition of vocational competence
3. RPL, immigration and gender
4. Theories of assessment in RPL
5. RPL and governance
6. Comparative studies of RPL.

Initially, the research focused mainly on RPL processes and on the results of pilot projects, where researchers were commissioned by the public bodies concerned to study and evaluate projects. Pilots were initiated in several municipalities, partly through national initiatives, partly through local initiatives, and the focus was mainly on recognising immigrants' prior vocational learning in relation to certificates at the upper secondary school level. More recently, extensive and independent studies have been conducted in relation to a wider range of RPL projects and implementation strategies. However, research focusing on specific projects is still the most common approach, perhaps unsurprisingly in a situation where RPL is not yet fully established as part of the mainstream education and training system.

Research has deployed various methodological approaches as well as theoretical perspectives. Qualitative approaches dominate thus far. Initially, these were characterised by exploratory studies using a general qualitative approach, based on semi-structured interviews. More recently, there have been more specialised approaches such as ethnographic studies combining participant observation with other types of data, phenomenographic analysis of interviews with participants and discourse analysis of RPL policy. The theories that have been utilised focus on phenomena such as learning, governmentality, communication, gender and processes of organising. Theoretical variation is also related to disciplinary involvement in the research field: educational research has been and is dominant, but researchers from human work science and from business administration have added new dimensions.[1]

Historical studies of RPL

The first theme is historical, including studies that trace the idea of RPL in Swedish education practice before the concept of validation was introduced. Andersson and Fejes (2005), Fejes and Andersson (2007) and Andersson and Fejes (2010b) have undertaken historical analyses of how validation emerged in Sweden. By tracing the idea of identifying, assessing and documenting a person's prior learning, they provide examples of several similar practices in Swedish history. For example, during the seventeenth century, the church used catechetical meetings as a way of checking that the population were good Christians and Lutherans, and could read *Luther's Little Catechism*. According to the canon law of 1686, the master of the household was to teach his children and his domestic servants to read, and to understand the central tenets of the Christian faith according to the catechism. The priests checked that the master had carried this out. If someone did not have the required knowledge, they risked being excluded from communion and therefore not allowed to get

---

[1] Human work science, or work science, is an interdisciplinary research field concerned with relationships between people and work.

married. From our perspective, these catechetical meetings contained ideas similar to validation. They were an assessment of the person's informally acquired competencies, documented formally by the priest. In this case, it was specific knowledge and specific experiences that were to be assessed. It was not validation as we know it today, which is often combined with ideas of economic growth. Rather, it was combined with the idea of social control.

Another form of validation was practised in the guilds. The guilds offered protection against illegal competition and acted to guarantee the social reproduction of vocational competencies. The idea behind the guilds' education was that the apprentice had to produce a qualifying piece of work when he was considered ready. Through different assessments, the apprentice would prove that he had mastered the craft. In other words, knowledge and competencies gained through practical training in the work context were validated by different tests (Fejes and Andersson, 2007). Similar ideas are present today. If a person has gained knowledge and competencies in working life (e.g. as a hairdresser), the idea is that it is possible to validate this through practical tests and to document it formally. However, the guilds' version of validation was combined with ideas about protecting the craft and social order; its focus was not primarily on the individual and societal benefits as is the case today.

A third example relates to Swedish initiatives in the 1970s to widen admission to higher education based on a general recognition of work-life experience and a general aptitude test. This system differed from those used in the United States at that time, where the focus was on specific competencies (Abrahamsson, 1989). Two new ways of admission were introduced in Sweden: the 25:4 scheme (originally 25:5); and the Swedish Scholastic Aptitude Test (SweSAT). The 25:4 scheme meant that anyone who was 25 years old with four years of work experience was basically eligible for higher education (grades at the upper secondary school level in English and Swedish were also required). Here, experience is construed as competence in a general way, independent of what the person has done during these years. Work experience is seen as giving the person a general introduction to society. This general introduction, and diversity amongst students, was seen as important for both higher education and working life. Thus, experience was valued on a general and collective level.

Recognition of vocational competence

Due to the fact that validation policy in Sweden has focused on vocational competencies, much of the research carried out is directed to this area, which is our second theme. This research focuses on different vocational areas and competencies, drawing on varying methodological frameworks. Studies are based on qualitative categorisation analysis, and semi-structured, qualitative interviews with project managers, teachers and participants in projects aiming to develop validation systems. Andersson (2001), Andersson, Hult and Fejes (2002) and Andersson, Fejes and Hult (2003b) have explored how systems for validating vocational competencies have been constructed in different municipalities, and the challenges in recognising prior learning in this area. The first study by Andersson (2001) focused on pilot validation projects that were organised in three municipalities as part of a national investigation. The latter two studies analysed eight validation projects initiated at a national level, involving 18 municipalities in total. One of these projects involved nine municipalities in one region and was the object of a separate analysis (Andersson, Fejes and Hult, 2003b). A main conclusion from these studies was that even though the aim was to create validation systems that were not based on the existing system, most of the cases studied ended up with validation systems adapted to the school system. Another conclusion concerned the role of language in the validation process. Immigrants were targeted in these initiatives. This highlighted the complex interface between competence in the Swedish language and vocational competence, and the need to be clear what is being assessed and why, and to ensure that language skills do not impede fair validation. These results are also presented in an international publication (Andersson, Fejes and Ahn, 2004).

A phenomenographic analysis of caretakers' experiences of validation is reported in a study by Andersson (2006a). The analysis is based on interviews with 11 caretakers, all of whom participated in an RPL project initiated by their employer, a property management company. Results indicated that the caretakers' experiences of validation varied from seeing it as an opportunity for self-development, to experiencing it in terms of control of their knowledge. Moreover, in some cases the view was that validation only 'scratched the surface' of their knowledge. In another study, Andersson (2007) focuses on the validation of ICT competencies. Such competencies can be seen as both work-related and general. In this ethnographic study, Andersson analyses an initiative where RPL was situated in the context of ICT courses in adult education at upper secondary level. The results illustrate how the validation process in this case was integrated into a learning process, instead of, as suggested by policy, being undertaken before further education and learning.

One of the major areas where validation is used to raise the formal competencies of workers is in care work with the elderly. Several studies have focused on this context (Fejes and Andersson, 2008, 2009; Sandberg, 2010). Fejes and Andersson (2009) discuss the relation between experience and learning in RPL from an experiential constructivist perspective. This study involves a case of in-service training, based on RPL. Data consist of interviews with nine supervisors, nine nursing home managers, six teachers, 18 health care workers participating in the programme and two project leaders working at different nursing homes in two municipalities. The interviews were analysed using a qualitative interpretative approach. Results show how prior learning plays a central role in the training process, both on an individual and a collective level. Participants' prior learning is taken as the starting point, particularly via learning conversations where prior learning is made visible and used, and where participants learn from each other. Further, new learning takes place as a consequence of the recognition process, and the study highlights how prior experience can create the basis for new learning through processes of reflection and discussion. In the same project, Fejes and Andersson (2008) explored the effects of validation on participants and the organisations in which they work. Results indicated that participants experienced an increase in self-esteem and became more engaged in discussions about their work during work hours.

Another case of validation in care work with the elderly in a municipality was studied by Sandberg (2010). His interest, drawing on Habermas' theory of communicative action, is directed towards a caring ideology that is, he argues, a central part of how the teachers implement validation. Through such an ideology, they construct a relation of trust with participants where validation, rather than focusing on assessment of knowledge, focuses more on acknowledging the personalities and identities of the participants. In this way, Sandberg argues, a normative discourse about what a good health care worker is in a female-dominant vocation is reproduced.

Validation in vocational/professional education at the tertiary level has also been a focus of research. Sandberg and Andersson (2010) draw on Habermasian theory in a study of how trade union representatives gain

233

recognition for competencies developed through their trade union work in relation to three undergraduate social sciences university courses. The analysis is based on data from the development of the RPL model in question, including documents, observations, interviews and informal conversations with 12 participants. A central conclusion from the analysis is that a focus on developing mutual understanding between assessor and assessee would create the basis for more fair and valid RPL.

Andersson and Hellberg (2009) focused on how childminders, with upper secondary school certificates and many years of kindergarten work experience, participated in a university validation programme to become pre-school teachers. The results, analysed from a situated learning perspective (Lave and Wenger, 1991), based on interviews with ten student teachers and additional information – for example, from conversations with a number of their university teachers – indicated that there was not much prior learning that could be recognised in relation to the university programme. Therefore, the participants had to study for almost as long as they would have done if they had entered the pre-school teacher programme in the normal way. However, the design of the programme made it possible for the participants to use their prior learning and experience *during* their studies, with very high success rates. Validation was in other words indirect, but still an important prognostic for successful study.

Berglund (2010) takes a different approach and analyses recognition processes in working life from a human work science perspective. The study does not focus on practices that are named 'validation', but on practices where prior learning is recognised in working life, irrespective of the terminology used. Based on theories of rationalisation, individualisation and organisation, and on empirical cases of two private and two public workplaces, Berglund shows that implicit systems exist for assessing competence in the workplace. However, such practices do not focus on giving individual employees formal recognition for their competence, but are based on the logic of production. Therefore, competences are made/kept invisible, based on the risk – from the employer's perspective – of losing competent employees or having to pay higher salaries.

RPL, immigration and gender

Our third theme is closely related to the second theme. The studies presented here also concern vocational competence, but with a particular focus on national background, ethnicity and/or gender. Validation of foreign vocational competence was and still is an area of particular interest in Sweden. Initiatives have been taken in policy and practice, motivated by a need to help immigrants enter the Swedish educational system and primarily the labour market. Such initiatives mean that this is a potential area for empirical research – there are actually cases available to study. Indeed, such initiatives have already been the subject of a number of studies with varying foci. One early exploratory study of the development of validation in Sweden studied how immigrant academics' professional competence was recognised in nine municipalities in one region (Andersson, Fejes and Hult, 2003a). Results revealed difficulties in ensuring fair assessments of knowledge developed in other countries and the challenge of assessing knowledge when the assessee does not have full mastery of Swedish professional/vocational language.

More recent qualitative studies in this area have focused on validation centres in three main urban areas in Sweden. Interviews were conducted with representatives from these centres as well as with 16 participants. An analysis of the meaning and consequences of RPL for the participants showed how the process of recognising immigrants' vocational competence enacts a 'sorting function' (Andersson, Hult and Osman, 2006). This sorting process takes place both at a macro-level, where RPL is offered mainly in vocations experiencing labour shortages, thereby excluding those with a background in other vocations from RPL opportunities, and at a micro-level through formal grading, based on the national system as well as informal recommendations to local employers.

A further analysis of these RPL processes (Andersson and Osman, 2008) utilised Foucauldian concepts of 'order of discourse', 'dividing practices' and 'technologies of power'. The concept of 'discourse' was used to describe utterances that are shared and are dominant in a vocation in a specific context at a specific time. The 'order' of discourse was understood in its double meaning: the order in which something is arranged or organised, but also the idea of a fraternity. Thus, an 'order of discourse' means that the discourse has a certain order and that it also forms an order. In this way, vocations in this analysis were understood as orders of discourse – fraternities that order and define 'valid' knowledge in the social practice (vocation). That is, the order of discourse defines and normalises how members in a profession are excluded/included. The use of the concept of 'dividing practices' was primarily intended to show how an RPL process and embedded 'technologies of power' construct what counts as valid professional competence – a professional subject in a vocation or profession. In the dividing practices studied by Andersson and Osman (2008), technologies of power embedded in the validation process were understood as performative in that they distinguished the insider from the outsider – that is, who is to be included and who is to be excluded, and what the excluded have to do in order to be included. In this process, technologies of power – surveillance, observation and examination – can act to produce the differential in/exclusion of immigrants, and of the knowledge they represent in relation to the 'orders of discourse' of working life in general and of certain vocations in Sweden. For example, inclusion could be subordinate: when a teacher got recognition as a childminder; or a registered nurse as a licensed practical nurse. This reflects Jones and Martin's (1997) notion of 'Procrustean RPL' – where competence is actually extensive but trimmed down to fit particular circumstances.

Some studies stress the lack of actual recognition via RPL for immigrant professionals. Comparisons between Canada and Sweden explore the politics of recognition. The results, based on national policy and individual cases from each country, show a general lack of recognition, even though there are differences in the systems and preconditions in the two countries (Guo and Andersson, 2006; Andersson and Guo, 2009). Despite aspirations of social transformation through prior learning assessment and recognition, a central conclusion from this discussion, based on Foucault's concepts of governmentality and techniques of governing, is that RPL 'has become a technical exercise and a governing tool rather than a form of social transformation' (Andersson and Guo, 2009, p. 423).

A review of Swedish research on immigration and RPL (Andersson and Fejes, 2010a) draws on socio-cultural theories of learning and knowledge to discuss RPL in relation to the mobility of people and knowledge. These issues are of great concern in Sweden. An open policy concerning the entry of refugees means that a lot of people come to Sweden with competences that are not directly needed in the labour market, as compared to countries where labour shortages govern immigration policy. This problem has to be met through different measures, and RPL is one possible way.

Diedrich (2008), working within the discipline of business administration and particularly organisational studies, discusses RPL that targets immigrants in terms of the 'management of difference'. In total, 73 people were interviewed – newly-arrived immigrants, caseworkers and other representatives of municipal and state organisations. In addition, observations were undertaken and documents analysed. The management of difference is described as a way of organising, within which the classification of competencies is central. This study, in common with those mentioned above, shows how the use of the Swedish norm is problematic – the assessment activities focus on what the immigrants are *not* able to do in their new context, rather than on finding out what they actually could do.

Another aspect of difference is the gender dimension in RPL, which has been emphasised in studies within human work science. Interviews and observations were undertaken in a project that aimed to develop a 'sustainable' competence development model in the field of caring. Lundgren and Abrahamsson (2005), and Abrahamsson and Lundgren (2006), investigated the Swedish discourse of validation and identified two different sub-discourses – the 'workplace learning discourse' and the 'education discourse'. From a broader perspective, they described how the concept of validation in work and vocational contexts is to a large extent part of a management discourse, where validation is related to concepts like 'knowledge management' and to ideas associated with the importance of measuring performance.

More specifically, their results show how two different cases within a larger validation and competence development project (see also Lundgren, 2005) illustrate a discursively constructed 'gender order' (referring to Hirdman, 1998) incorporating principles of segregation and hierarchy into the context and processes of validation/RPL. The cases were segregated. The first case was situated in a workplace dominated by men. Here, the initiative reflected a *workplace learning discourse*, where the men's prior knowledge was valued as competence and seen as valuable to the organisation. In the second case, the workplace was dominated by women, whose competencies were generally considered 'insufficient'. Here, an *education discourse* prevailed, where the focus was on 'adding' new knowledge. Thus, these cases were not only segregated but also hierarchical, in that men's competencies were more highly valued than women's.

Theories of assessment in RPL

Theories of assessment are central to knowledge measurement. Some researchers in Sweden have paid attention to such theories in relation to RPL; this forms the fourth theme in this chapter. A review report focusing on RPL (Andersson, Sjösten and Ahn, 2003) introduced a number of central concepts into the Swedish RPL discourse. For example, concepts like formative and summative assessment (see, for example, Wiliam and Black, 1996), and convergent and divergent assessment (see, for example, Torrance and Pryor, 1998), were introduced. Learning theories, primarily experiential learning (Kolb, 1984) and situated learning (Lave and Wenger, 1991; Wenger, 1998), have also been used to theorise different approaches to RPL.

The assessment aspect of RPL is elaborated further by Andersson (2006b). Different 'faces and functions' of RPL are discussed from an assessment perspective, based on ideas from Kvale (1996). The functions of selection and transformation are related to a focus on individuals and on knowledge respectively. The discussion shows how RPL – on the one hand – formatively contributes to the transformation of individuals and is also an instrument in the selection of individuals. On the other hand, what is particularly stressed is that assessment, including RPL processes, contributes to the selection of what is valid and valuable knowledge, and that an emphasis on informal and non-formal learning can also mean a transformation of what is seen as valuable knowledge.

Reliability and validity are central aspects of educational measurement and assessment (Wedman *et al.*, 2007; Stenlund, 2009). Andersson (2006b) takes these concepts into RPL. Wedman *et al.* (*ibid.*) conclude that problems of reliability and validity are endemic in assessment; avoiding them as far as possible is a matter of methods and resources. Reliability is a matter of stability; the results of multiple assessments ideally should be the same, independent of when or by whom they are made. Validity is defined in terms of 'content validity' – what knowledge is included in the assessment; 'empirical validity' – that other assessments with the same/opposite aim give the same/opposite result; and 'theoretical validity' – based on what prior knowledge/theories indicate the result of the assessment should be. Further, 'face validity' is also highlighted as important. This means the acceptance of the instrument by those who are exposed to it – otherwise it is likely that the relation between intention and result will weaken. For example, without face validity, it is reasonable to assume that an assessee will not provide results that are valid in relation to his/her actual competence.

Stenlund (2009) reviews international research with focus on the validity question in RPL; particularly RPL in higher education. She adopts a broad perspective on validity (based on Messick, 1989), where two dimensions are central. The first dimension is the *value* of RPL, which can be determined partly from the quality of the evidential basis of the assessment, and partly from its consequences. The other dimension is the *function* of RPL, where her model separates interpretation and use of results. These two dimensions result in four different quadrants of validity. The first is the quality of the evidence in relation to interpretation; that is, the quality of the assessment instruments. The second refers to the quality of the evidence in relation to the use of the results, meaning that relevance and usefulness are in focus. The third aspect is about the consequences of the assessment and particularly the consequences of the interpretation of the results, highlighting values and their implications for validity. The fourth and last aspect is the social consequences of how RPL results are used, and how these influence validity. The basic idea of the model is that validity as a whole can be assured based on these four aspects and in relation to the aim of the RPL process; that is, what is intended to be measured or assessed.

RPL and governance

Validation has also been researched as something that governs and shapes subjects in specific ways, which is our fifth theme. Based on a study of a validation project that aimed to recognise the competencies of 25 childminders in one municipality in relation to a teacher training programme, Säfström *et al.* (2004) problematise validation as an expression of the individualisation of education, the State's ambition to raise educational levels and a technocratic view on education. Validation is also described as a technique to govern the individual involved in lifelong learning, in the interests of economic development. Based on practical experiences, issues of democracy are also discussed regarding who should have access to validation, and how experience-based knowledge can be compared and assessed in relation to the more scientific views on knowledge that are prominent within academia.

In a similar vein, although based on a different theoretical framework, Andersson and Fejes (2005) draw on the Foucauldian concepts of 'governmentality' and 'genealogy' to argue that validation can be seen as a technique for governing the adult learner, and as a way of fabricating (or constructing) the learner as a subject. The authors trace this line of thinking historically by analysing 17 government Green Papers on adult and higher education published between 1948 and 2004. Results show that governing and fabricating the adult subject is not new, but present in all the periods analysed. There is, however, a difference in how the ideas of competence and knowledge are stressed. Today, the focus is on the subject's specific experience, which means competence. The subject is constructed as an adult with experiences that are to be evaluated. During the 1960s and 1970s, the focus was rather on general experience. There was also a discussion around the subject's ability to study. During the 1950s, the following line of thinking was dominant – only those with the talent/ability to study were accepted for adult education.

In a later article, also drawing on Foucault's theorisations, Andersson (2008) focuses on national policy-making regarding validation, and how such policies govern adult education and adult learning at the local level. The results of an ethnographic study on the development of RPL in one municipality, including data from observations, interviews and official documents, show how policy governs individuals indirectly through the organisation of the municipalities in terms of systems for adult education, which in turn mean that policies are to some extent rehearsed and recreated on the local level.

If Andersson (2008) is more interested in how validation governs at a more macro-oriented level, Fejes (2008) directs his interest towards the micro-practices of power in validation, where subjectivities are shaped and governed. Based on interviews with 26 participants, six managers, five supervisors and five teachers in a validation process in the context of care work with the elderly, he focuses on how reflection and reflective practices operate as 'confession' in the Foucauldian sense (Foucault, 2007). He argues that reflection as confession operates as a governing technology within the context studied. Each care worker is encouraged to reflect and scrutinise herself about her work as a way to improve her competencies and practice. Through appraisals, the nurse is invited to reflect about her/himself as a way to attain her/his desires. In this way, an active, responsible, problem-solving, self-governing nurse is constructed. In another article, Fejes (2010) develops this argument further, focusing on the pedagogical methods deployed in the validation process, such as the writing of diaries and learning conversations. These are seen as practices of confession where the care worker is both confessing to others and being confessed to, at the same time as confessing to herself or himself.

Comparative studies of RPL

Some RPL research compares Sweden with other countries, which is the sixth and last theme in this chapter. Andersson and Hult (2008), and Hult and Andersson (2008), describe and compare RPL systems and structures in the five Nordic countries (Sweden, Denmark, Finland, Iceland and Norway) in a cross-sector analysis, including the educational system as well as the labour market and the third sector (voluntary organisations, non-governmental organisations etc. in civil society). The comparison shows that all the Nordic countries have some RPL, even though concepts and practices are different in each country, and the stages of development differ. In all five countries, RPL/validation is most developed in the education sector, with assessment mainly carried out based on the criteria of the educational system. Although all Nordic countries have education systems that are based on individual competence, independently of how this is acquired, this individualisation process is not uniform across the countries. It should also be noted that in all five countries, RPL/validation is least developed in the third sector. In all countries, labour market stakeholders have been involved in the development of guidelines for RPL/validation, and ministries of education have been responsible for, or have participated in, the development work. Another common aspect is that validation is still being developed and modified. For example, in Finland, where a permanent system of validation has existed since 1994 (cf. Colardyn and Bjørnåvold, 2004), changes are still being made regarding how competence should be assessed and recognised. Concerning stages of development (*ibid.*), it is concluded that Denmark, like Norway, can be seen as an 'emerging' national system. Iceland was at the stage of 'experimentation and uncertainty', as was Sweden, despite many developmental efforts.

Another example of comparative analysis is between Canada and Sweden in the area of assessment/recognition of the prior professional learning of immigrants (mentioned above: Guo and Andersson, 2006; Andersson and Guo, 2009).

Conclusion

In this chapter, we have focused on examples of research that study and analyse RPL/validation as a phenomenon and practice in Sweden. As has been illustrated, research started to emerge at the turn of the millennium in relation to policy changes, and a focus on validation as a means to identify, assess and document people's prior learning and competence. Although the number of publications and research projects has increased during the last few years, there are only a few Swedish researchers that focus on validation as their research area. This might be because RPL/validation has been an explicit concept with developing policies and practices for a rather short period. We can also see how research on validation started amongst researchers within educational research, but as time has passed researchers from disciplines such as business administration and human work science have become interested and active. Therefore, it is likely that the research field will expand and develop further if RPL/validation continues to play a role in Swedish policy and practice.

It should be noted that qualitative approaches dominate. Quantitative ideas tend to be introduced at a theoretical level via discussions on reliability and validity. The lack of empirical quantitative research can partly be explained by the lack of official statistics and data on RPL results, making it impossible to follow up and analyse long-term effects. An exception is an ongoing project based on data from registers and official statistics, including a study of the effects of the 25:4 scheme. However, the results have not yet been published. More quantitative research on RPL in Sweden could be developed in the future, but this requires researchers to design projects that generate quantitative data; for example, broader surveys focusing on RPL processes, results and the effects of recognition practices on the candidates concerned.

Finally, this overview illustrates that a range of different theories are mobilised in studies of validation in Sweden. Some researchers use learning theories, drawing on Kolb's (1984) experiential learning cycle, or on Wenger (1998) and Lave and Wenger's (1991) ideas about situated learning and situated knowledge. Others draw on Habermas (1984, 1987) and his theory of communicative action, and Foucault's (2007) genealogy and governmentality. Yet others draw on gender theories such as those of Hirdman (1998). Theories of educational measurement/assessment and organisation theories are also utilised. This breadth should contribute to the developing theorisation of RPL in Sweden and in the research field internationally.

References

Abrahamsson, K. (1989) 'Prior life experience and higher education', in C. J. Titmus (ed.) *Lifelong Education for Adults: An International Handbook*, pp. 162–7. Oxford: Pergamon Press.

Abrahamsson, L. and Lundgren, A. (2006) 'Genus och lärande i arbetslivet' ['Gender and learning in the work life'], in L. Borgström and P.

Gougoulakis (eds) *Vuxenantologin* [*The Adult Anthology*]. Stockholm: Bokförlaget Atlas, pp. 409–34.

Andersson, P. (2001) 'Validering av utländsk yrkeskompetens – en studie av tre pilotprojekt' ['Validation of foreign vocational competence – a study of three pilot projects'], in *SOU 2001:78. Validering av vuxnas kunskap och kompetens* [*Validation of Adults' Knowledge and Competence*]. Stockholm: Utbildningsdepartementet.

Andersson, P. (2006a) 'Caretakers' experiences of RPL', *Journal of Vocational Education and Training*, Vol. 58, No 2, pp. 115–33.

Andersson, P. (2006b) 'Different faces and functions of RPL: an assessment perspective', in P. Andersson and J. Harris (eds) *Re-theorising the Recognition of Prior Learning*. Leicester: NIACE, pp. 31–50.

Andersson, P. (2007) 'Recognition of informal ICT competence', *Nordic Journal of Digital Literacy* [*Digital Kompetanse*], Vol. 2, No 3, pp. 173–88.

Andersson, P. (2008) 'National policy and the implementation of recognition of prior learning in a Swedish municipality', *Journal of Education Policy*, Vol. 23, No 5, pp. 515–31.

Andersson, P. and Fejes, A. (2005) 'Recognition of prior learning as a technique for fabricating the adult learner: A genealogical analysis on Swedish adult education policy', *Journal of Education Policy*, Vol. 20, No 5, pp. 595–613.

Andersson, P. and Fejes, A. (2010a) 'Mobility of knowledge as a recognition challenge – experiences from Sweden', *International Journal of Lifelong Education*, Vol. 29, No 2, pp. 201–18.

Andersson, P. and Fejes, A. (2010b) *Kunskapers värde: Validering i teori och praktik*, andra upplagan [*The Value of Knowledges: Validation in Theory and Practice*, second edition]. Lund: Studentlitteratur.

Andersson, P. and Guo, S. (2009) 'Governing through non/recognition: The missing 'R' in the PLAR for immigrant professionals in Canada and Sweden', *International Journal of Lifelong Education*, Vol. 28, No 4, pp. 423–37.

Andersson, P. and Hellberg, K. (2009) 'Trajectories in teacher education: Recognising prior learning in practice', *Asia-Pacific Journal of Teacher Education*, Vol. 37, No 3, pp. 271–82.

Andersson, P. and Hult, Å. (2008) 'Validation in the Nordic countries: A comparative analysis', *Lifelong Learning in Europe*, Vol. 8, No 3, pp. 150–7.

Andersson, P. and Osman, A. (2008) 'Recognition of Prior Learning as a practice for differential inclusion and exclusion of immigrants in Sweden', *Adult Education Quarterly*, Vol. 59, No 1, pp. 42–60.

Andersson, P., Fejes, A. and Ahn, S-E. (2004) 'Recognition of prior vocational learning in Sweden', *Studies in the Education of Adults*, Vol. 36, No 1, pp. 57–71.

Andersson, P., Fejes, A. and Hult, Å. (2003a) *Validering av invandrade akademikers yrkeskompetens: Erfarenheter från Nätverk Sörmland* [*Validation of Immigrant Academics' Professional Competence: Experiences from Network Sörmland*], Integrationsverkets rapportserie 2003:04. Norrköping: Integrationsverket.

Andersson, P., Fejes, A. and Hult, Å. (2003b) *Att visa vad man kan – erfarenheter från ett regionalt nätverk för validering av yrkeskompetens* [*To show what you know – experiences from a regional network for validation of vocational competence*], Vuxenutbildarcentrums skriftserie nr 18. Linköping: Linköpings universitet.

Andersson, P., Hult, Å. and Fejes, A. (2002) 'Validering av utländsk yrkeskompetens – en studie av den utökade försöksverksamheten' ['Validation of foreign vocational competence – a study of the extended experimental projects'], in *Validering av utländsk yrkeskompetens* [*Validation of Foreign Vocational Competence*], Redovisning av regeringsuppdrag, Dnr: 01-2001:03631, Bilaga 1. Stockholm: Skolverket.

Andersson, P., Hult, Å. and Osman, A. (2006) *Validering som sortering – hur värderas utländsk kompetens?* [*Validation as Sorting – How is Foreign Competence Valued?*]. Norrköping: Integrationsverket and Valideringsdelegationen.

Andersson, P., Sjösten, N-Å. and Ahn, S-E. (2003) *Att värdera kunskap, erfarenhet och kompetens. Perspektiv på validering* [*To value knowledge, experience and competence. Perspectives on validation*], Forskning i fokus, nr 9. Stockholm: Myndigheten för skolutveckling.

Berglund, L. (2010) *På spaning efter arbetsplatsvalidering. En studie av fyra organisationers synliggörande av kompetens* [*In Search of Workplace RPL: A Study of how Skills are made Visible in Four Organisations*]. Luleå: Luleå Tekniska Universitet.

Colardyn, D. and Bjørnåvold, J. (2004) 'Validation of formal, non-formal and informal learning: Policy and practices in EU member states', *European Journal of Education*, Vol. 39, No 1, pp. 69–89.

Diedrich, A. (2008) *Producing Difference in Organizing – Attempts to Change an Ethnic Identity into a Professional One*. University of Gothenburg, School of Business, Economics and Law, GRI-rapport 2008:3.

Fejes, A. (2008) 'Governing nursing through reflection: A discourse analysis of reflective practices', *Journal of Advanced Nursing*, Vol. 64, No 3, pp. 243–50.

Fejes, A. (2010) 'Confession, in-service training and reflective practices', *British Educational Research Journal*, published online 21 July 2010, DOI: 10.1080/01411926.2010.500371.

Fejes, A. and Andersson, P. (2007) 'Historicising validation: The "new" idea of validation in Sweden and its promise for economic growth', in R. Rinne, A. Heikkinen and P. Salo (eds) *Adult Education – Liberty, Fraternity, Equality? Nordic Views on Lifelong Learning*. Turku: Finnish Educational Research Association, pp. 161–81.

Fejes, A. and Andersson, P. (2008) *Validering integrerad i lärprocesser: Erfarenheter av kompetensutveckling av omvårdnadspersonal inom ramen för Kompetensstegen* [*Validation integrated in learning processes: Experiences from in-service training for elderly care workers within the Steps for Skills project*], HELIX research reports 08/01. Linköping: UniTryck.

Fejes, A. and Andersson, P. (2009) 'Recognising Prior Learning: Understanding the relation among experience, learning and recognition from a constructivist perspective', *Vocations and Learning: Studies in Vocational and Professional Education*, Vol. 2, No 1, pp. 37–55.

Foucault, M. (2007) *Security, Territory, Population: Lectures at the Collège de France 1977–1978*. Houndmills: Palgrave Macmillan.

Guo, S. and Andersson, P. (2006) 'The politics of difference: Non/recognition of the foreign credentials and prior work experience of immigrant professionals in Canada and Sweden', in P. Andersson and J. Harris (eds) *Re-theorising the Recognition of Prior Learning*. Leicester: NIACE, pp. 183–203.

Habermas, J. (1984) *The Theory of Communicative Action. Volume One. Reason and the Rationalization of Society*. Cambridge: Polity Press.

Habermas, J. (1987) *The Theory of Communicative Action. Volume Two. The Critique of Functionalist Reason*. Cambridge: Polity Press.

Hirdman, Y. (1998) *Med kluven tunga. LO och genusordningen. Svensk fackföreningsrörelse efter andra världskriget* [*In a Forked Tongue. LO and the Gender Order. Swedish Trade-Union Movement after Second World War*]. Stockholm: Atlas.

Hult, Å. and Andersson, P. (2008) *Validation in the Nordic Countries: Policy and Practice*. Kristianstad: fiora förlag/Nordiskt nätverk för vuxnas lärande.

Jones, M. and Martin, J. (1997) 'A new paradigm for recognition of prior learning (RPL)', in W. Fleet (ed.) *Issues in Recognition of Prior Learning: A Collection of Papers*. Melbourne: Victoria RPL Network, pp. 11–19.

Kolb, D. (1984) *Experiential Learning. Experiences as the Source of Learning and Development*. Englewood Cliffs, NJ: Prentice-Hall.

Kvale, S. (1996) 'Evaluation as construction of knowledge', in P. Hayhoe and J. Pan (eds) *East-West Dialogue in Knowledge and Higher Education*. Armonk, New York and London, England: M.E. Sharpe, pp. 117–40.

Lave, J. and Wenger, E. (1991) *Situated Learning: Legitimate Peripheral Participation*. Cambridge: Cambridge University Press.

Lundgren, A. (2005) *På längre sikt. 'Kompetenshimmel eller deltidshelvete?' En utvärdering av samarbetsprojektet Hållbar kompetensutvecklingsmodell under åren 2003–2004* [*In the longer run: Heaven of competence or part-time hell? An evaluation of the cooperation project Sustainable competence development model during the years 2003-2004*]. Luleå: Luleå Tekniska Universitet.

Lundgren, A. and Abrahamsson, L. (2005) 'Validation – in different ways'. Paper presented at *Researching Work and Learning (RWL)* conference, Sydney, Australia.

Messick, S. (1989) 'Validity', in R. Linn (ed.) *Educational Measurement*. New York: American Council of Education, pp. 13–103.

Säfström, C. A. (ed.) (2004) *Validering som utbildningspolitiskt instrument: en kritisk analys* [*Validation as an Instrument in Educational Policy: A Critical Analysis*]. Uppsala: Uppsala universitet, Institutionen för lärarutbildning.

Sandberg, F. (2010) 'Recognising health care assistants' prior learning through a caring ideology', *Vocations and Learning: Studies in Vocational and Professional Education*. Online First. DOI 10.1007/s12186-009-9031-8.

Sandberg, F. and Andersson, P. (2010) 'RPL for accreditation in higher education: As a process of mutual understanding or merely lifeworld colonization?', *Assessment and Evaluation in Higher Education*, published online 5 July 2010, DOI: 10.1080/02602938.2010.488793.

Stenlund, T. (2009) 'Assessment of prior learning in higher education: A review from a validity perspective', *Assessment and Evaluation in Higher Education*, published online 4 August 2009, DOI: 10.1080/02602930902977798.

Torrance, H. and Pryor, J. (1998) *Investigating Formative Assessment*. Buckingham: Open University Press.

Wedman, I., Stoor, M., Carling, E., Djuvfeldt, G., Holmström, P. and Linder, J. (2007) *Validering av kunskaper och kompetens* [*Validation of*

Knowledge and Competence]. Gävle: Högskolan i Gävle.

Wenger, E. (1998) *Communities of Practice: Learning, Meaning and Identity.* Cambridge: Cambridge University Press.

Wiliam, D. and Black, P. (1996) 'Meanings and Consequences. A basis for distinguishing formative and summative functions of assessment?', *British Educational Research Journal,* Vol. 22, No 5, pp. 537–48.

CHAPTER ELEVEN

United States of America: Prior Learning Assessment (PLA) research in colleges and universities

NAN L. TRAVERS

Abstract

The ways in which Prior Learning Assessment (PLA) policies and processes are established within educational institutions in the United States are totally individually based. Without set policies and practices across institutions, a framework within which to study and make generalisations regarding PLA programmes across institutions becomes difficult. As a result, research in PLA has depended on individual dissertations, institutions examining the effectiveness of their own practices and projects sponsored by foundations, and conducted by the Council for Adult and Experiential Learning (CAEL).

What is interesting in the US is the amount of doctoral research into PLA. This provides an academic resource that is lacking in other countries. Although early research indicated a low acceptance of PLA and an underutilisation of programmes, later studies suggest that PLA is increasing across the country. Research has consistently and unequivocally found that PLA students persist and have far greater success in their studies compared to non-PLA students. In addition, studies show that PLA students have increased academic and career outcomes over non-PLA students. Overall, studies suggest that participation in Prior Learning Assessment programmes has various 'transformational' effects on individual students − in terms of self-awareness and skill development.

As PLA practice has increased in colleges and universities, there is now a significant body of practice upon which future research can draw. There is scope for the further development and use of both quantitative and qualitative research to delve more deeply into the outcomes and effects of PLA, at both institutional and student levels.

Introduction

Education practices focused on adult learners, such as Prior Learning Assessment (PLA), are becoming more established in the United States (US) (Bamford-Rees, 2008; Hoover, 2010). Initially, Prior Learning Assessment (PLA) was developed to provide greater access to higher education for World War II veterans (Keeton, 2002), and later for adult learners more generally, as a way to balance the concentrated efforts most colleges and universities placed on reaching traditional-age students (Gamson, 1991; Keeton, 2002; Bamford-Rees, 2008). Over the last 40 years, there has been a growing focus on adult learners in higher education, and PLA opportunities for students have increased (Bamford-Rees, 2008).

On the other hand, research in Prior Learning Assessment is limited, mostly conducted through dissertations (LeGrow, 2000; Lamoreaux, 2005) by professionals within educational settings (Burris, 1997), and/or under the auspices of the Council for Adult and Experiential Learning (CAEL). For example, Travers (2009) reviewed 25 articles published in the 'PLA Corner' of the *Journal for Continuing Higher Education* over a nine-year period, and found that most articles focused on the anecdotal experiences of practitioners in the field. Lamoreaux (2005) reviewed 72 articles on PLA and found only 13 were research-based; all the others described practice. LeGrow *et al.* (2002) and Smith (2002) found similar results. After an extensive search for this chapter, over 30 dissertations, six peer-reviewed, research-based journal articles, ten CAEL research studies and seven institutional research studies were found that focused on Prior Learning Assessment in the United States between 1974 and 2010. Of these, 31 were focused on single institutions, 24 were multi-institutional studies and one was at a state level. Appendix 11.1 summarises these findings. This chapter concentrates on empirical research and cannot claim to have covered all of the available PLA research in the US. Of the dissertations reviewed, two (Hamilton, 1992; Guthrie, 1998) were theoretical and not empirical, and are not discussed.

The first sections of the chapter present contextual information pertaining to PLA in the United States. Thereafter, three main research themes are addressed in detail, leading to recommendations for further research.

Educational context

Governance and funding of higher education in the US

When comparing the research on Prior Learning Assessment within the United States with that in other countries, two points need to be clarified. First, the governing structure of higher education is locally controlled within each individual state, although financially supported through a combination of individual, local, state and federal dollars. Second, there are no federal curricular standards that all institutions of higher education must follow. Although some rules and regulations exist for institutions in receipt of federal support (e.g. financial aid rules that specify that well-defined curricula be established for programmes within which students receive federal aid), these do not regulate the particulars of curricular decisions.

State arrangements for PLA

Some states (e.g. Minnesota, Oklahoma, Pennsylvania and Vermont) have created state-wide systems for supporting and/or evaluating Prior Learning Assessment. The Pennsylvania Department of Education has developed the Pennsylvania Prior Learning Assessment Consortium, comprising institutions that have agreed to follow consortium guidelines. In Vermont, Prior Learning Assessment is conducted through an office within the Vermont State College System and the credits transfer into each of the state colleges by agreement. Most state systems of higher education (e.g. Arizona Board of Regents, New York State Department of Education, Texas Higher Education Coordinating Board) expect each institution to set its own standards regarding Prior Learning Assessment.

250

Accreditation and quality assurance of higher education and PLA

Accreditation is granted to institutions of higher education through non-profit agencies that are structured and operated independently from federal or state governing bodies. Regional accrediting bodies (e.g. Middle States Commission on Higher Education, New England Association of Schools and Colleges, Western Association of Schools and Colleges) are part of a system of peer review, whereby institutions analyse performance based on criteria they themselves have identified within overarching guidelines set by the accreditation agencies. The regional bodies specify that faculty within an institution are responsible for designing and maintaining the academic curricula. As a result, curricular policy is set through individual faculty governance, which regulates the curriculum within its own institution.

Regional accrediting bodies also set PLAR guidelines for institutions; these vary by body and, depending on the particular principle, allow institutional flexibility. For example, the New England Association of Schools and Colleges (2005) restricts individualised PLA to the undergraduate level, but allows flexibility in programme structure. The philosophy, policy and practice for accepting Prior Learning Assessment credits, established by individual institutions, must reflect local faculty agreement. As Cargo (1982, p. 7) states: 'College and university faculties are the custodians of academic credit, and real authority for awarding credit is almost always given to individual faculty members. Consequently, department policies and the practices of individual faculty members govern the actual practices of credit.'

The Council for Adult and Experiential Learning (CAEL) has developed ten standards of PLA practice (Willingham, 1977a; Whittaker, 1989; Fiddler *et al.*, 2006). These standards do not prescribe practice, but provide a philosophical foundation which most institutions use to structure their PLA programmes (Freed and Mollick, 2009). For example, the State University of New York (SUNY)-Empire State College structures its prior learning assessment programme using the standards and will accept other institutions' credits awarded through PLA, as long as that institution also adheres to the standards.

The above points are significant when exploring the development of Prior Learning Assessment and the direction of its research within the United States. There are no federal initiatives directed towards PLA since there are no regulations to monitor enforcement. Funding for extensive research by CAEL has mostly relied on independent foundations (e.g. Carnegie Corporation, Lumina Foundation) within larger initiatives examining innovation in educational practice. Guidelines and principles put forward by CAEL and regional accreditation bodies for establishing PLA policies and procedures within an institution are just that: guidelines and principles. The ways in which policies and processes are established within an institution are totally individually based. Without set policies and practices across institutions, the framework within which to study and make generalisations for PLA programmes across institutions becomes difficult. As a result, the body of research in PLA has depended on individual dissertations, institutions examining the effectiveness of their own practices, and projects sponsored by foundations and conducted by CAEL.

Historical context

Early developments

In 1945, the American Council on Education (ACE), through its Office on Educational Credit and Credentials, developed the high school equivalent General Education Development (GED) programme, and, through its Commission on Accreditation of Services Experiences, began evaluating military experience for college-level learning (American Council of Education, 1981). These efforts became the earliest recognised formal assessment of prior learning in the United States. The GED programme had two purposes:

1. to assist institutions in the appropriate placement of students returning from military service in a programme of general education; and
2. to help institutions determine the amount of academic credit that should be granted for learning that resulted from educational experiences in military service (*ibid.*, p. 3).

In 1974, the Office on Educational Credit and Credentials, and the Commission on Accreditation of Services Experiences, combined to become the Commission of Educational Credit and Credentials, with the responsibility to 'provide services that help [post-secondary] institutions determine appropriate credit awards for extra-institutional learning' (*ibid.*, p. 4).

252

The College Entrance Examinations Board (founded in 1900) began using exams to assess university-level learning as far back as the 1930s (Wolfson, 1996) and in 1967 created the College Level Examinations Program (CLEP):'the oldest and most widely used national examination program' (Cargo, 1982, p. 10). Later the College Entrance Examinations Board created the Advanced Placement Program.

The Educational Testing Service (ETS) was founded in 1947 – a collaborative not-for-profit venture by the American Council on Education, the Carnegie Corporation and the College Entrance Examination Board (CEEB). Standardised exams for college entrance were developed and research on formal educational testing was conducted.[1] Other standardised exams (e.g. The Defense Activity for Non-Traditional Education Support [DANTES], Thomas Edison College Examination Program [TECEP]) emerged and were increasingly accepted by institutions (Klein-Collins, 2006a, 2006b). Each of these exams has undergone rigorous validity and reliability studies to quality assure the award of college-level credits.

Moving beyond standardised exams

The above early efforts began to legitimise the assessment of prior learning through formal means and helped forge an early acceptance of college-level PLA. However, the principles and research underpinning these examinations were based on a behavioural model – to educate the masses to become a successful workforce for the industrial economy (ETS, 2008). The idea that everyone should know the same thing and in the same way was antithetical to another emerging idea – that an individual could gain college-level knowledge outside of the formal educational system which could not be evaluated through a standardised exam (Gamson, 1991). A schism emerged; some institutions would only accept the formal standardised means of evaluating prior learning, while others began to develop new ways to assess prior learning.

A Commission on Non-Traditional Study was founded in 1971, with funding from the Carnegie Corporation and the Educational Foundation of America, and jointly sponsored by the Educational Testing Service and the College Board (Bamford-Rees, 2008). This Commission examined current practices for non-traditional education, recommending that:'New

---

[1] www.fundinguniverse.com/company-histories/.

devices and techniques should be perfected to measure the outcomes of many types of non-traditional student and to assess the educative efforts of work experience and community service ... systems of quality control should be built into the instruction and evaluative aspects of non-traditional study whenever possible' (Bamford-Rees, 2008, p. 3).

Based on this work, a three-year research project was launched in 1974 – the Cooperative Assessment of Experiential Learning (CAEL) Project, funded by the Carnegie Corporation and organised by Morris Keeton under the auspices of the Educational Testing Service (Gamson, 1991; Knapp, 1991; Bamford-Rees, 2008). In 1977, CAEL separated from ETS as a non-profit organisation (first changing its name to the Council for the Advancement of Experiential Learning and then to its current name, the Council for Adult and Experiential Learning) to provide 'colleges and universities, companies, labor organizations and state and local governments with the tools and strategies ... for creating practical, effective lifelong learning solutions' (CAEL, 2009). Under the innovative leadership of Morris Keeton, CAEL began its first movements to organise a common agenda around assessing learning from experience through disciplined and quality means (Gamson, 1991).

Between 1968 and 1974, 13 colleges of higher education were founded (or expanded), with adult learners as the primary focus and some form of Prior Learning Assessment as part of the institutional offer (Keeton, 2002; Bamford-Rees, 2008).[2] These colleges evolved at a time of great ferment in higher education; institutions were beginning to realise that there was legitimacy to learning outside the classroom, that content and pedagogy should be relevant to students' concerns, and that minorities (including adults) had a right to higher education (Gamson, 1991). Keeton's hope was that this movement would 'seed the entire field of post-secondary education and thus ... have a salutary effect upon the standards of good practice throughout American higher education' (Gamson, 1991, p. 7). As a result, Prior Learning Assessment became a significant part of a movement for educational social justice, providing recognition of knowledge and access to post-secondary education that was unavailable in traditional higher education institutions.

---

[2] In the United States, the term 'college' refers to institutions of higher education granting at least a bachelor degree. Some colleges grant master's level degrees. The term 'university' refers to those institutions granting doctorate degrees.

These new 'adult-learner friendly' colleges (including State University of New York (SUNY)-Empire State College, the Community College of Vermont, the Thomas A. Edison State College of New Jersey and Minnesota Metropolitan State) took up this 'cause', and became leaders in establishing PLA policies and practices. They also began to conduct programme-based research, mostly investigating their own practices. Their PLA programmes embraced the philosophy that:

1. an adult could acquire college-level learning outside of the formal classroom setting;
2. an individual could have college-level learning that was not even currently taught in the academy; and
3. an individual could know something that formal testing could not assess.

These institutions (along with sister institutions in other countries) gave birth to the work on how prior learning could be assessed at an individual level.

The evolution of PLA research

As discussed, the earliest research on Prior Learning Assessment in the United States focused on validating standardised exams, on ascertaining their effectiveness and on the benefits they provided to institutions assessing students' knowledge. In an attempt to expand the knowledge base and validity of different types of assessment for sponsored and non-sponsored experiential learning, the Cooperative Assessment of Experiential Learning (CAEL) Project engaged multiple institutions in small projects, research and conferences between 1994 and 1997 (Gamson, 1991; Knapp, 1991).[3] Four priority areas were established: '1) Assessing the achievement of interpersonal skills, 2) Use of portfolios in assessing non-sponsored learning, 3) Assessing the learning outcomes of work or field experience, and 4) Use of expert judgment in assessing learning outcomes' (Knapp, 1976, p. ii).

---

[3] Sponsored experiential learning refers to learning situations structured by the institutions, such as field placements. Non-sponsored experiential learning refers to learning acquired by the individual that is not structured by the institution.

Faculty, students and administrators in about 50 institutions were interviewed regarding their practices and experiences of different methods of assessing prior learning. From these interviews, pilot projects and assessor training initiatives were launched via mini-grants to various institutions. Results were written up as a series of working papers and piloted in more than 80 institutional projects. In addition, CAEL organised 'assemblies' (i.e. conferences) twice a year during this period to disseminate research findings and gather further feedback from the 225–250 attendees at each assembly.

One key finding was that, although variations of practices clustered under themes, the themes themselves were consistent across institutions. Guiding principles for best practice were therefore derived from these overarching themes (Willingham, 1977b). This publication was revised by Urban Whitaker in 1989 and became *Assessing Learning: Standards, Principles, and Procedures*, which in turn was revised by Fiddler *et al.* (2006). From this point forward, CAEL became the leading organisation in the United States to sponsor research in Prior Learning Assessment, support workforce development, and provide an annual conference to disseminate the latest findings and practices in the field.

When CAEL became independent of the Educational Testing Service (ETS) in 1977, it continued its research agenda by exploring different PLA practices. In 1991, Morris Keeton gained funds from the Pew Charitable Trust to create the Institute for Research and Assessment in Higher Education (IRAHE) at the University of Maryland University College. The research conducted at IRAHE shifted the Trust's perspective on research in relation to adult learners from primarily pre-collegiate literacy development to concern with adult learning in higher education (Johnson, 2004).

As more institutions adopted PLA, CAEL continued to sponsor research to examine the practices that were emerging, publishing several books on the subject: *Earn College Credit for What you Know* (Simosko, 1985); *Assessing Learning: A CAEL Handbook for Faculty* (Simosko and Associates, 1988); as well as Whitaker's (1989) updated version of Willingham's work, *Assessing Learning: Standards, Principles and Procedures*. These publications became the foundation for the development of policies and practices at institutions across the country, and were pivotal for CAEL's recognition as a PLA authority. These publications have been updated and are still used extensively throughout the field.

256

In 1988, Thomas A. Edison State College of New Jersey, in cooperation with CAEL, created the National Institute on the Assessment of Experiential Learning, providing practitioners with a way to gather and learn more about practices and research in experiential learning. Annual proceedings were published to capture conversations and presentations. Most of these initial reports shared good practice and were used by institutions across the country (private and public, large and small) to initiate PLA programmes. Concurrently, there was an effort to collect smaller research studies and synthesise findings on adult learning. SUNY-Empire State College created the National Council on Adult Learning and, through mini-grants, sponsored practitioner-based research. The University of Maryland University College (UMUC), through IRAHE, began a research agenda to explore the effectiveness and efficiency of programmes focused on the adult learner.

The research on Prior Learning Assessment in the United States falls into three main categories: 1) research into practice; 2) research into student persistence, retention rates, and academic and career outcomes post-PLA; and 3) the 'transformational' effects of PLA on individuals and their learning. Each of these bodies of research is analysed and discussed in turn.

Research into practice

Large-scale studies into the scale and scope of implementation

A foundational study into the implementation of PLA was undertaken in 1975, supported by a Ford Foundation grant. Meyer (1975) surveyed 51 state governing boards or coordinating commissions of higher education, and 46 governing boards or community college commissions, to determine which institutions credentialed prior learning. Forty-two senior institutions and 25 community colleges were identified. Materials were gathered from 36 of the institutions and 14 of them were visited, and interviews conducted with faculty, administration and students. The results were published in *Awarding College Credit for Non-College Learning* (Meyer, 1975), and addressed different PLA practices, barriers to implementation and techniques/suggestions for implementing programmes.

In 1980, the American Council on Education (ACE) conducted a survey to determine the extent to which credits gained through PLA were accepted by institutions. The results indicated that of the 2,000 institutions that responded, most accepted credit assessed by exams. Of those accepting exams, 1,100 reported that they also used some form of portfolio evaluation of prior learning (Bamford-Rees, 2008).

A decade later, Swiczewicz (1990) surveyed 500 higher education institutions that were accredited through regional or other post-secondary accrediting agencies, and that were not proprietary, technical or vocational in nature. The selection was made on the basis of a randomised, stratified sample across regions and types of institutions. The survey aimed to determine the extent to which PLA had been 'diffused and disseminated across the higher education system' (*ibid.*, p. 16). To that end, the scope and frequency of different PLA practices were quantified. Swiczewicz found a disjuncture between policy and practice; that is, the number of institutions actually offering PLA was significantly less than those purporting to have policies and programmes in place. The most common form of PLA at that time was the award of credits for exams, military credit and learning evaluated by the American Council on Education (ACE). Little evidence was found of the assessment of individualised unstructured or unsponsored learning. Moreover, Swiczewicz found that even among those institutions offering PLA, relatively few students took advantage of it because of credit restrictions and institutional barriers.

By comparing practices and policies across states, CAEL has been able to determine the extent to which certain PLA practices exist in institutions. For example, in their 2006 survey, 272 community colleges, four-year colleges and universities reported on: the types of PLA credits accepted at their institution; how students learn about PLA; the ways in which PLA can be used towards a degree; and the fees charged. The results indicated that most institutions accept some form of PLA credit and that 66 per cent provide opportunities for individualised assessment of experiential learning. This was significantly higher than institutions reporting in 1996 (55 per cent) and in 1991 (50 per cent).

Much later, through CAEL, Glancey (2007) examined state-wide policies regarding prior learning in higher education institutions, and Klein-Collins (2006a, 2006b) examined policies and practices across the US. From these studies, CAEL determined a growing interest in PLA at the state level in that 'more than half of all states have at least one agency or entity that has instituted policies that support or encourage the adoption and use of prior learning assessment methods in higher education' (Klein-Collins, 2006a). The same study also documents the methods that are used to assess prior learning, how many credits it is possible to achieve via PLA, processes to review policies and practices, institutional autonomy in relation to PLA, and joint articulation arrangements between state-wide community colleges and universities.

Single institutional studies into barriers to the implementation of PLA

This type of research is common across the country, mainly as a result of doctoral research. Fisher (1991) undertook an in-depth study of one institution, interviewing a total of 51 individuals drawn from trustees, administrators, professional staff, full- and part-time faculty, and students. In addition, 96 faculty and students were surveyed over the phone, and documentary analysis was conducted. Findings indicated that many faculty members had concerns about the academic integrity of PLA assessment and a lack of institutional criteria for PLA; information exchange and communication between various constituents was patchy; and academic review processes for policies pertaining to prior learning assessment were in short supply. Moreover, the mission statement of the institution concerned was found to be incongruent with prior learning assessment.

Fisher's findings are consistent with other studies undertaken in the 1990s. In the same year, Harriger's (1991) doctoral thesis also examined barriers to the acceptance of PLA at a university. Administrators, faculty and students were interviewed regarding their understandings of the meaning of a college education, the status of adult students at the university, the concept of prior learning assessment, and their perceptions of the university's PLA programme. Major discrepancies in perceptions were found and Harriger recommended that the university develop a theoretical basis to support faculty acceptance of PLA, and also provide accurate information and consistent communication about the programme and associated practices. In a similar study, Raulf (1992) found that lack of awareness across constituents and restrictions in the ways in which assessed credits could be used reduced faculty commitment to and participation in PLA.

In an institutional evaluation, Topping (1996) found that a lack of accurate information and resources hindered the implementation of PLA. He also noted an interesting division in faculty attitudes towards PLA; faculty members in the liberal arts and sciences along with administrators were not supportive of prior learning assessment; while faculty in the career and applied arts were supportive. These findings echoed a much earlier piece of doctoral research. Stevens (1977) examined faculty knowledge and perceptions of PLA, and their opinions of what should be included in the process. It emerged that, in general, faculty were favourable towards assessing prior learning, but that faculty in the career areas were more favourable than faculty from other parts of the university. Furthermore, faculty who supported the use of behavioural objectives tended to be more sympathetic towards PLA practice than others.

In a case study of institutional change, Wolfson (1996) found a lack of awareness amongst faculty members of PLA policies and practices. Furthermore, there was confusion 'between PLA as a concept and specific methods of granting PLA credit' (*ibid.*, p. 6). The conclusion drawn was that 'PLA represents a major shift in both paradigm and process and requires faculty to make major shifts in the way they conceptualize their roles and student learning' (*ibid.*).

Multi-institutional studies into barriers to and enablers of PLA

Again, the majority of research under this sub-theme has been undertaken as doctoral study (both qualitative and quantitative). Geyer (1985) examined faculty perceptions of PLA across multiple institutions and found that although general support for the concept was reported, many faculty members did not endorse its use in their own institution.

In 1986, Halberstadt reported on faculty knowledge of and attitudes towards PLA practices across community colleges in a state system, finding that faculty knew very little about PLA and a lack of professional development opportunities for them to learn more. Gaerte (1996) surveyed 89 institutions and found that nearly half of them were opposed to PLA practices at the level of philosophy and principle.

Lee-Story (2001) conducted a multi-institutional doctoral study of 60 post-secondary hospitality management and 72 general management programmes (in the public and private sectors) to determine the extent and style of PLA practice. Respondents indicated a strong preference for formal testing rather than individualised assessment. However, portfolio-based assessment had a greater acceptance in private institutions. The reasons cited for opposition to portfolios included the difficulty that students experience in documenting learning outcomes and the difficulty that faculty experience when assessing them.

In a recent multi-institutional study, Hoffmann *et al.* (2009) studied institutional PLA practices across 32 institutions. They examined five critical factors impacting on PLA programmes:

1. institutional mission and commitment;
2. institutional support (administrative, faculty and financial);
3. programme factors, such as the number of different practices, ways in which learning was evaluated (e.g. matching course outcomes, individualised portfolio) and ways in which credits can be used (e.g. as elective credit, in the major);
4. assessor training; and
5. programme feedback and evaluation.

Results showed strong to moderate correlations across all the factors (range r=.84, p<.001 to .40, p<.04). Closer examination indicated that those institutions with mission, commitment and institutional support for PLA exhibited greater diversity of practices and use of credits. Conversely, institutions lacking the mission and commitment, and with less institutional support, tended to be more restrictive in their practices; for example, evaluation by exams only or strictly course-match evaluations and limited use of credits (e.g. electives only).

Research into how PLA takes place

Coulter *et al.* (1994) video-taped faculty members advising students about PLA and found two types of behaviours: a 'matching model', whereby students were advised using pre-existing learning objectives; and a 'discovery model', where prior learning was discussed without pre-existing assumptions about the learning and/or learning outcomes. More than a decade later, Travers *et al.* (2008) explored faculty-advising models at the same higher education institution, with similar results. Over 50 faculty members were interviewed. Some faculty believed that only learning taught somewhere in higher education should be assessed. Others believed that students may have acquired learning that is college-level, even if it had never been taught at any institution. Some were of the view that students' learning might shape future curricula at the college.

Arnold (1998) also examined faculty behaviour when assessing prior learning and found that although faculty members were familiar with the CAEL standards, they were uncertain about what they actually meant.

Although for the most part the standards were adhered to, some faculty awarded credit for experience rather than for learning (thereby flouting one of the most important standards). The need for more training in assessing prior learning was expressed.

Hoffmann and Michel (2010) interviewed PLA assessors with a view to identifying best practice in identifying college-level learning. They reported that rather than external standards, assessors relied on 'their personal knowledge, theoretical understanding, and experiences in the field in carrying out their responsibility to identify – and recommend credit for – college-level learning' (*ibid.*, p. 119). The assessors also noted that they 'focused on the student as they evaluate the portfolio', including observing their understanding of theories and principles, how they had applied their learning in different contexts, and how they utilised strategic approaches to problem solving. The researchers concluded that assessor judgements take 'not only the theoretical components into account but the students' learning, as it's embedded within their experiences' (*ibid.*).

Travers *et al.* (2011) have recently examined the written recommendations of 70 PLA assessors in terms of how the recommendations were expressed. Four overarching themes were identified concerning audience, voice, presentation of the learning and the language of assessment. Assessors wrote to three different audiences – to the student, to peer reviewers and to the administration. They used different approaches to describe the prior learning based on the source of their voice (e.g. professional authority, external authority). Some evaluators equated experience with learning, while others relied on the context of the learning to describe the learning that took place. On the basis of these observations, the researchers recommend institutions clarify expectations regarding audience and standards to be used, so that assessors are clearer about the approach to take.

Research into training for PLA assessors

Lee-Story's (2001) doctoral study of 60 post-secondary hospitality management and 72 general management programmes identified a lack of PLA training. The Hoffmann *et al.* (2009) multi-institutional study explored the strategies used to train assessors in how to assess portfolios. Data were analysed quantitatively regarding the number of different types of training opportunities, the frequency of training and the topics covered. The number of different types of training opportunities correlated strongly to institutional mission and commitment (r=.56, p<.01). The three most common topics covered in training were an overview of the PLA process (92 per cent), expectations of the evaluator (92 per cent) and expectations of the student (85 per cent). Although two of the topics identified as most useful were the overview of the process (100 per cent) and expectations of the evaluator (96 per cent), how to evaluate college-level learning (92 per cent) was also identified as useful. Topics identified for future training included how to evaluate college-level learning and an overview of national standards (such as the CAEL standards).

Research into the evaluation of PLA programmes

Freed's doctoral study (2006) examined the evaluation of PLA programmes and processes across Texan public universities offering non-traditional routes to baccalaureate degrees. Although similarities were found across the types of PLA processes, most institutions lacked evaluation practices for their programmes.

Evaluation is becoming a growing concern, especially as the number of institutions offering PLA increase. Hoffmann *et al.* (2009) found that only 18 out of 32 institutions reported having some type of formal process to seek feedback. Where institutions used multiple ways to gain feedback and gathered this feedback formally, the feedback was used to make programme improvements (r=.68, p<.003 and r=.65, p<.005, respectively). Further analysis explored the practices of those institutions with the strongest correlations across Hoffmann *et al.*'s (2009) five critical factors (see above). Most recently, Travers and Evans (2011) have proposed an evaluative framework utilising the CAEL standards and the five critical factors. Research has yet to commence on this framework.

Research that showcases best PLA practice

This line of inquiry has been the subject of many studies (e.g. Mandell and Michelson, 1990; Flint and Associates, 1999; Zucker *et al.*, 1999; Michelson and Mandell, 2004; Hart and Hickerson, 2008). Institutional practices are surveyed as a basis for the presentation of model PLA programmes. These 'best practices' are used as case studies to support institutional practice elsewhere and to provide resources for institutions wanting to develop PLA. For example, Flint and Associates (1999) compared six institutions noted for their best practices. Hart and Hickerson

(2008) published a representative collection of 11 current institutional practices complete with examples of policies, processes and sample student portfolios.

Reading across this body of research

Although the earlier research indicated a low acceptance of PLA (Swiczewicz, 1990; Harriger, 1991; Raulf, 1992) and an under-utilisation of programmes (Fisher, 1991), later studies suggest that PLA programmes are increasing across the country.

Research during the 1990s reported that faculty and administrators' views on PLA as an acceptable means to assess students' knowledge have acted as a barrier to programme implementation and acceptance. Other barriers to the development of PLA have included: incongruence between mission and PLA; inconsistency in the application of the PLA principles; lack of communication and information; and poor institutional understanding and definition of PLA.

A slice of research has examined the ways in which faculty assess prior learning. For the most part, the CAEL standards are followed. Some faculty, however, were found to assess experience rather than learning. Coulter *et al.* (1994) and Travers *et al.* (2008) found similar faculty advising behaviours, ranging from a course-match model to a 'learning discovery' model.

Faculty training was identified as an ongoing concern. In some studies, differences in faculty attitudes were discipline-based (Stevens, 1977; Topping, 1996). Evaluation of programmes has been identified as an area that institutions need to improve (Freed, 2006; Hoffmann *et al.*, 2009) and that needs greater study (Travers and Evans, 2011).

Best practices have frequently evolved from case study research. Despite recent research on institutional practices (Freed, 2006; Klein-Collins, 2006a, 2006b; Hoffmann *et al.*, 2009), more remains to be known about how PLA is implemented in institutions and the effectiveness of the practices.

In terms of methodology, the US benefits from a large number of doctoral studies. Where these research practices in depth, they tend to report problems with PLA. Research undertaken by CAEL, or to influence policy and institutional practice in favour of PLA, tends to be more optimistic and advocatory in style.

264

Research into student persistence, retention rates, and academic and career outcomes post-PLA

Retention and persistence in higher education

Studies at the Institute for Research on Adults in Higher Education (IRAHE) at the University of Maryland University College (UMUC) compared PLA and non-PLA students, finding higher rates of persistence in the PLA group (Hoffmann and LeMaster, 1996; Hoffmann *et al.*, 1996, 1997). Similarly, Fonte (2008) found that, over a ten-year period at one institution, students who completed a PLA portfolio graduated at a rate of 88 per cent. The research study does not provide comparative statistics for students not partaking in PLA, but the average five-year persistence rate across all groups of students at four-year institutions nationwide is 59 per cent (Horn and Berger, 2004).

Community colleges

Snyder (1990) and Freers (1994) (both doctoral theses) found that students completing a PLA programme in community colleges persisted at higher rates than those not undertaking PLA. Pearson (2000) studied the persistence of PLA and non-PLA students at a mid-western college, finding a significantly increased persistence rate for the PLA students, regardless of age, gender, high-school class rank, the number of prior credits, or grade point average (75 per cent versus 39 per cent). Stemm's (2009) doctoral thesis compared gender difference in persistence rates for PLA and non-PLA students. No significant difference was found, although there were differences in the types of PLA credits earned.

Academic and career outcomes after PLA

In doctoral research, Sargent (1999) found that of 253 students who engaged in PLA across a state-wide system, 88.9 per cent participated in degree programmes thereafter and 81.7 per cent completed their degree. One UMUC study examined graduation rates for 24,753 students over a four-year period, finding that students in the PLA programme had higher graduation rates (Hoffmann *et al.*, 1996). The same study also found higher grade point averages and more completed credits amongst PLA students. This was reinforced in a further study, which established that

265

87 per cent of the credits that students acquired through the PLA programme were at the upper level (Hoffmann and LeMaster, 1996). When examining the admissions criteria for accepting PLA students, Hoffmann *et al.* (1997) found that the orientation component of the PLA programme had a stronger effect on success than normal admissions requirements, including the usual writing assessment.

In addition, many studies have found that PLA students experience new and enhanced career opportunities (Boomazian, 1994; Rost, 2008). Brown (1999, 2002) found increased and better understanding amongst students of the role that work played in learning and development after participation in a PLA portfolio development programme. Freers (1994) also indicated that students reported an increase in promotions and salaries after a portfolio process. Furthermore, the same study found that PLA participants reported academic success and attainment of personal aspirations.

A recent CAEL study

Recently, CAEL has undertaken a comprehensive study to compare persistence rates for PLA and non-PLA students across 48 institutions offering a variety of types of PLA (Klein-Collins, 2010). The following data were used: student record data on the 2001–02 cohort; information on PLA policies and practices; institutional reasons for offering PLA; and institutional data gathered by each college from the Integrated Post-secondary Education Data System (IPEDS). In addition, interviews with administrators of PLA programmes were conducted to learn more about policy and practice at the institutions concerned. This is the largest study of its type, comprising 62,475 students, aged 25 or older, of whom 25 per cent (15,594) earned PLA credits from 2001 to 2008.

Overall, Klein-Collins (2010) reports that PLA students have higher rates of degree completion than non-PLA students, regardless of size, level or type of institution. The data also indicated that even if they did not complete their degrees, PLA students persisted for longer and took more credits than their counterparts. For example, the number of PLA students who did not continue after the first year was 37 per cent versus 60 per cent of the non-PLA students. In addition, 56 per cent of the PLA students who had not completed a degree by 2008 had completed 80 per cent of the credits needed, compared to 22 per cent of the non-PLA students. PLA students also had a slightly higher grade point average. Klein-Collins (2010, p. 57) concludes:

> *The data from the 48 post-secondary institutions … show that PLA students had better academic outcomes, particularly in terms of graduation rates and persistence, than non-PLA adult students. Many PLA students also shortened the time required to earn a degree; the average time to degree decreased as the number of PLA credits earned increased.*

Contrary to the myth that PLA takes students away from institutional credits, this research demonstrates that PLA students are, in fact, more likely to enrol in institutional credits. Overall, this study concludes that PLA helps 'adults earn degrees and progress more quickly to their goals' (*ibid.*, p. 60).

Although there were some community colleges in the above study, only seven of the 48 institutions were two-year institutions. CAEL conducted a follow-up study with an additional 88 community colleges (Brigham and Klein-Collins, 2010). The study found that although community colleges were relatively familiar with PLA and provided different prior assessment opportunities, certain populations (such as the returning adult student) were not taking advantage of the programmes. Brigham and Klein-Collins (*ibid.*, p. 3) reported that 'over 90% of the community colleges reported that they have students who likely have technical training that could be assessed for college-level credit, and nearly 70% of the respondents suggested that their institution should expand their PLA options'. These findings suggest institutional capacity could be developed and echo earlier research findings that explored the under-utilisation of PLA (e.g. Swiczewicz, 1990; Fisher, 1991).

Reading across this body of research

Research has consistently and unequivocally found that PLA students persist and have far greater success in their studies compared to non-PLA students, even at the same institution. In addition, studies show that PLA students have increased academic and career outcomes over non-PLA students.

The 'transformational' effects of PLA on individuals and their learning

The third body of research focuses on changes students experience as a result of engaging in PLA. Many studies report 'transformation' in various ways and at a range of levels.

Self-awareness and personal development

Burris (1997) found that many students experienced changes in self-concept through the critical reflection aspect of PLA, also reporting that PLA students experienced significant emotional experiences as they moved through the process. Brown (1999) found that students shifted from being uncertain about their abilities, and anxious about the possible outcomes of PLA, to recognising their accomplishments and exhibiting a 'sense of self-discovery and personal empowerment to achieve their professional and educational goals' (*ibid.*, p. 136).

Like Burris, Geerling (2003) identified strong feelings and emotions as students developed their prior learning portfolio. This study focused on six students' 'private' prior learning (e.g. learning acquired through emotional experiences such as divorce rather than through work-related experience).

Lamoreaux (2005) found seven areas in which students changed: '(i) affirmation of learning from experience, (ii) self-knowledge, (iii) self-confidence, (iv) acceptance of the past, (v) awareness of new/changed perspectives, (vi) awareness of new/changed learning perspectives, and (vii) consequences (related to other changes)' (*ibid.*, p. 126).

Stevens *et al.* (2010) surveyed 45 current and past students in terms of how PLA had impacted on the way they perceived their life, work, relationships with others and involvement in the community. Students reported positive changes in each category, and also changes in self-perception and increased self-confidence and self-worth. Some students reported that the peer-review process helped them to better understand changes in others, which in turn helped them to understand their own changes. The researchers claim that through extended reflection and writing, the PLA process 'has the capacity to change the learner's perspective on the meaningfulness of experience … to assign value to life's experiences through critical reflection and reflective discourse and to act on the newly constructed knowledge' (*ibid.*, p. 401).

In addition, a number of studies have reported that students developed a deeper understanding of the role that mentors and role models play in their lives (Mullen, 1995; Burris, 1997; Brown, 1999, 2002; Lamoreaux, 2005).

Problem solving

LeGrow *et al.* (2002) compared the problem-solving performances of PLA and non-PLA students in a business programme. Students had an option to enrol in the PLA-based or the traditional classroom-based programme. The researchers analysed the number of links within – and the complexity of – students' solutions during a talk-aloud problem-solving exercise. Results showed that PLA students consistently solved problems at a higher level of complexity and with more linkages than the classroom-based students, regardless of how much prior experience the student had in the field. In other words, low-experienced PLA students out-performed low-experienced classroom-based students, as did high-experienced students. This landmark study is the first to suggest the cognitive effects of PLA.

Study skills

Mullen (1995) researched the study habits and attitudes of 190 PLA students in two colleges, and compared students participating in a PLA programme (n= 92) with those not participating (n=98). The PLA students scored significantly higher than those not participating, across seven dependent variables: delay avoidance; work methods; study habits; teacher approval; education acceptance; study attitudes; and study orientation (*ibid.*, p. iii). Furthermore, they also scored higher on teacher approval ratings; that is, they developed 'a higher opinion of teachers and their classroom behaviour than students not participating in experiential learning' (*ibid.*, p. 92).

Self-direction and self-regulation

LeBerre (1997) examined the transfer of different types of prior experience and readiness for self-directed learning. Student focus groups reported that learning experiences requiring self-direction (such as military leadership) equated with more self-direction in a portfolio process. Travers *et al.* (2003) compared the impact of different teaching methods on students' regulation of their learning over a semester. They found that students in traditional lecture-style mathematics classes became less self-regulated and more teacher-regulated, while students who were taught mathematics using adult learning principles became more self-regulating. Travers (2008) compares the adult learning principles used in this study to PLA, and uses a self-regulated learning model to describe the ways in which students use self-concepts, choices, feedback-seeking, teacher-student alliance and metacognition to promote learning behaviours. She argues that the PLA process enhances students' abilities to regulate their learning.

Tacit knowledge

LeGrow's (2000) doctoral research found that PLA students exhibited slightly higher tacit knowledge ($\underline{d}$=.45, small effect size) than non-PLA students, as measured on the Tacit Knowledge Inventory for Business Managers (TKIM). In a post-hoc analysis, PLA students with high levels of previous experience scored significantly higher on the TKIM than similarly experienced classroom-based students ($\underline{d}$=2.11). LeGrow (*ibid.*, pp. 154–5) explains:

> *One characteristic of tacit knowledge is that it can influence perception, choice preferences or decision-making in the domain from which it was extracted [this study] suggest[s] that the intensive reflective process that is required to complete the [PLA] program may enable students who have high levels of experience to link that prior experience to knowledge elements across problem categories and to retrieve and apply that knowledge more easily … The process of delineating experiences and the knowledge acquired through them in order to verbalize the knowledge acquired from specific activities forces students to organize that tacit knowledge within the framework of the discipline or knowledge domain in which the student hopes to be granted college credit. This organization process requires the student to recognize the relationship of parts, that is, to recognize the structure of the body of knowledge within the domain.*

The process of reflection

Doctoral studies have also investigated the process of reflection in PLA. Lamoreaux (2005) examined portfolios and undertook in-depth interviews with 12 PLA students. The students saw the portfolio course as having changed their practice of reflection in four ways: how they reflected on and articulated learning from their experiences; increased 'self-questioning'; more questioning of assumptions; and more surfacing of tacit knowledge (*ibid.*, p. 126). Lamoreaux reported that students seemed to be 'internalizing the questioning process' as they worked through various exercises on the portfolio course (*ibid.*, p. 130).

270

Rausch (2007) studied the reflective practices of graduate students engaged in a portfolio process and found that perceptions changed during the development of the portfolio, from believing that the process was simply to document experience to an understanding that it was a representation of learning. This influenced the students' ability to demonstrate graduate-level competencies. Brown (1999, 2002) also found that students expanded their reflective processes and competence, and recognised the importance of reflection. McDonald (2000) found that the reflective portfolio process provided an effective resource for students to self-assess the type and amount of their prior learning.

Lamoreaux (2005) found that narrative writing includes drafting and re-drafting, provides a way for students to deepen their reflective processes, and 'objectifies' their experiences. This objectification provided enough distance for them to view their learning from new perspectives, thereby helping them to 'clarify and organize their knowledge' (*ibid.*, p. 129). Findings also suggest that peer and faculty feedback provide additional viewpoints that help students to objectify their experiences, and encourage and challenge them towards deeper thinking.

Conversely, Sheckley (2007) argues that when students are asked to reflect and recall experiences through writing, as expected in most PLA programmes, the linear nature of the narrative makes it difficult for them to explain what they have learned. This, he argues, is because cognitive functions in the brain are highly connective and associative. Consequently, the linear nature of the narrative cannot capture the ways in which the student has formulated his/her knowledge. He suggests that other formats, such as 'concept maps', may be more helpful and illuminative for students and assessors.

Michelson (2011) deploys literary analysis of students' essays to gain a better understanding about how they reflect and describe their experiences. In this work, the influence of society and education on the experiential narrative is examined. Michelson indicates that the narration may be as much a reflection of the mentor or assessor's knowledge as an accurate reflection of what the student has learned. In a similar vein, Travers *et al.* (2011) have also found that some assessor reports of student learning reflect what the assessor knows or expects, rather than the student's knowledge. These research studies raise important questions about commonly instituted PLA practices and their ability to evaluate students' knowledge authentically.

Reading across this body of research

Overall, studies suggest that participation in prior learning assessment programmes has various 'transformational' effects on individual students – in terms of self-awareness and skill development.

Future research

Studies in process

Some new research studies are under way. A collaborative project between SUNY-Empire State College and Thomas A. Edison State College is exploring faculty perceptions of 'college-level learning' (Travers *et al.*). Institutions do not work to a formal definition; rather, there is an assumption that faculty understand what is and what is not college-level learning. In *Assessing Learning: Standards, Principles, and Procedures*, Fiddler *et al.* (2006, p. 16) state that 'assessment should be based on standards and criteria for the level of acceptable learning that are both agreed upon and made public'. The overarching question posed by Travers *et al.* is: 'Do faculty share a common understanding of college-level learning?' The collaborative study seeks to determine if there is consensus across faculty at different institutions and in different disciplines/areas of study.

Stevens (in process) is also exploring the ways in which faculty perceive college-level learning. She interviewed 20 faculty members who assess prior learning and determined that college-level learning is difficult to define. In addition, her study determined that institutional standards and individual faculty member perceptions impact on the way in which the credit is defined as college-level learning.

Another study (Travers, in process) is exploring the impact of PLA on students' ability to self-regulate their learning. Building on previous research in self-regulation (Travers *et al.*, 2003; Travers, 2008), the study uses concept maps to record students' perceptions of their learning, and compares these perceptions pre- and post-PLA. The study also compares differences among students engaged in different forms of PLA (e.g. the College Level Examinations Program [CLEP], portfolio development) with students not engaged in PLA.

Research possibilities

As Bamford-Rees (2009, p. 8) states: 'We have indeed come a long way in the development and refinement of PLA policies and methods. In thirty-five years PLA has progressed through infancy and the teen years into adulthood and it seems a reasonably safe assumption that PLA is here to stay.' Possibilities for future research are almost endless. As the chapter has outlined, most PLA research has focused on the scope and scale of practice, barriers and enablers of practice, the impact of PLA on students' persistence and success rates, and the 'transformational' effects of PLA on individuals and their learning. These areas could be extended in a wide variety of ways. For example:

- Some of the studies that have compared practices across institutions have glossed over the nuances of practices, which could perhaps afford greater insight into the effectiveness of PLA.
- Although the recent CAEL study on the impact of PLA on student retention and persistence (Brigham and Klein-Collins, 2010) is the first comprehensive study of its kind, it did not take into account different types of PLA. For example, students undertaking standardised exams are in the same sample as students undertaking individualised portfolio assessment.
- Research examining various forms of 'transformation' for PLA students has often been based on small samples in single institutions. There is a lack of comparative study across students not engaged in PLA and/or across other institutions. Further research is needed to better understand these 'transformational' processes and to move us beyond the enticingly anecdotal.

As PLA practice has increased in colleges and universities, there is now a significant body of practice upon which future research can draw. Some existing research (e.g. Klein-Collins, 2010) uses quantitative strategies to give trends in PLA practices, while other research has used qualitative strategies to better understand the human qualities involved. There is scope for the further development and use of both types, to delve more deeply into the outcomes and effects of PLA, at both institutional and student levels. Further research will support inter-institutional learning and dialogue within the US and with other countries.

The author wishes to extend a special thank you to Alan Mandell, SUNY-Empire State College, for his invaluable comments.

References

American Council on Education (ACE) (1981) *Guide to Credit by Examination*. Washington, DC: American Council on Education.

Arnold, T. (1998) 'Portfolio-based Prior Learning Assessment: An exploration of how faculty evaluate learning'. Doctoral Dissertation, The American University, District of Columbia. Dissertations and Theses: The Humanities and Social Sciences Collection (Publication No AAT 9917494).

Bamford-Rees, D. (2008) 'Thirty-five years of PLA: We have come a long way', in D. Hart and J. Hickerson (eds) *Prior Learning Portfolios: A Representative Collection*. Chicago: Council for Adult and Experiential Learning, pp. 1–10.

Boomazian, S. (1994) 'Prior Learning Assessment using story: Academic access for underserved populations'. Doctoral Dissertation, The Union Institute, Ohio. Dissertations and Theses: The Humanities and Social Sciences Collection (Publication No AAT 9433568).

Brigham, C. and Klein-Collins, R. (2010) *Availability, Use and Value of Prior Learning Assessment within Community Colleges*. Chicago: Council for Adult and Experiential Learning.

Brown, J. (1999) 'A case study of adults in college who developed an experiential learning portfolio'. Doctoral Dissertation, Florida International University, Florida. Dissertations and Theses: The Humanities and Social Sciences Collection (Publication No AAT 9936897).

Brown, J. (2002) 'Know thyself: The impact of portfolio development on adult learning', *Adult Educational Quarterly*, Vol. 52, No 3, pp. 228–45.

Burris, J. (1997) 'The adult undergraduate's experience of portfolio development: A multiple case study'. Doctoral Dissertation, The University of Texas at Austin, Texas. Dissertations and Theses: The Humanities and Social Sciences Collection (Publication No AAT 98030914).

Cargo, R. (1982) *You Deserve the Credit: A Guide to Receiving Credit for Non-college Learning*. Columbia, MD: Council for the Advancement of Experiential Learning.

Coulter, X., Herman, L., Hodgson, T., Nagler, S. and Rivers de Royston, I. (1994) 'Assessing adults: Experiential learning'. Unpublished paper presented to the National Centre on Adult Learning (NCAL). Saratoga Springs, NY.

Council for Adult and Experiential Learning (CAEL) (2009) *Who We Are.* Available at: http://www.cael.org/who_we_are.htm.

Educational Testing Service (ETS) (2008) Positioning educational assessment for the 21st century (Flash, 12:09/58.4MB). Available at: www.ets.org.

Fiddler, M., Marienau, C. and Whitaker, U. (2006) *Assessing Learning: Standards, Principles and Procedures,* Second edition. Chicago: Council on Adult and Experiential Learning.

Fisher, V. (1991) 'An institutional evaluation of perceptions and expectations of a portfolio assessment program'. Doctoral Dissertation, Columbia University Teacher's College, New York.

Flint, T. and Associates (1999) *Best Practices in Adult Learning: A CAEL/APQC Benchmark Study.* Chicago: Council for Adult and Experiential Learning.

Fonte, L. (2008) 'Implications to the institution of awarding credit for prior learning assessment', *Journal of Continuing Higher Education,* Vol. 56, No 1, pp. 64–5.

Freed, R. (2006) 'An investigation of prior learning assessment processes in Texas public universities offering non-traditional baccalaureate degrees'. Doctoral Dissertation, University of Northern Texas, Texas. Dissertations and Theses: The Humanities and Social Sciences Collection (Publication No AAT 3214466).

Freed, R. and Mollick, G. (2009) 'Using Prior Learning Assessment in adult baccalaureate degrees in Texas', *Journal of Case Studies in Accreditation and Assessment,* Vol. 1, pp. 1–14.

Freers, S. (1994) 'An evaluation of adult learners' perceptions of a community college's assessment of prior learning program' (Doctoral Dissertation, Pepperdine University, Malibu, CA, 2004). Dissertations Abstracts International, 56, 0059.

Gaerte, D. (1996) 'An investigation of the prior learning assessment practices at member institutions of the Coalition for Christian Colleges and Universities'. Doctoral Dissertation, Purdue University, Indiana. Dissertations and Theses: The Humanities and Social Sciences Collection (Publication No AAT 9713515).

Gamson, Z. (1991) 'CAEL and change movement in higher education', in L. Lamdin (ed.) *Roads to the Learning Society.* Chicago: Council for Adult and Experiential Learning, pp. 3–18.

Geerling, F. (2003) 'Adults learning to reflect: A study of assessment of prior private learning'. Doctoral Dissertation, Michigan State University, Michigan. Dissertations & Theses: The Humanities and Social Sciences Collection (Publication No AAT 3115964).

Geyer, C. (1985) 'How faculty in Lutheran liberal arts colleges perceive non-traditional programs for adult learners (external degree, prior learning, CLEP)'. Doctoral Dissertation, University of Nebraska, Nebraska. Dissertations and Theses: The Humanities and Social Sciences Collection (Publication No AAT 8602111).

Glancey, K. (2007) *Statewide PLA Policy.* Chicago: Council for Adult and Experiential Learning.

Guthrie, D. (1998) 'The politics of designing and implementing a portfolio assessment process in continuing professional education'. Doctoral Dissertation, University of Georgia, Georgia. Dissertations and Theses: The Humanities and Social Sciences Collection (Publication No AAT 9828356).

Halberstadt, T. (1986) 'Faculty knowledge and attitudes regarding credit for prior learning in the community college system of the state of Massachusetts (life experience, non-traditional education)'. Doctoral Dissertation, University of Massachusetts Amherst, Massachusetts. Dissertations and Theses: The Humanities and Social Sciences Collection (Publication No AAT 8612043).

Hamilton, R. (1992) 'On experience: A critical review of the relationship between experience and adult learning'. Doctoral Dissertation, Columbia University Teachers College, New York. Dissertations and Theses: The Humanities and Social Sciences Collection (Publication No AAT 9228479).

Harriger, C. (1991) 'Barriers to the optimal use of Prior Learning Assessment: An institutional evaluation of perceptions of credit for prior learning'. Doctoral Dissertation, Columbia University Teacher's College, New York. Dissertations and Theses: The Humanities and Social Sciences Collection (Publication No AAT 9136394).

Hart, D. and Hickerson, J. (2008) *Prior Learning Portfolios: A Representative Collection.* Chicago: Council for Adult and Experiential Learning.

Hoffmann, T. and LeMaster, J. (1996) 'What percentage of EXCEL students earn lower and upper level credits?' Research presented at Montgomery Community College. Aldelphi, MD: University of Maryland University College.

Hoffmann, T. and Michel, K. (2010) 'Recognizing Prior Learning Assessment best practices for evaluators: An experiential learning approach', *The Journal of Continuing Higher Education*, Vol. 58, No 2, pp. 113–20.

Hoffmann, T., LeMaster, J. and Flickinger, S. (1996) 'The effectiveness of the EXCEL program in supporting efficient learning for adults: Study of UMUC's prior learning program linking UMUC's best practices in PLA to student retention to their degree'. Aldelphi, MD: Institute for Research on Adults in Higher Education.

Hoffmann, T., LeMaster, J. and Flickinger, S. (1997) *Efficiency of the EXCEL Program in Enhancing Effective Learning*. Aldelphi, MD: University of Maryland University College.

Hoffmann, T., Travers, N. L., Evans, M. and Treadwell, A. (2009) 'Researching critical factors impacting PLA programs: A multi-institutional study on best practices', *CAEL Forum and News*, September.

Hoover, E. (2010) 'Where life earns credit: "Prior Learning" gets a fresh assessment', *Chronicle of Higher Education*, Vol. 56, No 27, pp. A23–4.

Horn, L. and Berger, R. (2004) 'College persistence on the rise? Changes in 5-year degree completion and postsecondary persistence rates between 1994 and 2000 (NCES 2005-156)'. US Department of Education, National Center for Education Statistics. Washington, DC: US Government Printing Office.

Johnson, S. (2004) 'UMUC Senior scholar Morris Keeton wins prestigious Tolley medal', *FYI Online, UMUC's Faculty/Staff Newsletter*. Aldephi, MD: University of Maryland University College.

Keeton, M. (2002) 'Foreword', in T. Flint, P. Zakos and R. Frey (eds) *Best Practices in Adult Learning: A Self-evaluation Workbook for Colleges and Universities*. Kendall/Hunt Publishing, pp. v–ix.

Kent, E. (1996) 'User perceptions for transforming Prior Learning Assessment: A critical review of adult learners' insights'. Doctoral Dissertation, The Union Institute, Ohio. Dissertations and Theses: The Humanities and Social Sciences Collection (Publication No AAT 9710006).

Klein-Collins, R. (2006a) *Sneak Peek: Prior Learning Assessment – Current Policy and Practice in the U.S.* Available at: http://www.cael.org/forum_and_news/sneak_peek_prior_learning_assessment.htm.

Klein-Collins, R. (2006b) *Prior Learning Assessment: Current Policy and Practice in the U.S.* Chicago: Council for Adult and Experiential Learning.

Klein-Collins, R. (2010) *Fueling the Race to Postsecondary Success: A 48-institution Study of Prior Learning Assessment and Adult Student Outcomes.* Chicago: Council for Adult and Experiential Learning.

Knapp, J. (1976) 'The CAEL project: A case study'. Paper presented at the 60th Annual Meeting of the American Educational Research Association, San Francisco, California, 19–23 April.

Knapp, J. (1991) 'Portfolio assessment: Grounds covered and new frontiers', in L. Lamdin (ed.) *Roads to the Learning Society.* Chicago: Council for Adult and Experiential Learning, pp. 43–8.

Lamoreaux, A. (2005) 'Adult learners' experience of change related to prior learning assessment'. Doctoral Dissertation, Walden University, Minnesota. Dissertations & Theses: The Humanities and Social Sciences Collection (Publication No AAT 3180108).

LeBerre, M. (1997) 'The relationship between adult students' prior learning experiences and readiness for self-directed learning'. Doctoral Dissertation, George Mason University, Virginia. Dissertations and Theses: The Humanities and Social Sciences Collection (Publication No AAT 9721822).

Lee-Story, J. (2001) 'Crediting experiential learning: An examination of perceptions and practices in postsecondary hospitality management and general management programs'. Doctoral Dissertation, Florida Atlantic University, Florida. Dissertations and Theses: The Humanities and Social Sciences Collection (Publication No AAT 3013060).

LeGrow, M. (2000) 'Prior Learning Assessment: Impact of APL portfolio development on problem-solving skills and knowledge organization'. Doctoral Dissertation, University of Connecticut, Connecticut. Dissertations and Theses: The Humanities and Social Sciences Collection (Publication No AAT 9964785).

LeGrow, M. R., Sheckley, B. G. and Kehrhahn, M. (2002) 'Comparison of problem-solving performance between adults receiving credit via assessment of prior learning and adults completing classroom courses', *The Journal of Continuing Higher Education*, Vol. 50, No 3, pp. 2–13.

Mandell, A. and Michelson, E. (1990) *Portfolio Development and Adult Learning: Purposes and Strategies.* Chicago: Council for Adult and Experiential Learning.

McDonald, E. (2000) 'Reflection and assessment of experiential learning in graduate theological education'. Doctoral Dissertation, The University of Memphis, Tennessee. Dissertations and Theses: The

278

Humanities and Social Sciences Collection (Publication No AAT 9967041).

Meyer. P. (1975) *Awarding College Credit for Non-college Learning.* San Francisco: Jossey-Bass.

Michelson, E. (2011) 'Autobiography and selfhood in the practice of adult learning', *Adult Education Quarterly,* Vol. 61, No 1, pp. 3–21.

Michelson, E. and Mandell, A. (2004) *Portfolio Development and the Assessment of Prior Learning.* Sterling, VA: Stylus.

Mullen, S. (1995) 'A study of the difference in study habits and study attitudes between college students participating in an experiential learning program using the portfolio assessment method of evaluation and students not participating in experiential learning'. Doctoral Dissertation, Southwestern Baptist Theological Seminary, Texas. Dissertations and Theses: The Humanities and Social Sciences Collection (Publication No AAT 9707451).

New England Association of Schools and Colleges, Commission on Institutions of Higher Education (2005) *Standards for Accreditation, Section 4.34.* Bedford, MA: New England Association of Schools and Colleges. Available at: www.cihe.neasc.org.

Pearson, W. (2000) 'Enhancing adult student persistence: The relationship between prior learning assessment and persistence toward the baccalaureate degree'. Doctoral Dissertation, Iowa State University.

Raulf, J. (1992) 'An institutional evaluation of perceptions and expectations of prior learning assessment programs'. Doctoral Dissertation, Columbia University Teacher's College, New York.

Rausch, D. (2007) 'Demonstrating experiential learning at the graduate level using portfolio development and reflection'. Doctoral Dissertation, Andrews University, MI. Dissertations and Theses: The Humanities and Social Sciences Collection (Publication No AAT 3289968).

Rost, S. (2008) 'Itinerant job seekers and recognition of prior learning: An exploratory case study in employability and skills and experience utilization'. Doctoral Dissertation, Capella University, Minnesota. Dissertations and Theses: The Humanities and Social Sciences Collection (Publication No AAT 3313417).

Sargent, B. (1999) 'An examination of the relationship between completion of a prior learning assessment program and subsequent degree program participation, persistence, and attainment'. Doctoral Dissertation, University of Sarasota, Florida.

Sheckley, B. (2007) 'Mental models of how the world works: A foundation of adult learning'. Presentation at the International CAEL Conference, San Francisco.

Simosko, S. (1985) *Earn College Credit for What you Know.* Washington, DC: Acropolis Books.

Simosko, S. and Associates (1988) *Assessing Learning: A CAEL Handbook for Faculty.* Chicago: Council for Adult and Experiential Learning.

Smith, K. (2002) 'A phenomenological study conducted to further develop the base of knowledge to post-secondary student experiences with Prior Learning Assessment and Recognition'. Digital Dissertations Online, 41-03, 654.

Snyder, G. (1990) 'Persistence of community college students receiving credit for prior learning'. Doctoral Dissertation, University of Pennsylvania, Pennsylvania. Dissertations and Theses: The Humanities and Social Sciences Collection (Publication No AAT 9026650).

Stemm, W. (2009) 'The assessment of prior learning: Gender differences in experiential learning'. Doctoral Dissertation, Capella University, MN. Dissertations and Theses: The Humanities and Social Sciences Collection (Publication No AAT 3355386).

Stevens, C. (in process) 'Defining and assessing college-level learning: Perceptions from faculty assessors of prior learning assessment portfolios'. Doctoral Dissertation, Northern Illinois University, DeKalb, IL.

Stevens, K., Gerber, D. and Hendra, R. (2010) 'Transformational learning through Prior Learning Assessment', *Adult Education Quarterly*, Vol. 60, No 4, pp. 377–404.

Stevens, M. (1977) 'A strategy to gain faculty acceptance of and participation in the granting of credit for prior, non-sponsored learning at Black Hawk College'. Doctoral Dissertation, Nova University, Florida.

Swiczewicz, L. (1990) 'Segmentation and penetration of Prior Learning Assessment methodologies at American colleges and universities'. Doctoral Dissertation, University of Connecticut, Connecticut.

Topping, T. (1996) 'An institutional evaluation of perceptions and expectations of prior learning assessment options'. Doctoral Dissertation, Columbia University Teacher's College, New York. Dissertations and Theses: The Humanities and Social Sciences Collection (Publication No AAT 9636042).

Travers, N. L. (2008) 'Some thoughts on adult learning, self-regulated learning, and the Empire State College degree planning process', *All About Mentoring*, Vol. 33. Saratoga Springs, NY: Empire State College.

Travers, N. L. (2009) 'PLA research perspective on the United States of America'. Presentation at Thomson Rivers University, Open Learning, Kamloops, BC, July.

Travers, N. L. (in process) 'Prior Learning Assessment and self-regulated learning: A study of students' perceptions of their learning'. Saratoga Springs, NY: Empire State College.

Travers, N. L. and Evans, M. (2011) 'Evaluating prior learning assessment programs: A suggested framework', *International Review of Research in Open and Distance Learning*, Vol. 12 No 1. Available at: www.irrodl.org.

Travers, N. L., Sheckley, B. and Bell, S. (2003) 'Enhancing self-regulated learning: A comparison of instructional techniques', *The Journal of Continuing Higher Education*, Vol. 51, No 3, pp. 2–17.

Travers, N. L., Smith, B. Ellis, L., Brady, T., Feldman, L., Hakim, K., Onta, B., Panayotou, M., Seamans, L., Treadwell, A. (2011). 'Language of evaluation: How PLA evaluators write about student learning.' International Review of Research in Open and Distance Learning, Vol. 12, No 1. Available at: www.irrodl.org.

Travers, N. L., Smith, B., Johnsen, J., Alberti, P., Hakim, K., Onta, B. and Webber, E. (2008) 'Faculty voices: A Cinderella story at the PLA ball', *All About Mentoring*, Vol. 35. Saratoga Springs, NY: Empire State College.

Travers, N. L. and Negron, D. (in process) 'Faculty's perceptions of college-level learning: A multi-institutional study'. Saratoga Springs, NY: Empire State College.

Whitaker, U. (1989) *Assessing Learning: Standards, Principles and Procedures.* Chicago: Council for Adult and Experiential Learning.

Willingham W. (1977a) *The Principles of Good Practice in the Assessment of Experiential Learning.* Columbia, MD: Cooperative Assessment of Experiential Learning.

Willingham, W. (1977b) 'Foreword', in R. Reilly, R. Churchill, A. Fletcher, M. Miller, J. Pendergrass, J. Porter Stutz and J. Clark (eds) *Expert Assessment of Experiential Learning – A CAEL Handbook.* Cooperative Assessment of Experiential Learning.

Wolfson, G. (1996) 'Prior Learning Assessment: A case study of innovation and change'. Doctoral Dissertation, Nova Southeastern University, Florida.

Zucker, B. J., Johnson, C. C., and Flint, T. A. (1999) 'Prior learning assessment: A guidebook to American institutional practices'. The Council for Adult and Experiential Learning. Chicago: Kendall/Hunt.

Appendix 11.1 Summary of research on Prior Learning Assessment by year, source and type

Authors	Year	Source	Type
Institutional Practices			
Brigham, C. & Klein-Collins, R.	2010	CAEL	Multi-Institutional
Flint, T. & Associates	1999	CAEL	Multi-Institutional
Fisher, V.	1991	Dissertation	Multi-Institutional
Freed, R.	2006	Dissertation	Multi-Institutional
Freed, R. & Mollick, G. M.	2009	Journal (★)	Multi-Institutional
Gaerte, D. E.	1996	Dissertation	Multi-Institutional
Glancey, K.	2007	CAEL	Multi-State
Harriger, C. A.	1991	Dissertation	Single Institution
Hart, D. & Hickerson, J.	2008	CAEL	Multi-Institutional
Hoffmann, T., Travers, N., Evans, M. & Treadwell, A.	2009	CAEL	Multi-Institutional
Klein-Collins, R.	2006	CAEL	Multi-Institutional
Knapp, J.	1976	CAEL	Multi-Institutional
Lee-Story, J. H.	2001	Dissertation	Multi-Institutional
Mandell, A. & Michelson, E.	1990	CAEL	Multi-Institutional
Michelson, E. & Mandell, A.	2004	Book	Multi-Institutional
Meyer, P.	1975	Book	Multi-Institutional
Raulf, J. F.	1992	Dissertation	Single Institution
Swiczewicz, L. M.	1990	Dissertation	Multi-Institutional
Topping, T. E.	1996	Dissertation	Single Institution
Travers, N. L.	2009	Presentation	Multi-Institutional
Willingham, W.	1977	CAEL	Multi-Institutional
Wolfson, G. K.	1996	Dissertation	Single Institution
Institutional Practices (Faculty Focused)			
Arnold, T. M.	1998	Dissertation	Single Institution
Coulter, X. *et al.*	1994	Institutional	Single Institution
Geyer, C. K.	1985	Dissertation	Multi-Institutional
Halberstadt, T. L.	1986	Dissertation	Multi-Institutional
Stevens, C.	in process	Dissertation	Single Institution
Stevens, M. A.	1977	Dissertation	Single Institution
Travers, N. L. *et al.*	2008	Journal (★★)	Single Institution
Travers, N. L. *et al.*	2011	Presentation	Single Institution
Travers, N. L. & Negron, D.	in process	Institutional	Multi-Institutional
Student Outcomes (Persistence)			
Fonte, L. F.	2008	Journal	Single Institution
Hoffmann, T. & LeMaster, J.	1996	Institutional	Single Institution
Hoffmann, T., LeMaster, J. & Flickinger, S.	1996	Institutional	Single Institution
Hoffmann, T., LeMaster, J. & Flickinger, S.	1997	Institutional	Single Institution

282

Authors	Year	Source	Type
Klein–Collins, R.	2010	CAEL	Multi-Institutional
Sargent, B.	1999	Dissertation	Multi-Institutional
Stemm, W. M.	2009	Dissertation	Single Institution
Student Outcomes (Transformation)			
Boomazian, S. S.	1994	Dissertation	Single Institution
Brown, J. O.	1999	Dissertation	Single Institution
Brown, J. O.	2002	Journal	Single Institution
Burris, J. K.	1997	Dissertation	Single Institution
Freers, S. M.	1994	Dissertation	Single Institution
Geerling, F. S. H.	2003	Dissertation	Single Institution
Lamoreaux, A. J.	2005	Dissertation	Single Institution
LeBerre, M. L.	1997	Dissertation	Single Institution
LeGrow, M. R.	2000	Dissertation	Single Institution
LeGrow, M. R., Sheckley, B. G. & Kehrhahn, M.	2002	Journal (*)	Single Institution
McDonald, E. A.	2000	Dissertation	Single Institution
Mullen, S. K.	1995	Dissertation	Multi-Institutional
Rausch, D. W.	2007	Dissertation	Single Institution
Rost, S. J.	2008	Dissertation	Single Institution
Stevens, K., Gerber, D. & Hendra, R.	2010	Journal	Single Institution
Travers, N. L.	2008	Journal (**)	Single Institution
Travers, N. L.	in process	Institutional	Single Institution
Theoretical			
Guthrie, D. C.	1998	Dissertation	—
Hamilton, R. J.	1992	Dissertation	—
Travers, N. L. & Evans, M.	2011	Journal	—

Journal (*) – original research from dissertation
Journal (**) – institutional journal

CHAPTER TWELVE

Prior Learning Assessment and Recognition (PLAR) and the teaching–research nexus in universities

ANGELINA WONG

Abstract

Faculty resistance within universities, especially research-intensive universities, has often been cited as a major challenge to the growth of Prior Learning Assessment and Recognition (PLAR) in Canada over the past 20 years. While PLAR advocates and practitioners have regularly exhorted different levels of government to convene meetings of senior university decision makers to address this challenge, little effort has been made to analyse the relationship between university culture and faculty motivation to participate in the PLAR process. This chapter will analyse and discuss three issues that may help PLAR advocates understand this resistance and develop strategies to counter it: (1) the teaching-research nexus that impacts on academic identity and faculty motivation to engage in innovative approaches to assessment and curriculum development; (2) the university department as the focal point of discipline-based curricula reform, and changes in institutional policies and practices; and (3) the conundrum of growing university support for selected forms of experiential learning but declining support for PLAR. Two areas of potential collaborative research and development between academics and PLAR practitioners are identified.

Introduction

Prior Learning Assessment and Recognition (PLAR), also widely known as Prior Learning Assessment (PLA) in Canada and the United States, and Recognition of Prior Learning (RPL) in other countries, emerged from diverse starting places. In the case of Canada, the United Kingdom (UK), Australia, South Africa and New Zealand, after a period of practitioner activism the initiative has been primarily government-driven, in an attempt to harness human learning for economic and social purposes. In the United States, increasing numbers of ex-servicemen re-entering civilian society and seeking academic credentials during the 1960s and 1970s provided the driving force for a large number of education institutions to develop PLA. In all contexts, the rapid advance of the global knowledge economy has created a critical interest in widening participation in post-secondary education and training to support the development of a qualified workforce.

The Department of Human Resource Development Canada defined PLA as the process of identifying, assessing and recognising skills, knowledge or competencies that have been acquired through work experience, non-credentialed training, independent study, volunteer activities and hobbies. The Department also outlined how PLA can be applied 'toward academic credit, toward the requirement of a training programme, or for occupational certification' (HRDC, 1995, p. 1). As defined, it is not surprising that the early adopters and champions of PLAR were technical and vocational colleges, including Mohawk College in Ontario, Red River College in Manitoba, the Saskatchewan Institute for Science and Technology in Saskatchewan, and the University College of the Fraser Valley in British Columbia. For the most part, the introduction and development of PLAR was financed by separate monies additional to the regular funding of formal education. In British Columbia, three waves of special funding led to a decade of innovative pilot projects among all the publicly funded post-secondary institutions. However, when special funding ceased, PLAR services dramatically decreased or disappeared entirely.

Within higher education, PLAR is a means to facilitate individuals' access to a type of formal learning that is associated with credentials that have traditionally been under the authority of closed circles of academics. Recognising prior experiential learning is not an end in itself. Rather, as a process and a product it reflects the multiple goals of individuals with varied backgrounds and aspirations.

285

However, PLAR has had a cool reception and fragmented presence among Canada's universities since the early 1990s. University resistance has also been observed in Europe, Australia and South Africa, especially in research-intensive institutions (Andersson and Harris, 2006). The practice has been more warmly accepted among faculty who are familiar with the history of adult education and experiential learning. For example, John Dewey (1938), often referred to as the father of experiential learning, stated: 'The beginning of instruction shall be made with the experience learners already have ... this experience and the capacities that have been developed during its course provide the starting point for all further learning' (*ibid.*, p. 74). Other educators in subsequent decades (e.g. Knowles, 1970; Schön, 1983, 1987; Kolb, 1984; Brookfield, 1986) have also emphasised the importance of acknowledging prior learning in the development of independent and reflective learners.

Since the year 2000, more than 1,300 four-year universities and colleges in the US and Canada have participated in the National Survey of Student Engagement (NSSE). Institutions are using their data to identify aspects of the undergraduate experience inside and outside the classroom, which can be improved through changes in policies and practices more consistent with good practices in undergraduate education. NSSE-related publications over the past eight years have shown a promising trend towards integration of experiential learning and authentic assessment into undergraduate education, a trend that bodes well for wider acceptance of PLAR principles and processes.

Resistance is the focus of this chapter. Universities, unlike many other organisations, have unique organisational cultures that transcend national boundaries, many of which have remained unchanged for several centuries. It is to the advantage of individuals seeking recognition, and their advocates and associates in community-based organisations and/or vocational-oriented sectors, to understand the historical and contextual forces that shape university academics' attitudes towards PLAR, and their motivation to engage (or not) in PLAR-related processes. The chapter introduces three related issues to aid this understanding:

1. The teaching-research nexus that impacts on academic identity and faculty motivation to engage in innovative approaches to assessment and curriculum development such as PLAR.
2. The university department as the focal point of discipline-based curricula reform and changes in institutional policies and practices.

3. The conundrum of growing university support for selected forms of experiential learning and declining support for PLAR.

It is argued that PLAR can only succeed in universities with the committed participation of faculty and learners. On the basis of the above understanding, PLAR advocates and practitioners can work strategically with willing faculty in activities that could help provide the evidence to counter resistance to PLAR. Two areas of potential collaborative research and development are identified.

The teaching-research nexus, and its impact on academic identity and faculty motivation

One widespread perception among PLAR advocates is that most university faculty members place much greater value on research than teaching. Since most Canadian universities already have in place special admission policies for non-traditional students, PLAR can be regarded as a teaching practice rather than an admission practice. It is necessary to review some of the contextual and historical factors underlying the relationship between teaching and research in order to see if the emphasis on research, rather than teaching, is indeed a major reason for the lack of faculty support for PLAR at Canadian universities.

A large and diverse literature, mostly originating from the US and the UK, deals with the nexus (or interconnections) between teaching and research (Hattie and Marsh, 1996). This strand of research within higher education was triggered by public perception that an increased focus on research by universities and funding agencies was exerting a negative impact on teaching. Among the issues explored were: What is the nature of the university in the context of mass higher education? How do governments see research and higher education as part of the knowledge economy? What are the characteristics of a positive interconnection between teaching and research?

The work of Ernest Boyer has been particularly significant in terms of opening up discussions about the nature of the knowledge that universities need to support in their faculty and students. In 1990, Boyer, then president of the US Carnegie Association for the Advancement of Teaching, published his book *Scholarship Reconsidered: Priorities of the Professoriate*, challenging higher education to break out of the old teaching versus research debate. Boyer developed the role of 'scholarship' as bridging teaching and research, and saw the work of the university and its faculty as demonstrating four scholarships: discovery, teaching, integration and application (now often referred to as 'engagement'). A global dialogue emerged around Boyer's idea of the complementary roles of the four scholarships: scholars in the US and the UK responded to his ideas, in particular his seminal discussion of the scholarship of teaching (e.g. Clark, 1997; Glassick *et al.*, 1997; Healey, 2000; Barnett, 2003; Gordon *et al.*, 2003).

In Australia, Ramsden and Moses (1992), in a large-scale study, researched teaching-research relationships at the level of the individual academic and department across all subject areas in a range of institutions. They concluded that there was no evidence to suggest a simple functional relationship between high research output and the effectiveness of undergraduate teaching. In other words, the simple model of 'more research, therefore better teaching' is suspect. However, the authors did state that their study in no way refutes the proposition that the continuing study of and intellectual curiosity about a subject is necessary for effective teaching.

In a more recent Australian study by Zubrick *et al.* (2001), the authors observed a range of conceptions of the teaching-research nexus among three very different institutional contexts. At an elite research 'sandstone' university (University of Western Australia), the espoused culture was that 'whenever possible, research should not exist without teaching' (*ibid.*, p. 35). This institution included a large number of research-only staff and emphasised the development of strong postgraduate programmes. At a second institution, a university of technology (Curtin), the focus was on developing teachers' concept of themselves as scholarly resource specialists and professional mentors to students. At a third university formed from the merger of several non-research institutions (Ballarat), there were many faculty members who perceived academic work as limited to teaching. They focused on applying the Boyer (1990) framework of scholarship to integrate inquiry-based learning, teaching and community service in undergraduate programmes.

In the UK, the implementation of the Research Assessment Exercise (RAE) produced a dramatic rise in profile and funding of university research, and a corresponding devaluing of teaching. Jenkins (2007) notes that this has resulted in a growing separation of the research worlds of the university and student learning since a significant component of institutional funding has been linked to the outcomes of the RAE. This situation has been countered to an extent by the decision of the Higher Education Funding Council of England (HEFCE) to promote excellence in teaching and learning via the funding of 74 'centres for excellence in teaching and learning'.

After several years of national dialogue about teaching, Boyer spearheaded the Boyer Commission Report *Reinventing Undergraduate Education* (1998), which pointed out that US research universities have too often failed their undergraduate populations. He presented ten recommendations for changing undergraduate education that have had significant impact on thinking and action at the institutional level among research-intensive universities. A follow-up report three years later explored how those recommendations were being adopted. Actions undertaken by the National Science Foundation (NSF) to value the pedagogical dimensions of publicly-funded research was one positive outcome and continues to influence the landscape of undergraduate education. The NSF created funding streams that specifically target support for undergraduate students as researchers in institutions outside the elite research universities, including some community colleges. The 'scholarship of engagement' criterion for research funding applications now includes the extent to which undergraduates are involved in research, including research that benefits local communities.

In Canada, a commission of inquiry into university education observed that teaching excellence in most universities has not been accorded the same importance as research publications with respect to tenure and promotion (Smith, 1991). A controversial book by Pocklington and Tupper (2002) put forward the view that university research often detracts from the quality of teaching; research is elevated, while the quality of instruction is neglected. They claimed that within the scholarly enterprise, reflective inquiry-based research is undervalued compared to discovery research in science and medicine. Although Canadian universities are not assessed by a national system such as the RAE in the United Kingdom, data collected by Statistics Canada for the Canadian Association of University Business Officers (CAUBO) shows that progressively less money has been allocated to the teaching function since 1988 (Smith, 2010). Indeed, operating funds directed to teaching and non-sponsored research have fallen from 65 per cent in 1988 to 58 per cent in 2008. This represents a cutback of an average of $35 million at research-intensive universities and $45 million at the top five research universities. Moreover, only 57.6 per cent of this teaching budget goes to academic salaries. The 'savings' are used to fund increased costs for central administration, including non-academic staff. In contrast, sponsored research (by governments and corporations) consumed 25 per cent of university expenditures in 2008 compared to 15 per cent in 1988.

The prevailing view among many Western universities is that all faculty members must be teachers *and* researchers, and good research is essential to good teaching. The priorities of Canadian universities are heavily influenced by the inter-university struggle for prestige and recognition. The declining funding allocation for teaching is perhaps a manifestation of the exercise of pursuing higher rankings in global academic reputation (Smith, 2010), in which research excellence is the key indicator. The federal government, in the last decade, has invested in the creation of Canada research chairs in many discipline-based as well as inter-disciplinary programmes. These grants now constitute a major status symbol and a significant component of university-operating budgets.

There are signs that some 'elite' universities are paying more attention to the quality of teaching and learning. To counter the perception of privileging research over teaching, many Canadian universities have established or increased resources for centres dedicated to enhancing the quality of teaching and learning. Examples of a new emphasis on teaching include: the University of British Columbia's appointment of Carl Wieman, a Nobel Laureate in physics, to a special post designed to foster the quality of teaching; the University of Guelph's sponsorship of a round table on research, teaching and learning in 2006; the University of Saskatchewan's creation of a new position of vice-provost of teaching and learning in 2008, and re-allocation of significant resources to create a Learning Commons. The emerging focus on good practice in university teaching provides areas of common ground with selected processes in PLAR that could be fruitfully cultivated to increase support for PLAR.

Academic identity: the push and pull of teaching and research

For many university faculty members, motivations to work in higher education are shaped by strong values of the importance of a teaching-research nexus, though there seem to be significant individual and disciplinary differences in this regard. For example, research evidence suggests that individual academics have different conceptions of teaching. In the UK, Prosser and Trigwell (1999) highlighted studies that demonstrate clear differences between teachers with 'information transmission' conceptions and practices of teaching, and those with 'student change' models.

Henkel (2000) demonstrated the importance of the nexus to many faculty members' academic identity in a detailed three-year study of seven disciplines at11 English institutions (seven pre-1992 and four post-1992 institutions).[1] She observed that while academics are the strongest exponents of the argument that research and teaching are central to their work, only some see them as functionally complementary, and some regard themselves as essentially either researchers or teachers. Interviews with academics across a wide spectrum of universities showed that faculty members in the sciences strongly believe that exposure to active researchers, and the involvement of students in projects generated from their research, should be the basic features of an undergraduate education. Academics in the humanities and the social sciences tend to describe the research-teaching relationship in more complex and varied terms, with differing emphases on what Neumann (1994) calls the 'tangible' and the 'intangible' aspects of the research-teaching relationship. The tangible aspects are those in which transmission of new knowledge and research skills or techniques occurs, and the intangible aspects are those in which transmission of attitudes to knowledge takes place.

Australian researcher Brew's phenomenographic research (2001, 2003) of leading researchers at a major university concluded that when research and teaching are both viewed as founded on a traditional empiricist framework, the relationship is always problematic. If, on the other hand, knowledge is seen as a product of communication and negotiation, connections between research and teaching are quite different. She noted a move towards a more pluralistic view of knowledge that is accepting of the interpretive nature of academic work. For Brew (2003, p. 12), bringing teaching and research together centrally involves developing 'a

---

[1] Post-1992 institutions comprise former polytechnics and colleges of higher education. They are higher education corporations whose structures of governance derive from the 1988 Education Reform Act and the 1992 Further and Higher Education Act. In contrast to the pre-1992 universities, their model of governance specifies a more powerful role for the vice-chancellor as chief executive; a larger majority of external members on the governing body; limited participation of staff and students in governance; and a lesser role for the academic board. Similarly, in Canada, several provinces, notably British Columbia, have since 2005 granted university status to a number of former university colleges that offer a combination of academic and vocational programmes.

conception of teaching as being student focused, and concentrating on conceptual change'.

Research by Colbeck (1998, 2005) in the US indicates the importance of what 'counts' as research. Her research involved studying in detail the behaviours and roles of 12 academics, amongst other things, in order to understand how university, departmental and disciplinary contexts influence the ways and extent to which faculty integrate teaching and research. The faculties studied were in contrasting disciplines – physics and English – in two very different US institutions, with fictitious names: Vantage University, a high-prestige research university (a 'Research University 1', according to the Carnegie classification); and Cosmopolitan University, a 'Masters University 1' or comprehensive university.

Paradoxically, academics in the less well-resourced comprehensive university found it easier in one respect to link their teaching and research. At Vantage University, 'research' for faculty evaluation was narrowly interpreted to mean standing as an original researcher amongst peers in the discipline. By contrast, at Cosmopolitan University, faculty evaluation of 'research' included the writing of textbooks and creative works in the popular media. Colbeck (1998) draws a strong contrast between two physicists. In her sample of 12 academics, the person who demonstrated the strongest integration between teaching and research roles was a physicist at Cosmopolitan University whose research involved writing an introductory textbook that incorporated new pedagogical techniques. By contrast, at Vantage University, a physicist who previously had written an acclaimed computer-assisted physics course text had declined to write a follow-up because he realised his departmental colleagues would not recognise the value of such a project.

Academic identity is associated with having unique knowledge and skills, the ability to perform specific work tasks, and an association with a particular reference group. It is shaped incrementally by socialisation and the expectations of significant others, including peers and department heads. Colbeck (2005) later expanded her investigation to find out whether early-career academics (subsequent to the 1998 Boyer Commission Report) were likely to develop fragmented or integrated professional identities in terms of teaching and research. She found more instances of new academics being required to fragment their work in favour of research. Early-career academics in her sample integrate teaching and research nearly 20 per cent of their work time, even though they are often discouraged from doing so. The attempts at integration include enriching their classroom teaching with their research ideas and findings, engaging in reflective inquiry about student learning in their particular disciplines, and educating their graduate students to be reflective teachers.

Gibbs (1995), a UK researcher writing about his observations of several high-level conferences in the US and the UK, noted that university presidents and chancellors in both countries share a problem of how to reward excellent university teaching. In spite of many reports of innovations in valuing the scholarship of teaching, there was little evidence to show that research universities have adjusted the criteria for promotion and tenure to giving teaching excellence parity of esteem.

The literature on the teaching-research nexus and academic identity confirms that many academics work in university environments that reward research over teaching. Although there has been widespread discussion since the 1990s about valuing the complementary roles of the scholarships of discovery and teaching, it appears that many academics' motivations to work in higher education are shaped by their (often disciplinary-based) values about the importance of a teaching-research nexus. In addition, national policies and funding for research have resulted in structural separation between teaching and research. The desire of universities to pursue higher rankings within global academia has increased pressure on full-time faculty members to devote more time and energy to research. Since the reward system favours research, many academics find it hard enough to maintain quality in teaching, let alone engage in new practices such as assessment of non-formal, experiential learning.

How academics conceptualise teaching and research may be central to understanding their motivation to engage in effective teaching practices that positively impact on the student experience at both the undergraduate and graduate levels. Academics who subscribe to a more pluralistic view of knowledge and a conception of teaching as learner-focused are likely to be more empathetic towards PLAR. PLAR advocates need to actively seek out such faculty members and explicitly demonstrate to them the common ground between good practice in university teaching, and the principles and processes of PLAR. At an institutional level, PLAR advocates a need to add their voices to those seeking institutional reforms that will bring parity of esteem and reward between teaching and research.

Understanding disciplinary perspectives as a prelude to recruiting PLAR supporters

Learning and teaching occur for the most part within the framework of a discipline or domain, yet ever more approaches are needed that combine knowledge from different disciplines to respond to the problems that confront society, from the global economy to global warming. Contemporary university programmes are increasingly structured to reflect this need, but the curricula of many research-intensive universities remain traditionally structured according to the overall architecture of the major disciplines: the humanities, the natural and applied sciences, the social sciences, and professional programmes such as law and medicine.

A disciplinary area can be defined as a body of knowledge with a reasonably logical taxonomy, a specialised vocabulary, an accepted body of theory, a systematic research strategy, and techniques of replication and validation. However, Donald (2002, p. 7) states that disciplines have been found to be 'wildly flourishing jungles rather than orderly municipalities'. Disciplines sometimes behave more like warring tribes than peaceful communities – territorialism dominates decision making and competition limits access across borders to other domains of knowledge. Becher (1989) describes knowledge in the disciplines as a badly made patchwork quilt, full of gaps and overlaps. Because of such fragmentation, Donald encourages faculty to provide guidance for their students through explicitly described patterns of inquiry.

University disciplines have been categorised as hard versus soft and pure versus applied. This can be traced to a study by Biglan (1973), who had faculty members sort 36 academic areas into groups based on their similarity. He then used a process of multidimensional scaling to produce dimensions of hard versus soft, pure versus applied and life versus non-life. Hard disciplines have a logical structure and validation criteria that provide maximum direction to scholars in the field. In physics, for example, Newton's laws of classical mechanics form part of the curriculum around the world. Soft disciplines do not have a body of theory that is subscribed to by all members of the field; complexity is seen as a legitimate aspect of the knowledge such that the phenomena that can be studied are unrestricted or relatively unlimited. Whether a discipline is pure or applied also affects the manner in which it is organised epistemologically. Pure disciplines are more likely to use specific models, whereas applied disciplines are more open to environmental

294

eclecticism – using the most fitting model or method in a given circumstance.

In Canada, Donald (1995) analysed interview data from 40 professors in five disciplines and found that each discipline represented a different category of validation criteria and strategies, according to the Biglan dimensions of hard-soft and pure-applied. For example, physics represents hard-pure; engineering, hard-applied; psychology represents social science-pure; education, social science-applied; and English literature, soft-pure. In New Zealand, Robertson and Bond (2001, 2005) explored, through detailed interviews, how faculty members at the University of Canterbury perceived knowledge that shapes the teaching-research relationships in their environment. They found that the faculty members from 'hard' disciplines, with very hierarchical knowledge structures, generally believe that teaching-research relationships can only be activated at the postgraduate level; they tend to perceive undergraduate students as lacking the disciplinary frameworks to engage in inquiry. By contrast, faculty members from soft disciplines with low paradigm consensus are quite open to using new lenses to explore territory mapped by others.

When adult learners initiate a PLAR process, they enter a complex world of university learning with a maze of expectations, some explicitly stated, but many tacitly embedded in the perspectives and processes of the disciplinary areas in which recognition for their learning is sought. Articulating and documenting evidence for PLAR becomes an intellectual and emotional challenge as they forge their way through 'flourishing jungles' to find friendly borders to cross. It is beneficial for both PLAR applicants and PLAR advocates and practitioners in the community to build their understanding of the differences between disciplines, the kind of language used, the logical structure, the preferred criteria for validating knowledge, and the modes of inquiry deemed to be the most appropriate. Armed with this understanding, PLAR applicants can better organise and document their evidence of learning to obtain recognition.

To understand a discipline or a field of study, students must learn its perspectives and processes. Intellectual development requires linking domain knowledge (or the major concepts) and processes of inquiry (Donald, 2002). The concepts in a course and their relationships form the knowledge structure or core content of the course. A concept can be defined as a unit of thought or element of knowledge that allows us to organise experience. Concepts can exist at various levels of generality and abstraction, and may be simple or complex. A field of study is also characterised by a logical structure, which can be defined as the organisation of knowledge showing relationships between component parts. Validation criteria vary across disciplines. Although the criterion of consistency appears to be important in all disciplines, its measurement varies. In the sciences it would be concerned with external reality; in the humanities it might be consistency over time and across people; and in the social sciences, consistency could take the form of reliability over a series of observations.

Understanding the characteristics of various disciplines – their conceptions of knowledge, accepted modes of inquiry and validation criteria – can assist learners in preparing their applications for PLAR. Soft and applied disciplines are more likely to be open to idiosyncratic content and methods. Institutions that have both academic and vocation-preparation programmes are more likely to be sympathetic to boundary crossing. By understanding the disciplinary perspectives within the universities they wish to work with, PLAR advocates will be better positioned to recruit faculty members who would be open to engage in assessment and curriculum design practices that are beneficial for PLAR candidates.

The university department as the focal point for discipline-based curricula reform and changes in institutional policies and practices

University departments: unrecognised potential

Modern Western universities are internally complex. They are administratively divided into large faculties such as arts, science, medicine, business and law, and then into departments that yield further specialisation. Leadership in universities is highly political, and senior administrators cannot easily impose a common vision, a common curriculum or even common standards of evaluation. Kennedy (1995), a former president of Stanford University, points out that departments are the units in which the institution's strategy for academic development is formulated and practised. There is a powerful tradition, especially among research universities, of local control over most of the things that matter, including choice of new faculty, curriculum, and tenure and promotion criteria. It is often the department rather than the administration that determines how, if not which, policy decisions are implemented.

296

Within each department, the faculty member's work is unlike almost any other occupation. Most academics enjoy substantial freedom in how they teach their courses, the subjects in which they undertake research, and the performance of their obligations to their students, their colleagues and the university. The aforementioned study by Zubrick *et al.* (2001) illustrates how different institutional cultures influence different conceptions of the academic role, and subsequently how faculty members apply their time and energy. The studies by Colbeck (1998, 2005) further illustrate how some new academics are willing to devote time to integrating teaching and research in spite of pressures from their departments to focus on research.

In recent years, partially due to the influence of some prominent reports (Boyer, 1990, 1998; Byrne, 2000; National Survey of Student Engagement, 2003), many faculty members have been made aware of the imperative to provide high-quality learning experiences for their students. More university departments are re-designing their programmes to provide bridges between classroom-based learning and community-based or workplace-based learning. These departments are prime candidates for PLAR advocates to recruit as partners in developing assessment processes and curricula structures that would benefit both conventional age students and adult learners.

The future of PLAR at universities depends on achieving a critical mass of faculty who believe their engagement in the process will be valued and recognised. In lobbying government for more resources to kick-start or to sustain PLAR activities at universities, PLAR advocates should consider targeting resources for faculty development at the departmental level. For example, faculty members who have demonstrated an interest in teaching activities, such as the development of authentic assessment processes or supervision of experiential learning activities, could submit applications for 'PLAR awards' – grants that could be used to release time to undertake applied research and/or curriculum development that would benefit PLAR. Finding the resources to fund such awards will be a challenge; a later section will provide an example of innovation supported by private foundation funding.

Improving student experiences: trends with positive implications for PLAR

The aforementioned National Survey of Student Engagement (NSSE, 2003) was triggered by the recognition that established methods for assuring quality in higher education contain few external incentives for individual universities to engage in meaningful quality improvement, especially in the area of enhancing undergraduate education. Institutional accreditation processes, despite their recent emphasis on assessing student learning and development, deal largely with resource and process measures. Government oversight, as manifested in licence requirements and programme review mechanisms, in turn, continues to emphasise regulation and procedural compliance. Third-party judgements of 'quality' such as media rankings continue to focus on such matters as student selectivity and faculty credentials. None of these gets to the heart of the matter – the investments that institutions make to foster effective teaching practices, and the kinds of activities and experiences that their students receive as a result.

As one step towards addressing this condition, The Pew Charitable Trusts convened a working group of higher education leaders in February 1998. Collaborative actions were taken in the following decade to collect and publish student engagement data and case studies of high performing institutions to stimulate the integration of effective educational practices, including active and collaborative learning, student-faculty interaction, enriching educational experiences, and supportive campus environments. Enriching educational experiences as described in the NSSE include co-curricular activities, practicum, internship, field experiences, co-op experiences, clinical assignments, community service or volunteer work, foreign language coursework or study abroad, and culminating senior experiences such as capstone courses, senior projects or theses.

What do these educational experiences have in common with PLAR? They all subscribe to a more participative, learner-centred approach that places an emphasis on personal experience, rich learning events and the construction of meaning by learners. Learners analyse their experience by reflecting on, evaluating and reconstructing that experience (sometimes individually, sometimes collectively, sometimes both). PLAR also shares a common challenge with these university-sponsored learning activities in the development of effective methods and criteria for evaluating experiential learning. Evaluation plays an especially important role in situations where there is intensive immersion in the experiences and where other people are involved. Often, the evaluative activities themselves and the products generated for evaluation provide significant opportunities for those critical steps of observation, reflection and abstract conceptualisation that can lead to higher levels of active experimentation and application. It is likely that institutions that subscribe to the NSSE project will be more receptive to adopting policies and practices that enhance the learning experience, including the assessment and recognition of experiential learning.

The conundrum of growing support for experiential learning and declining support for PLAR

For many universities, the heart of their efforts to connect or reconnect the university to societal purposes has focused on developing institutional programmes and strategies to make the intellectual assets of the university more accessible to the community. After many years of contentious debate, teaching pedagogies associated with distance education and later e-learning have finally gained support, and achieved integration among faculties across the US and Canada. By contrast, teaching pedagogies that have potential for providing students with opportunities to link what they learn in the classroom to some real-world experience have been much slower in gaining widespread support.

University faculty members today are more familiar with and more accepting of community service learning (CSL) than PLAR. Practica or internships have been important experiential learning components of selected programmes within universities for many years, particularly in education and the health care professions. CSL is a more recent trend, but is seen as a contributor to the overall student experience and is supported by an expanding body of research (e.g. Zlotkowski, 1998; Eyler and Giles, 1999; Butin, 2005). Community service learning can be defined as a type of experiential education in which students participate in service in the community, and reflect on their involvement in such a way as to gain further understanding of the course content and its relationship to social needs and an enhanced sense of civic responsibility. In Canada, the rise of CSL at universities corresponds to the availability of private foundation funding, coupled with increased interest among senior administrators who perceive CSL as a manifestation of the institution's outreach and engagement mission. This situation contrasts sharply with declining government funding support for PLAR within post-secondary institutions and little internal interest in most universities.

In January 2005, the J.W. McConnell Family Foundation launched its National University-Based Community Service-Learning Programme.

To date, it has provided generous funding to ten Canadian universities to integrate CSL within their curricula and to build strong partnerships with local communities, as well as financial support for the Canadian Alliance for Community Service-Learning (CACSL). The institutional recipients of the awards include both large research universities (e.g. University of British Columbia and University of Alberta) as well as smaller comprehensive universities (e.g. St Francis Xavier University and Trent University). The Foundation's objective is to encourage active citizenship and to create resilient communities. Each of the ten programmes within the McConnell national CSL programme have unique characteristics, and are developing expertise with regard to certain specific elements of CSL design, delivery and/or assessment.[2]

The relative success of CSL at Canadian universities compared to PLAR raises the question of how PLAR advocates and practitioners could solicit resources from the private sector to support collaborative partnerships with selected universities for enhancing elements of PLAR design and delivery for targeted groups of learners.

Community service learning and PLAR: common ground

A pioneering publication by Weil and McGill (1989) provides a clue that language may be central to encouraging university academics to recognise the common ground between experiential learning and PLAR. Weil and McGill developed a 'village' metaphor to categorise the contexts of practice among a group of educators who had gathered at an international conference to share the approaches they adopt to champion experiential learning. The four villages are not mutually exclusive, but interact and intersect with each other. Village 1 concerns itself with the assessment and accreditation of experiential learning as a means of gaining access to educational institutions, employment and professional bodies. Village 2 focuses on changing the purposes, structure and curricula in post-secondary education. Village 3 is concerned with learning from experience as the core for consciousness-raising, and community action and social change. Village 4 takes as its focus personal growth and development to increase self-awareness and group effectiveness. In facilitating faculty development workshops on PLAR over a period of seven years,

---

[2] Descriptions of these projects are available at the CACSL website: http://www. communityservicelearning.ca/en/.

the authors noted that the village metaphor resonates with university academics. They begin to see the links between their individual teaching goals and practices, and the goals and processes of PLAR.

Development of a curriculum for experiential learning requires faculty members to appreciate different kinds of knowledge production, as well as the complexities of learning and the circumstances in which it can take place. As a typical course moves towards greater use of experiential components, pressures also develop for greater individualisation of purposes, substance and expectations concerning outcomes. Both CSL participants and PLAR candidates are required to make explicit and connect experiential learning outside the academy to the formal teaching and learning within the academy. However, only PLAR candidates are obliged to have their learning outcomes 'fit' into a programme post hoc. In addition, PLAR candidates, compared to participants in CSL and other university-sponsored experiential learning, lack the benefit of immersion in an academic culture that tacitly transmits many of its cultural norms and values. Faculty development workshops can address these similarities and differences within the context of improving assessment practices.

All learning necessarily involves experience of some sort, prior and/or current. Much of the impetus for experience-based learning outside the classroom has been a reaction against an approach to learning which is didactic, teacher-driven and involving discipline-focused transmission of knowledge. It supports a more participative, learner-centred approach that places an emphasis on the construction of meaning by learners. Many university programmes currently use a journal and/or a learning portfolio as the vehicle(s) of choice to document learners' observations, reflections, reconstruction of meaning, and proposals for experimentation or solution. The portfolio also features prominently within the PLAR process. Increasingly, university faculty members are engaged in the preparation of teaching portfolios (also called dossiers or case files) to support their application for promotion and tenure. These tools and processes provide common ground between PLAR advocates and university faculty interested in enhancing their teaching, and suggest a platform for some collaborative research and development between the academy and community-based organisations.

301

Potential areas of collaborative research and development

The recent trend among Canadian universities to allocate more resources to the expansion of university teaching and learning centres points to these units as the starting point for PLAR advocates and practitioners to identify ways and means of working with faculty members who are likely to be interested in collaborative research and development activities to further PLAR. Teaching and learning centres are dedicated to championing teaching at the university. They offer various programmes and workshops to both full-time and part-time faculty members to improve teaching effectiveness. They also work with academic departments to assist with curriculum and programme re-design. Some universities offer formal courses on teaching for graduate students and new faculty. Assessment methods, the application of learning portfolios and peer consultation are among the workshops commonly offered.

The issues discussed in this chapter illuminate two areas in which academics and community-based individuals, including PLAR advocates and practitioners, can engage in some collaborative research and development work that could benefit both conventional university students and adult learners – the development of learning communities and strategies to enhance student capacity for reflective practice.

The development of learning communities

One important outcome of a decade of participation in the NSSE is the increased attention higher education administrators and academics are paying to 'learning communities', a concept and instructional approach that holds promise for more institutional support for PLAR. Most learning communities incorporate active and collaborative learning activities, and promote involvement in complementary academic and social activities that extend beyond the classroom. Learning communities are intentionally structured to help students make two types of connection. The first is to encourage students to connect ideas from different disciplines, which is aided by being co-enrolled in two or more courses that are linked by a common theme. The second connection involves linking students to others through ongoing social interactions afforded by being with the same students for an extended period of time and engaging in collaborative learning processes (Zhao and Kuh, 2004).

According to Lenning and Ebbers (1999), learning communities take four generic forms. The fourth form, 'student-type learning communities', is specially designed for targeted groups, such as academically under-prepared students, historically under-represented students, honours students, students with disabilities and students with similar academic interests, such as women in maths, science and engineering. It is plausible that the university could support a learning community consisting of adult learners with varied informal and formal learning experiences, and seeking recognition of this learning. Institutional 'blessing' of such a community could qualify it for staff and other resources to facilitate the recruitment and retention of adult learners.

Emerging research in cognitive science stresses the importance of the learning context and developing schema that permit new learning through making connections with what was previously determined to be valid under specific conditions and contexts. For adult learners seeking advanced standing under PLAR, these conditions and contexts are usually related to work-based and community-based learning. A learning community that acknowledges the 'situatedness' of the learner in the workplace and the community – that the learner has a context in a particular setting at a particular time, with various demands placed on her or him – can become a powerful motivating force for adult learners to persevere in formal learning (Brandford *et al.*, 2000).

Strategies to enhance student capacity for reflective practice

Students going out into community service placements and adult learners seeking PLAR from the university can both benefit from an orientation to the theory and practice of reflection. Writers such as Kolb (1984) have cautioned that experiential learning often appears too thoroughly pragmatic for the academic mind, while practitioners in the community often feel university students in their midst are too focused on book learning. In mentoring novices in unfamiliar contexts, both academics and practitioners should help learners to reflect on their experiences, and learn from both the process and outcomes of that reflection. Collaboratively, academics and PLAR advocates/practitioners can build much stronger 'scaffolds' to help learners develop meta-cognition, the capacity to build mental maps within which one can locate one's learning and to which one can make explicit references in subsequent situations.

303

Whether the goal is to provide evidence of learning from a CSL experience or for PLAR, all learners must use disciplinary, professional or work-related frameworks as appropriate to examine their learning – to appreciate both its achievements and limitations. The development of awareness about what is actually being learned or has been learned so far, and the ability to articulate this convincingly, are strongly influenced by how clearly the teacher explains the criteria for evaluating critical reflection. Collaboratively, academics and practitioners can equip learners with conceptual and practical resources to enable them to identify and monitor their own learning, a key step in developing a habit of lifelong learning. Practitioners, through providing situation-specific examples of reflection in work-based or community settings, can help academics anticipate and plan learning activities that bridge theory and practice. Academics, through explicating the levels and standards that underpin their programmes, can help practitioners become more effective advisors to PLAR candidates.

Concluding comments

This chapter has introduced three issues that illuminate university faculty's resistance to and/or reluctance to adopt PLAR at a time when many universities, including research-intensive universities, are devoting more attention and resources to enriching the learning experience for their students. PLAR as a social movement is pressing universities for institutional change to facilitate the achievement of credentials by non-traditional groups of learners. On the other hand, universities as cultural institutions have a centuries-old tradition that has withstood wars, revolutions and industrial transformations, and come out less changed than almost any other segment of their societies (Carnegie Council on Policy Studies in Higher Education, 1980).

There are encouraging signs that some universities are at the cusp of shifting from resistance to inspired action. Byrne (2000), Executive Director of the Kellogg Commission on *The Future of State and Land-Grant Universities*, states that as the Commission investigated the issue of access, it became apparent that 'the issue is not really access to or admission into our institutions, but a more important issue – access to a successful life in society resulting from a higher education experience' (*ibid.*, p. 15).[3] He further points out the importance of universities to provide opportunities for faculty, staff, students and the public to learn together in seeking solutions to real problems; to create and use knowledge for society's benefit; and to organise opportunities for lifelong learning.

Universities have been given the authority to be the gatekeepers of credentials that reflect the achievement of specific levels of knowledge and skills in disciplinary-based fields of study. Because of today's societal value of university credentials as proxy evidence of capability for selection into many desirable occupations, universities are being pressured to meet the goals of many individuals who may not be ready for or personally suited to the type of formal learning required in universities. It is important that PLAR advocates and adult learners beyond the academy understand that the type of learning that universities value represents only one type of learning, and does not denigrate other types of learning. It is a type that does not favour delineating a 'universe' of outcomes such as those derived from industry-based occupational standards, and used in vocational education and training. Rather, university education seeks to promote an individual's integration of knowledge, skills and personal qualities to respond to and deal with new and changing circumstances. Collaboration between PLAR practitioners and faculty members from disciplines (and departments) with an affinity for using new lenses to explore territory mapped by others can provide useful guidance and resources for both conventional and non-traditional students.

In spite of cultural pressures to privilege research over teaching, there are faculty members who are sympathetic to the concept of PLAR as a means of enhancing diversity and equity among university students. However, under the current reward system, most feel that they cannot

---

[3] The Kellogg Commission on *The Future of State and Land-Grant Universities* was created with funding from the W.K. Kellogg Foundation, and consisted of the presidents and chancellors (past and present) of 26 American public universities. The Commission was created at a time when a sceptical public appeared convinced that students were being ignored and that research was deemed to be more important than teaching, when enrolment was projected to increase significantly at the same time that funding was limited, and would continue to be so. The Commission identified five issues for discussion and campus action: the student experience; student access; the engaged institution; a learning society; and campus culture. The Commission has achieved significant impact on public universities in both the US and Canada.

afford to devote time to learning and practising the PLAR assessor role. By shifting the focus to enhancing aspects of the teaching and learning process that academics are already interested in, PLAR advocates and practitioners stand a much better chance of inspiring and recruiting a pool of committed faculty.

It is also useful to recognise that there are different types of universities with different histories and academic cultures; within any one university, there are different disciplinary and departmental cultures. Research-intensive universities may be better suited to educating large numbers of graduate students and have advantages in some professional programmes. For example, several Canadian research universities now have programmes to assist internationally trained pharmacists, physicians, engineers and lawyers to practise in their adopted countries. At the same time, many conventional-age undergraduates and adult learners may do as well or better in regional comprehensive and undergraduate-focused universities. Equipped with knowledge of the complex interaction of academic culture, identities and motivation, PLAR advocates can strategically choose 'dance partners' who could help PLAR to transit from pilot projects to institutionalised practice.

Two initial research questions emerge from this study that would begin to address the move from resistance to inspired action:

1. Does involvement in experiential learning pedagogies, including PLAR, stimulate new interest and vitality for the faculty role?
   - Are there differences among different departments or across different disciplines?
   - Are there differences among faculty at different stages of their careers?
2. Does involvement in experiential learning pedagogies, including PLAR, open up collaborative opportunities for faculty in teaching, research and community engagement? If it does open up opportunities, in what ways does it do so and in relation to what type of opportunity?

References

Andersson, P. and Harris, J. (eds) (2006) *Re-theorising the Recognition of Prior Learning*. Leicester, UK: National Institute of Adult Continuing Education (NIACE).

Barnett, R. (2003) *Beyond All Reason: Living with Ideology in the University.* Buckingham: Society for Research into Higher Education and Open University Press.

Becher, R. (1989) *Academic Tribes and Territories.* Bristol, PA: Open University Press.

Biglan, A. (1973) 'The characteristics of subject matter in different academic areas', *Journal of Applied Psychology,* Vol. 57, No 3, pp. 195–203.

Boyer, E. (1990) *Scholarship Reconsidered: Priorities of the Professoriate.* San Francisco: Jossey-Bass.

Boyer Commission on Educating Undergraduates in the Research University (1998) *Reinventing Undergraduate Education: A Blueprint for America's Research Universities.* Stony Brook: State University of New York at Stony Brook. Available at: http://naples.cc.sunysb.edu/Pres/boyer.nsf.

Branford, J., Brown, A. and Cocking, P. (eds) (2000) *How People Learn: Brain, Mind, Experience, and School.* Washington, DC: National Research Council and National Academy Press.

Brew, A. (2001) *The Nature of Research: Inquiry in Academic Contexts.* London: Routledge/Falmer.

Brew, A. (2003) 'Teaching and research: New relationships and their implications for inquiry based teaching and learning in higher education', *Higher Education Research and Development,* Vol. 22, pp. 3–18.

Brookfield, S. (1986) *Understanding and Facilitating Adult Learning.* San Francisco: Jossey-Bass.

Butin, D. (ed.) (2005) *Service-learning in Higher Education: Critical Issues and Directions.* New York: Palgrave Macmillan.

Byrne, J. (2000) 'Engagement: A defining characteristic of the university of tomorrow', *Journal of Higher Education Outreach and Engagement,* Vol. 6, No 1, pp. 13–21.

Carnegie Council on Policy Studies in Higher Education (1980) *Three Thousand Futures: The Next Twenty Years in Higher Education.* San Francisco: Jossey-Bass.

Clark, B. (1997) 'The modern integration of research activities with teaching and learning', *Journal of Higher Education,* Vol. 68, No 3, pp. 242–55.

Colbeck, C. (1998) 'Merging in a seamless blend', *The Journal of Higher Education,* Vol. 69, No 6, pp. 647–71.

Colbeck, C. (2005) 'Creating academic identity and the impact of the Boyer Commission Report'. Presentation at the Canadian Summit on the Integration of Teaching and Research, University of Alberta, 3–5 August.

Dewey, J. (1938) *Experience and Education*. New York: Macmillan.

Donald, J. (1995) 'Disciplinary differences in knowledge validation', in N. Hativa and M. Marincovich (eds) *Disciplinary Differences in Teaching and Learning*. New Directions for Teaching and Learning, No 64. San Francisco: Jossey-Bass.

Donald, J. (2002) *Learning to Think: Disciplinary Perspectives*. San Francisco: Jossey-Bass.

Eyler, J. and Giles, D. (1999) *Where's the Learning in Service Learning?* San Francisco: Jossey-Bass.

Gibbs, G. (1995) 'Promoting excellent teaching is harder than you'd think', *Change*, May/June, pp. 17–20.

Glassick, C., Huber, M. and Maerof, G. (1997) *Scholarship Assessed: Evaluation of the Professoriate*. San Francisco: Jossey-Bass.

Gordon, G., Andrea, V., Gosling, D. and Stefani, L. (2003) *Building Capacity for Change: Research on the Scholarship of Teaching*. Bristol: Higher Education Funding Council for England.

Hattie, J. and Marsh, H. (1996) 'The relationship between research and teaching: a meta-analysis', *Review of Educational Research*, Vol. 66, No 4, pp. 507–42.

Healey, M. (2000) 'Developing the scholarship of teaching in higher education: A discipline-based approach', *Higher Education Research and Development*, Vol. 19, No 2, 169–89.

Henkel, M. (2000) *Academic Identities and Policy Change in Higher Education*. London: Jessica Kingsley Publishers.

Human Resource Development Canada (HRDC) (1995) *Prior Learning Development Newsletter*, Vol. 1, No 2. Ottawa, ON: HRCD.

Jenkins, A. (2007) 'Towards sane UK national policies: or learning from some US policies'. Paper presented at the Marwell 2007 Colloquium on International Policies and Practices for Academic Enquiry, Winchester, UK, 19–21 April. Available at: http://portal-live.solent.ac.uk/university/rtconference/2007/colloquium _papers.aspx.

Kennedy, D. (1995) 'Another century's end, another revolution for higher education', *Change*, Vol. 27, No 3, pp. 8–15.

Knowles, M. (1970) *The Modern Practice of Adult Education*. Chicago: Follett.

Kolb, D. (1984) *Experiential Learning: Experience as the Source of Learning and Development*. Englewood Cliff, NJ: Prentice-Hall.

Lenning, O. and Ebbers, L. (1999) *The Powerful Potential of Learning Communities: Improving Education for the Future.* ASHE-ERUC Higher Education Report, Vol. 26, No 6. Graduate School of Education and Human Development, George Washington University, Washington, DC.

National Survey of Student Engagement (2003) *Converting Data into Action: Expanding the Boundaries of Institutional Improvement.* Bloomington: Center for Postsecondary Research, Indiana University.

Neumann, R. (1994) 'The teaching-research nexus: Applying a framework to university students' learning experiences', *European Journal of Education*, Vol. 29, No 3, pp. 323–39.

Pocklington, T. and Tupper, A. (2002) *No Place to Learn: Why Universities aren't Working.* Vancouver, BC: UBC Press.

Prosser, M. and Trigwell, K. (1999) *Understanding Learning and Teaching: The Experience in Higher Education.* Buckingham: SRHE and Open University Press.

Ramsden, P. and Moses, I. (1992) 'Associations between research and teaching in Australian higher education', *Higher Education*, Vol. 23, No 3, pp. 273–95.

Robertson, J. and Bond, C. (2001) 'Experiences of the relation between teaching and research: What do academics value?', *Higher Education Research and Development*, Vol. 20, No 1, pp. 5–19.

Robertson, J. and Bond, C. (2005) '"Being" in the university', in R. Barnett (ed.) *Reshaping the University: New Relationships between Research, Scholarship and Teaching.* Maidenhead, UK: McGraw-Hill and Open University Press.

Schön, D. (1983) *The Reflective Practitioner.* New York: Basic Books.

Schön, D. (1987) *Educating the Reflective Practitioner: Toward a New Design for Teaching and Learning in the Professions.* San Francisco: Jossey-Bass.

Smith, S. (1991) *Report of the Commission of Inquiry on Canadian University Education.* Ottawa: Association of Universities and Colleges in Canada.

Smith, W. (2010) 'Where all that money is going', *McLean's*, 18 January issue, p. 38.

Weil, S. and McGill, I. (1989) *Making Sense of Experiential Learning: Diversity in Theory and Practice.* Buckingham, UK: SRHE and the Open University Press.

Zhao, C. and Kuh, G. (2004) 'Adding Value: Learning communities and student engagement', *Research in Higher Education*, Vol. 45, No 2, pp. 115–38.

Zlotkowski, E. (ed.) (1998) *Successful Service-learning Programs: New Models of Excellence in Higher Education.* Boston, MA: Anker Publishing Company.

Zubrick, A., Reid, I. and Rossiter, P. (2001) *Strengthening the Nexus between Teaching and Research.* Australian Department of Education, Training and Youth Affairs, Canberra. Available at: http://www.dest.gov.au/archive/highered/eippubs/eip01_2/01_2.pdf.

CHAPTER THIRTEEN

Research into Prior Learning Assessment and Recognition (PLAR) in university adult education programmes in Canada

CHRISTINE WIHAK AND ANGELINA WONG

Abstract

Using a survey methodology, this research study explored the use of Prior Learning Assessment and Recognition (PLAR) in the context of Canadian university-based Adult Education programmes. Of 11 institutions responding, only three reported using PLAR for advanced standing in degree-level credit programmes, while an additional four reported using PLAR only in non-credit programmes and one institution used it only for admission to a graduate degree. Information provided from these institutions is discussed in terms of fees, supports for students, assessment methods, faculty compensation, institutional barriers and supports, and challenges. An important finding was the lack of clear articulation concerning the theoretical basis for PLAR use. The study concluded that Adult Education programmes need a stronger theorisation of PLAR in order to increase the availability of PLAR within degree-level Adult Education programmes, to overcome faculty resistance to PLAR, and to fulfil the potential of Adult Education programmes to take leadership with regard to PLAR implementation in the larger university community.

Introduction

In Canada and the United States, PLAR (Prior Learning Assessment and Recognition) is considered a central element of an 'adult-focused' post-secondary institution (Council on Adult and Experiential Learning, 2000). Thomas (2000) argued that the use of PLAR in post-secondary education rests on theoretical foundations in adult learning. But how is PLAR practice faring within its original field of adult education? A review of Canadian and international empirical literature on PLAR (Wihak, 2006) revealed very little evidence that university certificate, degree and diploma programmes in Adult Education[1] make use of the practice, at either the undergraduate or graduate level. Further, a recent survey of Canadian university websites investigating PLAR implementation (Wihak, 2007) found only one specific mention of PLAR with regard to Adult Education programmes.

What could explain the lack of PLAR activity in Adult Education programmes in Canadian universities? One possibility is that PLAR is being practised in such programmes but not reported or publicised, or it is being practised informally (Kennedy, 2003). Another possibility is that university-based adult educators suffer from some or all of the influences that have impeded PLAR implementation in the Canadian university context in general (Wong, 2000; Wong and Wihak, 2007). These influences have included rigid curriculum considerations, faculty resistance, administrative concerns and cost issues. A third possibility is that problems with the theoretical foundations of PLAR and consequent implications for practice are impeding its use within university-based Adult Education programmes.

The theoretical underpinning for PLAR is derived from ideas of reflective learning within the constructivist tradition (Conrad, 2010). For example, Wong (2000) described the use of Kolb's experiential learning cycle in relation to PLAR. This theoretical basis has, however, recently come under criticism because of its restricted nature. Harris (2006) has argued that experiential learning theories such as Kolb's ignore differences in types of knowledge and make the assumption that knowledge 'can transfer unproblematically between contexts' (*ibid.*, p. 14). Harris challenges this theoretical assumption by using Bernstein's curriculum theory to explore knowledge creation and transmission in the context of a university-based Adult Education RPL project. Implemented in post-apartheid South Africa, the project was designed to afford experienced

---

[1] 'Adult Education' refers to formal programmes of study to prepare individuals to become educators of adults, with the capitalisation used to distinguish it from 'adult education', the broad activity of providing education for adults (cf. Spencer, 2008).

adult educators who lacked degrees the opportunity to access a post-graduate diploma programme. Although a process for prior learning assessment was designed with this intention, Harris found that candidates' expression of their knowledge nevertheless had to conform to academic practices and standpoints that were important in the diploma curriculum. Advantaged candidates were those who had developed skill in reflection, had a well-developed and active learner identity, and had experience in areas such as policy and curriculum development. Those with back-grounds in areas such as business administration, with informal animator educator experience, and those lacking reflective skills, were disadvantaged. The diploma programme and the RPL process designed in relation to it 'had a hidden curriculum which rewarded particular ways of thinking and acting' (*ibid.*, p. 68), which unintentionally undermined the goal of recognising certain types of prior learning. Harris further noted that this drift to the academic was 'unconscious' (*ibid.*) on the part of the RPL programme facilitators, who subscribed strongly to the social justice goal of the project.

Two recent Canadian papers have highlighted significant differences in how adult education scholars believe PLAR should be approached in university Adult Education programmes. Sullivan and Thompson (2005) described the development of a self-assessment instrument used in PLAR processes for the CACE (Certificate in Adult and Continuing Education), a non-credit programme offered through distance education by a consortium of four Canadian universities. The self-assessment instrument was based on the premise that the knowledge and skills that adult educators need can be identified and stated in terms of behavioural outcomes. Through a DACUM-like process involving consultation with 42 practising adult educators, the authors created an instrument reflecting 13 competencies, with 229 associated performance elements. Several of the competencies are specific to the Adult Education field, involving, for example, 'Theory' (of adult learning), 'Instructional Design' and 'Facilitation'. Other competencies are more generic, including 'Professionalism', 'Critical Thinking' and 'Interpersonal Communication'. Although the authors recognised that adult educators use 'rich and complex knowledge and skills every day', the self-assessment instrument is intended to allow these knowledge and skills to be self-assessed in a systematic and transparent way.

Fenwick (2006), describing a much less formalised process used in PLAR at the University of Alberta, took issue with the notion that knowledge in Adult Education should be codified in the form of desired competencies. Using examples of portfolios submitted by an Aboriginal student who worked with Elders in passing on traditional knowledge and by a corporate trainer, she asserted that a competency-type approach privileges the mainstream voice. Similar to Harris (2006), she found that only knowledge that fits pre-existing definitions is considered valuable, while the learner's own knowledge is 'stripped of subjectivity, location, and embeddedness in social and material conditions' (*ibid.*, p. 286). Adopting a stance derived from complexity theory, Fenwick (2006) argued that PLAR should focus on the process of knowledge creation, rather than on knowledge as a product. Such an approach to PLAR would shift the emphasis to portfolios and interviews, rather than checklists such as those developed by Sullivan and Thompson (2005). Instead, the educator would be involved in assisting the students to interpret their experiences through extended conversations.

The current research was intended to investigate, first, whether Adult Education programmes are making more use of PLAR than was apparent in Wihak's (2006, 2007) previous research, and, second, to what extent each of the three possible explanations (informal PLAR, institutional barriers and theoretical uncertainty), identified in Wong and Wihak (2007), was responsible for the apparent lack of PLAR implementation in Canadian university-based Adult Education programmes. By surveying representatives of such programmes, we hoped to shed light on the extent and nature of PLAR activity, policies and practices, and theoretical justification. The research findings formed the basis for recommendations for further research.

Method

Sample

Although Canada has no formal accreditation process for degree-granting institutions, membership in the Association of Universities and Colleges of Canada (AUCC) is recognised as ensuring that an institution meets Canadian standards for university level education. Ninety-two Canadian public and private not-for-profit universities and university-degree level colleges comprise the AUCC membership. Member institutions range from small liberal arts colleges to large comprehensive universities, offering graduate-level training as well as professional

314

programmes. The sample for this study was drawn from the AUCC membership.

The AUCC website provides a searchable database of programmes offered by its member institutions.[2] This database was used to identify institutions offering university-level Adult Education programmes. In total, the database yielded 18 institutions offering some form of university credential (certificate, diploma, undergraduate degree, graduate degree) in the discipline.

For each institution, a search of the institutional website was conducted to identify contact people for the Adult Education programme, who were then sent an email invitation to participate in the study. A total of 12 institutional respondents (66 per cent) agreed to participate, a response rate that compares favourably with the response rate in a recent PLAR-related email survey conducted with Canadian universities (Kennedy, 2003). One institutional respondent, however, had to withdraw from the study because of illness and was unable to complete the study questionnaire. Thus the findings are based on responses from a total of 11 institutional respondents. At five of these universities, the Adult Education programmes in question are delivered through distance education, supported in part or whole by electronic technology.

Questionnaire

Contact people agreeing to participate were emailed a questionnaire containing 12 open-ended questions concerning PLAR policies and procedures used at their institution. These questions related to: use of PLAR for admission and/or advanced credits; information provided about PLAR to programme applicants; support provided to applicants in having their learning assessed; methods used to assess prior learning; use of course-specific or programme-based PLAR; fee structures for PLAR assessments; faculty compensation; number of PLAR applications per year; challenges in offering PLAR; supports and barriers from central institutional administration; and the theoretical basis of the PLAR practice. The questionnaire concluded by giving the respondents the opportunity to offer advice to other Adult Education programmes with regard to PLAR or to make any other comments. Respondents were asked to return the completed questionnaire by email to the first author.

---

[2] http://www.aucc.ca/can_uni/search/index_e.html.

Findings

Use of PLAR

Eight of the 11 responding universities reported making use of PLAR in their Adult Education programmes for admissions (i.e. allowing students who do not meet usual educational requirements to enter the programme) and/or for advanced standing (i.e. acknowledging learning from experience in the form of academic credits). In four of the institutions, PLAR is used with regard to non-credit certificates in Adult Education. Three respondents indicated that PLAR is used at bachelor degree level (BA or BEd in Adult Education). At one university, PLAR is used for admission to an MEd programme. Three respondents reported that they do not use PLAR in any of their programmes.

Information provided to students about PLAR availability

All eight of the universities using PLAR indicated that they make considerable effort to inform students about its availability. Information is provided in university calendars, programme brochures, and on the institution and/or programme website. In addition, informing prospective students about PLAR is considered a normal part of the advising process prior to admission to the programme. Two respondents further commented that their particular institutions offer PLAR to all students, in all programmes, so that PLAR for Adult Education is part of that process.

Support provided to applicants in having their learning assessed

Responses to this question showed that considerable variability exists in the amount and nature of support offered to students to prepare to have their learning assessed. Two institutions offer portfolio development courses, which provide elective credits towards a university-level credential. At one of these institutions, students wishing to submit a PLAR application are required to take the portfolio development course first. Two institutions provide individual guidance to the applicants in how best to (re)present their learning. At another institution, individual guidance used to be offered, but now 'very little' support is provided. The remaining two institutions provide written information but little personal guidance.

Methods used to assess learning

The predominant method used to assess learning is the paper-based portfolio, reported by seven of the eight universities. One of these respondents, however, commented that the portfolio is 'not a good tool unless absolutely necessary'. That particular institution prefers to use interviews and/or demonstration, which are also used by other surveyed institutions to supplement portfolio-based evidence.

Interestingly, none of the respondents reported using e-portfolios, even though four of the Adult Education programmes in question make use of online technology for programme delivery. This reflects a dilemma facing some adult educators. The e-portfolio, compared to the paper-based portfolio, creates potential barriers for those adult learners who are not computer literate or do not have convenient access to computers, (Wong, 2004). There are three primary concerns: (1) the time needed to master the software; (2) compatibility of computer hardware and software; and (3) privacy. Students who wish to add graphics, photos and other multimedia elements to their portfolios need to master a broad set of skills – writing and organising text, designing page layouts, creating graphics, scanning photos, and creating and editing videos and sound clips. Some educators question whether the time and effort to create e-portfolios are worth the effort. When e-portfolios are used to support job applications, interviews are not always conducted in places with easy access to technology. Even those interviewers with access to computers, who are disposed to taking the time to view the e-portfolio, must know how to access it. The third issue of privacy raises several policy questions for the institution, including who will have access to the e-portfolio, and whether password protection can and should viably be implemented and supported.

One school reported using 'challenge for credit exams' with regard to Adult Education courses, while another school reported that challenge exams could be used to earn further credit in addition to petitioning for credit through the adult education portfolio system.

Use of course-specific or programme-based PLAR

Two respondents reported that their institutions used only course-specific PLAR. One of those respondents commented: 'The term PLAR is not used at the university'; the term 'challenge for credit' is used instead.

Another respondent replied that their programme allows both course-specific and programme-based PLAR applications. Two respondents reported using a form of programme-based PLAR, with the assessed learning being shown on the student's transcript as 'unassigned credit'.

One respondent reported using a form of PLAR that is based on the applicant having taken a specific non-credit programme with a non-profit organisation, after that programme had been reviewed by the faculty. A respondent from a second institution indicated using a similar approach: 'If an applicant has a trade, business, or journeyperson certificate, and two years teaching/training experience, we automatically grant 30 university credits (1st year).'

Fee structures for PLAR assessments

Fee structures for PLAR assessments varied widely, ranging from no fee being charged (two institutions) to a charge of 75 per cent of the tuition for the course module for which the applicant is attempting PLAR credit (two institutions). One institution reported charging a fee based on service provision; the fee is designed to cover administrative costs and an honorarium for the assessor. At two institutions, PLAR assessment for admissions is covered through the normal admission fees.

Faculty compensation

Compensation practices for PLAR assessors also vary widely. In the institution with the most generous compensation, the respondent reported a very complex compensation scheme, which is embedded in the institution's collective agreement with faculty members. Under this scheme, a faculty member who performs a PLAR assessment can choose whether to count the assessment towards the core work assignment, to be paid an honorarium based on the number of course credits the applicant is petitioning for, or to bank 'student equivalencies' (which reflect the time involved in the assessment) towards teaching release. At another institution, sessional instructors are hired at an hourly rate to perform the assessment, based on a maximum of four hours. At the remaining institutions, assessment of PLAR is considered part of academic duties, with no additional compensation.

Number of PLAR applications per year

Two of the respondents were not able to provide any institutional figures on PLAR activity. One respondent estimated that in her institution, which offers a non-credit certificate programme, three out of 50 applicants to the programme would petition for PLAR credit for one course module, and one of those three would be granted the credit. These figures are similar to those reported by a respondent whose institution allows PLAR for admission to a graduate-degree programme; out of 30 applicants, between two and five request admission based on PLAR, and typically only one would be granted it. Another respondent reported much higher figures, with approximately 20 PLAR applicants every year in which the programme was enrolling a new cohort.

Challenges in offering PLAR

The respondents articulated a wide range of challenges in offering PLAR, some of which appear to be institution-specific rather than cross-cutting issues. At one institution, for example, a major issue is the lack of a mechanism to consider work experience or non-formal training; Challenge for Credit exams is the only allowable form of PLAR. Cost was an issue mentioned by two respondents, although for different reasons. One respondent worked at an institution that lacked resources to support faculty to perform assessments. At the other institution, the respondent reported that applicants assume 'assessment is free and that the overall tuition should be reduced directly by the cost of the challenged module'.

Four respondents alluded to faculty resistance to the concept and practice of PLAR. Three of these respondents expressed the opinion that resistance was stronger from faculty members who were not involved in Adult Education, while one respondent reported resistance within the Adult Education programme itself. One respondent who reported faculty resistance also commented that some faculty members embrace PLAR 'enthusiastically', while others remain 'confused' about the concept.

Supports and barriers from central institutional administration

Three respondents reported that they were working at institutions that support university-wide PLAR. Another respondent described her university as supporting PLAR in principle, but being inconsistent in its implementation. In contrast, three respondents characterised their institutions as lacking mechanisms for PLAR. One of these further reported that because the university does not want to 'acknowledge' PLAR, the Adult Education programme has 'had to work quietly'.

Theoretical base

Respondents offered terse comments with regard to their theoretical base: as one respondent commented: 'tough question to answer'. Respondents referred to adult learning theory in general, rather than offering any specific comments about competing theoretical possibilities.

Advice to other Adult Education programmes

While respondents' comments offered to other Adult Education programmes covered a range of topics, two themes dominated. The first theme focused on being realistic with students about PLAR, and giving them both theoretical and practical support in preparing their PLAR petition (e.g. making sure the student understands the difference between transfer credit and PLAR). The second theme focused on the importance of having strong advocates from within the faculty, and of educating faculty and administrators about PLAR. Additional comments included the need to develop processes that are meaningful to the student. One respondent emphasised that Adult Education programmes need to 'stress the academic aspect of this process' and to 'justify it with supporting knowledge of other credible institutional practices'.

Discussion

The results of this survey suggest that PLAR is more often used in university-based Adult Education programmes than was apparent from the earlier web-based survey of Canadian university websites (Wihak, 2007). Nevertheless, the practice is far from pervasive. While the majority of survey respondents reported using PLAR, half of the institutions offer it only in relation to non-credit, certificate-level programmes.

How PLAR is practised within the Adult Education programmes shows considerable variation in terms of factors such as fees, supports for students, assessment methods, faculty compensation, and so on. Variation exists because Canada is a huge country with ten provinces and regional populations that reflect different histories of immigration. The universities, depending on the constituencies that they serve, perceive and support PLAR differently. Some universities that co-exist with competing universities in large urban regions may regard PLAR as a 'loss leader' in their student recruitment, a service that earns its keep by attracting enrolment gains from non-traditional groups of students. Universities with a virtual monopoly in their regions support PLAR in principle but invest minimally in the process, as they already have more qualified traditional students than they can accept into their programmes.

Regardless of where they are situated in the country, Canadian universities tend to consider the financial impact of PLAR and the cost to the institution if no additional budget is forthcoming from government. Institutions that favour the development of electronic portfolios have to contend with the cost of developing and maintaining infrastructures that will support the storage of and access to e-portfolios by students, faculty and potential employers. Provincial government grants for developing PLAR services at universities were in full flush in the early 1990s, faded in the late 1990s and are now almost non-existent. Until the issue of cost is addressed, PLAR services will not be integrated into the mainstream of student services at Canadian universities.

The survey findings also show that with the exception of Adult Education programmes operating within a PLAR-friendly institution, similar institutional barriers to PLAR implementation exist as have been identified for PLAR in the higher education context in general (Wong, 2000; Wihak, 2007; Wong and Wihak, 2007). Indeed, the barriers may be more severe for Adult Education programmes than for more mainstream disciplines. Adult Education units within Canadian universities, especially the research intensive ones, tend to have marginal status. Faculty members who have specialist training in Adult Education tend to be a minority group in faculties of education, or hold their appointments within continuing education or extension units. Although Adult Education is historically the home of PLAR (Keeton, 2000; Thomas, 2000), not all adult educators are familiar with the concept and processes of PLAR. Some actually resist the intent of PLAR, feeling that the service dilutes their hard fought-for credibility as university scholars.

Although the philosophical commitment and expertise for supporting PLAR *potentially* resides within Adult Education programmes, individual faculty members are increasingly pressured to engage in mainstream research, rather than in implementing PLAR as a mechanism for social inclusion. Likewise, at faculties that have expressed some interest in PLAR in the past because of demands from mid-career professionals wanting advanced standing in graduate studies, the reward system works against faculty members who invest time and energy in advising and supporting PLAR candidates to present their experiential learning for assessment.

While the respondents to this survey showed a commitment to PLAR, their expression of its theoretical underpinnings was not fully articulated. One of the most influential theoretical models referenced by Canadian PLAR advocates (cf. Wong, 2000) has been Kolb's (1984) model of the experiential learning cycle. The model depicts learning as a cycle of grasping and transforming information – adults learn either through direct contact with concrete experience or through detached comprehension of abstract concepts; the learning is then personalised through reflection and experimentation.

Fenwick (2006) recently critiqued Kolb's model for perpetuating an institutionally imposed template for presenting knowledge and skills, acquired via experiential learning. Fenwick's concern is that the model oversimplifies the complexity of learning and devalues the learner's experiential process. Issues raised include: 'who is doing the recognizing, and how is this actor (whether a goal, institutional checklist, language, knowledge discipline, or individual assessor) now implicated in the emergence of learning and action connected with the situation being examined?' (*ibid.*, p. 295). Harris (2006), in contrast, has argued that experiential learning models such as Kolb's ignore or downplay significant differences in the nature and structure of knowledge gained through experience, and knowledge gained through formal studies. She argues that unexamined adoption of these models as the theoretical basis for the assessment of prior learning can do disservice to both formal disciplinary knowledge and experiential knowledge. The tendency by many PLAR practitioners and advocates to conflate different forms of knowledge may be one of the reasons for resistance to PLAR in parts of the post-secondary world.

Both Fenwick (2006) and Harris (2006) have called for a closer scrutiny of the prior learning assessment process in Adult Education programmes, in light of new and different theoretical perspectives on knowledge and knowledge creation. The difficulty that respondents from Adult Education programmes in this study had in articulating their theoretical basis for PLAR suggests that such an examination would be valuable. Systematic research is needed that turns different theoretical lenses on both the learning that adult learners who apply to Adult Education programmes bring with them and the learning required in Adult Education programmes. Such research needs to look both at the content of the learning and learning processes within and outside the higher education context.

For example, a comparison of Adult Education curricula across Canada, in relation to the adult education competencies developed by Sullivan and Thompson (2005) for a particular programme, might be one place to start. Exploring how Canadian Adult Education curricula would fare in an analysis using Bernstein's concepts, such as that employed by Harris (2006), would also be very illuminating. A different study might look at comparing the experiences of aspiring adult educators who apply for PLAR using the competency approach with that of applicants who use a portfolio approach.

University-based Adult Education programmes have a leadership role to play in encouraging greater use and acceptance of PLAR within the broader academic community. In order to play this leadership role, however, Adult Education scholars must have a theoretically articulated stance with regard to PLAR within their own discipline.[3] When differing theoretical perspectives and related research on PLAR become more thoroughly embedded in Adult Education curricula, graduates from these programmes can be confident spokespersons as they participate in PLAR implementation in other university-based disciplines and outside the university setting.

References

Conrad, D. (2010) 'Achieving flexible learning through recognition of prior learning practice: a case-study lament of the Canadian academy', *Open Learning: The Journal of Open and Distance Learning*, Vol. 25 No 2, doi:10.1080/02680511003787479

Council on Adult and Experiential Learning (CAEL) (2000) *Serving Adult Learners in Higher Education: Principles of Effectiveness – Executive Summary*. Chicago: CAEL. Available at: http://www.cael.org/pdf/publication_pdf/summary%20of%20alfi%20principles%20of%20effectiveness.pdf (Accessed 9 December 2009).

Fenwick, T. (2006) 'Reconfiguring RPL and its assumptions: A complexified view', in P. Andersson and J. Harris (eds) *Re-theorizing the Recognition of Prior Learning*. Leicester, England: National Institute of Adult Continuing Education (NIACE).

---

[3] This is the subject of Wong's chapter in this volume.

Harris, J. (2006) 'Questions of knowledge and curriculum in the recognition of prior learning', in P. Andersson and J. Harris (eds) *Re-theorizing the Recognition of Prior Learning*. Leicester: National Institute of Adult Continuing Education (NIACE).

Keeton, M. (2000) 'Recognizing learning outside of schools in the United States of America', in N. Evans (ed.) *Experiential Learning around the World*. London: Jessica Kingsley.

Kennedy, B. (2003) *A Spring 2003 Snapshot of the Current Status of Prior Learning Assessment and Recognition (PLAR) in Canada's Public Post Secondary Institutions*. Toronto: Council of Ministers of Education, Canada.

Kolb, D. (1984) Experiential Learning. Englewood Cliffs, N.J.: Prentice Hall.

Spencer, B. (2008) 'Have we got an adult education model for PLAR?' Proceedings of the Canadian Association for the Study of Adult Education (CASAE) Annual Conference. Available at: http://www.oise.utoronto.ca/CASAE/cnf2008/OnlineProceedings-2008/CAS2008%20Proceedings.html (Accessed 27 July 2010).

Sullivan, S. and Thompson, G. (2005) 'The development of a self-assessment instrument to evaluate selected competencies of Continuing Education practitioners', *Canadian Journal of University Continuing Education*, Vol. 31, No 2, pp. 59–94.

Thomas, A. (2000) 'Prior Learning Assessment: The quiet revolution', in A. Wilson and E. Hayes (eds) *Handbook of Adult and Continuing Education*. San Francisco: Jossey-Bass.

Wihak, C. (2006) *State of the Field Review: Prior Learning Assessment and Recognition (PLAR)*. Ottawa: Canadian Council on Learning.

Wihak, C. (2007) 'Prior Learning Assessment and Recognition in Canadian universities: View from the web', *Canadian Journal of Higher Education*, Vol. 37, No 1, pp. 95–112.

Wong, A. (2000) *University-level Prior Learning Assessment and Recognition: Building Capacity for an Institutional Response*. Saskatoon: University of Saskatchewan.

Wong, A. (2004) *E-portfolios: Implications for University Teaching and Learning*. University of Saskatchewan sabbatical research report. Saskatoon: University of Saskatchewan.

Wong, A. and Wihak, C. (2007) 'Canadian perspectives on recognizing prior learning: Barriers to implementation of Prior Learning Assessment and Recognition (PLAR) in the university setting'. Paper presented at the European Distance Education Network (EDEN) conference, Naples, Italy, June.

324

Reflections on research for an emergent field

Dr Norm Friesen,
Canada Research Chair in E-learning Practices,
Thompson Rivers University

Social, governmental and business pressures sometimes provide the necessary impetus for research and development in an emerging field. However, the specific outputs and results most valued by government and business do not always align with the priorities of a solid research agenda. It is evident from this edited collection that the pressures driving Prior Learning Assessment and Recognition (PLAR) research are many and powerful, and that these are poised to increase in their force and urgency. It is equally clear that the responses of researchers in PLAR to these developments have been varied and resourceful. Speaking as a researcher with experience primarily in the field of online and distance learning – an area similarly subject to pressures of policy and profit – I would like to take this opportunity to conclude this book with a few words of encouragement and reflection.

In education as in other fields, those responsible for shaping policy and funding priorities are understandably interested, as they often say, in 'what works'. Determining what is effective and efficient, and what is optimal given a range of alternatives, sounds like a laudable and even critical goal for research. However, it is often not the best starting point for complex and emerging fields. To begin by making determinations about optimisation and efficiency is to put the cart before the horse: it means that research begins by comparing outcomes of different programmes and conditions, and by seeking causal relationships between these conditions and the results they ostensibly produce. But in focusing on quantifiable answers to such narrowly-defined questions, research of this kind fore-closes on a range of important issues and questions that need to be asked first.

These questions, fortunately, are at the very heart of this book: How can PLAR be usefully theorised? How and why is PLAR different from one jurisdiction to another? What are the commonly-held but changing assumptions and values of PLAR researchers and practitioners? Can PLAR and its variants be described through a common vocabulary and what might that vocabulary be? What are the different outputs and criteria against which PLAR policy and services might be judged? Is quality of paramount importance, or is the potential or actual value of the learning recognised as the priority – or is some other criterion altogether to be seen as most significant?

It is important to address, carefully and openly, these types of questions because they will likely determine how issues about efficiency and 'what works' will eventually be framed. And the answers to these more instrumental questions, in turn, will lead to decisions about policy, priorities and funding. The kinds of questions that I have suggested – particularly those related to common presuppositions and terminology – are questions that are associated with what is sometimes called 'theory building'. But some of the connotations of this term are misleading.

'Theory building' suggests for some the construction of a shared, comprehensive and monolithic theory – the product of a unified collaborative enterprise. This has been an ideal that researchers in e-learning and particularly distance education have pursued (e.g. see Keegan, 1990), but to little avail: these fields are too far from the realm of physics and even psychology to be characterised by paradigmatic unity. The phenomena at issue in research in e-learning or distance education are not timeless and universal, nor are they reducible to some kind of common physical or biological substrate. They are products of policy and practice, not of nature, and as such are contingent and contextual.

Consequently, what I recommend here and elsewhere (Friesen, 2009) is a 'multivocal' approach to research: the application of multiple theories and methodologies to a field of practice and research. I believe that PLAR, like e-learning or distance education, would benefit from being illuminated from a multiplicity of perspectives, rather than defined in terms of an overarching explanatory edifice. First and perhaps most modestly, a multivocal approach offers room for both theoretical and a-theoretical contributions. It has a place for project reports and comparative studies of all kinds, which are already strongly represented in this collection. Whether qualitative or quantitative in orientation, these studies and reports help to identify differences and similarities in policy, practice and vocabulary, and thereby contribute to the formation and stabilisation of a common vocabulary and discourse – necessary preconditions for an emergent and productive research community.

A multivocal approach would of course encompass both qualitative and quantitative research. In recommending theoretical and method-ological approaches for PLAR, I especially emphasise those which are qualitative or mixed. Methods of this kind include descriptive and com-parative case studies; discursive and textual analyses of PLAR policies and other documents; phenomenological explorations of the quality of PLAR experiences and services; action research into programme development, implementation and modification; or grounded theory for generating new categories and linkages. The critical, social-justice orientation of some PLAR practitioners (again illustrated in this collection) also provides a valuable perspective. Moreover, as population and labour mobility continue to increase, critical comparisons of the status, credentialing and experiences of different groups in relationship to PLAR remain important.

There are paradigmatic reasons for my emphasis on descriptive, com-parative and exploratory research. These types of investigation do not take the place of, but provide the preconditions for, the hypotheses, variables and treatments of quantitative, quasi-experimental research. Positing a null hypothesis for a quantitative, experimental investigation requires a rela-tively stabilised field of study, one characterised by widely understood practices and outcomes. Only in this way can a hypothesis isolate two variables and their interrelationship from a welter of phenomena. And only in this way can research designate a treatment that would differ meas-urably from established practice. The kind of research I recommend above would first help to resolve these variables, variations, and established out-comes and practices.

These ways of doing research will help, each in its own way, to estab-lish and stake out aspects of the geography and landscape of the PLAR field. In this sense, the approaches I recommend might be categorised as 'topological' or 'topographical' in nature. Topology involves seeing and studying the terrain as someone who inhabits it. It implies a close con-nection with practice, stakeholder experience and – to stretch the landscape metaphor perhaps too far – the perspectives of those working in the 'trenches'. Types of research that might fit with this approach include project reports, case studies, action research and phenomenology. The topographical view involves a mapping out of what is visible from an elevated perspective. But it is important to keep in mind that episte-mologies of research are slightly more complex than those implied in surveying a place from an aeroplane or using Google Earth. Research approaches allied with the topographical include comparative case stud-ies, surveys of programmes and the literature itself, or grounded theory generating broad categories and structures.

Fortunately for PLAR, its subject–matter focus readily complements the requirements of defining and forming the field itself: both are con-cerned with the development and organisation of knowledge, and its institutional legitimisation. And given the urgency of the formation of this field, this bodes well for building a community of scholarship in PLAR.

References

Friesen, N. (2009) *Re-Thinking E-Learning Research: Foundations, Methods and Practices*. New York: Peter Lang.

Keegan, D. (1990) *Foundations of Distance Education* (third edition). London: Routledge.

Index